CRIMINAL EVIDENCE

CRITICAL READINGS

CRIMINAL EVIDENCE

CRITICAL READINGS

FIRST EDITION

Edited by Pamela Newell, Esq.

cognella®

SAN DIEGO

Bassim Hamadeh, CEO and Publisher
Amy Smith, Senior Project Editor
Christian Berk, Production Editor
Emely Villavicencio, Senior Graphic Designer
Stephanie Kohl, Licensing Coordinator
Natalie Piccotti, Director of Marketing
Kassie Graves, Vice President of Editorial
Jamie Giganti, Director of Academic Publishing

Cover image copyright © 2019 iStockphoto LP/digicomphoto.

Printed in the United States of America.

cognella® | ACADEMIC PUBLISHING
3970 Sorrento Valley Blvd., Ste. 500, San Diego, CA 92121

For Mark II, Joey, Lanier, Jon, and Lauren for making me so proud.

For Derrick Maynard for your unwavering support and love.

CONTENTS

PREFACE

I was a frustrated criminal evidence professor at the University of North Georgia. I had gone through three different textbooks in six semesters. None of them had the right college-level mixture of terminology and practical information. There are dozens of evidence textbooks out there for law students, but that was not my audience, nor was I looking for a casebook. When Cognella reached out to me about participating in its anthology series, I jumped at the chance to become the editor of my own criminal evidence book I could use in my classes for criminal justice majors.

As aforementioned, this book is for college-level criminal justice majors taking a criminal evidence course. There will only be snippets on civil law. This book focuses on criminal trials and the evidence used in them. The text covers the sources of evidentiary law, crime scene evidence, direct and circumstantial evidence, crime scene evidence, interrogations, confessions, evidentiary basics, witnesses, and hearsay.

This book is written in an objective manner and does not advocate for a particular perspective, although there are some sections that highlight the pros and cons of specific approaches. This anthology differs from other books because it covers a distinctly limited subject instead of throwing all manner of data at the student without context or organization. It also includes practical scenarios and real-world discussions.

INTRODUCTION

The content of this book revolves around the evidence that is dealt with in a criminal investigation and trial. The book is organized in a logical way by first focusing on an introduction to criminal evidence, then sources of law, and finally the issues that may come up in an investigation and trial. Each chapter will have an introduction, featured reading(s), key terms, and study questions.

This book is specifically addressed to criminal justice majors in a collegiate setting. In order to maximize the book's effectiveness as a tool for learning, students should make sure to cover the introductory material and the key terms. The introduction gives context to when the upcoming topic will apply. The key terms will help students familiarize themselves with basic legal terms that will reappear in the reading material. Additionally, each chapter includes at least one real-life instance of the topics and theories discussed in the chapter, which will allow students to see evidence in a practical setting.

This book is designed for students who seek a philosophical and practical understanding of criminal evidence that will directly apply in their careers.

Evidentiary Law

Sources of Law—Judicial Precedent

by Raluca Lupu

1. Introduction

The legal meaning of the notion "formal source of law" captures many aspects, ways of turning the content of the rule of law into a rule of conduct, and enforces respect as role model in relationships between people.

Study of formal sources of law reveals their diversity. This diversity is motivated by the multitude and variety of social relations, which require legal regulation in the long evolution of society.

All types of law so far have seen a multitude of sources—acts of state authorities, customary law, judicial precedents, doctrine, etc. Similar legal systems can be expressed in different forms, as, in fact, a specific legal system, during its existence, may be reproduced in many forms. Supremacy of a certain formal source of law changes in relation to the degree of its development, the complexity of social relations. Thus, if feudal law is based mainly on customary law, bourgeois revolutions radically change the ratio between customary and normative act in favor of the latter.

M. Djuvara points out that positive law must be acknowledged, must be revealed in specific crystallization. There must be forms in which to find it. Formal sources of law are these forms which show what positive law represents.[1]

From a legal perspective, formal sources of law are of particular interest. They are the externalization of rules of conduct by a certain form of legal language, corresponding to an optimal reception by its recipients. Formal sources of law are one of

---

1   Djuvara. M., Bereceanu B., Ioan M. (1995), "General theory of law", *Legal encyclopedia*, Bucharest: ALL, 302.

the requirements actually the most important, providing legal order, corresponding to a deep need, namely the need for security of the society.

Formal sources of law consecrated by evolution are: customary law, legal doctrine, judicial precedent, normative contract and normative act. Each source of law will be explained in order to allow clear differentiation between them and to highlight the peculiarities of the judicial precedent.

2. Customary Law

It is the oldest source of law. Customary law appears in the stage of development of primitive society, being the expression of needs felt by any society, bound to conservation of community values. Law takes over a series of customs and adjusts them to the specific reality of a political society. People apply some rules in the process of their interaction, often unconsciously. That specific rule is concluded to be useful and necessary. Not all customs created by society are sources of law.

As far as existing customs are concerned, state power takes the following stand: recognition and consecration, enforcing those considered useful for strengthening the rule of law; reception and toleration of those which, by their meaning and importance, do not require transformation into legal rules and their stipulations do not contradict with the rule of law; forbidding those which contradict established order, protected by the state power.

Two conditions are required for a custom to become source of law: a material, objective condition, namely an old and undeniable custom and a psychological, subjective condition, according to which, the specific rule (custom) is compulsory.

Custom is based on actual cases later referred to and evoked as precedents. The legislator may validate the custom in a legal act or may refer to it. At the same time, it is possible that, once a new law coming into force, the legislator to remove certain habits, to no longer recognize their validity, contesting them expressly. It is obvious, however, that the legislator cannot stop the formation of new customs.

Custom remained a main source of law throughout antiquity and middle ages.

Although the role of customary law in modern times decreased, it rules to a considerable extent in Anglo-Saxon law system and former British colonies, now independent states. Custom is still a source of maritime law, due to the characteristics of maritime trade rules, particularly of harbor activities.

It should be noted that the status of source of law is not recognized for a custom that contains a rule contrary to public order and morals, or a custom that would abolish a law in force.

3. Doctrine (Specialized Legal Literature)

Doctrine includes analyzes, investigations, interpretations that specialized people give to legal phenomenon. Romanian researcher S. Popescu states that "doctrine is law, as conceived by theory, its scientific explanation, generalization and systematization."[2]

Doctrine is legal science. In general, the role of science is theoretical-explanatory, scientific interpretations of the normative material helping the legislator or judge, in the process of creating, or law enforcement.

Legislative practice and practicing law (enforcement by the administration and courts) could not exist and so more could not be effective without legal theory. Meanwhile, solutions and interpretations of the doctrine are always based on practical cases, start with facts and then, as a generalization, interpret and explain them theoretically. The current system of sources of law can no longer consider the doctrine as the direct creative source of law. Some authors talk about the indirect (mediated), creator role of the doctrine.

Doctrine played an important role in the middle ages. Facing the obscurity and uncertainty of customary law, judges seek solutions in the comments of scientific works. Scientists' consensus was highly valued, due to their important role. When customs were collected and published, the role of the doctrine decreased without disappearing.

Legal doctrine is therefore a rigorous and systematic way of knowledge of the legal phenomenon, with a theoretical and critical constructive role, particularly manifested by promoting new ideas in law, by reception of the social changes that must find an echo in law. It is interesting to note that under formation of new legal typologies (Community law for example), the entire system of sources of law is reproduced, doctrine being recognized as a source of law.

4. Legal Practice (Case Law) and Judicial Precedent

Judicial precedent is a decision of a court in a specific case, which is a binding rule of law. Jurisprudence (multiple judicial precedents) consists of all decisions pronounced by all courts at all levels. According to their purpose, courts examine certain causes and sentence based on the law. Cases are private or public. Notified (by action or indictment), the judge should hear the case and sentence by interpreting and enforcing a legal norm.

Recognition of jurisprudence as a source of law is reluctant, founded on the principle of separation of powers. Indeed, in a state of law, creating laws is the task of legislative bodies, judicial bodies enforcing laws to specific cases. Recognizing the courts' right of direct normative elaboration would mean to force the door of legislative creation, disturbing the balance of power.

Historically, the jurisprudence has played an important role as a source of law, in Roman law. Praetorian law (which included the creative solutions of pretor) constitutes an important source of the institutions of Roman law.

---

2   Popescu. S. (2000), *General theory of law*. Bucharest: Lumina Lex, 159.

As judicial precedents (decisions of the Supreme Court), jurisprudence is recognized to have a creative role, indirectly. This is the situation for the legal systems belonging to the Roman-Germanic family. In Anglo-Saxon legal system (common law) jurisprudence is recognized as source of law. Common law consists of legal judgments and customs. Judicial precedent has an important role, and the judge is not simple interpreter of the law, but a law maker. A case can be solved on the basis of precedent pronounced hundreds of years before. There are collections of precedents but still the many complications and controversies are not eliminated.

According to Vǎllimǎrescu, jurisprudence role is to interpret the law and apply it to specific cases, to complete law when it is silent on an issue, to adapt the law to new conditions of life of society.[3] The importance of this source of law is established since slave law. In Roman times, for example, Praetorian law included rules introduced to correct or adapt old Roman civil law. Praetors had the right to establish binding rules expressing the government interest in a number of situations that were not stipulated by civil law in force.[4] In feudal law, precedent becomes source of law, especially in Europe, after the reception of Roman law (XV and XVI centuries). Once the power of the feudal State centralized and absolute monarchies formed, a tendency to strengthen the role of normative acts issued by the absolute monarch at the expense of the precedent and the other sources of law is ascertained. The most important social relationships begin to be governed by written laws, in comprehensive codes. Thus, in Germany, the Criminal Code of 1794 stated that the decisions to be issued should not consider any views of scientists or previous decisions made by the courts[.]" The French Civil Code of 1804 and the Austrian Civil Code of 1811 include similar provisions.

With the bourgeois revolutions, the problem of judicial precedent as a source of law was differently considered in various legal systems. Thus, if in countries such as those mentioned above case law was not included among the sources of law, then in England, USA, Canada, it held a very important place and role. Judicial precedents are considered sources of law in countries with different legal system. So for example, in Switzerland there is an opinion that some decisions of the Federal Court are true sources of law.[5]

In doctrine, there was no unified view on judicial precedent as a source of law due to its complexity. Therefore, positivism, which was the basis of the exegetical school, prevented judicial practice to be recognized as a source of law, admitting that no rule can result from a mere practice, even if judicial. In France a strong doctrine current was manifested—scientific school which denounced inadequacy and insufficiency of formal law, the deceitfulness of omnipotence idea. The first and main representative of this school was Fr. Geny who rehabilitated the free initiative of the judge outside the law enforced.[6]

---

3   Vǎllimǎrescu, A. (1999), *Legal encyclopedia treatise,* Bucharest: Lumina Lex, 239.

4   Cocoş, Ştefan (2000), *Roman Law,* Bucharest: All Beck, 32.

5   Smochinǎ, A. (2002), *Istoria universalǎ a statului şi dreptului. Epoca anticǎ şi medievalǎ. [Universal history of state and law. Antique and medieval period.]* Chişinǎu: Tipografia Centralǎ, 83–105.

6   Aramǎ, E. (2007), "Problema precedentului în doctrina juridicǎ [The precedent issue in the legal doctrine]", *National Revue of Law.* Special edition, International scientific and practical conference "Judicial Precedent, theoretical and practical aspects". Chişinǎu, 29 September, 80–15.

5. Normative Contract

Contract is an individual legal document meaning that it establishes rights and obligations for determined subjects (seller and buyer, locator and lessee and so on). Civil Code defines contract as an agreement between two or more persons to constitute or put out a legal report. This accepted, the contract can be a source of law.

The contract results from legal stipulations and is fulfilled in strict compliance with them. There is one category of contracts which do not relate directly to issues of rights and obligations as determined, so it governs no specific legal relations, but considers general stipulations that establish certain rules of conduct. They are called normative contracts and, as such, are intended sources of law.[7]

Opposed to specific contracts which establish rights and obligations for the subjects, the history of law knows the conventional form of the creation of legal rules, when the rights and obligations come as a rule of conduct binding legal rules for the parties, in their behavior.[8]

In constitutional law, the normative contract represents a source of law in the matter of organization and function of federal structures of the states. Federations are created as contracts (treaties) between states that want to build up the federation are concluded.

In labor law and social security law, normative contract is source of law in the form of collective labor contracts, which provide general conditions of organizing labor process in a determined branch and on which individual lab M. our contracts are then concluded.

Finally, in public international law, normative contract, as a treaty, is the main source of law. A treaty is always the expression of free consent of the states and only to that extent it is a source of rights and obligations for the signatory states. In contemporary international law, the treaty is the most important mean for governing the relations between states, of cooperation, based on the sovereign equality of states, in support of respecting their sovereignty and independence.

6. Normative Act

Legal normative act is the most important in the system of sources of law. Prominent place of the normative act is explained by historical reasons and by reasons related to the characteristics of content and form of this legal source, relative to other sources.

The normative legal acts system—published technical legal forms in which legal rules are set by the state authorities—is made up of laws, decrees, resolutions and ordinances, regulations and orders of ministries, decisions and resolutions of local administrative bodies.

---

7   Craiovan, I. (2001), *Tratat elementar de teoria generală a dreptului [Elementary treatise of general theory of law]*, Bucharest: All Beck, 237.

8   Baltag. D., Guţu. A. (2002), *Teoria generală a dreptului. Curs teoretic. [General theory of law. Theoretical course]*, Chişinău: Reclama, 189.

Supreme force of law is the privilege of the rule of law and is part of the democracy essence. Law is, as reflected by the Declaration of Human Rights of 1789 "an expression of the general will and all citizens have the right to be involved personally or by their representatives to its elaboration" (art. 6 of the Declaration).

Federal Rules of Evidence

Article I. General Provisions

Rule 101. Scope; Definitions
Rule 102. Purpose
Rule 103. Rulings on Evidence
Rule 104. Preliminary Questions
Rule 105. Limiting Evidence That Is Not Admissible Against Other Parties or for Other Purposes
Rule 106. Remainder of or Related Writings or Recorded Statements

Article II. Judicial Notice

Rule 201. Judicial Notice of Adjudicative Facts

Article III. Presumptions in Civil Cases

Rule 301. Presumptions in Civil Cases Generally
Rule 302. Applying State Law to Presumptions in Civil Cases

Article IV. Relevance and Its Limits

Rule 401. Test for Relevant Evidence
Rule 402. General Admissibility of Relevant Evidence

Legal Information Institute, "Federal Rules of Evidence."

Article V. Privileges

Article VI. Witnesses

Article VII. Opinions and Expert Testimony

Rule 701. Opinion Testimony by Lay Witnesses
Rule 702. Testimony by Expert Witnesses
Rule 703. Bases of an Expert's Opinion Testimony
Rule 704. Opinion on an Ultimate Issue
Rule 705. Disclosing the Facts or Data Underlying an Expert's Opinion
Rule 706. Court-Appointed Expert Witnesses

Article VIII. Hearsay

Rule 801. Definitions That Apply to This Article; Exclusions from Hearsay
Rule 802. The Rule Against Hearsay
Rule 803. Exceptions to the Rule Against Hearsay—Regardless of Whether the Declarant Is Available as a Witness
Rule 804. Hearsay Exceptions; Declarant Unavailable
Rule 805. Hearsay Within Hearsay
Rule 806. Attacking and Supporting the Declarant's Credibility
Rule 807. Residual Exception

Article IX. Authentication and Identification

Rule 901. Authenticating or Identifying Evidence
Rule 902. Evidence That Is Self-Authenticating
Rule 903. Subscribing Witness's Testimony

Article X. Contents of Writings, Recordings, and Photographs

Rule 1001. Definitions That Apply to This Article
Rule 1002. Requirement of the Original
Rule 1003. Admissibility of Duplicates
Rule 1004. Admissibility of Other Evidence of Content
Rule 1005. Copies of Public Records to Prove Content
Rule 1006. Summaries to Prove Content
Rule 1007. Testimony or Statement of a Party to Prove Content
Rule 1008. Functions of the Court and Jury

Article XI. Miscellaneous Rules

Rule 1101. Applicability of the Rules
Rule 1102. Amendments
Rule 1103. Title

Effective Date and Application of Rules

Pub. L. 93–595, §1, Jan. 2, 1975, 88 Stat. 1926, provided: "That the following rules shall take effect on the one hundred and eightieth day [July 1, 1975] beginning after the date of the enactment of this Act [Jan. 2, 1975]. These rules apply to actions, cases, and proceedings brought after the rules take effect. These rules also apply to further procedure in actions, cases, and proceedings then pending, except to the extent that application of the rules would not be feasible, or would work injustice, in which event former evidentiary principles apply."

Historical Note

The Federal Rules of Evidence were adopted by order of the Supreme Court on Nov. 20, 1972, transmitted to Congress by the Chief Justice on Feb. 5, 1973, and to have become effective on July 1, 1973. Pub. L. 93–12, Mar. 30, 1973, 87 Stat. 9, provided that the proposed rules "shall have no force or effect except to the extent, and with such amendments, as they may be expressly approved by Act of Congress". Pub. L. 93–595, Jan. 2, 1975, 88 Stat. 1926, enacted the Federal Rules of Evidence proposed by the Supreme Court, with amendments made by Congress, to take effect on July 1, 1975.

The Rules have been amended Oct. 16, 1975, Pub. L. 94–113, §1, 89 Stat. 576, eff. Oct. 31, 1975; Dec. 12, 1975, Pub. L. 94–149, §1, 89 Stat. 805; Oct. 28, 1978, Pub. L. 95–540, §2, 92 Stat. 2046; Nov. 6, 1978, Pub. L. 95–598, title II, §251, 92 Stat. 2673, eff. Oct. 1, 1979; Apr. 30, 1979, eff. Dec. 1, 1980; Apr. 2, 1982, Pub. L. 97–164, title I, §142, title IV, §402, 96 Stat. 45, 57, eff. Oct. 1, 1982; Oct. 12, 1984, Pub. L. 98–473, title IV, §406, 98 Stat. 2067; Mar. 2, 1987, eff. Oct. 1, 1987; Apr. 25, 1988, eff. Nov. 1, 1988; Nov. 18, 1988, Pub. L. 100–690, title VII, §§7046, 7075, 102 Stat. 4400, 4405; Jan. 26, 1990, eff. Dec. 1, 1990; Apr. 30, 1991, eff. Dec. 1, 1991; Apr. 22, 1993, eff. Dec. 1, 1993; Apr. 29, 1994, eff. Dec. 1, 1994; Sept. 13, 1994, Pub. L. 103–322, title IV, §40141, title XXXII, §320935, 108 Stat. 1918, 2135; Apr. 11, 1997, eff. Dec. 1, 1997; Apr. 24, 1998, eff. Dec. 1, 1998; Apr. 17, 2000, eff. Dec. 1, 2000; Mar. 27, 2003, eff. Dec. 1, 2003; Apr. 12, 2006, eff. Dec. 1, 2006; Sept. 19, 2008, Pub. L. 110–322, §1(a), 122 Stat. 3537; Apr. 28, 2010, eff. Dec. 1, 2010; Apr. 26, 2011, eff. Dec. 1, 2011; Apr. 16, 2013, eff. Dec. 1, 2013; Apr. 25, 2014, eff. Dec. 1, 2014; Apr. 25, 2019, eff. Dec. 1, 2019.

The Justice Process

by Lawerence F. Travis III

C ases move through the justice system from the first stage of detection by law enforcement through subsequent stages to final discharge from the system. While there are some feedback mechanisms by which a case can move back to an earlier decision point, on the whole, cases flow in one direction through the system. This processing of cases represents the "total system" of criminal justice. It includes the subsystems of law enforcement, the courts, and corrections.

In this chapter we will trace the criminal justice system of the United States. In doing so, we will skip many of the details and nuances of criminal justice processing in the interests of developing an understanding of the total justice system. In other words, to some extent we will ignore the "trees" in order to get a better look at the "forest." Later chapters will examine the subsystems of criminal justice in more detail.

Perhaps the greatest constant of criminal justice is variety. Even things as simple as titles differ among jurisdictions. For example, prosecutors are variously known as state's attorneys, district attorneys, U.S. attorneys, prosecutors, and other titles. In most states, the highest court is called the state supreme court; in New York, the supreme court is a trial court, and the highest court is the New York Court of Appeals. With an appreciation that what follows here is a sketch of the justice system, we are ready to proceed.

The Decision Points of the Criminal Justice System

The President's Commission on Law Enforcement and Administration of Justice (1967a) created the flow chart of the justice system presented as Box 3.7 in the previous chapter. While we follow the general model of the President's Commission, we use slightly different terminology. The criminal justice system begins with the detection of crime, proceeds through investigation, arrest, initial appearance before the court, preliminary hearing, charging (arraignment), trial, sentencing, and possible revocation, and ends with discharge. We will examine these decision points.

Detection

As the formal social institution charged with the control of deviance that is identified as crime, the justice system does not start until a criminal offense is detected. Crime that goes undetected does not influence the justice process directly. It is only when the justice system (usually through the police) notices a possible criminal offense that the process begins.

Perhaps more than half of all crime is never discovered by the justice system (Rand, Lynch & Cantor, 1997). Many crimes remain undetected because no one realizes that a crime was committed. Many others are detected but are not reported to the police, so that the justice system is not aware that criminal offenses have occurred.

Have you ever reached into your pocket or wallet for money you knew you had, only to discover that it was missing? Most of us at some time have experienced missing money. We cannot be certain that we did not spend it or lose it, but we also cannot remember when it was spent. Have we been the victims of theft? Do we report the money as stolen?

If we assume that we spent or lost the money and do not believe it was stolen, a theft may go undetected. Similarly, if we are convinced the money was stolen, we may still not report it because the sum is so small and the chance of recovery so slim. In the latter case, a crime has gone unreported. **Undetected crime** is crime that is not known to the criminal justice system or the victim—crimes that are not recognized as crimes. An **unreported crime** is one that victims recognize as law-breaking behavior but is not brought to the attention of authorities.

If a person has a fight with a friend or relative and assumes it is "personal," an assault may go undetected or at least unreported. The first decision to influence the criminal justice process is determining whether a crime may have occurred. This decision is made most frequently by a civilian rather than a justice system official. A second decision is reporting a crime; again, this decision is made most often by someone other than a justice system official (Avakame, Fyfe & McCoy, 1999). Surveys of crime victims indicate that most crimes are not reported to the police, and that the rates of reporting crime have been relatively stable over the past several years (Catalano, 2006; Hart & Rennison, 2003; Rand, 1998). Over the past few decades, while the number of crimes reported to the police decreased slightly, the number of crimes recorded by the police increased dramatically (Rand, Lynch & Cantor, 1997). In recent years, the rate at which crimes have been reported to the police has increased, especially the rate of reporting for violent crimes (Rennison & Rand, 2003).

Violent crimes have traditionally been reported at higher rates than property crimes, with the exception of sexual assault and rape. Still, nearly half of violent crimes are not reported to police. In a study of reasons for reporting or not reporting domestic violence, Felson, Messner, Hoskin, and Deane (2002) found that victims don't report crime for reasons of privacy, protecting the offender, or fear of reprisal. They note that researchers have focused on reasons for not reporting, but have ignored reasons to report victimization. Felson and his colleagues found that victims of domestic violence were encouraged to report the crime for self-protection, because they viewed the offense as serious, and because they felt the police would take the offense seriously. Goudriaan, Lynch, and Nieuwbeerta (2004) studied crime reporting across several nations and found that social and individual characteristics of the victims influence the likelihood of crime reporting.

Nonreporting of crime limits the ability of criminal justice agents and agencies to respond to crime. Box 3.1 presents the frequency with which different types of crimes are reported to the police, and Box 3.2 describes reasons typically given by people for not reporting violent crimes.

BOX 3.1   Percent of Crimes Reported to Police by Type of Crime, 2005

Type of Crime	Percent of Responses
Violent Crimes:	47.4
Rape/Sexual Assault	38.3
Robbery	52.4
Aggravated Assault	624
Simple Assault	42.3
Personal Theft	35.2
Property Crimes:	39.6
Burglary	56.3
Motor Vehicle Theft	83.2
Theft	32.3

Source: S. Catalano (2006). *Criminal Victimization, 2005.* Washington, DC: Bureau of Justice Statistics:10.

BOX 3.2   Reasons Given for Not Reporting Violent Crimes, 1992–2000

Reason	Percent of Cases
Private/Personal Matter	20
Not Important Enough	17
Reported to Other Official	14
Not Important to Police	6
Fear of Reprisal	5
Not Clear a Crime Occurred	4
Lack of Proof	4
Protect Offender	3
Inconvenient	3
Other	25

Source: T. Hart & C. Rennison (2003). *Reporting Crime to the Police, 1992–2000.* Washington, DC: Bureau of Justice Statistics: 7.

When a crime or suspected crime is reported to the police, the justice system is mobilized. If agents of the justice system decide that crime has occurred, they have made the detection decision. The police respond to the report of a crime. It is then that case decisionmaking rests with official agents of the justice process. Once the police come to believe that a crime may have been committed, it is their decision whether and how to proceed. We can say that the criminal justice system starts when justice system officials (usually the police) believe a crime has occurred. At that point, the agents of the justice system take control over the official societal response to the crime.

Investigation

Upon deciding that a crime may have been committed, the next decision is whether to investigate, and if so, how thoroughly to investigate. **Investigation** is the search for evidence that links a specific person to a specific crime. It is a process in which the results of initial inquiries often determine the intensity of the investigation. If, for example, someone reports a prowler, the responding officers may make a visual check of doors and windows, find nothing suspicious, and leave. Alternatively, they may note footprints near a window or find scratch marks on a door or window frame, and then intensify their investigation.

At the conclusion of the investigation, three outcomes are possible. First, no evidence of criminal activity may be found and, thus, the possible crime is classified as **unfounded,** or not real. Second, evidence of possible criminal activity may support the finding that a crime was committed or attempted, but there is not sufficient evidence for an arrest. In this case, the crime will be left **unsolved** (i.e., no offender is known), and the investigation, at least theoretically, will continue. Finally, the investigation may yield evidence of both a crime and a probable guilty party. In the last outcome, the next decision stage is reached: arrest.

Arrest

Despite expectations, media portrayals, or legal mandates, police officers do not have to arrest every violator of the criminal law. The police officer makes a decision whether to arrest a suspected offender. Many factors affect the arrest decision.

Perhaps the two most important factors that determine whether an **arrest**—i.e., taking a person into custody—will be made are (1) the seriousness of the suspected offense, and (2) the quality of the evidence against the suspect. The officer can exercise tremendous discretion in this decision, especially for less serious offenses. For example, if a traffic officer stops you for speeding, a citation is not the only possible outcome, even if you actually were speeding. How often does a person give the officer excuses for his or her violation of the traffic laws? How does a person feel about the officer who issues a citation when he or she knows that the officer could have given a warning?

Discretionary decisions not to arrest are often the result of an officer's attempts to achieve "street justice." Street justice is a term used to describe attempts by police to deal with problems without formal processing. For example, an officer may counsel or warn loitering juveniles, rather than arresting them. In these cases, the officer tries to solve the problem in a way that avoids the negative consequences of formal processing. As we shall see in our discussion of the police, much police work is problem solving, and arrest is only one tool used for that purpose. Many times, however, police officers do decide to arrest a suspect. If an arrest is made, the next decision stage is reached: initial appearance.

Initial Appearance

Persons arrested for crimes are entitled to a hearing in court to determine whether they will be released pending further action. This **initial appearance** or hearing occurs relatively quickly after arrest, usually within a matter of hours. The hearing does not involve a determination of guilt, but rather an assessment of the defendant's likelihood of appearing at later proceedings. Arrested suspects are usually entitled to release before trial. With the exception of some serious crimes (murder, terrorism, kidnapping, etc.) specified in some statutes, arrested persons may be released while awaiting trial. Traditionally, this release has been accomplished by the posting of bail.

The primary purpose of bail is to ensure that the suspect will return to court for later hearings. The theory of bail is that a person will return to court if it would cost too much not to return. Thus, traditional bail involves the defendant "posting bond," or leaving money on deposit at the court. If the defendant returns, the bond is refunded. If the defendant does not return for the next hearing, the court keeps the bail money and issues a warrant for his or her arrest.

Since the 1970s, criminal justice reforms have witnessed the rebirth of "release on recognizance" systems whereby suspects obtain pretrial release without posting bond as long as they have a job, house, family, and other ties to the community. If a person is expected to appear in court to avoid losing a few thousand dollars, it seems reasonable that he or she would also appear to keep a home, job, or family ties.

In some jurisdictions, it is possible for the prosecutor to ask for "preventive detention." In these cases, the prosecutor believes that, if released on bail, the defendant will present a danger of continued crime in the community. Upon a hearing that establishes that the defendant is indeed dangerous, the magistrate is authorized to deny pretrial release.

In many courts, bail schedules have been developed by which different levels of bail amounts are tied to different types of crime. For instance, the rate for burglary might be $5,000, but for robbery, $10,000. The bail decision, however, is not automatic. If the magistrate believes that the suspect will flee or fail to appear for later hearings, a higher bail may be set. In other cases, a lower bail than usual may be set to allow the defendant to keep his or her job or to maintain family contacts. In either case, after the initial appearance, the next decision relates to the justification for governmental (i.e., justice system) intervention in the life of the citizen.

Charging

Between the time of arrest and arraignment, the prosecutor reviews the evidence in the case and determines a formal criminal charge. The offense for which a person is arrested is not necessarily the one with which he or she will be charged. For example, the police may arrest someone for armed robbery, but be unable to prove that a weapon was used in the crime. The prosecutor may then formally charge the offender with traditional (unarmed) robbery.

Charges are brought in two principal ways: indictment by grand jury or by information. With the indictment, the prosecutor presents the case in secret to a grand jury, which decides whether the evidence is strong enough to warrant the issuance of an indictment. With the information, the prosecutor presents the case in open court before a magistrate, who determines if the evidence is sufficient to warrant a formal charge.

In the information process, a judge reviews the strength of the evidence against a suspect and decides if it is sufficient to have the defendant "bound over" to the felony court. While not a determination of guilt or innocence, the **preliminary hearing** involves a judge ruling on the strength of the case against the defendant. While the defendant ultimately may be found not guilty, if the available evidence supports probable cause to believe the defendant may be found guilty, the judge will typically order the case bound over to trial, allowing the state to continue.

A courtroom artist rendering of Atlanta Falcons quarterback Michael Vick appearing at his arraignment hearing at the federal courthouse in Richmond, Virginia. Vick pleaded not guilty on July 26, 2007, to federal dogfighting charges. Vick was eventually sentenced to 23 months in prison for promoting and funding the dogfighting operation. *Photo credit: AP* Photo/Dana Verkouteren.

About a quarter felony arrests in large counties are dismissed before trial (Rainville & Reaves, 2003). The number of cases resulting in dismissal has been dropping over the past decade. Earlier studies of criminal prosecution (Boland, Mahanna & Sones, 1992) reported that nationally, 45 percent of felony arrests were dismissed before trial. Nearly one-half of these are dismissed by the judge. The rates of dismissal of charges at preliminary hearings vary based on the procedures used to bring cases to court. In places where the prosecutor reviews evidence before appearing in court, the weakest cases are rejected before a preliminary hearing is held, and the number of cases dismissed by the judge is low. Where no such review occurs, the rate of dismissal at the preliminary hearing may exceed 40 percent.

Arraignment

At the **arraignment**, the defendant is notified of the formal criminal charges against him or her and is asked to plead to the charges. The arraignment is not a hearing on the facts of the case. The defendant may plead not guilty, guilty, or *nolo contendere* (no contest), or may stand silent. When the defendant pleads guilty or *nolo contendere*, a finding of guilt is entered. If the defendant remains silent, a plea of not guilty will be entered on his or her behalf and a trial date will be set. Most criminal defendants plead guilty at arraignment, often as part of an agreement negotiated with the prosecutor (McDonald, 1979; Newman, 1966; Rosett & Cressey, 1976). In the typical plea bargain, the prosecutor drops charges or otherwise changes the seriousness of the formal charge in exchange for certain conviction without trial arising from a guilty plea from the defendant.

Trial

While most cases result in a guilty plea, those that receive the most media attention and publicity are those that involve a trial at which the defense and prosecution contest the facts and law before a neutral decisionmaker. Most cases that go to trial are what Samuel Walker (2001:29) terms "celebrated cases." In these cases, defendants receive full-blown trials, very often jury trials. Because these are the cases that receive the most publicity, much of the public believes that the jury trial is the normal operating procedure of the justice system.

At trial, the state (prosecutor) must prove, beyond a reasonable doubt, that the defendant committed the criminal offense for which he or she has been charged. The defense attorney seeks to discredit the state's case and, at a minimum, establish that there is some doubt as to whether the defendant committed the offense. Depending upon the nature of the case, one of two types of trials will be requested by the defense: a jury trial or a bench trial.

The jury trial is the ideal of the justice system. A panel of the defendant's peers hears all of the evidence and decides whether the defendant is guilty or not guilty. The bench trial is held before a judge alone, who hears all of the evidence and then decides whether the defendant is guilty or not guilty. If the verdict is "not guilty," the justice process ends with the acquittal of the defendant. On the other hand, if the verdict is "guilty" (or if the defendant pleads guilty), the defendant stands convicted of the crime and the next decision point in the justice system is reached: sentencing.

Sentencing

The sentencing decision has been described as bifurcated (i.e., having two parts). First, the judge decides the type of sentence. This can range from a fine to incarceration and covers a wide variety of alternatives, including probation, confinement in jail or prison, and combinations such as probation with a fine. In capital cases, such as murder, the type of sentence may be death. The second part of the decision involves the conditions of sentence. These include the conditions of supervised release (probation), such as curfew, employment, and so on, as well as the length of prison term for those incarcerated. In states where offenders are convicted of capital crimes, this part of the decision may involve the method of execution (see Box 3.3).

Sentencing power is shared among the three branches of the government. The legislative branch sets limits on penalties by establishing minimum and maximum prison terms and fine amounts, by declaring some offenses ineligible for probation, and by other similar actions. The judicial branch is where the sentencing judge selects the actual type and conditions of sentence from alternatives allowed by the legislature. The executive branch has the power to pardon, to offer clemency, and, often, to authorize parole. This shared power is indicated in Box 3.4.

Most convicted offenders are sentenced to probation or a fine and are not incarcerated. Fewer than half of those convicted of felonies in 2000 were sentenced to prison (Rainville & Reaves,

2003). Those who are incarcerated most frequently gain release from prison through parole or mandatory release, and are required to live in the community under supervision and to obey conditions of release similar to those placed on probationers (Travis & Latessa, 1984). Failure to obey these conditions can lead to the next possible decision point in the justice process: revocation.

BOX 3.3 **Method of Execution**

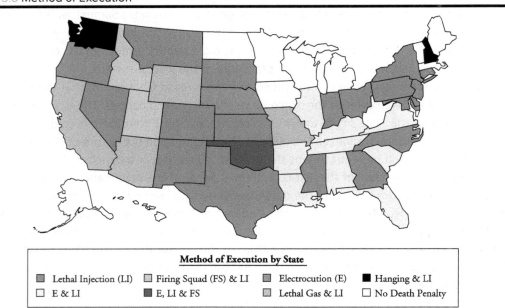

Method of Execution by State

■ Lethal Injection (LI)	□ Firing Squad (FS) & LI	■ Electrocution (E)	■ Hanging & LI
□ E & LI	■ E, LI & FS	□ Lethal Gas & LI	□ No Death Penalty

Source: K. Donovan & C. Klahm (2007). Cincinnati: Center for Criminal Justice Research, University of Cincinnati.

Revocation

The overwhelming majority of criminal offenders who are sentenced to correctional custody serve some portion of their sentence under community supervision on either probation or parole. Both of these sentences are a form of **conditional release**, whereby the offender is allowed to remain in the community if he or she abides by certain conditions, such as reporting regularly to a supervising officer, observing a curfew, or refraining from further criminal activity. Violation of the conditions of release constitutes grounds for the **revocation** of liberty. For instance, a probationer who is ordered not to consume alcohol can lose his or her liberty if caught drinking. The revocation process is a miniature justice system in which the probation or parole officer detects and investigates violations of conditions, and arrests and prosecutes violators who are tried by the sentencing judge (if on probation) or parole authority (if on parole). Upon "conviction" of violating the conditions of release, the violator may be sentenced to incarceration or continued supervision.

BOX 3.4 Distribution of Sentencing Power Among Branches of Government

States vary in the degree of judicial and parole board discretion in sentencing and release decisions provided by law. Today, the range of state sentencing systems involves the following:

Indeterminate sentencing. The judge has primary control over the type of sentence given (such
as prison, probation or fine, and the upper and lower bounds of the length of prison sentences within statutory limits), but the actual time served is determined by the parole board.

Determinate sentencing. The judge sets the type of sentence and the length of prison sentences within statutory limits, but the parole board may not release prisoners before their
sentences have expired, minus time off for good behavior, or "good time."

Mandatory prison terms. Legislation requires imposition of a prison sentence, often of specified length, for certain crimes and/or categories of offenders.

Presumptive sentencing. The judge is required to impose a sentence whose length is set
by law for each offense or class of offense. When there are mitigating or aggravating
circumstances, however, the judge is allowed to shorten or lengthen the sentence within
specified boundaries.

Some states have other practices that affect sentencing and the actual time served:

Sentencing guidelines. The courts set sentences by using procedures designed to structure
sentencing decisions, usually based on offense severity and criminal history.

Parole guidelines. Parole boards use procedures designed to structure release decisions
based on measurable offender criteria.

Good-time policies. In nearly all states, legislation allows for reduction of a prison term
based on the offender's behavior in prison.

Emergency crowding provisions. These are policies that relieve prison crowding by systematically making certain inmates eligible for early release.

In recent years many states have been moving away from sentencing systems that allow judges and parole
boards wide discretion in sentences and time served. They are moving toward more certain and fixed
punishments for crimes through mandatory sentences, sentences of fixed length (determinate sentencing),
and the abolition of parole boards.

Source: Bureau of Justice Statistics (1989), *BJS Data Report, 1988* (Washington, DC: U.S. Department of
Justice):20–21.

When the author of this book was employed by the Oregon State Board of Parole, nearly half of all inmates admitted to that state's prisons each year were admitted as probation or parole violators. Between 1990 and 2000, the percent of prison admissions in the United States accounted for by parole violators rose from 29 to 35 percent (Hughes, Wilson & Beck, 2001:13), and parole violators still comprised one-third of prison admissions in 2002 (Harrison & Beck, 2005:6).

With the exception of the death penalty, incarceration in prison is this country's most severe penalty. Convicted offenders receive this sentence either directly from the court or, more circuitously, through the revocation of conditional liberty.

In comparison to the total number of convicted offenders, less than 1 percent is sentenced to death or life imprisonment (Rainville & Reaves, 2003). Thus, for most offenders, a day comes when they are no longer under the control of the justice system. The last point in the justice process is discharge.

Discharge

Most criminal offenders will eventually be discharged from their sentences. **Discharge** is final release from criminal justice control or supervision. For some, this discharge will occur at the expiration of their term. For someone sentenced to a 10-year prison term, discharge will take place 10 years after the date of sentencing, whether the person was incarcerated for the full 10 years or was granted an earlier release by parole or reduction in term for good behavior.

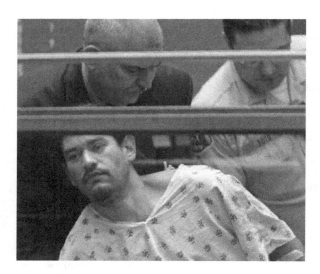

Juan Manuel Alvarez appears in a Los Angeles courtroom for his arraignment on murder charges, January 28, 2005, in Los Angeles. Alvarez, who faced murder charges for allegedly triggering the deadly collision of two commuter trains during an aborted suicide attempt, was granted a delay of his arraignment for further medical evaluation. *Photo credit: AP Photo/Nick Ut, Pool.*

Many states, however, have adopted procedures for "early" discharge. An offender serving a 10-year term may be paroled after serving three years, and then, after successfully completing three years (for example) under parole supervision, may receive an early discharge; thus, the offender may be released from sentence after serving only six years. Other jurisdictions in which no formal early discharge procedure exists may place similar offenders on "unsupervised parole status" after some time. In this case, the offender technically is still under sentence but is not being supervised in the community, and, for all practical purposes, has been discharged.

Upon discharge from sentence, the convicted offender becomes a member of the free society again. In most cases, the record of conviction and collateral effects of conviction (limits on civil rights, employability, and the like) will haunt the ex-convict. Conviction of a crime, especially a felony, often disqualifies the offender from certain types of occupations, such as those requiring licensure or certification (teaching school, practicing law or medicine, and the like). In some cases, felony conviction leads to "civil death," that is, the offender has no rights to enter contracts (including marriage), borrow money, vote, or hold public office (Buckler & Travis, 2003; Burton, Cullen & Travis, 1987).

BOX 3.5 **Method of Execution**

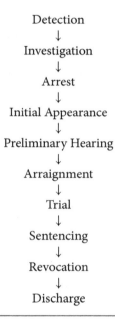

Detection
↓
Investigation
↓
Arrest
↓
Initial Appearance
↓
Preliminary Hearing
↓
Arraignment
↓
Trial
↓
Sentencing
↓
Revocation
↓
Discharge

Box 3.5 graphically portrays the decision points of the criminal justice system.

The Total Criminal Justice System

As our brief description of the justice system illustrates, cases move through the various decision points on a contingency basis. If a crime is detected, an investigation may begin. If the investigation yields sufficient evidence, an arrest may be made. If an arrest is made, formal charges may be brought. The operative word is "if." Approaching this issue from the other direction, the sentence depends upon the conviction, which depends upon the charge, which depends upon the investigation, which depends upon the detection of crime. To paraphrase an old song about how bones are connected, we might say detection is connected to investigation; investigation is connected to arrest; arrest is connected to charging; charging is connected to arraignment;

arraignment is connected to sentencing; sentencing is connected to correction; and correction is connected to discharge.

Each decision in the justice process is in large part determined by previous decisions. To a certain degree, earlier decisions depend upon past practices in later points of the justice process. For example, if a county prosecutor routinely dismisses cases involving possession of minor amounts of marijuana, law enforcement officers are more inclined to stop arresting persons for possession of small amounts of that drug.

As the concept of a system implies, the various components of the justice process (the decisions) are interdependent. As a result, the practices of all the justice agencies affect those of every other agency to some extent. Similarly, environmental pressures will affect the operations of each justice agency to some degree. Some examples illustrate the manner in which environmental pressures and agency changes have system-wide effects: the effort to control drunk driving, the "war" on drugs, and the redefinition of domestic violence arrest policies.

Controlling the Drunk Driver

Drunk driving, while a serious safety problem on the nation's highways, was not viewed as a particularly serious offense historically. In the 1980s, however, drunk driving came to be seen as a serious crime. It was no longer fashionable to drink and drive, and sketches and jokes about drunk drivers in the entertainment media were replaced with dramas depicting the devastating effects of drunk driving. "In short, attitudes have changed. Today's drunk driver is a pariah. It is no longer socially acceptable to stagger out from a pub and sit behind the wheel" (Balko, 2003:9). Applegate et al. (1996) noted that surveys generally reveal that the public takes a punitive stance toward drunk driving. However, the punitiveness of the public is related to how much harm is caused by the drunk driving, with drunk drivers who injure or kill others most likely to be seen as deserving harsh penalties. Over the past quarter century all states have taken steps to control drunk driving, most often by redefining the offense as a more serious misdemeanor or felony, and by requiring mandatory incarceration of those convicted of drunk driving, regardless of harm. Every state now has defined a blood alcohol content (BAC) of .08 as a presumptive standard of intoxication. That is, if the BAC measures .08 or higher, the driver is assumed to be impaired. Box 3.6 describes statutory provisions affecting driving under the influence. Persons convicted of driving while intoxicated accounted for nearly 6 percent of the jail population nationally and around 10 percent of convicted offenders serving sentences in jails (see Box 3.7).

This shift in public attitude regarding drunk drivers—and the associated legislative changes—placed considerable strains on the criminal justice system. More persons were arrested for driving under the influence of alcohol; more of those arrested refused to plead guilty; and many more of those found guilty were incarcerated in jails. Further, many of those sent to jail were first offenders with no prior record, and were not typical jail inmates. In many ways, these offenders required a different institutional setting than the jail, which is generally used for other types of criminal offenders.

BOX 3.6 Statutory Provisions Concerning Driving Under the Influence

Statutory Provision	Jurisdictions With Provision	Jurisdictions Without Provision
Felony D.U.I.	46	5
Mandatory Jail for 2nd Offense	47	4
Zero Tolerance	51	0
Penalty for Test Refusal Greater than for Test Failure	34	17
Vehicle Confiscation	30	21
.08 BAC Per Se Intoxicated	51	0

Source: Mothers Against Drunk Driving. Found at: http://www.madd.org (accessed July 7, 2007).

BOX 3.7 Impact of DUI Enforcement on Jail Populations

Percent of persons in jail by sex, race, and conviction status with most serious offense being DUI.

Offender Characteristic	Percent
Sex:	
Male	6.6
Female	4.9
Race/Ethnicity:	
White	10.9
Black	1.1
Hispanic	7.7
Status:	
Convicted	8.9
Unconvicted	2.3

Source: D. James (2004), *Profile of Jail Inmates, 2002* (Washington, DC: Bureau of Justice Statistics):3, 4.

With drunk driving defined and viewed as a more serious offense, police officers are more likely to investigate erratic drivers, to charge the offender with driving under the influence (DUI) rather than with reckless operation, to arrest rather than warn, and, generally, to "process" offenders. Robyn Cohen (1992) reported that between 1980 and 1989 the number of arrests for drunk driving rose by 22 percent, while the number of licensed drivers increased by only 14 percent. In addition, prosecutors are more likely to charge drunk drivers. Moreover, with higher stakes (e.g., loss of driving privileges, stiff fines, mandatory incarceration), defendants are less likely to plead guilty (Meyer & Gray, 1997). As a result, the courts must hold more trials, and mandatory sentences create overcrowding in the jails. All three components of the justice process had to adapt to this new emphasis on DUI enforcement, as is seen in Box 3.8.

BOX 3.8 **Effects of Mandatory Jail Terms for Drunk Driving**

To gauge the impact of tougher sanctions on the criminal justice system, National Institute of Justice researchers examined the effects of mandatory confinement for drunk driving in jurisdictions in Washington, Tennessee, Ohio, and Minnesota. The findings revealed:

- When mandatory confinement is introduced and well publicized, drunk driver arrests usually increase.
- The introduction of mandatory confinement imposes new and heavy demands on courts, incarceration facilities and probation services.
- The adoption of mandatory confinement is frequently accompanied by increased public concern about drunk driving and is associated with a decline in traffic fatalities.
- Mandatory confinement can be imposed either through legislation or through judicial policy.
- The implementation of mandatory confinement often requires additional resources for the criminal justice system.
- Appropriate systemwide planning can minimize dysfunction and substantially reduce the impact of mandatory confinement on criminal justice operation.

Source: National Institute of Justice (1985), "Jailing Drunk Drivers: Impact on the Criminal Justice System." *NIJ Reports* (July):2.

The effort to control drinking and driving has continued and gotten more intense. Balko (2003) reports more than 100 new pieces of drinking-and-driving legislation were considered in 31 states between 2002 and 2003. In 2000, the U.S. Congress passed a law creating a federal presumptive intoxication standard at a blood alcohol level of .08. This legislation tied federal highway money to adoption of the new standard. States that did not adopt the lower standard would not receive federal highway funds. Some states estimated that the increased costs of criminal justice processing of drivers found to have blood alcohol levels between .10 and .08 would exceed the amount of highway funds they received from the federal government. Those states initially chose not to adopt the new standard (Vartebedian, 2002), but all states now have this standard.

Interestingly, an early evaluation of changes in drunk driving enforcement (1985) revealed how justice agency policies can affect the total system as well. In Memphis, Tennessee, with little publicity about drunk driving, law enforcement attitudes did not change, and thus arrest rates, court loads, and jail populations of drunk drivers also did not change. In Minnesota, however, although no legislation was enacted, judges adopted a policy of mandatory incarceration; successfully anticipated problems for police, courts, and corrections; and took steps to minimize the problems.

Other analyses of drunk driving laws and enforcement practices show that organizational patterns of police agencies affect arrest decisions (Mastrofski, Ritti & Hoffmaster, 1987). Individual officer characteristics also were found to be related to arrest decisions in drunk driving cases

(Meyers et al., 1987). These studies indicate that an understanding of the effect of justice reform is difficult. Knowledge of the changes in the law is only part of the answer. Organizational and individual characteristics of justice agencies and agents affect how a reform is implemented. Finally, research on the effects of stiff punishments for drunk driving reveals that the deterrent effect of these laws is limited. Yu, Evans, and Clark (2006) reported that persons having an alcohol addiction or serious drinking problem were not likely to be deterred by DUI penalties.

The War on Drugs

In 1973, the state of New York adopted legislation hailed as "the nation's toughest drug law" (U.S. Department of Justice, 1978). This law was intended to "crack down" on those who sold heroin and other dangerous drugs. It had provisions for very stiff sentences and placed controls on plea bargaining. Further, to cope with the anticipated increase in drug offense cases, it provided for the creation of 49 new judgeships. The intent of the legislation was clear: to apprehend, convict, and punish those who sold heroin.

The effect of the law, however, is less clear. The officers and agencies of the justice system appear to have adapted to the changes in order to reduce the potentially disruptive effects on normal court operations that would result from the new law. While there were no dramatic increases in arrests for sale of heroin, fewer of those arrested were indicted, fewer of those indicted pleaded guilty, and fewer were convicted. For those convicted, both the rate of incarceration and the length of prison terms increased after the law took effect. However, in the final analysis, three years after the law was passed, the percentage of those arrested for heroin sale or possession who went to prison remained stable at 11 percent, a figure identical to that occurring before the law was passed in 1973.

There are several possible explanations. First, a probable reason why the number of arrests did not increase was because the sale and possession of large quantities of heroin were already considered serious offenses (even before the new law was enacted). Neither law enforcement nor public attitudes were changed by the new legislation. The fact that fewer defendants pleaded guilty meant that prosecutors needed to be more certain of getting a guilty verdict before taking a case to trial. Thus, indictments decreased as marginal cases were dismissed or downplayed. The increased number of trials created a backlog for the courts so that fewer cases were processed, and further, acquittals were handed down in some cases in which previously a plea of guilty had ensured conviction.

The mandatory sentencing provisions of the legislation may account for the higher incarceration rate and more severe prison terms imposed after the legislation was enacted. This suggests that there was no conscious effort to undermine the intent of the tough anti-drug law, but rather, the court component of the justice process adapted to new pressures reflexively. As part of a system, the courts sought to maintain equilibrium and adapted to stresses and strains so as to minimize their impact.

In this example, the effect of the legislation was initially and most specifically directed at the criminal courts, and an effort was made to alleviate the strains through the creation of new courts. Had these new courts not been provided, it is likely that even more cases would have been dismissed and/or the backlog of cases would have been even greater. The law did not directly affect law enforcement. The effect of changes in prison sentences on corrections was not dramatic for two reasons. First, because heroin dealers are only a very small proportion of all those sentenced to prison, even large increases in their terms or rate of incarceration would not dramatically affect prisons. Second, the percentage of those arrested who were actually sentenced to prison did not change, and the effects of longer terms would not be felt until several years after those who received longer sentences had been imprisoned.

The war on drugs, having raged now for more than a two decades in its most recent form, has produced changes in the characteristics of prison populations, with convictions for drug law violations being the most common crimes for which persons are sentenced to prison (Durose & Langan, 2003; White & Gorman, 2000). Most offenders serving prison terms at any time were convicted of violent crimes, but drug offenders account for the largest part of total prison population growth (Harrison & Beck, 2003). This has contributed to the continued problem of prison and jail crowding and prompted the development of intermediate sanctions, specialized drug courts, and other adaptations in the criminal justice system. It has also had a disproportionately harsh impact on the poor, women, and members of minority groups (Welch, Wolff & Bryan, 1998).

Domestic Violence Arrest Policies

The redefinition of domestic violence also illustrates the interdependency of the criminal justice system. The movement toward policies calling for mandatory arrests in cases of domestic violence has been complicated (Sherman, 1992). Some evaluators have noted that despite clear policy statements requiring arrest, police officers arrest domestic violence offenders in less than half of all cases (Belknap & McCall, 1994). This may be a result of the fact that the offender is not present when the police arrive (Feder, 1996), as well as because prosecutors and courts often still do not treat the offense as a serious matter (Kane, 1999). Whatever else has happened, there is some evidence that victims are increasingly likely to complain to the police, and that the police are increasingly likely to write formal reports, even if no arrests are made (Lanza-Kaduce, Greenleaf & Donahue, 1995).

Johnson and Sigler (2000) compared public opinion about violence against women over a 10-year period and reported that public tolerance for violence has decreased as criminalization of such behavior has become more common. A more recent study indicates that the public is still intolerant of domestic violence, whether in the form of physical or verbal abuse (Boatwright-Horowitz, Olick & Amaral, 2004). It is not possible to tell if opinion changes cause legal changes, or if the reverse is true. Still, domestic violence policy and law demonstrate the link between public opinion and criminal justice practice. Jones and Belknap (1999), studying the practices of the Boulder, Colorado, police, report that the police response to domestic violence appears more formal and serious currently than it has in the past. Again, public perceptions of offense seriousness and the severity of justice system response are related.

One of the most important policy changes in the response to domestic violence has been a proliferation of preferred or mandatory arrest policies and laws. These reforms require the police to arrest offenders involved in domestic assaults. The impact of such policies is unclear. It appears that arrest generally reduces later instances of domestic violence, but the impact of arrest is different for white offenders and for black offenders, and may be different for people of different economic levels (Maxwell, Garner & Fagan, 2002). There is also evidence that mandatory arrest policies have increased the arrests of domestic violence victims (Chesney-Lind, 2002). In most jurisdictions adopting these policies, the numbers and rates of arrests for both male and female parties to the incidents have increased dramatically. The unintended consequences of these policies, such as deterring victims from reporting offenses, increasing the number of victims subjected to arrest,

Actress Carmen Electra is escorted by police to the Miami-Dade County jail after she and then-husband, former basketball star Dennis Rodman, were arrested at a hotel on charges of domestic violence. Mandatory and preferred arrest policies have increased the numbers and rates of arrest for both male and female parties to domestic violence incidents. *Photo credit: AP Photo/ Wilfredo Lee.*

and long-term effects on relationships and families, are still unknown (Humphries, 2002). Efforts to make prosecution of domestic violence easier may result in less effort by police to obtain victim cooperation, and ultimately in weaker cases and fewer convictions (Davis, Smith & Taylor, 2003). What is clear is that the adoption and implementation of policy reforms in this area has been neither easy nor trouble-free (Ostrom, 2003; Whitcomb, 2002).

All of these issues have proven to be difficult for criminal justice policymakers and reformers to manage. Experience with these efforts to change criminal justice practices in dealing with drunk drivers, drug offenses, and domestic violence illustrates how the justice system interacts with its environment. In some cases, changes occur in all aspects of the justice process, such as drug enforcement, resulting in more arrests, convictions, and changes in the correctional population. In other cases, the system is sometimes able to adapt so as to minimize the impact of a reform by increasing rates of case dismissal or plea bargaining, or reducing the severity of sentences. All of these examples show that the criminal justice process operates as a system, adapting to change and pressure. They also indicate the complexity of evaluating the operations of the criminal justice process. This complexity becomes clearer when one examines the structure and organization of the agencies that comprise system of criminal justice in the United States.

The Components of Criminal Justice

As was done in Chapter 1, it is common to divide the criminal justice system into three parts: law enforcement, courts, and corrections. Each of these three parts of the justice system is itself comprised of a multitude of separate agencies and actors. The organizations that make up the total criminal justice system are differently structured and funded, and draw from different personnel pools.

One of the most important distinctions among similar agencies is jurisdiction. Police departments, courts, and correctional agencies may be municipal (village, township, city, or county), state, or federal in nature. They may be specialized, like the United States postal inspectors, or they may have general duties, as does a typical police department. They may be public or private (such as security guards, many halfway houses, and other entities that provide crime control services). In this section, we will examine the nature of criminal justice agencies in law enforcement, courts, and corrections.

Law Enforcement

There are so many agencies with law enforcement mandates that it is not possible to state their true number with confidence. In 1967, the President's Commission on Law Enforcement and Administration of Justice (1967b) estimated (in its task force report on police) that more than 40,000 police agencies were in existence. Later, the U.S. Department of Justice reported that there were close to 20,000 state and local law enforcement agencies. This report, however, did not include townships with populations of less than 1,000 (1980:24), nor did it include federal law enforcement agencies. Most recently, the Bureau of Justice Statistics (Reaves, 2007) identified about 18,000 state and local police agencies.

Federal Law Enforcement

A number of federal law enforcement agencies exist. These agencies tend to be small with specific mandates, yet in total, federal law enforcement is very complex. We are all aware of the Federal Bureau of Investigation (FBI), and most of us have heard of the U.S. Marshals; the Postal Inspectors; the Drug Enforcement Administration (DEA); the Bureau of Alcohol, Tobacco, Firearms, and Explosives (ATF); the Immigration and Naturalization Service; Customs; the Internal Revenue Service (IRS); and the Secret Service. Yet, many are unaware of the law enforcement duties of the National Park Service, the United States Supreme Court Police Department, the National Gallery of Art Protection Staff, and other federal "police" agencies. We seldom consider the military police, the tribal police departments on Native American reservations, or the investigative duties of auditors and staff of such organizations as the Federal Trade Commission (FTC) (Travis & Langworthy, 2008). Reaves and Bauer (2003) reported that in mid-2002, the federal government employed about 93,000 full-time officers with arrest powers who were authorized to carry firearms. The bulk of these employees worked for the Immigration and Naturalization Service, and they included 14,000 employees of the Federal Bureau of Prisons. At least 16 other federal agencies employed 500 or more such officers and agents. These numbers excluded law enforcement personnel in the military and those working overseas, but did include some 1,300 federal officers in U.S. Territories. These federal employees do not include the officers of the Transportation Security Administration, created in the wake of the September 11, 2001, terrorist attacks.

Creation of the Department of Homeland Security resulted in organizational changes in federal law enforcement. The Department of Homeland Security is now the single largest employer of federal law enforcement officers, administering the U.S. Coast Guard, Secret Service, Federal Protective Service, and U.S. Customs Service (except for some revenue functions), and has taken over the responsibilities of the Immigration and Naturalization Service, which was abolished. With these changes, the Department of Homeland Security employs 38 percent of federal officers, and the Department of Justice employs 37 percent (Reaves & Bauer, 2003:5).

Because they serve the entire nation, these agencies recruit nationally and tend to have more stringent entry requirements than do most police departments. The FBI, for example, requires a bachelor's degree in combination with investigatory experience or postgraduate training. Because federal law enforcement is funded at the federal level, salary and benefits for federal law enforcement officers are often higher than those paid to municipal police.

State Law Enforcement

The most common form of state police agency is the highway patrol. The highway patrol is charged with enforcing traffic laws on state and federal highways. Many states, however, also charge their state police with general law enforcement duties (International Association of Chiefs of Police, 1975). The New York State Police, for example, not only serve as traffic officers on that state's highways, but also have as a primary duty the provision of general law enforcement service to residents in rural and unincorporated areas. In addition, several states have specialized state units to combat drug offenses, organized crime, liquor and cigarette tax violations, and the like. Finally, many states also charge their park services with law enforcement obligations. Reaves and Hickman (2002) reported that 49 primary state police agencies employed more than 87,000 officers.

Like federal agencies, state agencies recruit from a pool of candidates that is considerably larger than that tapped by most local police departments. Moreover, in many states, the salary and benefits paid to state police officers are higher than those paid in most local departments (Bureau of Justice Statistics, 1989).

Municipal Law Enforcement

The bulk of law enforcement services are provided through municipal or local police departments, as shown in Box 3.9. These include the traditional city or township police department, as well as the county sheriff. The majority of police departments in the United States are local ones, and most police agencies are small, employing fewer than 25 officers (Reaves, 2007:4). Most police officers, however, work for large departments, because the relatively few large departments employ a great many officers.

BOX 3.9 Distribution of Police Personnel and Costs by Level of Government

Level of Government	% Police Personnel	% Police Costs
Federal	14.0	16.7
State	9.5	9.6
Local	76.5	73.6

Source: A. Pastore & K. Maguire (eds.) (2007). *Sourcebook of Criminal Justice Statistics* [online]. Found at: http://www.albany.edu/sourcebook/ (accessed August 1, 2007).

Municipal police departments rarely conduct national searches or recruitment drives, with the exception of a few (usually larger) police departments. Most local police departments recruit locally and employ civil service testing to enlist new officers (Sanders, Hughes & Langworthy, 1995). Sheriffs generally are elected, but many sheriff's deputies are recruited through civil service. It is common for police protection to comprise a major portion of a municipality's budget. In more than 40 states, law enforcement officers must first pass a required training curriculum before being sworn in, and new recruits must complete at least 800 hours of academy and field training. Recruits in the largest agencies must complete about twice as many hours of training (nearly 1,600) than those employed in smaller ones (Hickman & Reaves, 2003:5).

On average, there are about 1.5 local police officers for every 1,000 residents. In 2000, local police agencies costs were approximately $179 per resident per year. The average starting salary for a full-time local police officer was $31,700 per year. As might be expected, departments serving smaller communities generally pay lower salaries than those serving larger communities (Hickman & Reaves, 2003:6–7). By 2004, local police departments employed more than 446,000 full-time sworn officers (Reaves, 2007). The more than 3,000 sheriff's offices employed another 175,000 sworn officers, bringing the total number of sworn officers in general-purpose local police and sheriff agencies to more than 600,000 full-time sworn officers (Reaves, 2007:5).

Private and Other Public Law Enforcement

In addition to the agencies described above, there are hundreds of special-purpose law enforcement agencies in cities and counties, ranging from parkway and transit authority police to housing authority police. Reaves (2007) identified nearly 1,500 public, special purpose police agencies including housing authority, school, airport, university, and park police. Further, there are thousands of private and semi-public law enforcement agencies in the United States. For example, most factories, amusement parks, and hospitals have security staff, as do most retail chain stores. Many residential buildings and developments also have private security. Private police and private security personnel outnumber the public police by a ratio of at least three to one (Maahs & Hemmens, 1998). Additionally, the coroner or medical examiner is often considered to be a law enforcement official because of the investigative duties of that position.

As we have seen, it may not be possible to speak accurately of law enforcement—or even of the police—in the United States. The diversity of agencies, standards, and duties is nearly mind-boggling. Because law enforcement is the largest (numerically) component of the justice process, a review of justice agencies in courts and corrections is less complicated, but only marginally so.

Courts

In 1977, the U.S. Department of Justice reported that there were more than 3,600 courts of general or appellate jurisdiction in the United States, exclusive of tribal courts and the federal judiciary. In 1994, the Bureau of Justice Statistics surveyed a sample of more than 3,000 state felony courts of general jurisdiction (Langan & Brown, 1997). There are thousands of courts of limited jurisdiction also in operation. Ostrom, Kauder, and LaFountain reported that there are more than 15,550 state courts alone. Like law enforcement, the court system is fragmented and complicated (National Survey of Court Organization, 1977). There are federal, state, and municipal courts. These courts are divided further in terms of the types of cases they may hear and the types of decisions they may reach.

There are more than 300 justices of the Supreme Court and other courts of last resort in the 50 states, District of Columbia, and federal systems. More than 1,100 additional justices serve in intermediate courts of appeal, with more than 9,000 judges serving in general trial courts (Rottman et al., 2000). State supreme court justices are paid an average of $107,905 per year, with intermediate and trial court judges earning average salaries of $106,395 and $96,475, respectively (Maguire & Pastore, 1999:68).

Federal Courts

In 1996, there were more than 1,850 federal justices, judges, and magistrates, with a total judiciary staff exceeding 24,000 (Administrative Office of the U.S. Courts, 1996; Maguire & Pastore, 1996). Federal judges and justices of the U.S. Supreme Court are nominated by the President and appointed with the advice and consent of the United States Senate. These judges have lifetime tenure. Federal magistrates are appointed to eight-year terms by federal district judges.

The federal courts are organized by **circuits**, with 11 circuits covering the entire nation. Within these circuits, 89 district courts are trial courts. In addition, more than 400 federal magistrates within these districts may hear minor offenses and conduct the early stages of felony trials and more serious civil trials. Compensation for federal judicial officers ranges from more than $142,000 per year for magistrates to more than $198,000 per year for the Chief Justice of the U.S. Supreme Court (Maguire & Pastore, 2003:75).

Federal courts decide cases of federal interest: for example, charges of federal law violation. Federal appeals courts also decide federal constitutional issues, even if such issues were raised during state trials or proceedings.

State Courts

State judicial systems are similar to the federal judiciary in structure. They are generally comprised of trial courts, intermediate appellate courts, and a state supreme court. State judges and justices are either appointed (as is the federal judiciary) or elected. Members of most state judiciaries are in office for specified terms of office (unlike federal judges, who have lifetime tenure). Rhode Island's judges have lifetime tenure, and judges in Massachusetts and New Hampshire serve terms that do not expire until the judge reaches age 70 (Ostrom, Kauder & LaFountain, 2003).

While federal judges are recruited nationally (although district court judges and circuit court judges are generally selected from among candidates residing in the particular district or circuit), state court judges are elected statewide (or appointed) for statewide posts (e.g., the office of justice of the state supreme court), or from the jurisdiction of the lower court (e.g., the county of a specific county court). While there may be no constitutional provision (Maine and Massachusetts do not require a law degree), as with United States judges, or statutory requirement that judges be members of the bar, most judges are attorneys. By late 2002, the average salaries for judicial officials in state courts were $123,525 for justices of the highest court, $121,086 for intermediate appellate court justices, and $111,222 for general trial court judges (Maguire & Pastore, 2003:81).

Local Courts

There are a plethora of local courts in the United States. These are courts of limited jurisdiction because they are not allowed to decide felony cases, serious misdemeanors, or civil suits seeking damages above fairly low dollar amounts. Often these are known as "justice of the peace" courts. In many places, these limited-jurisdiction courts are known as police courts or mayor's courts. They usually decide traffic offense cases, hear violations of local ordinances and petty offenses, and make bail determinations.

Some of these judgeships are "ex officio." For example, upon being elected mayor in Ohio, the new mayor becomes the "judge" of mayor's court. In states that still retain the office of justice of the peace, frequently there is no formal legal training required for this position. These limited-jurisdiction courts are not authorized to conduct jury trials, and their decisions may be appealed to courts of general jurisdiction, which are also known as "trial courts."

Salaries for these local courts are usually not commensurate with what an attorney could earn in the private practice of law. However, many of these courts operate on a part-time basis, and members of the bar may serve as justices of the peace.

Other Courts

Every court system has a number of special-jurisdiction courts. For example, the federal judiciary has a tax court, and states usually have a court of domestic relations and/or a juvenile court. Several jurisdictions also have bankruptcy courts and other special jurisdiction courts. A relatively recent innovation is what may be called a **private court**. In some places, offices or commissions for dispute resolution have been developed to divert cases away from the formal courts (Aaronson et al., 1977). Here, the parties to a dispute sit with a lay negotiator (or team of negotiators) and attempt to resolve their problem without resorting to the courts. Most of these private courts are staffed by volunteers or by paid staff whose salaries are lower than that of a judge. An example of this type of private court was seen on television as "The People's Court." Court specialization within the criminal justice system has also increased with the development and spread of special **drug courts** dedicated to the processing and supervision of drug cases, as illustrated in Box 3.10. Other special courts are increasingly common. Rottman and Casey (1999) describe these as "problem-solving courts" where courts (judges, prosecutors, and the defense bar) work with offenders, victims, service providers, and the broader community to develop long-term solutions to the problems that bring cases to court.

BOX 3.10 Special Jurisdiction/Problem Solving Courts in the United States, 2004

Court Specialty	Number of Courts
Drug Court	1,315
Family Court	202
Domestic Violence	123
Mental Health	115
Community	25
Re-entry	14
Other	214

Source: D. Rottman & S. Strickland (2006), *State Court Organization 2004* (Washington, DC: Bureau of Justice Statistics):185–186.

Prosecution

At all levels of courts, from local to federal, the interests of the state (not the victim) are represented by the prosecutor. In the federal system, the prosecutor is the U.S. Attorney or the Deputy U.S. Attorney. These are lawyers appointed by the nomination of the President with the consent of the Senate. Local prosecutors are common in most states; for the most part, they are lawyers elected at the county level. Prosecutors have many titles, including district attorney, state's attorney, county attorney, circuit attorney, commonwealth's attorney, solicitor, and others (DeFrances, 2002:11). The Bureau of Justice Statistics reported the existence of more than 2,300 prosecutor's offices responsible for felony cases in state criminal courts in 2001 (DeFrances, 2002). These offices employed more than 79,000 people, including more than 31,000 attorneys (DeFrances, 2002:3).

The salary of a prosecutor generally is not very high in comparison to potential private practice earnings or judicial salaries. The median salary for chief prosecutors in all jurisdictions was $85,000. In large jurisdictions in 2001 the median salary was $136,700 per year (DeFrances, 2002:2). Many assistant prosecutors (also known as assistant district attorneys) seek these positions at the start of their careers in order to gain trial experience prior to starting their own practices (Rubin, 1984).

Defense

There are three basic structures for the provision of defense counsel: private retention, public defenders, and assigned counsel. Private retention refers to the possibility of the defendant retaining his or her own attorney. Private retention is unusual because most criminal defendants cannot afford attorney fees. However, in cases involving wealthy or notorious defendants, celebrated defense attorneys are often retained. Fewer than one-fifth of felony defendants in the largest counties and less than one-third of defendants in federal courts used privately retained counsel (Harlow, 2000:1). Public defenders are organized like prosecutors; that is, they usually work with an appointed director or administrator who hires a sufficient staff of attorneys to represent indigent clients in court (*Guide to Establishing a Defender System*, 1978). The most common form of criminal defense system is the public defender, but most criminal courts use two or more methods of providing defense counsel, including assigned counsel and contract systems. In the provision of assigned counsel, judges are presented either with a list of all attorneys practicing in their jurisdiction, or with a list of those attorneys willing to take on criminal defense cases. The judge then appoints an attorney for each indigent defendant from this list; he or she usually moves down the list from the first name to the last. The attorneys selected and assigned are then paid a set fee, which is usually on an hourly rate not to exceed some upper limit per case. In contract systems, the court enters an agreement with a law firm, bar association, or private attorney for indigent defense services for a specified period of time at a specified rate (Harlow, 2000).

Like prosecutors, defense attorneys employed in public defender offices (and most assigned counsel schemes) are not paid as well as judges, nor are they paid as much as they could earn in private practice as retained defense attorneys. Again, like prosecutors, young attorneys often seek this kind of work to gain trial experience.

In the cases of both prosecutors and defense attorneys, staff are recruited from local bar associations. While the local nature of the recruitment is comparable to recruiting for most police officers and judges, the requirement of membership in the bar limits the pool of possible applicants.

Witnesses and Jurors

Many other persons are involved in the court process in addition to prosecutors, defense counsel, and judges. There are court support staff members, such as court clerks, stenographers, bailiffs, and administrators; however, we will focus here on witnesses and jurors.

A variety of persons may serve as witnesses in a criminal case (Victim/Witness Legislation, 1984). Generally the arresting officers and any investigators are called as witnesses in a criminal case. If any passersby saw the offense, they too may be called to testify. Sometimes the defendant (or a codefendant) is called to testify in criminal cases (but the defendant cannot be required to be a witness). Depending on the nature of the case, or of the defense, expert witnesses may be called. These individuals are first established as having special knowledge not commonly available to the average citizen. Experts in areas such as ballistics, forensic medicine, and psychology or psychiatry (for instance, when an insanity defense is raised) are asked to bring special knowledge to bear on issues at trial. The victim of a crime is "useful" only as a witness. Crimes are public wrongs; individual suffering is not at issue in criminal trials. In recent years, however, there has been an increased emphasis on using the criminal process to redress the harms suffered by individual victims. Balancing the interests of the victim with those of the defendant is a complicated task (Office for Victims of Crime, 2002).

Citizens participate directly and most strongly in the criminal justice process in the courts. Citizens make up the two types of juries used in the courts. Grand juries of citizens sit and listen to the prosecutor's case before deciding whether an indictment should be issued. Trial juries sit and listen to the criminal trial before deciding if the defendant should be convicted. In several states, and in death penalty cases, the jury also recommends a sentence to the judge after deciding to convict the defendant. Box 3.11 describes the use of jurors in the federal courts.

BOX 3.11 Juror Usage in the Federal Courts, 2005

Grand Juries:	
Total number of:	
Sessions	9,854
Jurors in Session	196,197
Hours in Session	48,582
Average number of:	
Jurors per Session	19.9
Hours per Session	4.9
Petit Juries	
Jury Trial Days	30,775
Total Jurors Selected	612,032

Source: A. Pastore & K. Maguire (eds.) (2007). *Sourcebook of Criminal Justice Statistics* [online]. Found at: http://www.albany.edu/sourcebook/ (accessed August 1, 2007).

Jurors are selected from lists of residents in the court's jurisdiction. Often these lists are voter registration rolls, telephone books, or the billing records of utility companies. Trial jurors are then subjected to voir dire, a process by which the prosecutor and defense attorney seek to discover whether the jurors have any prejudices that could affect their decision in the trial. A juror suspected of being unable to make an objective decision may be challenged by the attorneys and dismissed by the judge.

Corrections
Corrections can be divided into the general categories of incarceration and community supervision. This general classification, however, grossly oversimplifies this complex component of the justice system. In the area of incarceration are found both prisons and jails, while both probation and parole comprise the nonincarceration sectors of corrections. With this dichotomy, it is not clear where such sanctions as halfway houses or "split sentences" fall.

Incarceration

The most frequent place of incarceration for criminal offenders and those suspected of criminal acts is the jail. There are more than 3,300 jails in the United States (Perkins, Stephan & Beck, 1995), most of which are municipal—either city or (more frequently) county jails. Most jails do not have treatment staffs of counselors, psychologists, and therapists. The major occupational group in jails is correctional officers. Most jail correctional officers are poorly trained and low-paid. Often, jail officers are members of the police department or the sheriff's department that is responsible for jail operation. Starting salaries for jail officers in 1982 were reported to be at an average of less than $11,000 per year (Kerle & Ford, 1982), which was $1,700 per year lower than the average starting salary of a patrol officer in the same jurisdiction. In 1996, the average starting salary for a jail officer was about $22,600 (Camp & Camp, 1996). Jail officers often are recruited in the same way as police officers, which is through local searches and civil service testing.

The nation's jails supervise some 690,000 inmates on any given day, but because of the relatively short time most persons stay in jail, 10 million or more people may "do time" in jail each year. The U.S. Department of Justice reported more than 13 million admissions to jails in 1993 (Perkins, Stephan & Beck, 1995). More than half of those held in jail are not yet convicted and are awaiting trial (Harlow, 1998). It is not possible to determine how many jail admissions are repeat offenders.

The nation's more than 1,600 prisons and state and federal correctional facilities house more inmates than do jails on any given day (more than 1.2 million), but because of the longer terms, fewer people serve prison time each year than jail time. While jails usually are municipal, prisons are operated by the state or federal governments. Prisons are more apt than jails to have counselors, therapists, industries, and educational programs, partly because prisons are larger and hold inmates longer, and partly because they have a larger resource base (state taxes) than do city and county jails. Still, the most common occupational category in prisons is that of correctional officers (Stephan & Karberg, 2003). Like jail officers, correctional officers in prisons are typically selected through civil service and are not particularly well paid (Camp & Camp, 1984). State and federal correctional facilities employed almost 350,000 personnel in 1995, with about two-thirds of these designated as custody or security staff (Maguire & Pastore, 1999:81).

Nonincarceration

The most common form of nonincarcerative sanction (after fines, perhaps) is probation. On any day there are more than 3.9 million persons under probation supervision (Glaze, 2003:1). Probation officers supervise these persons in the community and are also responsible for writing presentence investigation reports and other programs, depending upon the jurisdiction.

Probation officers are typically assigned to courts, although more than one-half of the probation departments in the country are run by states. Unlike police or correctional officers, it is common for a probation officer to be required to have a college degree. Recruitment of probation officers tends to be local, on the basis of the court's jurisdiction. In 1996, Camp and Camp (1996) reported that there were more than 29,500 probation and parole officers (not counting supervisory staff). The average salary for entry-level probation officers reported by Camp and Camp (1996:135) was $25,126 per year.

Parole is similar to probation, except that parole is handled by a state agency; parole officers are, therefore, state employees. At any given time, more than 750,000 persons are under parole supervision. These persons have been granted an early release from incarceration (mostly from prison) and are supervised by parole officers. Thirty-eight states have parole boards in the executive branch of government that are responsible for deciding which inmates to whom early release will be granted, as well as what should be the proper conduct of the prisoners' parole periods.

A parole officer is often required to have a college education and to perform duties similar to those of a probation officer, except that a parole officer typically has a smaller caseload comprised of ex-inmates. Parole officers, on the average, receive slightly higher wages than do probation officers, and are selected from statewide pools through civil service procedures. Camp and Camp (1996) reported that the average annual salary for an entry-level parole officer was $26,829.

Private-Sector Corrections

As with law enforcement and the courts, there is also private involvement in corrections as well. Traditionally, many correctional practices were the province of voluntary or private initiatives. Throughout the 1980s until the present, there has been a growing movement to "privatize" corrections, with private companies constructing and operating prisons and jails in addition to providing other services on a contract basis (Travis, Latessa & Vito, 1985). Box 3.12 gives an indication of the growth of private involvement in corrections.

BOX 3.12 Growth of Private Correctional Facilities, 1995–2000

	Number	
Facility Characteristics	**1995**	**2000**
Confinement Facility	29	101
Community-Based	81	163
Total Personnel	5,248	24,357
Custody/Security Personnel	3,197	14,589
Size:		
Fewer than 250 Beds	93	175
250 to 1,499 Beds	17	79
1500 Beds and Larger	0	10
Rated Capacity	19,294	105,133
Percent Occupied	86%	89%

Source: A. Pastore & K. Maguires (eds.) (2007). *Sourcebook of Criminal Justice Statistics* [online]. Found at: http://www.albany.edu/sourcebook/ (accessed August 1, 2007).

In addition to these for-profit private correctional enterprises, volunteer service is relatively common in corrections. Volunteers write to and visit prison inmates, provide services to probation and parole offices and clients, and serve on a variety of boards and commissions. The boards and commissions range from those that govern halfway houses to citizen court-watching groups. "Neighborhood Watch" programs and other citizen crime-prevention projects have also increased the citizens' role in law enforcement. One of the most important trends in criminal justice over the past decade has been the resurgence of private initiative in the criminal justice system. Corrections is being affected by this development.

Systems and Criminal Justice Structure

What this chapter has demonstrated is that the criminal justice system in the United States is extremely complex. The various agencies that comprise the system are organized at different levels of government, utilize different resource bases, and select differentially qualified personnel in different ways. In short, although the justice system appears too diverse to be a system, the interdependence of its parts and its sensitivity to environmental changes support a systems approach.

There are at least 52 criminal justice systems in the United States: one for each state, the federal government, and the District of Columbia. This may, in fact, be an underestimate of their numbers. For example, if city police can arrest someone for violating a city ordinance, and that person can be convicted and fined in mayor's court, do we have a city justice system? While it may be argued that there are many criminal justice systems in the United States, we will continue to examine and discuss the criminal justice system as a whole.

This systems approach to the study of criminal justice seems especially appropriate. Without a prevailing approach, we might be forced to throw up our hands in despair, unable to make sense of the confusion. Why do we have so many agencies? Why do these different agencies have conflicting and sometimes competing jurisdictions and goals? The answer is because they are part of an open system. The large number of agencies and the various levels and branches of government involved can be understood as a manifestation of the environmental impact on American criminal justice. Given our political and cultural values of federalism, local autonomy, and the separation of powers, we should not be surprised at the confusion in the justice system; it would be more surprising if there was no confusion. A single, well organized, monolithic criminal justice system for the entire nation may well be "un-American."

Review Questions

1. Identify the ten decision points of the criminal justice process discussed in this chapter.
2. How does the justice process work as a directional flow of cases in the total system?

3. Give two examples of how the environment of the justice process affects the operations of all justice agencies.
4. What are the basic components of the justice process?
5. Describe the different types, levels, and staffing patterns of the components of the justice process.
6. Why is the "systems" approach especially appropriate to the study of American criminal justice?

References

Aaronson, D.E., N.N. Kittrie, D.J. Saari & C.S. Cooper (1977). *Alternatives to Conventional Criminal Adjudication.* Washington, DC: U.S. Government Printing Office.

Administrative Office of the U.S. Courts (1996). *Annual Report of the Director, 1995.* Washington, DC: Administrative Office of the U.S. Courts.

Applegate, B., F. Cullen, B. Link, P. Richards & L. Lanza-Kaduce (1996). "Determinants of Public Punitiveness Toward Drunk Driving: A Factorial Survey Approach." *Justice Quarterly* 13(1):57–80.

Avakame, E.F., J.J. Fyfe & C. McCoy (1999). "'Did You Call the Police? What Did They Do?' An Empirical Assessment of Black's Theory of the Mobilization of Law." *Justice Quarterly* 16(4):765–792.

Balko, R. (2003). "Back Door to Prohibition: The New War on Social Drinking." *CATO Policy Analysis* 501.

Belknap, J. & K. McCall (1994). "Woman Battering and Police Referrals." *Journal of Criminal Justice* 22(2):223–236.

Boatwright-Horowitz, S., K. Olick & R. Amaral (2004). "Calling 911 During Episodes of Domestic Abuse: What Justifies a Call for Help?" *Journal of Criminal Justice* 32(1):89–92.

Boland, B., P. Mahanna & R. Sones (1992). *The Prosecution of Felony Arrests, 1988.* Washington, DC: Bureau of Justice Statistics.

Buckler, K. G. & L.F. Travis (2003). "Reanalyzing the Prevalence and Social Context of Collateral Consequence Statutes." *Journal of Criminal Justice* 31(5):435–53.

Bureau of Justice Statistics (1989). *Profile of State and Local Law Enforcement Agencies, 1987.* Washington, DC: U.S. Department of Justice.

Bureau of Justice Statistics (1991). *Census of Local Jails 1988.* Washington, DC: U.S. Department of Justice.

Bureau of Justice Statistics (1996). *Correctional Populations in the United States, 1994.* Washington, DC: U.S. Department of Justice.

Burton, V.S., F.T. Cullen & L.F. Travis III (1987). "The Collateral Consequences of a Felony Conviction: A National Study of State Statutes." *Federal Probation* 51(3):52–60.

Camp, G.M. & C.C. Camp (1984). *The Corrections Yearbook.* South Salem, NY: Criminal Justice Institute.

Camp, G.M. & C.C. Camp (1996). *The Corrections Yearbook.* South Salem, NY: Criminal Justice Institute.

Chesney-Lind, M. (2002). "Criminalizing Victimization: The Unintended Consequences of Pro-Arrest Policies for Girls and Women." *Criminology and Public Policy* (2)1:81–90.

Cohen, R. (1992). *Drunk Driving*. Washington, DC: Bureau of Justice Statistics.

Davis, R., B. Smith & B. Taylor (2003). "Increasing the Proportion of Domestic Violence Arrests that are Prosecuted: A Natural Experiment in Milwaukee." *Criminology and Public Policy* 2(2):263–282.

DeFrances, C.J. (2002). *Prosecutors in State Courts, 2001*. Washington, DC: Bureau of Justice Statistics.

Durose, M. & P. Langan (2003). *Felony Sentences in State Courts, 2000*. Washington, DC: Bureau of Justice Statistics.

Feder, L. (1996). "Police Handling of Domestic Calls: The Importance of Offender's Presence in the Arrest Decision." *Journal of Criminal Justice* 24(6):481–490.

Felson, R., S. Messner, A. Hoskin & G. Deane (2002). "Reasons for Reporting and Not Reporting Domestic Violence to the Police." *Criminology* 40(3):617–648.

Glaze, L. (2003). *Probation and Parole in the United States, 2002*. Washington, DC: Bureau of Justice Statistics.

Goudriaan, H., J. Lynch, & P. Nieuwbeerta (2004). "Reporting to the Police in Western Nations: A Theoretical Analysis of the Effects of Social Context." *Justice Quarterly* 21(4):933–969.

Guide to Establishing a Defender System (1978). Washington, DC: U.S. Government Printing Office.

Harlow, C. (1998). *Profile of Jail Inmates 1996*. Washington, DC: Bureau of Justice Statistics.

Harlow, C. (2000). *Defense Counsel in Criminal Cases*. Washington, DC: Bureau of Justice Statistics.

Harrison, P.M. & A.J. Beck (2003). *Prisoners in 2002*. Washington, DC: Bureau of Justice Statistics.

Harrison, P.M. & A.J. Beck (2005). *Prisoner and Jail Inmates at Midyear 2004*. Washington, DC: Bureau of Justice Statistics.

Hart, T.C. & B.A. Reaves (1999). *Felony Defendants in Large Urban Counties, 1996*. Washington, DC: Bureau of Justice Statistics.

Hart, T.C. & C. Rennison (2003). *Reporting Crimes to the Police, 1992–2000*. Washington, DC: Bureau of Justice Statistics.

Hickman, M.J. & B.A. Reaves (2003). *Local Police Departments, 2000*. Washington, DC: Bureau of Justice Statistics.

Hughes, T. A., D.J. Wilson & A.J. Beck (2001). *Trends in State Parole, 1990–2000*. Washington, DC: Bureau of Justice Statistics.

Humphries, D. (2002). "No Easy Answers: Public Policy, Criminal Justice, and Domestic Violence." *Criminology and Public Policy* (2)1:91–96.

International Association of Chiefs of Police, Division of State and Provincial Police (1975). *Comparative Data Report*. Gaithersburg, MD: IACP.

Jailing Drunk Drivers (1985). Washington, DC: U.S. Department of Justice.

Johnson, I. & R. Sigler (2000). "Public Perceptions: The Stability of the Public's Endorsements of the Definition and Criminalization of the Abuse of Women." *Journal of Criminal Justice* 28(3):165–179.

Jones, D. & J. Belknap (1999). "Police Responses to Battering in a Progressive Pro-Arrest Jurisdiction." *Justice Quarterly* 16(2):249–273.

Kane, R. (1999). "Patterns of Arrest in Domestic Violence Encounters: Identifying a Police Decision-Making Model." *Journal of Criminal Justice* 27(1):65–79.

Kerle, K.E. & F.R. Ford (1982). *The State of Our Nation's Jails, 1982*. Washington, DC: National Sheriffs' Association.

Langan, P. & J. Brown (1997). *Felony Sentences in State Courts, 1994*. Washington, DC: Bureau of Justice Statistics.

Lanza-Kaduce, L., R. Greenleaf & M. Donahue (1995). "Trickle-up Report Writing: The Impact of a Proarrest Policy for Domestic Disturbances." *Justice Quarterly* 12(3):525–542.

Maahs, J. & C. Hemmens (1998). "Guarding the Public: A Statutory Analysis of State Regulation of Security Guards." *Journal of Crime and Justice* 21(1):119–134.

Maguire, K. & A. Pastore (1996). *Sourcebook of Criminal Justice Statistics—1995*. Washington, DC: U.S. Government Printing Office.

Maguire, K. & A. Pastore (1999). *Sourcebook of Criminal Justice Statistics—1998*. Washington, DC: U.S. Government Printing Office.

Maguire, K. & A. Pastore (2003). *Sourcebook of Criminal Justice Statistics—2002*. Washington, DC: U.S. Government Printing Office.

Maguire, K., A. Pastore & T. Flanagan (1993). *Sourcebook of Criminal Justice Statistics—1992*. Washington, DC: U.S. Government Printing Office), 90.

Mastrofski, S.D., R.R. Ritti & D. Hoffmaster (1987). "Organizational Determinants of Police Discretion: The Case of Drinking-Driving." *Journal of Criminal Justice* 15(5):387–402.

Maxwell, C. D., J.H. Garner & J.A. Fagan (2002). "The Preventive Effects of Arrest on Intimate Partner Violence: Research, Policy and Theory." *Criminology and Public Policy* 2(1):51–80.

McDonald, W. (ed.) (1979). *The Prosecutor*. Beverly Hills, CA: Sage.

Meyer, J. & T. Gray (1997). "Drunk Drivers in the Courts: Legal and Extra-Legal Factors Affecting Pleas and Sentences." *Journal of Crime and Justice* 25(2):155–163.

Meyers, A., T. Heeren, R. Hingson & D. Kovenock (1987). "Cops and Drivers: Police Discretion and the Enforcement of Maine's 1981 DUI Law." *Journal of Criminal Justice* 15(5):361–368.

National Survey of Court Organization (1977). Washington, DC: U.S. Department of Justice.

Newman, D.J. (1966). *Conviction: The Determination of Guilt or Innocence without Trial*. Boston: Little, Brown.

Office for Victims of Crime (2002). "The Crime Victim's Right to Be Present." *Legal Series Bulletin #3* (January). Washington, DC: Office for Victims of Crime.

Ostrom, B., N. Kauder & R. LaFountain (2003). *Examining the Work of State Courts 2002: A National Perspective from the Court Statistics Project*. Washington, DC: National Center for State Courts.

Ostrom, B. (2003). "Domestic Violence: Editorial Introduction." *Criminology and Public Policy* 2(2):259–262.

Perkins, C., J. Stephan & A. Beck (1995). *Jails and Jail Inmates, 1993–94*. Washington, DC: U.S. Department of Justice.

President's Commission on Law Enforcement and Administration of Justice (1967a). *The Challenge of Crime in a Free Society.* Washington, DC: U.S. Government Printing Office.

President's Commission on Law Enforcement and Administration of Justice (1967b). *Task Force Report: The Police.* Washington, DC: U.S. Government Printing Office.

Rainville, G. & B. Reaves (2003). *Felony Defendants in Large Urban Counties, 2000.* Washington, DC: Bureau of Justice Statistics.

Rand, M. (1998). *Criminal Victimization 1997: Changes 1996–97 with Trends 1993–1997.* Washington, DC: Bureau of Justice Statistics.

Rand, M., J. Lynch & D. Cantor (1997). *Criminal Victimization, 1973–95.* Washington, DC: Bureau of Justice Statistics.

Reaves, B. (2007). *Census of State and Local Law Enforcement Agencies, 2004.* Washington, DC: Bureau of Justice Statistics.

Reaves, B. & M. Hickman (2002). *Census of State and Local Law Enforcement Agencies, 2000.* Washington, DC: Bureau of Justice Statistics.

Reaves, B.A. & L.M. Bauer (2003). *Federal Law Enforcement Officers, 2002.* Washington, DC: Bureau of Justice Statistics.

Rennison, C. & M.R. Rand (2003). *Criminal Victimization, 2002.* Washington, DC: Bureau of Justice Statistics.

Rosett, A. & D. Cressey (1976). *Justice by Consent.* Philadelphia: J.B. Lippincott.

Rottman, D. & P. Casey (1999). "Therapeutic Jurisprudence and the Emergence of Problem-Solving Courts." *National Institute of Justice Journal* (July):12–19.

Rottman, D., C. Flango, M. Cantrell, R. Hansen & N. LaFountain (2000). *State Court Organization, 1998.* Washington, DC: Bureau of Justice Statistics.

Rubin, H.T. (1984). *The Courts: Fulcrum of the Justice System,* 2nd ed. New York: Random House.

Sanders, B., T. Hughes & R. Langworthy (1995). "Police Officer Recruitment and Selection: A Survey of Major Police Departments in the U.S." *Police Forum* 5(4):1–4.

Sherman, L. (1992). *Policing Domestic Violence: Experiments and Dilemmas.* New York: Free Press.

Smith, S. & C. DeFrances (1996). *Indigent Defense.* Washington, DC: Bureau of Justice Statistics.

Stephan, J. & J. Karberg (2003). *Census of State and Federal Correctional Facilities, 2000.* Washington, DC: Bureau of Justice Statistics.

Travis, L.F. & R.H. Langworthy (2008). *Policing in America: A Balance of Forces,* 4th ed. Englewood Cliffs, NJ: Prentice Hall.

Travis, L.F. & E.J. Latessa (1984). "A Summary of Parole Rules Thirteen Years Later: Revisited Thirteen Years Later." *Journal of Criminal Justice* 12(6):591–600.

Travis, L.F., E.J. Latessa & G.F. Vito (1985). "Private Enterprise in Institutional Corrections: A Call for Caution." *Federal Probation* 49(4):11–16.

U.S. Department of Justice (1978). *The Nation's Toughest Drug Law.* Washington, DC: U.S. Government Printing Office.

U.S. Department of Justice (1980). *Justice Agencies in the United States.* Washington, DC: U.S. Government Printing Office.

Vartebedian, R. (2002). "A Spirited Debate Over DUI Laws." *Los Angeles Times* (December 30, 2002):A1.

Victim/Witness Legislation: An Overview (1984). Washington, DC: U.S. Department of Justice.

Walker, S. (2001). *Sense and Nonsense about Crime and Drugs: A Police Guide*, 5th ed. Belmont, CA: Wadsworth.

Welch, M., R. Wolff & N. Bryan (1998). "Decontextualizing the War on Drugs: A Content Analysis of NIJPublications and their Neglect of Race and Class." *Justice Quarterly* 15(4):719–742.

Whitcomb, D. (2002). "Prosecutors, Kids, and Domestic Violence Cases." *National Institute of Justice Journal* (March):2–9.

White, H.R. & D.M. Gorman (2000). "Dynamics of the Drug-Crime Relationship." In G. LaFree (ed.), *The Nature of Crime: Continuity and Change*. Washington, DC: National Institute of Justice, Criminal Justice 2000, Volume 1.

Yu, J., P. Evans & L. Clark (2006). "Alcohol Addiction and Perceived Sanction Risks: Deterring Drunk Drivers." *Journal of Criminal Justice* 34(2):165–174.

Chapter 1: Key Terms and Discussion Questions

Key Terms

Arraignment: initial appearance; bringing a defendant before a judge to hear the criminal offenses charged and to plead guilty or not guilty

Arrest: the act of taking an individual into custody in a manner such that the individual would reasonably disbelieve that he or she is free to leave in order to charge the individual with a criminal offense

Bail: the temporary release of a defendant before trial in exchange for security given for the defendant's appearance at a later hearing

Booking: a procedure at the police station following an arrest where information about the arrest and the arrestee is entered into police records; usually includes mug shot, fingerprinting, and inventory

Brady Rule: part of discovery; prosecution must disclose potentially exculpatory evidence to the defense

Circuit Court: federal intermediate appellate court

Circumstantial Evidence: evidence that allows proof of one fact by drawing inferences or conclusions from the proof of another fact(s)

Common Law: judge-made law; body of law based on general principles and embodied in case law; originated in English courts and used in early colonial law; also known as customary law

Competent: evidence that is admissible, material, and relevant to the fact(s) at issue

Congress: the federal legislature

Courts of Appeal: federal circuit courts; intermediate appellate courts for state and federal courts

Direct Evidence: evidence, if credible, will immediately establish a fact; does not need inferences; comes directly from a witness's observations and knowledge

Discovery: methods used to obtain evidence for trial from opposite parties

District Court: federal trial court

Evidence: anything used to prove or disprove a fact in a case

Federal Rules of Evidence: a set of standardized rules that guide the use of evidence in federal trials

Grand Jury: a group of citizens that examines evidence of a defendant's action to determine whether charges should be pressed against the defendant via indictment; not necessary if there has been a preliminary hearing

Legislature: a body of representatives that have the power to pass laws

Magistrate: judicial officer vested with limited legal power; can authorize and issue warrants

Motion to Suppress: a motion filed to squash evidence because the evidence was obtained illegally

Preliminary Hearing: adversarial hearing required for prosecutor to show there is sufficient probable cause for the case to go forward; not needed if there have been grand jury proceedings

Pre-Trial Motions: motions filed by either party after arrest and before trial

Probable Cause: justification for police action that is based on more than 50 percent certainty that a crime has been or is being committed; more than reasonable suspicion, less than beyond a reasonable doubt

Relevant: evidence that is admissible, reliable, competent, and material to the fact(s) at issue

Reliable: evidence that is admissible, competent, and relevant to the fact(s) at issue

Search: an exploratory investigation of an individual or location by the government that infringes on the individual's reasonable expectation of privacy

State Supreme Court: highest state appellate court

Statutes: laws that have been promulgated by legislatures; codified law originating from passed bills

Superior Court: state trial court

US Supreme Court: highest court of the land; hears cases from state and federal courts

Discussion Questions

1. What is the difference between customary/common law and doctrines?
2. Explain jurisprudence as a source of law.
3. Describe the steps of the criminal justice process from arrest to trial.
4. Are video arraignments fair?
5. Do you agree with mandatory arrests in domestic violence investigations?

What Is Evidence?

The Crime Scene

Discovery, Preservation, Collection,
and Transmission of Evidence

by James W. Osterburg and Richard H. Ward

Defining the Limits of the Crime Scene

The crime scene encompasses all areas over which the actors—victim, criminal, and eyewitness—move during the commission of a crime. Usually it is one, readily defined area of limited size, but sometimes it comprises several sites. A case example of the latter is to be found in the abduction of a bank manager as he left for work one morning. The car that conveyed him to the bank, the vault and other areas in the bank, the vicinity of the place in the woods where he was found tied to a tree—each site is a part of the crime scene. Another example is a homicide in which the murder is committed in one place and the body is dumped or buried in another.

Although the precise boundary lines of a crime scene are most often well-defined, sometimes they can be in dispute. In the case of an attempted murder of a prominent black civil rights leader as he returned to his motel, the question was whether the shots came from one spot or from three different areas. Had a lone shooter lay hidden in the patch of weeds across the street from the motel? If so, it would support the local police view that the ambush was a response to the victim's visit with a white woman, a local civil rights activist. On the other hand, the three separate matted areas found in the weeds the next day supported federal investigators' belief in a conspiracy—and the presence of three shooters would put the crime under federal as well as local jurisdiction. Disputing a conspiracy theory, the police asserted that the weeds were trampled by reporters converging on the scene and not by one restive shooter.

In the world of cyberspace, the crime scene may be less obvious, and may involve multiple sites and multiple victims. For example, in cases involving child pornography distributed over the Internet, there may be several crime scenes: a crime scene in which children were victimized and photographed, a location where the photographs or images were later distributed (for sale or otherwise) on the Internet or by mail, and a buyer or user who may also be liable if a law is violated. Other examples may involve identity theft or fraud involving multiple locations and victims.

It is clear from the preceding cases that the crime scene must be conceptualized. Once its position and boundaries are defined, the scene must then be made secure, the physical evidence discovered and collected, and the crime reconstructed (if needed). Had the correct procedure been followed in the ambush investigation—boundaries defined and protected, and the area within them recorded—there would not have been a question of whether there were one or three sites or perpetrators. In this case, ensuring that the boundaries were "properly protected" would have meant cordoning it off until daylight, when the cursory search in the dark turned up little evidence. In all cases it means excluding reporters, government officials, even superior police officers who are not directly involved in the investigation; not to mention local residents and curiosity seekers. In any ambush investigation it is important to establish where the perpetrator was concealed and to record details of activity within that area. Afterward, it can be searched for other physical evidence, such as spent cartridges, food containers, or discarded cigarettes and matches. In this ambush, a thorough search conducted the next morning led to the discovery of a spent shell casing (from a 30.06 rifle) that had been overlooked.

The in-flight bombing of Pan Am Flight 103 over Lockerbie, Scotland, gave new meaning to the concept of the limits of a crime scene. Fragments of physical evidence—plane parts, bomb bits, personal belongings, body parts—were scattered over 800 square miles of countryside (see Figure 4.1). The painstaking recovery of four million pieces of physical evidence attests to the diligence and thoroughness of the effort to solve the case.

In cases involving cybercrime, the evidence may lie in a computer, or in some cases on disks or "jump" drives, as well as hard copies of materials, such as e-mails between individuals. In most cases, evidence recovery will require the assistance of experts. Nevertheless, it is important that the investigator recognize the broad dimensions of such cases and be familiar with the *modus operandi* of this type of criminal activity.

FIGURE 4.1 Scene of the crash of Pan Am Flight 103 in Lockerbie, Scotland. Crucial fragmentary evidence was recognized and collected in an area about 25 miles away from Lockerbie. The Pan Am Flight 103 evidence scene is the largest crime scene ever (more than 800 square miles) that needed to be searched.

The Crime Scene as an Evidence Source

An offender brings physical evidence to the crime scene: in burglary cases, tools needed to break into the premises or a safe; in robbery or homicide cases, a weapon used to threaten, assault, or kill; in arson cases, a container of flammable fluid; in technology-related cases, a hard drive or the messages on a cell phone. During the commission of a crime, an offender may inadvertently leave evidence behind (*in situ*): fingerprints, tool marks, shoe prints, blood-spatter patterns, spent bullets, fired cartridge casings. Other physical evidence can by its very nature be unavoidably left behind: in kidnapping cases, the ransom note; in bank robbery cases, the note handed to the teller. For instance, it may be left on a record tape. In one homicide case, the suspect's name first emerged in a message left on the deceased's answering machine.[1] The caller asked that a meeting be set up at a specific time in the owner's home, and when the latter was found dead there and time of death was determined to be an hour or two after the proposed meeting, this crucial piece of information had to be followed up. In this instance, it was—with success.

When searching the crime scene (and afterward), an investigator's observations and interviews might develop intangible evidence. For example, the emotional factors involved in motivating and carrying out a homicide become manifest as intangible evidence through an assessment of such observations as: grossly excessive stab wounds, bones unnecessarily broken, parts of the body cut out or cut off, or the choice and kind of lethal weapon employed. A shrewd appraisal of intangible evidence (as in psychological profiling) can provide leads to possible perpetrators. Interviewing also can be used to develop intangible evidence. Witnesses or victims may report on the language used during the commission of the crime. How exactly did the robber convey intentions and demands? What did the rapist say, before, during, and after the assault? Because such commands and comments are elements of the perpetrator's *modus operandi,* they have investigative and probative value.

The CSI Effect

Television programs written about crime scene investigation (CSI) are among the most popular. From a forensic scientist's perspective, or more correctly, a criminalist's viewpoint, such shows have been both meaningful and detrimental. They have alerted the public that forensic science exists and should be employed on their behalf. Unfortunately, they have also led many members of the public to believe they are knowledgeable about crime scene evidence and what should be collected, rather than leaving it to the CSI or criminalist to decide. Thus, sometimes the so-called evidence pointed out by the complainant and reluctantly collected by the crime scene investigator merely covers the analyst's lab work space with mostly irrelevant clue material. For example, a smudged fingerprint or a shoe impression with no details with which to compare the suspect's finger or shoe are often collected merely to satisfy the "expert" complainant.

---

1   Shannon Tangonan, "Accused Levin Killers Due to Be Arraigned," *USA Today,* (June 9, 1997), 9A.

Opportunity for Discovery

The crime scene provides the major opportunity to locate physical evidence. The initial response should be regarded as the only chance to recognize, record, and collect physical evidence. The investigator must make the most of it. This search, however, must be conducted properly and lawfully, or the evidence will be suppressed in the course of a trial. Police should not relinquish control over the scene and its environs until all evidence has been discovered and collected. If it must be gone over again later, legal difficulties may be created because pertinent evidence was not recognized or collected initially.

In 1984, the U.S. Supreme Court in *Michigan v. Clifford* reversed a decision based on evidence obtained by investigators who entered the scene of a suspected arson five hours after the blaze had been extinguished.[2] Another case, *Michigan v. Tyler*, also illustrates the need to collect evidence without unnecessary delay, otherwise a warrant must be obtained.[3] In the *Tyler* arson case there were three searches. The first was within one and a half hours after the fire; the second, four hours later (dense smoke having caused the delay); but the third was made three weeks later. Evidence from the first two was held admissible, but the evidence seized in the third attempt was not, because no emergency validated the warrantless search. The court found that investigators were able to stay inside the building after the fire was exhausted, but are required to obtain a warrant to conduct a search for evidence of crime not related to the cause of fire. Courts have consistently followed precedent from the *Tyler* case, including the case of *United States v. Mitchell*, in which firefighters entered a building 12 hours after the fire was exhumed to continue looking for evidence on how the fire started. The detectives were not able to continue the search immediately after the fire because of adverse conditions of the scene. All evidence retrieved during the second search was admissible as evidence.[4] Delayed or late attempts are legal if the permission of the owner or occupant of the premises is obtained, preferably in writing. Figure 4.2 is a consent form for this purpose.

In *Mincey v. Arizona*, involving the homicide of a narcotics officer, the identity of the offender (Mincey) was known from the outset.[5] Investigators took four days to search his apartment, and the evidence they discovered led to a conviction. On appeal, the Court noted that no occupant of the premises had summoned police and that the search continued for four days. It held, therefore, that no justification for the warrantless search existed under the Fourth Amendment. Police officers are able to search a home when exigent circumstances exist, such as the case in *United States v. Richardson*, in which a 911 call was made to report a homicide victim in the basement of Richardson's residence. A similar call was made approximately one week before, and no evidence of homicide was found. When police investigated this call, with no warrant, they found evidence and charged Richardson with unlawful possession of a firearm and possession

---

2   *Michigan v. Clifford*, 464 U.S. 1 (1983).

3   *Michigan v. Tyler*, 436 U.S. 499 (1978).

4   *United States v. Mitchell*, 85 F.3d 800 (1st Cir. 1996).

5   *Mincey v. Arizona*, 437 U.S. 385 (1978).

State of _____

County of _____

I, _____ , hereby permit

(name of searcher) _____ of the

(name of agency or dept.) _____

to search my * _____

located at _____

described as ** _____

I authorize them to process, collect, and take *any* relevant object including, *but not limited to,* latent fingerprints, hairs, fiber, blood, tracks, impressions, clothing, criminal instruments, contraband, and fruits of a crime.

I further authorize the making of photographs, videotapes, and sketches of the area being searched.

I understand that I have the right to refuse such consent.

I freely and voluntarily give this consent this _____ day of _____, 19_____.

Witnessed

_____
    (name)   (date)

* Entire home; basement only, if one or more rooms, specify which; garage; locker; automobile or truck; and so on.

** Single family house; condominium, apartment number; a four-door sedan (make and model); mobile home; and so on.

FIGURE 4.2 Consent-to-search form.

with intent to distribute cocaine. No homicide victim or evidence of a homicide was found. Richardson appealed on the notion that the 911 call did not suffice for exigent circumstances; the court rejected the claim.[6]

An extended discussion of the need to comply with the search requirements of the Fourth Amendment can be found in an *FBI Law Enforcement Bulletin* article.[7] Its author, Special Agent Kimberly Crawford, points out that the Supreme Court, in *Katz v. United States*, created the presumption that all searches conducted without warrants are unreasonable. Accordingly, a valid search warrant must be secured before any crime scene search is undertaken; that is, unless it falls under the exceptions allowed by the Court (consent-to-search or emergency situations).

A consent to search must be given voluntarily by a person reasonably believed to have control over and legal access to the premises.[8]

There are two kinds of emergency situations:

1. Those involving an attempt or opportunity to carry off or destroy evidence. To support this contention, belief must meet the standard of probable cause.
2. Those involving threats to safety or life. In these cases, a lower level of proof—reasonable suspicion—is acceptable.

In an emergency situation, a warrantless search is lawful, but it must not go beyond the limits of the emergency; thus, a general exploratory search of the premises cannot be conducted lawfully. This limitation also applies in a consent search.

Crawford offers an example of a crime scene search for evidence that exceeded the scope of the emergency.[9] In this case, a 14-year-old kidnap victim, upon being liberated by police officers, told them where the kidnapper kept his guns and ammunition. Beyond retrieving the weapons from a closet, no further search of the apartment was made. On appeal, it was held that the emergency situation ("exigent circumstances," in the Court's language) justified entry into the apartment, but the emergency ended when it was determined that neither the defendant nor anyone else was in the apartment. Entering the closet to locate the weapons exceeded the scope of the emergency search. The evidence, therefore, was not admissible. Because the 14-year-old victim did not have control over the apartment, the consent exception was not applicable.

In recent years, the use of roadblocks by police departments to gain information on recently committed crimes and to prevent drunk driving has increased considerably. In *Illinois v. Lidster*, a roadblock was set up to elicit information about a fatal hit-and-run accident that occurred one week before at the same location at about the same time. As Lidster approached the road block, his vehicle swerved, almost hitting an officer. When an officer noticed the smell of alcohol on

---

6   *United States v. Richardson*, 208 F.3d 626 (7th Cir. 2000).

7   Kimberly A. Crawford, "Crime Scene Searches: The Need for Fourth Amendment Compliance," *FBI Law Enforcement Bulletin*, 68:1 (1999), 26–31.

8   *Illinois v. Rodriquez*, 497 U.S. 177 (1990).

9   Crawford, op. cit., 29.

Lidster's breath, a field sobriety test was performed, which Lidster failed. Lidster was cited for driving under the influence of alcohol (DUI), which he appealed. The Supreme Court found that the roadblock did not violate Lidster's Fourth Amendment rights against unreasonable search and seizure because its purpose was not for crime control but rather to gain public information to solve a crime.[10]

Historically, police officers were required to knock and announce themselves and wait a reasonable amount of time before entering a home to serve a search warrant. The consequences for not abiding by these requirements was losing all evidence under the exclusionary rule guidelines. The Supreme Court decided in *Hudson v. Michigan* that the evidence found in such searches would have been discovered anyway, and that all evidence should be admissible in court. The understanding is that the "reasonable wait time" was ambiguous and the proper consequence of not meeting this requirement should not be the loss of all evidence found in the search.[11]

Purpose of Search

To understand the numerous precepts imposed on police behavior at a crime scene, one must be aware of the reasons for conducting a search. The most common reason is to develop associative evidence; that is, to find evidence that could link a suspect to the crime or the victim. Should some linkage be developed, its probative strength can range from an intimation of who may have been involved up to actual proof of something (as when a fingerprint is developed at the scene). Accordingly, nothing at the crime scene should be touched or stepped on.

Another purpose for the crime scene search is to seek answers to: What happened? How, when, and where did it happen? In a homicide the forensic pathologist is usually able to provide answers after the autopsy, and sometimes (in other kinds of cases) answers are obvious even to the detective. When they are not, however, it is essential that nothing be moved or altered. Then, at least some of the questions may be satisfied when a reconstruction of the crime is attempted. In all events, before the criminalist can collect associative evidence or undertake a reconstruction, the scene must first be carefully recorded and photographed.

The police sometimes have other reasons for making a crime scene search: (1) to recognize evidence from which a psychological profile may be developed, and from which, conceivably, a motive may be determined (i.e., why the crime was committed); (2) to identify an object the use or purpose of which is not readily apparent or is foreign to the scene, thereby calling for efforts to trace ownership—through a serial number (as with Oswald's rifle in the Kennedy assassination) or by locating its source, through point of sale (as in an item of clothing bought in the Pan Am Flight 103 bombing case) or manufacturer; or (3) to recognize a perpetrator's *modus operandi* (MO). In a burglary, for example, the use of a push drill to make a hole in the top sash of the

---

10   *Illinois v. Lidster*, 540 U.S. 419 (2004).

11   *Hudson v. Michigan*, 547 U.S. 586 (2006).

bottom half of a window (to insert a wire and open the catch) is sufficiently unusual to be viewed as the MO of that criminal. Pooling clues from several burglaries with the same tell-tale marks increases the chances of a suspect's apprehension.

Arrival of the First Police Officer

When the criminal has not been caught red-handed and has fled the scene before the first officer arrives (which is what generally happens), several responsibilities devolve upon the first officer on the scene:

1. To call for medical aid for the injured. In those cases in which a person is seriously injured, the steps (below) may be deferred until this is attended to. Medical personnel should be admonished not to step on footprints or other clues, and not to move anything beyond what is required to assist the injured. They should be instructed to carry a victim out on a stretcher. This is preferred because a wheeler or cart makes it difficult to avoid disturbing blood spatters, foot or shoe impressions, or other evidence on the floor or pathways to and from the scene.
2. To ascertain any facts pertinent to the criminal(s) that should be immediately transmitted to the patrol force—personal description, make and model of vehicle used, direction fled from scene.
3. To isolate the crime scene (and if necessary, its environs). To limit access to those with responsibility for its examination and processing.
4. To detain and separate any eyewitnesses so they cannot discuss their individual observations with each other.
5. To continue to protect the scene until the officer who is to be responsible for the continuing investigation arrives. This authority is determined by departmental policy.

The time of any significant subsequent action (as well as its nature, the reasons for taking it, and people involved) should be carefully noted and recorded. Not doing so permits defense counsel to create the impression that an investigator is lazy, not thorough, or incompetent. Being well-informed on the rules of evidence, attorney's often attack the collection and handling of physical evidence at the crime scene. Their aim is often to have it ruled inadmissible should there have been any procedural lapse. In the Nicole Brown Simpson/Ronald Goldman double-murder case, for example, investigators left the original scene early on, only to run into what they believed to be a second crime scene. As a consequence, the protection of the original scene, the reasons for leaving it, and the processing of both scenes for physical evidence became matters of intense interest to the defense. In such cases it is crucial that the investigator take good notes in a timely fashion, recording the investigative actions taken and the reasons why.

Arrival of the Investigator

On arrival at the crime scene, the investigator must note the following details to write a report and, possibly much later, to answer questions by defense counsel at trial:

1. Who made the notification; the time of arrival; and how long it took to respond.
2. The weather conditions and visibility.
3. The names of persons at the scene; in particular, the names of those who already went through the scene or any part of it.
4. The facts of the case as ascertained by the first officer(s) at the scene.
5. Subsequent actions on taking responsibility for the crime scene from the uniformed officer who was in charge up to that point.

Other Sources of Physical Evidence

In addition to the crime scene, there are several other possible sources of physical evidence:

1. The clothing and body of the victim (if not at the crime scene).
2. The suspect: the body, clothing, weapon, automobile, house, garage, or other area or article under his or her control.
3. Electronic evidence that may be stored on a movable device.

Whatever the source—crime scene, victim, or suspect—the basic precepts governing the discovery, preservation, and collection of physical evidence apply equally.

Discovery of Physical Evidence

Barry Fisher, the Crime Laboratory Director of the Los Angeles County Sheriff's Department, and author of the landmark text on crime scene investigation notes:

> Forensic scientists, crime scene specialists, and latent print experts are the individuals whose jobs apply science and technology to the solution of criminal acts. They shoulder an important role in the criminal justice system. Their skill and knowledge in the criminal investigation may establish the innocence or guilt of a defendant. Professional ethics and integrity are important to their work (p. 15).[12]

It should be noted, however, that before any physical evidence can be collected and transported, it must first be recognized as such. Recognition is a routine matter when clue materials are familiar,

---

12   Richard F. Fox and Carl L. Cunningham, *Crime Scene Search and Physical Evidence Handbook*, reprint (Washington, DC: U.S. Government Printing Office, 1973), iii.

like bullets, cartridge casings, tool marks, and blood. When materials are unfamiliar, recognition depends on the investigator's education, training, and imagination. Large police departments today have technicians and scientific equipment available for collecting and preserving physical evidence. In small departments the investigator shoulders this responsibility, responding to the extent possible with skills acquired through training, self-study, and experience on the job.

For readers who are looking for vicarious hands-on experience, a book such as *The Crime Laboratory: Case Studies of Scientific Criminal Investigations* includes some of the common and, more important, some of the uncommon types of physical evidence encountered at crime scenes.[13] It is illustrated with police photographs (one-to-one or photomacrograph) of evidence discovered at the crime scene, together with those of a known comparison specimen (exemplar) obtained from the suspect (see Figures 4.3 and 4.4). By comparing the two pieces of evidence, the reader determines whether an identity exists. For many of the case examples, solutions arrived at by the criminalist who worked on the investigation are provided. When the exercises are mastered, the details upon which an identity depends will be recognized. The trainee will appreciate what specific aspects of physical evidence covered in the exercises need protection when being collected and transmitted to the laboratory. In addition, he or she will better understand the principles underlying the various protocols for handling of physical evidence. For those already in law enforcement, a local laboratory may be able to provide photographs of crime scene evidence and known comparison samples.

FIGURE 4.3 Impression in wood.
Clark Boardman Co., Ltd. and Herbert Mac-Donell, Laboratory of Forensic Sciences, Corning, NY

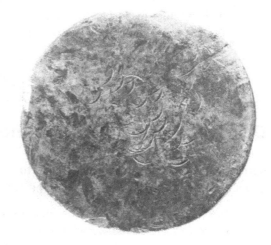

FIGURE 4.4 Hammer face is reproduced to permit a direct comparison with Figure 3.3. These pieces of potential evidence can be compared to determine whether a common origin exists.
Clark Boardman Co., Ltd. and Herbert MacDonell, Laboratory of Forensic Sciences, Corning, NY

13   James W. Osterburg, *The Crime Laboratory: Case Studies of Scientific Criminal Investigation*, 2nd ed. (New York: Clark Boardman, 1982), 161–381.

Overview, Walk-Through, and Search

The process of discovery begins after the complainant (and often before an eyewitness, if any) has been questioned. When information is not otherwise available, the investigator's experience with that type of crime is put to use in forming a general impression of what happened and where to look for physical evidence. The search should include:

1. The most probable access and escape routes. When fleeing the scene, some criminals deliberately discard a weapon or burglar's tools, or on occasion, the proceeds of the crime.
2. Any area where the perpetrator waited before committing the crime. Burglars often gain entrance to a building just before closing time, then wait until it has been vacated. Killers or robbers also wait in ambush for their victims. In these areas, such clues as used matches, burned cigarettes, spent cartridge casings, food containers, etc., may be found.
3. The point of entry to the premises.
4. The route used within the premises where signs of the perpetrator's activity—such as objects that have been moved or places broken into—are apparent.
5. Any objects that seem to have received the attention of the criminal, such as a safe.
6. Some unusual places where evidence might be discovered:
   A. refrigerator
      a) half-eaten food (this actually happens)
      b) latent fingerprints on handle
   B. bathroom
      a) toilet seat—fingerprints—hairs
      b) trash can
   C. computer
   D. videotapes or other storage devices

A walk-through of the crime scene is first undertaken to observe the actual physical evidence and to ascertain which locations and articles require processing; namely, dusting for fingerprints or photographing blood-spatter details. If an outdoor search must be made during the hours of darkness, the scene should be protected and searched again in daylight. Under these circumstances, the first search should be confined to the fairly obvious and to what could be of immediate value in identifying or apprehending the perpetrator. Priority must be given to evidence that has a short life and is easily destroyed unless prompt action is taken to preserve and protect it. Whether indoors or out, sufficient illumination is crucial: it will help to prevent the mistake of walking on or missing evidence that cannot be seen.

The preliminary walk-through process helps to define the boundaries of the areas to be examined. Regardless of the search pattern employed, it must be systematic and thorough. When the area is large, a piecemeal probing of small sections (or strips) is effective. However, this task can be shortened. In a homicide committed in a sand pit, in which the victim's skull was fractured, the search for the missing weapon could start where the body was found. A better idea, however, would be to divide the area surrounding the sand pit area into a large grid. Those cells in the grid along the possible escape route (which, owing to foliage, offered a place to discard and conceal the weapon) might be searched after the sand pit area. If unsuccessful, the search could be directed to other cells in the grid and, upon completion, the entire process reviewed to make certain none were overlooked.

Recording Conditions and Evidence Found at the Crime Scene

For a number of reasons, it is essential upon arrival to record the investigative evidence or clue materials that were noted during the search of the crime scene:

1. Some investigators use a tape or digital recorder, dictating observations and other information.
2. Writing an official report of the day's activities provides a record of information that will be useful later for jogging the memory and assuring accuracy.
3. Details that the criminalist can use for reconstructing the crime or developing associative evidence will be available.
4. As an investigation progresses and the suspect or witness makes statements, some aspects of the crime scene that did not initially appear significant can become important. A record made before anything was disturbed will permit such a reevaluation.
5. Records are useful in preparing for the interrogation of a suspect.
6. Defense attorneys, legitimately, will be curious about where and when the evidence was found and by whom. The investigator's preparation for cross-examination should begin at this early stage, not delayed until the trial date is set.
7. The effectiveness of courtroom testimony is enhanced when more than mere memory is available to recall events.

Methods of recording the situation, conditions, and physical evidence found at the crime scene include: notes, photographs, and sketches. Other methods used by some agencies require audio or video recording equipment. Each method has a distinct value in that it supplements the others; in general, however, all three should be used to document the crime scene.

Notes

Recording the activities upon the arrival of the first officer and investigator at the scene is best accomplished with notes kept on a chronological basis. Many believe that a loose-leaf notebook is preferable to a bound one for logging the arrivals, departures, and assignments of assisting personnel, as well as the directions given to evidence technicians for processing the scene. It facilitates having material pertinent to the case at hand. If the notes are needed to refresh the investigator's memory when testifying, or should the court grant defense permission to examine them, then only the applicable jottings are open to inspection. If in a bound notebook, all information—confidential and otherwise, or pertaining to other cases—could be revealed.

Some people believe a bound notebook is best because it makes it difficult to change facts as first recorded should there be an attempt later to corrupt the officer. For the same reason, ink is preferable for crime scene notes. Should a correction be necessary, it is admissible to draw a line through the original notes and initial the alteration. Regardless of what form they take, the notes may become part of the *res gestae*, a record of what was said or done by the complainant, witness, or suspect in the first moments of the investigation. *Res gestae* (statements or acts), being an exception to the hearsay rule, may be admitted as evidence for consideration by a jury.

Photographs

Photography is a key component of any police department's inventory of tools. Larry Miller, a former crime scene investigator, identifies the following uses of different types of photography:

- Identification files.
- Communications and microfilm files.
- Evidence.
- Offender detection.
- Court exhibits.
- Reproduction and copying.
- Personnel training.
- Crime and fire prevention.
- Public relations.[14]

Two kinds of photographs are taken at the crime scene. The first is intended to record the overall scene: the approach to the premises used by the criminal, the point of entrance, the pathway through the premises, the various rooms the criminal entered, and the location of any physical evidence (see Figure 4.5). The second kind records details needed by the criminalist to reconstruct the crime or establish an identity. They are preserved by life-size or one-to-one photographs (of fingerprints, blood spatter patterns, tool marks) or occasionally by a photomacrograph of the evidence. A

FIGURE 4.5 A photograph of a crime scene. The square in the forefront was included in the photograph to aid in perspective and mapping.
Police Photography, 5th ed., by Larry S. Miller

14   Larry S. Miller, *Police Photography*, 5th ed. (Newark, NJ: LexisNexis Matthew Bender, 2006), 4–5.

specially designed camera for one-to-one recording of fingerprints and other objects is commercially available and simple to operate. A photomacrograph, which requires a camera with a bellows extension, sturdy tripod, suitable focal length lenses, and illumination, should be left to a trained evidence technician. The introduction of the video camcorder and digital camera with a power zoom lens and macro capability has simplified both the taking of record pictures and the preservation of evidence details by photograph or photomacrograph.

Sketches

The advantage of a sketch is that it includes only essential details; in addition, it best indicates distances or spatial relationships between items of evidence, indoors or out. There are two kinds: rough and finished. The rough sketch, a relatively crude, free-hand representation of all essential information, including measurements, is made at the crime scene (see Figure 4.6). Because there is great variation in individual sketching ability, changes are often needed in tracing outlines. It is best to use pencil for this task. The finished sketch is more precise: its lines are clean and straight and its lettering is either typeset or typewritten. Usually prepared later when time is available, it uses information from the rough sketch, notes, and photographs taken at the crime scene.

When the distances in the finished sketch are precise and proportional, with lines drawn by a skilled drafter, it is termed a *scale drawing* (see Figure 4.7). Scale drawings can be helpful in court to demonstrate exact distances. For example, in a case involving an unsuccessful attempt to choke the victim, the issue of manslaughter versus murder came up at trial. The jury had to decide whether the time it took for the killer to run down a hallway to the kitchen for a knife and return to the bedroom to finish the job was sufficient to constitute premeditation. A scale drawing would help in making this determination.

Commercially available crime scene sketch kits provide several templates: some for house furnishings, others for store and office layouts, and so on. Computerized systems (such as Compu-Scene, by Allied Security Innovations, Inc.) are also available. In addition to routine drawing materials, a 100-foot steel tape and two people are needed to make the measurement. Each person must verify the distance between the item (the physical evidence) and a fixed object (a wall, boulder, house, telephone pole, or tree). Indoor measurements (from item of evidence to wall) are made along the shortest perpendicular lines, with two such right-angle measurements required to locate it. Each measurement is best made to the nearest walls not parallel to each other. This is known as the coordinate method for locating an object (see Figure 4.8). Another method (the triangulation method) is employed outdoors, the measurements being made from two fixed objects such as the corner of a house, a telephone pole, fence post, or tree (see Figure 4.9). If the direction and angle (obtained from a compass) are known for each measurement, the location of the object or item of evidence can be established (see Figure 4.10). Even when the angles are unknown, if each distance is considered the radius of a circle, the two circles can intersect at two points only, and the evidence will be located at but one of these two points. If the measurer records the general direction of the evidence from each fixed object, it is possible to select the correct intersecting point of the two circles.

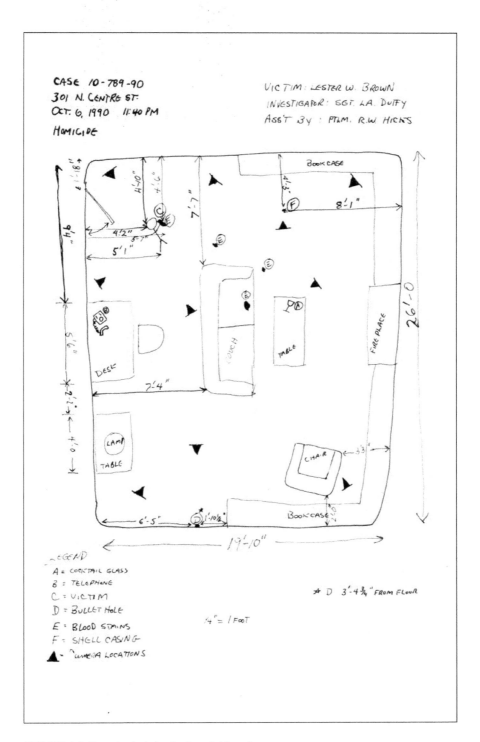

FIGURE 4.6 Rough sketch of a homicide crime scene.
Courtesy, Sirchie Finger Print Laboratories, Inc., Raleigh, NC

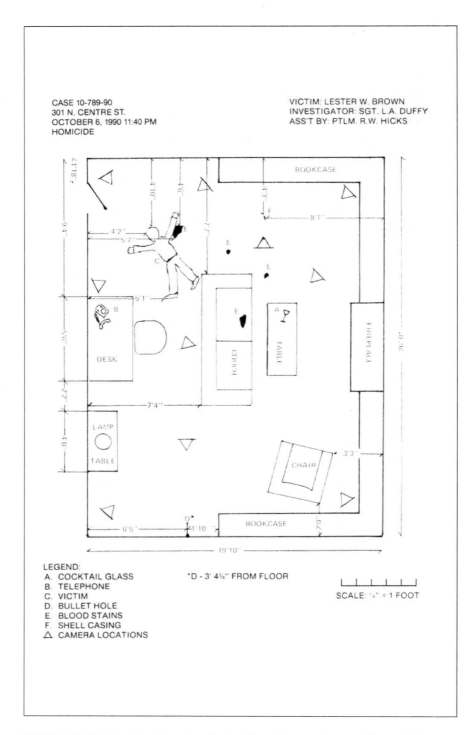

FIGURE 4.7 Finished sketch and scale drawing of same scene as Figure 4.6.
Courtesy, Sirchie Finger Print Laboratories, Inc., Raleigh, NC

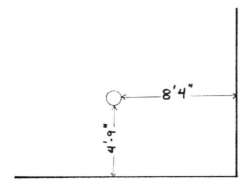

FIGURE 4.8 Coordinate method for locating an object.
Courtesy, Sirchie Finger Print Laboratories, Inc., Raleigh, NC

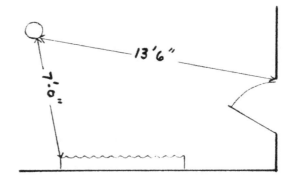

FIGURE 4.9 Triangulation method for locating an object.
Courtesy, Sirchie Finger Print Laboratories, Inc., Raleigh, NC

Exact measurements are important for two reasons: one, to reconstruct the crime—namely, to check the account given by a suspect or witness; and two, to give clear-cut, precise answers to defense counsel's questions, and ensure that counsel is provided no opportunity to impugn the investigator's competence or confidence.

Collection and Preservation

When each item of physical evidence has been properly recorded, it must then be collected separately and preserved for examination in the laboratory and eventually in court. The requirements of both scientist and lawyer therefore must be kept in mind. Because improperly collected or preserved evidence will fail to meet the tests defense counsel can apply in court, legal requirements will be considered first.

Preservation—Legal Requirements

The same information used by the criminalist to reconstruct the crime serves to answer defense counsel's questions at trial. For example, the distribution pattern of spent cartridges ejected from an automatic pistol may allow the criminalist to determine where the shooter stood when firing the weapon, and defense counsel will certainly ask how he or she knows the exact position of each cartridge. An admissible set of photographs and a sketch can defuse this challenge. Other tests lawyers can apply in attempting to exclude evidence involve the certainty of the identification (of the cartridges in this example) and the issue of continuity of possession—the chain of custody of each item of evidence.

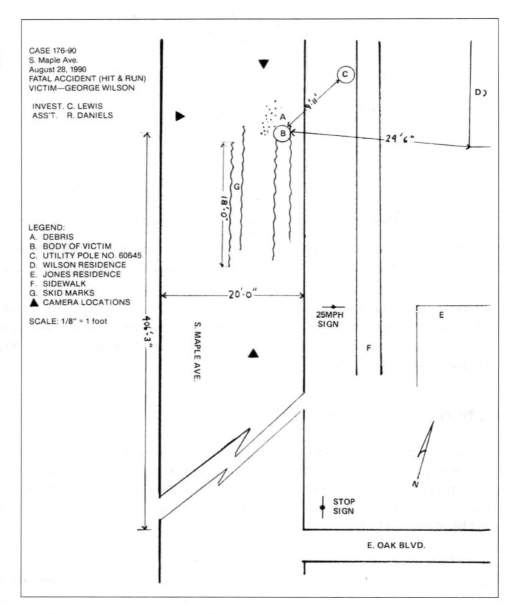

CASE 176-90
S. Maple Ave.
August 28, 1990
FATAL ACCIDENT (HIT & RUN)
VICTIM—GEORGE WILSON

INVEST. C. LEWIS
ASS'T. R. DANIELS

LEGEND:
A. DEBRIS
B. BODY OF VICTIM
C. UTILITY POLE NO. 60645
D. WILSON RESIDENCE
E. JONES RESIDENCE
F. SIDEWALK
G. SKID MARKS
▲ CAMERA LOCATIONS

SCALE: 1/8" = 1 foot

S. MAPLE AVE.

25MPH SIGN

STOP SIGN

E. OAK BLVD.

FIGURE 4.10 Finished sketch and scale drawing of a homicide that took place outdoors.
Courtesy, Sirchie Finger Print Laboratories, Inc., Raleigh, NC

Identification

To be admissible in court, an item of evidence must be shown to be identical with that discovered at the crime scene or secured at the time of arrest. Thus, any alleged marijuana cigarettes found in the defendant's possession on arrest or bullets removed from the bedroom mattress after a homicide must be shown to be the cigarettes or the bullets acquired originally. To make identifications with certainty and thereby preclude a successful challenge, some method of marking each item of evidence must be devised, the marks serving to connect each bit of evidence to both investigator and defendant or scene. If possible, they should include the date and location of the acquisition of the evidence. Attempting to squeeze this information onto a small item would be impractical, but an envelope, bottle, or other container provides an enlarged labeling surface. Plastic containers are preferred because this material is less likely to break or contaminate the evidence. Any receptacle must be sealed and initialed on the seal. In cases involving computers or other storage devices, special handling may be required, and care must be taken not to alter or destroy data. For this reason, an expert in this area should be consulted. The Federal Bureau of Investigation has established specialized units in major cities to assist local law enforcement in cases involving computers and other electronic storage devices.

An all-in-one evidence tag/label is available that can be used for the identification of many kinds of evidence. Printed on heavy-duty stock, it can be either threaded using tamper-proof ties through a pre-punched hole to form an evidence tag or made into an adhesive backed evidence label by peeling off the protective backing (see Figure 4.11).

FIGURE 4.11 An all-in-one evidence tag/label. It is supplied with tamper-proof ties for tagging and peel-off backing with a permanent adhesive to make it into a label.
Courtesy, Lynn Peavey Co., Lenexa, KS

In large police departments the storage and retrieval of evidence from the property clerk or evidence custodian is somewhat complicated. For simplification, a voucher number system may be utilized to account for the evidence. Some large departments use a computer to inventory and track evidence as it is examined within the laboratory. This has little to do with the identification of the original evidence by the detective; rather, it is related to the other legal requirement: chain of custody.

Continuity of Possession/Chain of Custody

Evidence must be continuously accounted for from the time of its discovery until it is presented in court. Anyone who had it in their possession, even momentarily, may be called upon to testify as to when, where, and from whom it was received; what (if anything) was done to it; to whom it was surrendered, and at what time and date. The greater the number of people handling the evidence, the greater the potential for conflict in, or contradiction of, their testimony. Any disruption in the chain of custody may cause evidence to be inadmissible. Even if it is admitted, a disruption can weaken or destroy its probative value. Accordingly, the rule is to have the least possible number of persons handle evidence. If at all practical, the investigator should personally deliver evidence to the laboratory. If the facility is far away, the use of the U.S. Post Office (Registered) or United

Parcel Service (Acknowledgment of Delivery) is permissible. Their signed receipts usually suffice to satisfy the court. The court appearance of a postal or delivery clerk is not usually required.

Police departments normally specify how physical evidence should be marked, transported, and stored. These procedures are not specified here, as they vary from department to department, but the general considerations can be met in a number of ways. Any practice that ignores them can create major problems regarding the admissibility of evidence in court.

Vulnerability

If investigators do not comprehend the legal aspects intrinsic to the preservation of physical evidence, they become vulnerable to attack by defense counsel. The lessons of the Nicole Brown Simpson/Ronald Goldman murder case underscore how effective such challenges can be. In this double homicide, numerous bloodstains were discovered at the original crime scene and, subsequently, at O.J. Simpson's home.

A (known) sample of O.J. Simpson's blood was drawn for comparison purposes. The investigator had the option of logging it into one of two forensic evidence facilities nearby. Instead, he opted to deliver it (almost three hours later) to the criminalist, who was still collecting evidence at the crime scene. He took this step because he did not have the case number needed to log it in. Keeping the chain of custody as short as possible may also have motivated his decision to hand-deliver the blood sample to the criminalist. Although the bureaucratic mind-set may well account for believing that a case number is required before evidence can be logged in, this is an administrative rather than legal requirement. Moreover, chain of custody was in no way shortened by delivering the tube to the criminalist who had to in turn deliver it to the evidence custodian. Rather it was lengthened, because a serologist (or DNA expert) would most likely be the next person to handle the tube had the crime scene criminalist not been involved.

The main lesson to be learned is that bringing exemplars (or a suspect) back to the crime scene provides defense counsel with an opportunity to raise a doubt as to whether the questioned evidence was there originally or was there because it was taken to the scene. This is exactly the opportunity the defense grasped in the Simpson case, as one of the jurors remarked after the trial:

> Juror Brenda Moran told the press that the jury found Vanatter's decision to carry Simpson's blood sample around with him for several hours "suspicious because it gave him the opportunity to plant evidence": he's walking around with blood in his pocket for a couple of hours. How come he didn't book it at Parker Center or Piper Tech? He had a perfect opportunity. Why walk around with it? He was my biggest doubt ... There was an opportunity to sprinkle it here or there.[15, 16]

---

15   Fox and Cunningham, op. cit., 41–46.

16   Alan M. Dershowitz, *Reasonable Doubts: The Criminal Justice System and the O.J. Simpson Case* (New York: Simon & Schuster, 1996), 74.

Preservation—Scientific Requirements and Means

Scientific Requirements

The criminalist also has scientific requirements for the preservation of evidence, the primary one being that there be no alteration in its inherent quality or composition. Sometimes, deterioration may occur in such biological materials as blood, semen, and vomit before the investigator arrives at the scene. Any change after that must be minimized by taking proper precautions promptly. Physical evidence may undergo change in the following ways:

1. Loss by leakage (of a powder) from an opening in the seam of an envelope; or by evaporation (of a volatile liquid) from an improperly stoppered container.
2. Decomposition through exposure to light, heat, or bacteria; for example, direct exposure to summer sun can alter a bloodstain in a very short time. It may not be recognized.
3. Intermingling of evidence from various sources and locations in a common container. In a sex crime, the suspect's and victim's underwear should not be placed in the same bag. Such commingling, surprisingly, is not uncommon.

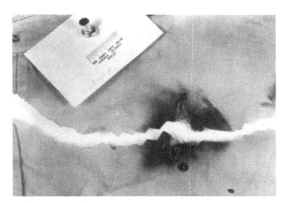

FIGURE 4.12 Powder mark on victim's shirt cut through by hospital personnel unmindful of its potential evidentiary value.
Courtesy, New Jersey State Police

4. Alteration by the unwitting addition of a fresh fold or crease in a document; or a tear or cut in a garment. For example, hospital personnel in haste to remove clothing, have cut right through the powder mark on the victim's shirt (see Figure 4.12). They also have disposed of such clothing. If it has any potential as evidence, immediate measures must be taken to retrieve it.
5. Contamination, bacterial or chemical, resulting from the use of unclean containers.
6. Alteration of data on computers or electronic storage devices.

A few precautions can minimize or eliminate these problems:

1. Use only fresh, clean containers.
2. Use leak-proof, sealable containers.
3. Uphold the integrity of each item of evidence by using separate containers.
4. Keep evidence away from direct sunlight and heat. Refrigerate biological evidence (such as whole blood, urine, and rape kits) when not being transported.
5. Deliver evidence as quickly as possible to the laboratory.
6. Handle evidence as little as possible.

7.   Do not attempt to access or remove computer files without competent assistance.

Biological specimens, particularly blood and semen stains, are best preserved by permitting them to dry at room temperature, away from direct sunlight. No air currents (e.g., from a fan) or heat (e.g., from a blow dryer) should be directed at them. For more information, see http://www.fbi.gov/hq/lab/pdf/Evidence%20Reference%20Guide.pdf

Collection—Scientific Requirements and Means

Scientific Requirements
It was pointed out earlier that the comparison and interpretation of details in physical evidence—especially the development of associative evidence—is a major activity for the criminalist. As part of this process, the criminalist requires that a specimen from the suspect be checked against the evidence from the crime scene. Therefore, an inked set of the suspect's fingerprints must be at hand for comparison with a latent print found at the scene, or a bullet fired from the suspected weapon must be available to link the crime scene bullet to a certain weapon. Generally, comparison specimens of known origin (exemplars) must be collected and made available to criminalists. Three considerations should govern the collection:

1.   Whenever possible, variables must be controlled.
2.   Background material must be collected.
3.   The quantity of the sample must be sufficient.

Control of Variables
It is fundamental to scientific experimentation that, where feasible, all variables except one be controlled during the test. Because controlling the variables is not always possible in criminalistics, all variables that can possibly be eliminated should be. Thus, when collecting handwriting specimens for comparison with a forged check, variables to be eliminated include: the size, color, and printing on the check; and the type of writing instrument (by employing the same type—ballpoint pen, pencil, pen nib with nutgall ink, etc.—used in the original forgery). Similarly, when examining a firearm, the same ammunition used in the commission of the crime, if available, should be employed in the test firing. The aim in controlling variables is to have the evidence specimen duplicated to the fullest extent possible in the exemplar.

Background Material
A material that has been bloodstained or has had paint transferred to it (in a hit-and-run accident, for instance) contains valuable physical evidence. Something, however, may have been present on the material prior to the crime that could interfere with the tests that the criminalist performs. For this reason, an unstained sample that is quite close to the stained area should be collected. A bloodstained mattress, for instance, can yield misleading results if perspiration or saliva was already on the ticking when the crime was committed. By testing an unstained sample of the ticking, blood type antigens can be discovered and dealt with by a serologist. Another

example: When a bicycle is struck by an automobile, each vehicle's paint can be transferred to the other. To evaluate the spectrograms of each paint, a specimen of the original paint on each vehicle must be taken from a spot near the collision-transfer point. These specimens, like the unstained ticking, constitute the background samples.

Sample Sufficiency

It is accurate to say that most investigators do not collect comparison samples of adequate size or quantity. This may partly be a result of misunderstanding, for the sensitivity of modern instrumental methods of analysis has certainly been exaggerated. Still, it is better that samples be too large rather than too small. The investigator or evidence technician, naturally, is limited to what is available at the crime scene. In general, this factor does not pertain to the known specimen (exemplar), which usually is large. As a result, the criminalist is able to establish the conditions and method of examination before comparing the crime scene evidence with it.

Means

Various tools are required to separate and remove material from its setting when collecting physical evidence at the crime scene. Special means are employed to gather trace evidence. Similarly, an assortment of containers is needed to isolate and protect each material.

Tools

In general, tools that cut, grip, or force are needed for the collection of physical evidence. They can be classified as follows:

1. Cutting Implements
   Scissors—compound-action metal snips or shears
   Saws for wood and metal
   Scalpels and razors
   Chisels for wood and metal
   Knives
   Drills with assorted bits
   Axes
   Files
2. Gripping Devices
   Assorted wrenches
   Assorted pliers
   Tweezers—straight and angled
3. Forcing or Prying Tools
   Screwdrivers—various sizes of regular and Phillips-head types
   Hammers—claw, ball-peen, chipping, mallet
   Crowbars

Containers

All items listed below are available in most communities. They are best collected in advance, in anticipation of future need:

1. Bags   paper, plastic
2. Boxes   pill (drug store type), shoe, large cartons
3. Envelopes   assorted sizes and types; mail, brown manila with metal clasp, plastic
4. Other containers
   Plastic   used by druggists to dispense tablets and capsules; or used to store or freeze foods
   Glass   bottles with stoppers, Mason jars with lids
   Cans   with tight covers

Expansion envelopes; heat-sealable, extra-strength polyethylene bags; and other items for the collection of crime scene evidence are available from police equipment specialists such as Sirchie Finger Print Laboratories, Lynn Peavey Company, Ames Safety Envelope Company, and Kinderprint Company (see Figures 4.13–4.16).

FIGURE 4.13 **Kraft bags.**

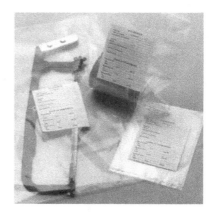

FIGURE 4.14 **Heat sealable, clear polyethylene bags.**

FIGURE 4.15 **Evidence bags for rifles or other long items.**

FIGURE 4.16 **Clear evidence jars with tight-fitting screw-on caps.**

Courtesy, Lynn Peavey Co., Lenexa, KS

Collection—Special Considerations

In addition to the routine collection of physical evidence, today's investigator should not over-look the possibility of trace evidence, and also must keep in mind the hazard imposed by HIV-infected blood.

Trace Evidence

Trace evidence, differing from ordinary physical evidence mainly because of its small size, calls for special methods. Three techniques for discovering and gathering trace evidence are: vacuuming, shaking, or sweeping, and adhesion to tape. An ordinary vacuum cleaner with good suction, equipped with a special attachment to hold filter paper in place, can be used to trap the debris as a deposit on the paper. Each item of evidence processed requires a fresh filter. Particulate matter and fibers (on clothing, automobile rug, bed sheet, blanket, etc.) are dis-lodged by vigorous shaking over a clean white sheet of paper laid on a large table. The adhesion technique involves pressing a three- or four-inch piece of transparent tape on the evidence to be examined; with the tape placed sticky side down on a glass slide, the debris adhering to it can be studied directly under the microscope. A stereomicroscope is employed to sort out the fibers or particles obtained from vacuuming or shaking; a polarized light microscope is used for comparison and identification.

Detective Nicholas Petraco (New York Police Department), who specializes in trace evidence examination, believes that even in this day of highly advanced laboratory instrumentation "the microscope, especially the polarized microscope, is the most important and versatile instrument available to the criminalist for the study of trace evidential materials."[17] He cites several cases that were solved because of the "vital role that the microscope and trace evidence played."[18]

AIDS as a Concern for Crime Scene Investigators

The potential of Acquired Immune Deficiency Syndrome (AIDS) as a serious hazard to the health of those charged with collecting physical evidence at scenes of violent crimes has been acknowl-edged.[19] A research paper by Kennedy and others points to the special vulnerability of crime scene investigators:

> [For] ... unlike the doctor, nurse, or health worker who most often works in a controlled environment, the criminal investigator may be confronted with less manageable conditions.[20]

> ... using conventional methods such as latex gloves for protection against the potential risk of AIDS or other infectious diseases may not be adequate at every crime scene ... While the human skin and protective garments are barriers to exposure to the AIDS virus, there are

---

17   Nicholas Petraco, "Trace Evidence—The Invisible Witness," *Journal of Forensic Sciences*, 31:1 (1986), 321–327.

18   Ibid., 321–327.

19   D.B. Kennedy, R.J. Homant, and G.L. Emery, "AIDS Concerns Among Crime Scene Investigators," *Journal of Police Science and Administration*, 17:1 (1990), 12–18.

20   Ibid., 13.

objects and conditions present at a crime scene which may, through abrasion, puncturing, or cutting action, provide an avenue for transmission and infection.[21]

The authors raise the following problem:

... If investigators believe they are not properly protected from the AIDS virus, they may limit their evidentiary searches, consciously or unconsciously, to only those scenarios they believe to be "safe." Physical evidence may only be cursorily dealt with, hunches may not be followed up, and officers may avoid specialized forensic assignments. If evidence of poor quality must be relied upon by the courts, the truly guilty may not be convicted. Worse yet, the innocent may fail to be exonerated.[22]

They conclude with some recommendations, to wit:

... Notwithstanding these clear concerns for the AIDS problem in general and their own safety in particular, the vast majority of crime scene investigators and evidence technicians report that the quality of their work is not adversely affected. While policy makers at all levels of the criminal justice system may be pleased by the perseverance of forensic line officers, it is clear that their efforts must be supported by stronger departmental measures if they are to continue effectively in their work. At the very least, clear guidelines that incorporate the latest information on AIDS prevention should be developed and publicized. The feasibility of issuing various support equipment, such as specialized clothing, also needs to be explored.[23]

Transmission of Evidence to the Laboratory

Delivering physical evidence to the laboratory is best done in person for legal and scientific reasons. In the case that this is not possible, the U.S. Postal Service or United Parcel Service (UPS) can be used to deliver the packaged evidence. Proper packing, wrapping, and sealing is extremely important when evidence is to be shipped. With this in mind, the FBI has prepared a helpful set of explicit recommendations and instructions, which are available at their web site.

This text thus far has treated investigations as though the detective and his or her partner are conducting the crime scene search by themselves. However, when a high-profile case, a large crime scene, or multiple scenes are involved, a more elaborate evidence collection process is desirable. To this end, the FBI has published a booklet with the aim of ensuring that search efforts are conducted in an organized and methodical fashion.[24] It describes the duties and responsibilities of the response team, which includes: a team leader, a photographer and photographic log recorder, an evidence recorder/custodian, and specialists (e.g., bomb expert,

---

21 Ibid., 14.

22 Ibid.

23 Ibid., 18.

24 Federal Bureau of Investigation. *Suggested Guidelines for Establishing Evidence Response Teams*. (Washington, DC: Department of Justice, no date).

geologist, etc.). Other issues treated include: organization and basic stages in a search operation, documentation procedures, and equipment recommendations.

While largely concerned with how to conduct a search, the booklet also warns the user of the pitfalls involved in blindly following their recommendations. Considering the gravity of high-profile crimes, the booklet's suggestions help investigators recall things to do that can be overlooked in the heat of the moment.

Finding Physical Evidence by Canvassing

Canvassing is employed most often to search out witnesses who do not know they have useful information about a crime under investigation. It is also used to track down the source of crime scene evidence. For example, in the Sam Sheppard murder case, a nationwide canvass was undertaken to find a surgical instrument matching the contours of a bloodstained impression found on the pillow of the victim, Marilyn Sheppard—the defendant's wife. Despite intense efforts, it was not successful.

In kidnapping cases, a modified form of canvass for physical evidence has proved successful. A document examiner selects handwriting (or printing) characteristics in the kidnapper's ransom note that are outstanding and easily recognized. A photograph illustrating these unusual characteristics is prepared and distributed to each investigator after the document examiner has explained their significance. Then investigators are sent out systematically to examine numerous public documents for handwriting or printing characteristics resembling those in the photograph. They examine applications for state license plates, automobile operator's licenses, and marriage licenses. They scan the signatures on election voting records, financial transactions, and probation and parole records. The Lindbergh/Hauptmann kidnapping case would have been solved earlier had this procedure (which was suggested at the time) been followed. With numerous clues indicating that the kidnapper came from the Bronx, it would have been feasible to initiate and confine the search to that borough; and, had driver's license or automobile registration files been examined, the kidnapper's distinctive brand of handwriting could have been recognized.

The lessons of the Lindbergh case were not forgotten, however. They were applied successfully in the LaMarca/Weinberger kidnapping case, in which the writer of a ransom note (left in the victim's carriage) was found by assigning investigators to comb through various public documents until one was located that apparently bore the same handwriting. The discovery involved 150 detectives and FBI agents who, in a brief training session, were taught to recognize the unusual characteristics in the handwriting of the ransom note. After examining 2 million public documents, an FBI agent discovered one that appeared to contain characteristics similar to those in the note; when examined by an expert, the agent's preliminary judgment was proved correct.

Supplemental Readings

Adams, Thomas F., Allen G. Caddell, and Jeffrey L. Krutsinger. *Crime Scene Investigation*, 2nd ed. Upper Saddle River, NJ: Prentice Hall, 2004.

Bevel, Tom, and Ross M. Gardiner. *Blood Stain Pattern Analysis*. Boca Raton, FL: CRC Press, 1997.

Bodziak, William J. *Footwear Impression Evidence: Detection, Recover, and Examination*, 2nd ed. Boca Raton, FL: CRC Press, 2000.

Cowger, James F. *Friction Ridge Skin: Comparison and Identification of Fingerprints*. Boca Raton, FL: CRC Press, 1992.

Davis, Randal. *Evidence Collection and Presentation*. San Clemente, CA: LawTech, 2005.

DeForest, Peter R., R.E. Gaensslen, and Henry C. Lee. *Forensic Science: An Introduction to Criminalistics*, 2nd ed. New York: McGraw-Hill, 1995.

Eckert, William G., and Stuart H. James. *Interpretation of Bloodstain Evidence at Crime Scenes*. Boca Raton, FL: CRC Press, 1993.

Fisher, Barry A.J. *Techniques of Crime Scene Investigation*, 7th ed. Boca Raton, FL: CRC Press, 2004.

Fox, Richard H., and Carl L. Cunningham. *Crime Scene Search and Physical Evidence Handbook*. Boulder, CO: Paladin Press, 1987.

Gardner, Ross M. *Practical Crime Scene Processing and Investigation*. Boca Raton, FL: CRC Press, 2005.

Goodall, Jean, and Carol Hawks. *Crime Scene Documentation*. San Clemente, CA: LawTech, 2005.

Hawthorne, Mark R. *First Unit Responder: A Guide to Physical Evidence Collection for Patrol Officers*. Boca Raton, FL: CRC Press, 1999.

James, Stuart H., Paul E. Kish, and T. Paulette Sutton. *Principles of Bloodstain Pattern Analysis: Theory and Practice*. Boca Raton, FL: CRC Press, 2005.

Kirk, Paul L. *Crime Investigation*, 2nd ed. Edited by John I. Thornton. Reprint. New York: Wiley & Sons, 1974; Melbourne, FL: Krieger, 1985.

Lee, Henry C. *Crime Scene Investigation*. Taoyuan, Taiwan (Republic of China): Central Police University Press, 1994.

Lee, Henry C., and Robert F. Gaensslen, eds. *Advances in Fingerprint Technology*. Boca Raton, FL: CRC Press, 1994.

Lewis, Jon M.A. *Criminalistics for Crime Scene Investigators*. San Clemente, CA: LawTech, 2005.

McDonald, Peter. *Tire Print Identification: Practical Aspects of Criminal Forensic Investigation*. Boca Raton, FL: CRC Press, 1992.

Miller, Larry S. *Police Photography*, 5th ed. Newark, NJ: LexisNexis Matthew Bender, 2006.

Miller, Larry S., and Daniel J. Moeser. *Report Writing for Criminal Justice Professionals*, 3rd ed. Newark, NJ: LexisNexis Matthew Bender, 2007.

Moody, Kenton J., and Patrick M. Grant. *Nuclear Forensic Analysis*. Boca Raton, FL: CRC Press, 2005.

Nordby, Jon J., and Stuart H. James. *Forensic Science: An Introduction to Scientific and Investigative Techniques*, 2nd ed. Boca Raton, FL: CRC Press, 2005.

Osterburg, James W. *The Crime Laboratory: Case Studies of Scientific Investigation*, 2nd ed. Eagan, MN: West Group, 1982.

Pederson, Daniel. "Down on The Body Farm." *Newsweek*, (October 23, 2000), 50–52.

Petraco, Nicholas, and Hal Sherman. *Illustrated Guide to Crime Scene Investigation*. Boca Raton, FL: CRC Press, 2006.

Redsicker, David R. *The Practical Methodology of Forensic Photography*, 2nd ed. Boca Raton, FL: CRC Press, 2001.

Rynearson, Joseph M., and William J. Chisum. *Evidence and Crime Scene Reconstruction*, 3rd ed. Redding, CA: National Crime Investigation and Training, 1993.

Safferstein, Richard. *Criminalistics: An Introduction to Forensic Science*, 5th ed. Englewood Cliffs, NJ: Prentice Hall, 1995.

Staggs, Steven. *Crime Scene Photography*. San Clemente, CA: LawTech, 2005.

U.S. Department of Justice. *Handbook of Forensic Services*. Quantico, VA: Federal Bureau of Investigation, 2003.

Proper Handling of Evidence

Key Pieces of Evidence Are Only as Good as They Way They Were Seized

by J. L. Sumpter

In the age of precision, law enforcement is put under a powerful microscope to assure department protocol was properly carried out. From OJ Simpson to countless other trials where the handling of evidence played a role in an acquittal, it is imperative officers follow strict procedures.

There must be a series of checks and balances in place to ensure proper chain of custody. Ideally, this is a streamlined process where the intake and transfer of evidence is documented so well, there is little room for error. This starts at the scene.

The rushing must stop when the investigation begins. Once the scene is deemed safe, the rushing stops. All focus is on cause and effect, and nothing is out of the question. While starting from the outside in, officers should concentrate on taking as many pictures as possible. If a body is lying in a field, every angle leading to the victim is documented.

In a house, all rooms are photographed before documenting the point of entry or victim. This is so simple but could have a major influence on the outcome as evidence may show up in photos not seen with the human eye at the scene.

When getting closer to the focal point, and before seizing evidence, all focus is on the victim. Before this occurs, who is assuring proper procedures are being met? In rural areas, a buddy system works great. They are the investigator's eyes when focus is on the evidence. Two officers testifying the same gives the defense little wiggle room.

All scenes are different, so an officer must ask how he/she can best paint a detailed description of the scene for the jury and others. Diagraming the scene is very important for reconstruction purposes. Officers want to put the jury at the scene when explaining it on the stand. By giving them a detailed diagram with measurements not to scale, they can put the scene in better perspective.

Handling evidence under a buddy system is ideal.

Proper documentation is a non-negotiable.

What can go wrong, may indeed go wrong. Unfortunately, everyone is a detective in today's "CSI" rage. Potential jurors are not only educated on the different types of potential evidence, they are aware of the terminology too. As for the actual handling of evidence, it is vital that cross-contamination does not occur. Not only should each piece of evidence be properly documented, but handled as its own entity. They make gloves every day, so use them.

Keep in mind, what you think is a small case could catch national attention. Don't be that officer left to explain why contaminated fingerprint or DNA evidence came from the scene.

Great documentation is needed when anything whatsoever is taken from the scene. Precise documentation is critical when seizing evidence at the scene. From location to bagging, to transport vehicle, everything is photographed or videotaped with an accurate time stamp. At this point, it is also good practice for the second officer to play devil's advocate. After each piece of evidence is located and seized, constantly asking if every "I" was dotted and every "T" was crossed is important.

There are many officers out there sitting on the stand kicking themselves for something they could have done better. It's a much safer avenue taking all the time needed to document seized evidence. The officer's time on the stand should be spent explaining the evidence, not how the process was improperly handled. The less doubt for the jury, the better.

Due diligence pays off when the evidence is where it should be. Once the evidence is transported back to the department, it should be under the same magnifying glass as it was at the scene. The officer must precisely follow the department's evidence intake policy and procedures. It is also good protocol to have logs showing officers are periodically trained in the department's evidence collection process. Ignorance is no excuse when handling key pieces of evidence.

There are a number of records management systems out there to streamline this process. Anything to make sure the chain of custody is not broken reaps benefits in the end and if a digital system prevents errors, then cost should not be an issue.

There are many departments still relying on the trusted paper method. If this is a fine-tuned procedure, then great, but a fail-safe system (if there is such a thing) could be a great addition to this process.

From here, the property control officer should have specific procedures in place for proper documentation and placement purposes. Mistakes at this level are just as important as the actual seizing process. Lost evidence is not an option.

Can you imagine what could happen if defense attorneys found out the property control officer left the evidence room door open? This small mistake could be detrimental to every case and the department's reputation. This is a small example why a buddy system can help to eliminate small but potentially critical mistakes.

Documenting digital evidence is no different. In the digital world, it is required to show the evidence was not altered in any way, i.e., Photoshopped. The "originated" and "last modified" labels attached to the photo are important, but there are many other tools to prove the integrity of a photo. In a case where digital evidence, i.e., photos, computers, etc. play a major role, the prosecutor should seek testimony from an expert.

When taking hundreds of photos at the scene, the officer is bound to experience flash or lighting issues. Should the unreadable photos be deleted? Absolutely not. If the defense notices missing or out- of-sequence photos, it's likely red flags are raised. No investigation is perfect, but any opportunity to quash doubt is ideal.

Because of the possibilities for error, evidence collection and chain of custody are two of the most highly criticized procedures in law enforcement. This is only a fragment of ways to seize and document evidence, but if officers are properly trained in department protocol, use a buddy system, and constantly question every piece of seized evidence, the room for error is minimal.

Interviews

Obtaining Information from Witnesses

by James W. Osterburg and Richard N. Ward

Questioning People

The investigator spends a great deal of professional time talking with people after a crime is committed. The victim and eyewitness(es) are first; next are those whose identities develop in the course of the investigation. Some people furnish complete and candid information, but some are less cooperative or will deliberately mislead authorities; others must be coaxed to come forward.

The terms used to describe the questioning process are *interrogation* and *interviewing*. Interrogation applies to a suspect and a suspect's family, friends, or associates—people who are likely to withhold information or be deceptive. Interviewing applies to victims or eyewitnesses who can reasonably be expected to disclose what they know. Hence, the guiding principles and techniques of interrogation (discussed in Chapters 10 and 11) differ considerably from those of interviewing.

Interviewing

There are few people who have neither been interviewed nor conducted an interview themselves. Whether formal or informal, it is the same process that is involved in job hunting, shopping, or talking over a child's progress with a teacher. Its purpose is the exchange of information. Investigators also are engaged in this exchange, and as practiced professionals they generally take in far more information than they give out. Seeking facts not divulged because there is little comprehension of their significance, the investigator needs to be intuitive, alert, and skillful—much more than a passive information-recorder. If interviewing at the crime scene is unavoidable and there is any chance that the suspect or accomplices are within hearing distance, absolute discretion is a must. The following questions—"five Ws and one H": Who?, What?, When?, Where?, Why?, and How?—should be regarded as the minimum to be covered in an interview.

Who: The question of who involves the name, address, sex, age, and occupation of the interviewee. Interviewees can be victims, witnesses, or others suggested by witnesses or friends of the victim. Who is the perpetrator? Who gains some advantage from committing the crime? The investigator taking information from a witness must make a point of verifying the name and address given. A driver's license or other identification can prevent a subpoena's being returned marked: "Addressee Unknown." It is not uncommon to lose a case because a witness could not be contacted; numerous cases have been lost for precisely that reason.

What: What was observed by the eyewitness? What was heard or learned through any of the other senses (smell, touch, taste)? What relationship exists or existed between victim and perpetrator? Between the complainant and witness? Between complainant and other witnesses? Between participants in the crime? What objects were moved, taken, or damaged?

When: When was the crime committed? When did the interviewee acquire this information? When did a suspect last see or talk to the victim?

Where: Where did the crime take place? Where did the interviewee observe, hear, or otherwise learn what he or she is reporting? Where did the interview take place?

Why: Why was the interviewee in a position to observe the incident? Why did the crime occur (possible motive)? Why was the victim, target, or object selected? Why was a particular object moved, taken, or damaged?

How: How was the crime consummated? How was it originally conceived?

Modus Operandi: As previously discussed, the manner in which a crime was committed can serve as the trademark or *modus operandi* (MO) of that criminal. For example, the language used to convey to the victim that a robbery is to take place differs among holdup perpetrators. In a sexual assault, a rapist's threats, demands, and remarks characterize him just as the means of breaking and entering—cutting a hole in the roof, breaking through a wall with a jack hammer, hiding in the stairwell until the building is closed, picking a lock—distinguish a burglar. Some aspects of MO must be sought at the crime scene; others are furnished by the complainant (and perhaps by witnesses) at the initial interview. The well-maintained MO file can tie several crimes together through crime analysis. Individual clues collected in each crime may not suffice, but a pool of clues from crimes sharing a common MO could suggest a strategy for identifying and apprehending the perpetrator.

Acquiring the Facts

One method of acquiring the facts is to utilize a standardized form dealing with the significant details a complainant or witness may possess. Termed *complaint report* or *investigation report*, such forms are designed with questions framed to ensure that vital information is not overlooked. At the same time the forms are intended to ferret out facts that witnesses fail to volunteer because their potential value is unrealized. A note of caution:

> ... it is not true that more information necessarily is more productive. In some circumstances the use of precoded incident forms may be counterproductive.
>
> ... [Although] information is essential to apprehension and prosecution, [there are those who] are pessimistic about the way in which this notion has been implemented in some departments where investigating officers must wade through long, general lists of questions and precoded investigation forms ... . [It can be argued] that the key to enhanced productivity lies in collecting only that information likely to be useful in identifying and apprehending an offender.[1]

Thus, specialized forms need to be developed and tested. Their primary function is to minimize the amount of information collected and maximize its usefulness. If investigative efficiency is to be improved, applied research in this vein is essential. A simplified identification chart designed to focus a victim's or witness's immediate attention on a particular aspect of the crime or its perpetrator is needed. Also helpful would be a greater use by business establishments of a height line marker; placed on the exit doorjamb, it allows the height of the perpetrator passing through the door to be estimated.

A concept known as *Frame-by-Frame Analysis* (FFA) involves the detailed analysis of a victim or suspect's statement that focuses on very specific details. Savino and Turvey note that:

> The best way to understand this particular method is by comparing it to a movie. If we watch a movie in real time we may understand what is going on, but we might not observe all of the details. However, if we run the same movie in slow motion, frame-by-frame, we may better recognize the details of the action as it occurs.[2]

Failing to heed the importance of recording details when handling interviews, though obvious, is one of the major mistakes made by investigators, and it is not unusual for an interviewer to screen out or fill in important points because of carelessness, preconceived notions, time constraints, or misperceptions. Consider, for example, watching a movie, and then seeing the movie a second or third time. How much information is added with each viewing?

Another important aspect of the interview is observation of the facial expressions of the interviewee. Gary Faigin has studied facial expressions in great detail. He notes that the slightest change in a person's facial movements may reveal lying, fear, anger, or a host of other subtle clues that can further the investigation. Is the subject being evasive, perhaps afraid or fearful, or maybe hiding something? If a subject has a tendency to avoid eye contact, what does that mean? Even further, what can a person's eyes reveal? Do they evince sadness, lack of interest, anger, or hostility? As Faigin notes, "The eyes and brow together are easily the most magnetic

---

1   W.G. Skogan and G.E. Antunes, "Information, Apprehension, and Deterrence: Exploring the Limits of Police Productivity," *Journal of Criminal Justice*, 7 (1979), 234–235.

2   John O. Savino and Brent E. Turvey, *Rape Investigation Handbook* (Oxford, UK: Elsevier Science & Technology, 2004), 110–111.

and compelling part of the face ... We instinctively feel that the eyes provide our most direct link to the person within."[3]

Describing the Offender

The victim or eyewitness can make a major contribution by providing a good description of the perpetrator. Several procedures have been developed to accomplish this. The earliest, the *portrait parlé* (loosely translated, "verbal picture"), was suggested by Bertillon of the Sûreté. It was a supplement to his identification scheme, anthropometry (the recording of certain body measurements—especially bone length), which, despite his own fanatical opposition, was eventually dropped in favor of fingerprints. But *portrait parlé*, utilizing facial and bodily features to describe an individual, continues to this day.

Three other methods have emerged. In one, an artist draws a likeness of the person observed. People capable of this can be found in most communities; they may be on the staff in large police departments. Another method employs a series of pre-drawn facial features—hairlines, mustaches, eyebrows, eyes, ears, noses, lips, chins, and so on. Choosing the one feature from each series most closely resembling the perpetrator's feature (see Figure 6.1), the eyewitness makes selections that form a composite picture of the perpetrator. Composite kits are commercially

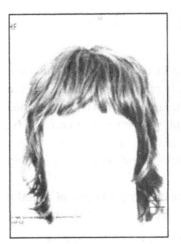

FIGURE 6.1 A few of the 193 forehead/hair styles available in the Photo-Fit female Caucasian front face kit.
Sirchie Finger Print Laboratories, Raleigh, NC

---

3   Gary Faigin, *The Artist's Complete Guide to Facial Expression* (New York: Watson-Guptill, 1990), 64.

available. Identi-Kit is well known; other makes, such as the Penry Photo-Fit, are equally satisfactory (see Figure 6.2).

FIGURE 6.2 A comparison of a Photo-Fit composite with a photograph of the same person. Sirchie Finger Print Laboratories, Raleigh, NC

The third (and latest) method exploits the graphics capability of the computer. A number of software programs have been designed to produce images of suspects or wanted persons: Compu-Sketch and ComPHOTOfit.

Compu-Sketch, offered by Allied Security Innovations, Inc., evolved in conjunction with a California police officer, Tom Macris, who served for 12 years as sketch artist for the San Jose Police Department.[4] It has been described:

> [Compu-Sketch] combines and creates over 100,000 facial features by simply pressing a button; one feature quickly falls over another until the composite is complete. The positioning of features in their relation to each other is unlimited, while refinement of resultant images is by electronic "paint box" techniques. The product is printed out as a highly credible composite sketch for leaflets or wanted posters.
>
> At the system's heart is a comprehensive interview program. It provides maximum help to the witness to recall critical suspect features, while assuring completely unbiased answers with non-leading and non-suggestive queries. Incorporated into the computer program is the key interview process enabling the operator to assist the witness step-by-step with memory enhancement questions triggering other memory processes, with consistency from case to case and agency to agency.[5]

4   R. Bocklet, "Suspect Sketches Computerized for Faster Identification," *Law and Order,* 35:8 (Aug. 1987), 61–63.

5   Ibid., 62.

Some facial features available in the Compu-Sketch library are shown in Figure 6.3. ComPHO-TOfit works with five features to draft the composite sketch, e.g., forehead, eyes, nose, mouth, and chin; a mustache, beard, eyeglasses, and headgear can be added if needed. ComPHOTOfit's developers claim that "the image generated is virtually photo quality after the image section lines of the component parts are blended out with a mouse, or moles and scars are 'painted' in."[6]

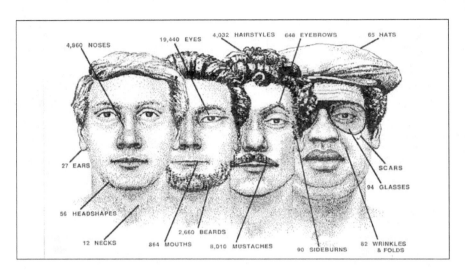

FIGURE 6.3 Compu-Sketch feature library.
Digital Descriptor Systems, Inc., Langhorne, PA

People normally see the features on a face in totality, unless one feature stands out. The totality (or gestalt) can be caught by the police artist, who offers the choice of an infinite number of facial features. Sirchie Finger Print Laboratories claims that more than 12 billion faces can be composed using the Photo-Fit system. If an artist's sketch or a composite picture is distributed, the likelihood of its utilization by the patrol force, community merchants, and the general public is greater than if a verbal description alone were circulated. When the general public must be looked to for help, prospects for its involvement increase if resentment is felt about the crime, or if the request is a novelty. Of course, the ultimate result is an identification; short of that, productive results could include leads that send detectives in search of additional facts from a record file or another person.

Describing Stolen or Lost Property

The task of identifying stolen property arises when the stores of loot of a burglar or fence are located. Because theft is largely a means of acquiring cash by pawning or selling stolen goods,

---

6   Ibid., 201.

police monitoring of property sold to secondhand dealers or pledged as security in pawn shops can bring about its identification. For this to result, it must be described twice:

First: by the owner to the investigator handling the case
Second: by the pawnbroker or secondhand dealer to the stolen property bureau of a
            police department

Because it would practically take a miracle to bring owner/victim and pawnbroker reports together (filing dates can be 30 or more days apart), the information generated by each report must be similar. To achieve this, the Stolen/Lost Property Report Form is a requisite. In some jurisdictions the law stipulates that pawnshop owners file such forms; in others, their voluntary cooperation must be sought. Owing to the nature of this business, however, it is not uncommon for pawnbrokers to contact police when merchandise brought to them arouses suspicion. Whether filing is required by law or voluntary, both reports (owner/victim and pawnbroker) should ultimately come together in the stolen property bureau records, thereby helping to clear the case as well as facilitating a return of the stolen goods to their rightful owners.

A Stolen/Lost Property Report Form can be developed in accordance with the following (or similar) taxonomy:

KIND OF OBJECT	Camera, TV, stereo set, credit card, watch, binoculars, jewelry
NAME OF MANUFACTURER (OR OTHER SOURCE) MODEL NUMBER	
IDENTIFYING FEATURES	Serial number, initials, or other personal inscription
MATERIAL USED	Shiny chrome or dull black body of a camera
IN ITS CONSTRUCTION	Wood or plastic in a TV set; gold or silver in jewelry
PHYSICAL APPEARANCE	Size, shape (as of a diamond), condition (like new, scratched)
MARKINGS	In many cases an object may have markings or identifiable damages known to the victim

Dealing with the Reluctant, Fearful, or Unaware Witness

Securing Cooperation

It is a fact that many crimes occur in which no witnesses come forward. Several reasons account for this disinclination: a person may be concerned over loss of pay through court continuances, harbor a fear of the police, or dread the offender's retaliation. In addition, some people have information, but are unaware of its usefulness to the police. An effective way to secure cooperation is to set up a special, 24-hour "hotline"; this allows witnesses to telephone police while remaining anonymous. Offering a reward is another time-honored formula. When the investigator learns the name of a potential witness who has not come forward, the rationale for this behavior must be ascertained. The means of dealing with this phenomenon vary with the reasons that foster it.

The growth of Crime Stoppers, local organizations of citizens that operate hotlines and offer rewards for information on crimes and criminals, has proven to be of assistance in investigations. Generally, an individual who provides information may remain anonymous, but in many cases the informant can be encouraged to come forward.

The Reluctant Witness

It does not require great imaginative ability to reassure the reluctant witness. Recognizing and realistically dealing with a legitimate complaint will usually suffice. For instance, many people are concerned about loss of pay when repeatedly called to court only to have the case continued (set for a later date). Should this be the basis for hesitancy, the investigator can arrange to have the witness placed on a telephone alert, to be called only when the case is actually on trial and the testimony wanted within an hour or so. In the course of duty, detectives continuously work out such arrangements.

The Fearful Witness

Witnesses who dread reprisal should their identity become known can be difficult to handle. For a key witness in an important case, protective custody (agreed to or imposed) may be required—a harsh measure that is seldom taken because it is hard on the individual and expensive for the state. A sympathetic attitude and a reliable appraisal of the danger (for example, by citing a witness's safety in the jurisdiction) may remove any remaining hesitancy. Just the same, there will be those who, for cultural or other reasons, cannot be persuaded to divulge what they know.

The witness who is reticent owing to fear of the police presents both short-term and long-term challenges. The short-term challenge is for the detective on the case to induce a person to divulge what he or she knows; the long-term challenge is for the department to surmount the misgivings that cause people to dread contact with the police. It may surprise many police officers to learn that law-abiding citizens fear them. In small communities with relatively homogenous populations, the degree of fear is not as great and usually is not manifest, but a latent fear may well exist.

This should not be surprising to those in large communities like New York, especially in the aftermath of the notorious Kitty Genovese case. It was in March of 1964 that Genovese was stalked by an assailant from a parking lot to a point near her apartment house door, where she was stabbed repeatedly. The time was 3:20 A.M. and her screams for help awakened the neighborhood, producing a hue and cry. Seeing lights go on and hearing people's shouts, the attacker was frightened off; however, 10 minutes later, when no police cars had responded to the scene, he came back for the kill. Knowing the extent of the injuries he had inflicted, and surmising that his victim had crawled to the refuge of an apartment doorway, he searched and found her there. Again she screamed for help, but this time he cut her throat and stopped the cries.

Some 38 neighbors heard Kitty Genovese that night. Yet it was not until 3:55 a.m.—about 30 minutes after the first scream, by which time the killer had long departed—that one of them called the police. Not an unfamiliar experience for many large city departments, this phenomenon is usually written off as citizen indifference or unwillingness to get involved. Is this the answer? Thirty-eight people were right at the scene, safe in their homes, with telephones available. Why the hesitation? Why was not one in this larger-than-average number of witnesses motivated by enlightened self-interest or plain civic duty to call the police?

To clarify the issue, one of the authors made informal queries among civilians in several sections of the United States. One fairly common retort stood out: a defensive "Have you ever called the police?" Even an inexpert poll-taker is alerted when rhetoric is employed to dodge an awkward question. Respondents, therefore, were asked to explain further. Upon doing so, they confronted, perhaps for the first time, the fundamental cause of their hesitancy: the fact that police emergency operators invariably put callers on the defensive and require them to justify the call.

Whatever its cause, this barrier is real; this became apparent from some respondents' replies. When an operator's voice is an irritated monotone, it communicates "This is nothing new; what are you excited about?" To the caller, of course, the event is indeed new and unusual enough to cause great concern. By turning off the civic-minded with a seemingly indifferent response, law enforcement agencies probably forfeit future cooperation. Moreover, because any contact with police is a rare event for most people, the experience is likely to be recounted to family and friends, producing more reticent witnesses who are unwilling to come forward.

Generating Long-Term Cooperation

Progressive police departments have begun to take seriously the recommendation of President Johnson's Commission on Law Enforcement and the Administration of Justice that

> ... the officials of the criminal justice system itself must stop operating, as all too many do, by tradition or by rote. They must re-examine what they do. They must be honest about the system's shortcomings with the public and with themselves. They must be willing to take risks in order to make advances. They must be bold.[7]

In keeping with the Commission's spirit, many departments have instituted victim-witness assistance units. In rape cases, for example, a female officer (who may be a trained social worker) responds to a reported rape scene. She supports the victim in a personal way throughout the questioning, then accompanies her to the hospital for medical examination, where physical evidence (semen, pubic hairs, blood) is acquired. Later, she provides follow-up counseling and sees the victim (now the witness) through the criminal justice process, explaining each step along the way—why it is necessary and what is next. A humanely treated victim is likely to be a willing witness, more so certainly than one who must—because official concern is focused only on the investigation—go over details of the ordeal while being inadvertently embarrassed by various male officers.

---

7   U.S. President, 1966–1972 (Johnson), The President's Commission on Law Enforcement and Admin-istration of Justice, *The Challenge of Crime in a Free Society* (Washington, DC: U.S. Government Printing Office, 1967), 15.

Some assistance programs concentrate on what is expected of the victim/witness when called to the stand. They supply transportation to court, child care, and a lounge or service center separated from the defendant. Some agencies even see to the repair of broken windows or damaged door locks in the home of a witness who has been threatened. For the witness or victim who feels intimidated, "hotline" telephones have been set up for advice, reassurance, and action.

The Unaware Witness

There are times when someone in the neighborhood sees the criminal on the way to or retreating from the crime scene. The observer could be sitting in a car, looking out a window, walking a dog, or driving a cab. Yet such observers are generally unaware of having seen anything that could be of value to the police. By revisiting the scene the following day or two, and exactly one week after the crime, the investigator may find a person who was passing when the crime was about to be (or was being) committed. In a well-publicized crime, the observer may realize he or she has something to contribute and come forward. In a major case, broadcasting an appeal is sometimes effective, as are leaflets distributed in shopping and transportation centers.

Canvass

If the case warrants it after all other measures have failed, a neighborhood canvass may be undertaken to discover the offender or unaware witness. Expensive and time-consuming, a canvass requires careful administrative control to ensure that every person in the area is contacted and interviewed. Large cities pose the greatest number of problems in conducting a store-to-store, building-to-building, house-to-house canvass. But if the area can be reasonably well-defined, its size and number of inhabitants limited, and the search is marked by patience and thoroughness, the chances of success are enhanced.

In the United States, a canvass is often considered in cases of homicide. The tactic works for other crimes as well. It can be productive when based on the possibility that someone saw or heard something that he or she did not bother to report until confronted by the inquiries of a police officer knocking on the door. Then, there is always the chance that the officer will knock on the very door of the perpetrator, who will be exposed by the combined effect of surprise and guilty knowledge.

Indifferent Complainants

At times a complainant may display indifference or claim that he or she is too busy to be questioned. Since most victims are anxious to be helpful, such resistance raises the question: "Why?" Sometimes the answer can be found through a crime scene examination focused on how the crime was committed, e.g., through a reconstruction of the event. Re-examining the alleged facts and the physical evidence may reveal that the crime was simulated, and account for a complainant's reluctance to be interviewed and possibly exposed as the perpetrator. An interrogation then may have greater success. In addition, when evidence of a crime (a burglary, for instance) is recognized as having been simulated, Horowitz's condition that evidence be available against the individual is met. This factor can be effective when interrogating the complainant who is falsely claiming to have been the victim of a burglary. (See Chapter 11.)

Behavioral Analysis Interviews

The Behavioral Analysis Interview (BAI) is an investigative technique that seeks to capitalize on the fact that a person being questioned unwittingly emits nonverbal signals. Called an interview, yet nearer to an interrogation in purpose, BAI can be likened to a bridge between the two. It also is described as an effective substitute when the polygraph is not available or acceptable for use.[8] So far, it has been of greatest help in private security work and for screening numbers of suspects when polygraph tests would be too time-consuming.

The objectives of the BAI technique include:

1. To develop investigative information, including statement inconsistencies or procedural/policy violations that may have contributed to the problem, as well as insight into the relevant activities of others;
2. To develop behavioral information indicative of the suspect's truthfulness or deception regarding the issue under investigation; and
3. To determine whether or not the person being interviewed did, in fact, commit the act that is under investigation.[9]

Behavior Analysis Interviews are based on the three levels of communication, including the verbal channel, paralinguistic channel, and the nonverbal channel. The most noticeable form of communication is verbal communication, in which word choice and arrangement are used. The paralinguistic channel involves the characteristics of speech that fall outside the spoken word, and nonverbal communication involves all nonverbal behavior, such as leg and arm movements, eye contact, and facial expressions.[10]

Based on an empirical study, the following symptoms are to be noted during the interview, because:

> ... it was clear that the innocent suspects revealed their truthfulness by their behavior, and the guilty revealed their deception by their behavior.
>
> ... truthful suspects were more at ease during the interview. They were able to sit comfortably without shifting while being questioned. These suspects were straightforward in their answers and looked at the interviewer with sincere eyes.

---

8   D.E. Wicklander, "Behavioral Analysis," *Security World*, 17:3 (Mar. 1980), 41.

9   From the Reid Behavior Analysis Interview (BAI).

10   F.E. Inbau, J.E. Reid, J.P. Buckley, and B.C. Jayne. *Criminal Interrogation and Confessions*, 4th ed. (Sudbury, MA: Jones and Bartlett, 2004), 125.

The guilty suspects appeared to be more nervous and uneasy during the interview. Some acted resentful or aggressive. The guilty suspects were often evasive, would not look at the examiner, and moved around frequently during the interview.

... It is important to note that the interviewer does not look for just one behavior symptom from the suspect. Rather, he is evaluating a cluster of behavior symptoms.[11]

To provoke a response, the person under suspicion is told that a specially trained interviewer will do the questioning and take fingerprints. If any other physical evidence has been found, this fact is also utilized; if, for instance, the evidence was a hair, the individual can be asked to provide a sample. The interviewer then begins with a review of some details of the crime, and watches for behavioral responses. Next, the person is turned over to another interviewer who has several prepared questions relevant to the crime; again, any behavioral reaction is noted. Finally, a third interviewer asks formulated questions based on previous responses, then terminates the session with the taking of fingerprints, watching all the while for any behavioral symptoms of guilt or innocence.

Sometimes a bait question is employed to draw the individual into modifying or even repudiating the original assertion of noninvolvement. An example: "Why would anyone say they saw you come out of the bar and go to the parking lot just before Joe was shot there?" A truthful response would be a direct denial such as "That can't be; I wasn't there" or "Whoever told you that is full of shit." A guilty response, based on the possibility that he or she was indeed seen in the lot, would either produce a denial—usually after some hesitation—or an admission that he or she was in the lot (but on another day), and a claim that the witness made a mistake as to when this occurred.

A response suggestive of guilt requires follow-up: by surveillance; perhaps seeking an informant; tracing the weapon used—if it was recovered; questioning associates; and so on. When and if further evidence is developed, a full-scale interrogation may be in order. Proponents claim that a professional BAI interviewer can "confidently eliminate over 80% of the innocent and can identify the guilty without the use of the polygraph technique."[12]

Hypnosis

The primary function of forensic hypnosis is that of an investigative tool. All information elicited should be independently verified as much as possible. Forensic hypnosis is used with the victim or a witness. It is not recommended for use with a suspect (remember: if you can lie when not in a "trance," you can lie when induced!). The following are some guidelines recommended for the hypno-investigator:

1. The hypno-investigator should not be involved in the direct investigation of the case.
2. Before hypnosis is induced, a written record should be made that includes a description of the subject matter and the information that was provided.

---

11   Wicklander, op. cit.

12   Ibid., 61.

3. The session should be both videotaped and audiotaped.
4. There should be no "line-up" or mug shot viewing prior.
5. Explain hypnosis to the subject before the session.
6. After an introductory relaxation, the victim/witness should be allowed to give a verbatim account of the incident.
7. The session should be conducted in a comfortable, "homey" atmosphere that is soundproofed and free of distractions.
8. Only the hypnotist and victim/witness should be allowed in the session, unless the hypnotist determines that it is necessary for a parent/guardian, case investigator, or police artist to be present.

Hypnosis, when properly used, can be a valuable tool for the investigator. Hypnosis is no longer considered to be "black magic voodoo witchcraft" but a positive and reliable information-gathering, crime-solving tool for the twenty-first-century criminal investigator.[13] The use of hypnosis by law enforcement as a means of interviewing has met with some criticism. Two concerns are expressed: (1) in some crimes the victim suffers severe psychological trauma, and reliving the experience through hypnosis could make it worse; and (2) "facts" may be implanted to cue or lead the witness under hypnosis, he or she being suggestible in this condition. To avoid criticism while retaining the benefits of hypnosis, the FBI has established elaborate guidelines for its use as an investigative tool.

> The FBI's policy basically states that the FBI is to use hypnosis only in selected cases. This would include bank robbery, where force is used or a large amount of money is involved, kidnapping, extortion, and crimes of violence which occur where the FBI has jurisdiction. Hypnosis is confined to use with key witnesses or victims of crimes only. No one who has the potential of becoming a suspect or subject in a case is to be hypnotized for any reason. For the sake of brevity, the term "witness" will be used in this article as a substitute for "witness/victim." The FBI uses only highly qualified hypnotists to do the actual induction. The use of hypnosis must be discussed with the U.S. attorney and his permission obtained. The U.S. attorney must then obtain written permission from the Assistant Attorney General of the Criminal Division, U.S. Department of Justice. The current policy also states that no Agent may participate in a hypnotic interview without written permission from the Attorney General. Further, the hypnotic interview must be recorded in its entirety, either by audio or videotape, with video the preferred method.
>
> The guidelines specify the use of a psychiatrist, psychologist, physician, or dentist who is qualified as a hypnotist. The use of a qualified health professional provides additional protection for the witness, the cost of which is minimal. Agents have used the services of professionals who have given generously of their time, or who have charged only a modest fee for the sessions, because of their desire to help in what is for some a new area of hypnosis. Furthermore, the FBI has found that this added protection has not restricted Agents in their use of hypnosis.[14]

---

13 E.G. Hall, "Watch Carefully Now: Solving Crime in the 21st Century," *Police*, (June 1999), 42–45.

14 R.L. Ault, "Hypnosis: The FBI's Team Approach," *FBI Law Enforcement Bulletin*, 49:1 (Jan. 1980), 5–8. Available at: http://www.ncjrs.gov/App/Publications/abstract.aspx?ID=64620

The FBI has utilized hypnosis in numerous cases; in many of these investigations, additional intelligence was obtained. Some was relevant and produced immediate results (e.g., an accurate sketch drawn from the witness' recall), but some is still open to question because the imprecise nature of hypnosis-based information makes corroboration difficult.

Often overlooked as a member of the investigation "team," sketch artists have sometimes proved invaluable in hypnosis sessions. Several cases in which the FBI was involved were resolved dramatically because artists provided satisfactory composite sketches of suspects. An FBI artist will travel to various field offices to work with the witness, coordinator, and doctor to produce composite drawings of suspects. Outside artists should be familiarized with the FBI guidelines and the use of hypnosis in aiding recall.

The Future of Hypnosis

Hypnosis continues to be a minor tool in the investigator's repertory. Nevertheless, it can be an effective one. Not only will it save many work hours, the potential also exists for its use by investigators themselves to enhance their own recall of events or details.

The team approach has proved valuable to the FBI. Introducing a "doctor-patient" relationship into an investigation, it ensures additional protection for witness and victim, while minimizing the hazards (potential and real) of hypnosis. Most important, the team approach helps to offset doubts about professionalism. There may well be a few individuals in law enforcement whose techniques are unscrupulous, but the same might be said of the health professions, both mental and physical. Law enforcement agencies may wish to consider some of the FBI's guidelines for improving an existing program or establishing the place of hypnosis in their departments.[15]

The National Board of Professional and Ethical Standards is one provider of Professional Board Certification and Teaching Credentials in hypnosis. Their Director of Ethics is a sitting Police Chief whose job it is to oversee the Ethics Committee for the organization and its members and students. The Board reminds users of hypnosis that the credibility of information obtained through hypnosis is enhanced when the facts disclosed are supported by independent evidence. It is important that such disclosures be followed up with additional investigative efforts involving other individuals, objects (physical evidence), and records to secure corroborative evidence.

Eyewitness Evidence: The Role of Perception and Memory

Most people have strong convictions about what they see with their own eyes, thus jurors tend to believe eyewitness testimony. However, experienced detectives have learned that eyewitnesses can be mistaken; indeed, it is not uncommon to find various eyewitness reports on an identical event to be incompatible. It is the task of the investigator to resolve such contradictions. One way is to reconstruct how the crime was committed (the use of physical evidence and the crime

---

15   Ibid., 8.

laboratory for this purpose are treated in Chapter 2). Another way to evaluate eyewitness reports is by understanding the psychological process involved: it begins with the original observation and proceeds to its retelling to the detective later and ultimate presentation to the court if the case goes to trial. A rather complicated process of observing and recalling, it can be divided into the following stages:

1. *Sensory input*: Information is encountered through visual observation or other senses, then encoded for storage in memory;
2. *Memory*: The storage and retention of what was observed and encoded;
3. *Retrieval*: The recovery of information through search of memory and its communication to others. The availability of cues to assist the search process is important at this stage.

Sensory Input

To understand how information is acquired, it is important to know the difference between perception and attention. Borrowing from Huxley's plain-talking style (which serves well for explaining the scientific method in Chapter 13) should be helpful. In one example, a person absorbed in reading hears a loud noise that seems to come from just outside the window. The reader, his or her attention diverted from the book, then interprets the meaning of the noise. Perception based on previous experience permits the likely cause to be determined. The sound could be of automobiles colliding, thunder, a scream, or a gunshot.

Now, consider a new baby asleep in its crib who is awakened by an identical noise. Though its attention would also be directed at the sound, having acquired no experience or knowledge in his or her brief life span, the baby is unable to interpret what the noise means. Like the reader, the baby's attention might be directed toward the sound; unlike the reader, however, the baby lacks any perception of its cause.

Perception is an important concept in comprehending the process of sensory input. Memory (essentially stored perceptions) and perception are intertwined, but for didactic reasons they are usually considered separate processes. To possess memory a person must have experiences. Something—a thought, emotion, object—must be comprehended through the mind or the senses. The person then perceives a new event in terms of experiences already stored up in memory and builds expectations and attitudes on them. So long as biases and stereotypes that can color expectations and attitudes are operative, perception may be faulty.

Perception can be considered the interpretation, classification, and conversion of sensory stimuli into a more durable configuration for memory. In other words, sensory input is assimilated to established knowledge stored in long-term memory. The discrete elements of an event are organized by the mind into meaningful categories, and stored. The aim is to assimilate the event, then reconcile it with prior experience and knowledge so as to avoid any discrepancy between them—bringing both the perceived event and prior experience into harmony and making them compatible. The mind's need to effect such a reconciliation is, however, a possible source of error. Perception also can be affected by stress or arousal felt at the time cognizance was taken of the event. Thus, the perception of how long it took for a crime to be committed (or for the police to respond) is often much greater than the actual elapsed time. Other factors affecting perception include age, health, and gender.

Memory

What the witness to a crime sees is etched on the brain; and later, on request, it can be recollected precisely. This belief is pervasive—witnesses (particularly victims) often asserting: "I'll never forget that face!" Common sense would seem to concur, yet clinical and laboratory experimentation demonstrate that memory is a complex phenomenon that cannot be explained with assumptions or beliefs. For example, common sense rejects the idea that sensory input received after an event can affect the memory of that event. Nonetheless, there is considerable empirical evidence that post-event information is indeed integrated with what already exists in memory. As a result, modifications may include: a change in the person's memory, enhancement of existing memory, or nonexistent details becoming embodied in the previous existing memory. Post-event information may arise from reading a newspaper article about it, from questions asked by an investigator or attorney, or from overhearing or talking about the event (particularly with other witnesses). The mind, therefore, is not like a videotape recorder that captures and retains what was seen (or heard) and remains unaffected by subsequent input.

Psychologists use the term *unconscious transference* to describe a witness's mistaken recollection about a crime—a recollection implicating an individual who was not involved. In one case, for instance, a young adult identified in a lineup (composed of several bank tellers) as the person who had robbed a bank was, in fact, an innocent depositor who had been in the bank the previous day. He was otherwise not connected with the institution, and certainly not with the robbery. This case illustrates the critical need to check out an accused person's explanation or alibi. Here, a review of the bank's deposit records would have challenged (and precluded) the lineup misidentification.

Information Retrieval

Two kinds of remembering are of interest to the detective: recall and recognition. In recall a previous event (e.g., a crime) is described verbally—in narrative form, in a *portrait parlé*, or to a police artist. In *recognition* there is an awareness that something was seen previously; some aspect of an event is remembered and selected from a group of similar items, persons, or photographs. This occurs when a mug shot is picked from the mug shot file or an individual is selected from a lineup. Generally, a person's ability with regard to recognition is better than it is for recall.

For retrieving information from a witness through an interview, a new technique, the result of psychological research into memory retrieval, is a major step forward. (See the section on The Cognitive Interview later in this chapter.)

Witness Errors

In addition to the possible errors associated with perception and memory, other sources of error include environmental conditions and personal factors.

Environmental Conditions

A person's ability to observe an event is limited by such factors as: the illumination of the scene, the distance of the observer from the scene, the noise level (if hearing is involved), and the weather (if the event occurred outdoors). If the evidence in a case depends largely on eyewitness testimony, it is desirable to verify whether environmental conditions existing at the time permitted such observations. Basic to the protection of the innocent, a verification can also deflect criticism by defense counsel and strengthen the confidence of the witness by establishing that there were no impediments to making the reported observations.

Personal Factors

Although sight and hearing most often provide the basis of witness testimony, any of the five senses can be involved. Again it is desirable to verify that the relevant sensory organs are or were not impaired. Taking this precaution enhances the credibility of the witness.

The Cognitive Interview

In 1908 Harvard's Hugo Munsterberg (the first experimental psychologist in America) proved that although eyewitness testimony was remarkably faulty, it could be improved upon.[16] His effort was ignored by lawyers, judges, and law enforcement, and not until the 1970s would psychologists reexamine ways to improve eyewitness testimony. This kind of empirical research may have been further prompted by the RAND Corporation report noting that the single most important factor as to whether a case would be solved is the information provided by a witness or victim.[17]

This observation led R. Edward Geiselman and others to research the effectiveness of memory retrieval techniques; their program was labeled the *cognitive interview*.[18] Reminiscent of Munsterberg's earlier experiment, an incident was staged and 16 undergraduates became "eyewitnesses." Divided into two groups, only one group (the cognitive interview group) was given instruction in memory-retrieval techniques. It included four recommendations for completing the test

---

16   Hugo Munsterberg, *On the Witness Stand* (Littleton, CO: Fred B. Rothman, 1981) [A reproduction of the original 1908 edition].

17   Peter Greenwood and Joan Petersilia, *The Criminal Investigation Process. Vol. III: Observations and Analysis* (Santa Monica, CA: RAND, 1975).

18   R. Edward Geiselman, R.P. Fisher, D.P. MacKinnon, and H.L. Holland, "Enhancement of Eyewitness Memory: An Empirical Evaluation of the Cognitive Interview," *Journal of Police Science and Administration*, 12:1 (1984), 74.

booklet, which had an open-ended question and some pointed (short-answer) questions. The recommendations were:

> First, try to reinstate in your mind the context surrounding the incident. Think about what the room looked like and where you were sitting in the room. Think about how you were feeling at the time and think about your reactions to the incident.
>
> Second, some people hold back information because they are not quite sure about what they remember. Please do not edit anything out. Please write down everything, even things you think may not be important. Just be sure to indicate at the right how sure you are about each item.
>
> Third, it is natural to go through the incident from beginning to end, and that is probably what you should do at first. However, many people can come up with more information if they also go through events in reverse order. Or, you might start with the thing that impressed you the most and then go from there, proceeding both forward and backward in time.
>
> Fourth, try to adopt the perspective of others who were present during the incident. For example, try to place yourself in the experimenter's role and think about what she must have seen.[19]

The researchers concluded:

> The results of this study illustrate that the cognitive interview has substantial promise as a technique for the enhancement of eyewitness memory retrieval. The cognitive interview produced significantly more correct information without an accompanying increase in the amount of incorrect information. This advantage for subjects using the cognitive interview held for both an open-ended question and for pointed questions. Overall, 84 percent of the information generated with the cognitive interview was found to be accurate. Further, the confidence of the witnesses in their correct responses was enhanced with the cognitive interview, while confidence in their incorrect responses was not reliably affected. All but one of the subjects who received the cognitive interview reported that they found the methods to be useful.[20]

The next step for the Geiselman team was to compare the cognitive interview against hypnosis, another memory enhancement technique. Then both were matched against results obtained from a standard police interview.[21] This research revealed that both the cognitive and hypnosis procedures elicited a significantly greater number of correct items of information from the subjects than did the standard interview. This result, which held even for the most critical facts from the films, was most pronounced for crime scenarios in which the density of events was high. The number of incorrect items of information generated did not differ across the three interview conditions. The observed memory enhancement was interpreted in terms of the memory-guidance techniques common to both the cognitive and hypnosis interviews. Neither

---

19   Ibid., 76.

20   Ibid., 79.

21   R. Edward Geiselman, R.P. Fisher, D.P. MacKinnon, and H.L. Holland, "Eyewitness Memory Enhancement in the Police Interview: Cognitive Retrieval Mnemonics Versus Hypnosis," *Journal of Applied Psychology*, 70:2 (1985), 401–412.

differential questioning time nor heightened subject or interviewer motivation could explain the results.[22] Three years later, Geiselman and Fisher reported on the effort to refine and revise the cognitive interview technique which, they stated, was based on four core principles: memory-event similarity, focused retrieval, extensive retrieval, and witness-compatible questioning.[23]

Memory-Event Similarity

Memory-event similarity involves an attempt to have the witness mentally recreate the environment surrounding the incident. A psychological environment similar to that which existed at the time of the crime is reproduced at the interview.

> The interviewer, therefore, should try to reinstate in the witness's mind the external (e.g., weather), emotional (e.g., feelings of fear), and cognitive (e.g., relevant thoughts) features that were experienced at the time the crime occurred.[24]

The witness is requested to think about the crime—the scene and what it looked like, where he or she was standing (or sitting), and the reaction to the crime at that time. This is a mental exercise; the witness is not physically placed at the scene. "In fact, if the crime scene has changed considerably, going back to the scene could conceivably interfere with the witness's recollection."[25]

Focused Retrieval

Because memory retrieval requires concentration, the interviewer helps witnesses to focus by refraining from asking too many short-answer, undirected, or irrelevant questions that tend to break concentration. Just as asking a series of questions can create a barrier that obstructs memory, so can interrupting the eyewitness who is responding to an open-ended question or providing a narrative description of the event. Another means of focusing memory retrieval is to have witnesses write everything down, even details they consider unimportant or about which they are unsure.

Extensive Retrieval

Memory retrieval is hard work, and witnesses are apt to terminate the effort after the first attempt. It is especially likely that the elderly will do so; they need to be encouraged to make other attempts. The usual mode is to begin at the beginning and continue chronologically to the end, but there are other ways. For example, witnesses can be asked to start with whatever detail is most indelibly inscribed in their memory, and from there, encouraged to go backward and forward. Another way is to reverse the order, urging witnesses to describe how the incident ended, and then proceed backward to the beginning.

---

22   Ibid., 401.

23   R.E. Geiselman and R.P. Fisher, "The Cognitive Interview: An Innovative Technique for Questioning Witnesses of Crime," *Journal of Police and Criminal Psychology*, 4:2 (October 1988), 3.

24   Ibid.

25   Ibid.

Witness-Compatible Questioning

Just as the eyewitness is better able to retrieve memory when the environment surrounding the event is recreated, so are interviewers better able to ask questions if they can place themselves in the witness' frame of mind. The aim is to ask questions compatible with the situation in which the witness found himself or herself. To accomplish this, interviewers should try to place themselves in the witness' situation, and then frame questions on the basis of what was likely to have been observed at the time. This means adjusting to the witness' perspective rather than having the witness adjust to the investigator's. Geiselman and Fisher conclude by remarking:

> ... cognitive interviewing reliably enhances the completeness of a witness's recollection, and without increasing the number of incorrect or confabulated (replacing facts with fantasy) bits of information generated ... .The procedures are easy to learn and can be readily adopted in routine police interview procedures. In fact, the cognitive interview is in use as standard training at several police departments and other law enforcement agencies.[26]

Supplemental Readings

Interviewing

Bennett, Margo, and John E. Hess. "Cognitive Interviewing." *FBI Law Enforcement Bulletin* 60:3 (Mar. 1991), 8–12.

Fisher, Ronald P. *An R.E. Geiselman Memory-Enhancing Technique for Investigative Interviewing; the Cognitive Interview*. Text. Ed. Springfield, IL: Charles C. Thomas, 1992.

Fisher, R. P., K.L. K.L Falkner, M. Trevisan, and M.R. McCauley. "Adapting the Cognitive Interview to Enhance Long-term Recall of Physical Activities." *Journal of Applied Psychology*, 85 (2000), 180–89.

George, R., and B. Clifford. "The Cognitive Interview—Does It Work?: In G. Davies, S. Lloyd-Bostock, M. McMunan, and C. Wilson, eds., *Psychology, Law and Criminal Justice: International Developments in Research and Practice* (New York: Walter de Gruyter), 1996, 146–154.

Gorden, Raymond L. *Basic Interviewing Skills*. Englewood, CO: Peacock Publications, 1992.

Rabon, Don. *Interviewing and Interrogation*. Durham, NC: Carolina Academic Press, 1992.

Shearer, Robert A. *Interviewing in Criminal Justice*, 3rd ed. Acton, MA: Copley, 1989.

Spaulding, William. *Interviewing Child Victims of Sexual Exploitation*. Arlington, VA: National Center for Missing and Exploited Children, 1987.

Starrett, Paul, Esq., and Joseph N. Davis. *Interview and Interrogation with Eyewitness Evidence*. San Clemente, CA: LawTech, 2004.

Zulawski, David E., and Douglas E. Wicklander, eds. *Practical Aspects of Interview and Interrogation*. Boca Raton, FL: CRC Press, 1993.

---

26 Ibid., 4–5.

Dealing with Witnesses

Cain, Anthony, A., and Marjorie Kravitz. *Victim/Witness Assistance: A Selected Bibliography*. Rockville, MD: National Criminal Justice Reference Service, 1978.

Cannavale, Frank J., Jr., and William D. Falcon. *Witness Cooperation*. Lexington, MA: Lexington Books, 1976.

Nonverbal Communication

Ekman, Paul, and Wallace V. Friesen. *Unmasking the Face*, 2nd ed. Palo Alto, CA: Consulting Psychologist Press, 1984.

Fast, Julius. *Body Language*. New York: M. Evans and Company, 1972.

Speigel, J.P., and P. Machotka. *Messages of the Body*. New York: The Free Press, 1974.

Weaver, Richard L. *Understanding Interpersonal Communications*, 7th ed. Glenview, IL: Harper College Division, 1996.

Hypnosis

Arons, Harry. *Hypnosis in Criminal Investigation*. Springfield, IL: Charles C Thomas, 1967.

Niehaus, Joe. *Investigative Forensic Hypnosis*. Boca Raton, FL: CRC Press, 1992.

Reiser, Martin. *Handbook of Investigative Hypnosis*. Los Angeles: Lehi, 1980.

Perception, Memory, and Witness Error

Ellison, Katherine W., and Robert Buckout. *Psychology and Criminal Justice*, Chapter 5. New York: Harper & Row, 1981.

Wall, Patrick M. *Eyewitness Identification in Criminal Cases*. Springfield, IL: Charles C Thomas, 1971.

Yarmey, A. Daniel. *The Psychology of Eyewitness Testimony*. New York: The Free Press, 1979.

Interrogations and Confessions

by Jacqueline R. Kanovitz

> No person shall be ... compelled in any criminal case to be a witness against himself ...
>
> Fifth Amendment

Introduction

The law of **interrogations** and confessions is not set out in any single article or amendment to the Constitution. The restrictions come from five constitutional provisions, combined with federal and state statutes requiring prompt **arraignment** of suspects in **custody**. The five constitutional provisions that bear on the admissibility of confessions are the Fourth Amendment exclusionary rule, the Fifth Amendment privilege against self-incrimination, the Sixth Amendment right to counsel, and the Fifth and Fourteenth Amendment due process clauses.

Constitutional restrictions on the admission of confessions are designed to ensure that confessions are voluntary and trustworthy. Coerced statements are considered unreliable. However, even if this were not so, restrictions on admission serve to discourage police officers from engaging in practices that our society does not tolerate.

Five Requirements for Admissibility

Admission of a confession may be challenged on at least five different grounds. The first stems from the Fifth and Fourteenth Amendment due process clauses. It is a violation of due process to admit an involuntary confession into evidence.[1] Coerced confessions are considered unreliable because even an innocent person may confess when the pressures become unbearable.

The second requirement stems from the Fourth Amendment exclusionary rule, which was covered in Chapter 4. The Fourth Amendment exclusionary rule applies to confessions as well as to physical evidence. Police are aware that people tend to

---

1   *See* § 6.2 *infra*.

confess when the "cat is out of the bag." To reduce the temptation to force the cat out of the bag illegally, the Fourth Amendment requires suppression of confessions that are causally related to an illegal *Terry* stop, **arrest**, or **seizure** of property, even if the confession was voluntary and its reliability is not in question.[2]

Confessions that fail to satisfy any of the following requirements are inadmissible as evidence of guilt.

1. The due process free and voluntary rule,
2. The Fourth Amendment exclusionary rule,
3. The Fifth Amendment privilege against self-incrimination, and
4. The Sixth Amendment right to counsel.

Confessions may also be suppressed for violating federal and state delay-in-arraignment statutes.

FIGURE 7.1 Legal Hurdles That Confessions Must Pass in Order to be Admissible as Evidence

---

The third requirement, known as the *McNabb-Mallory* delay-in-arraignment rule,[3] is based on federal and state statutes that require suspects to be taken before a magistrate for arraignment "without undue delay" after the arrest. The period between arrest and arraignment is inherently coercive, because the suspect is generally held incommunicado, without counsel or access to the outside world. Concerns for the voluntariness of confessions given during this period prompted the Supreme Court to adopt the *McNabb-Mallory* rule, which requires suppression of confessions given during the interval between a suspect's arrest and arraignment if police officers are guilty of unnecessary delay in taking the arrestee before a magistrate.

The fourth requirement, known as the *Miranda* rule,[4] is grounded in the Fifth Amendment privilege against self-incrimination.[5] This requirement applies to confessions elicited during police **custodial interrogations**. Confessions given by suspects while in police custody will be suppressed unless the prosecution proves that the suspect was warned of his or her *Miranda* rights and voluntarily waived them before making the statement.

The fifth requirement stems from the Sixth Amendment right to counsel.[6] The Sixth Amendment right to counsel attaches upon initiation of prosecution. During all subsequent investigative contacts pertaining to the charges, police must obtain a valid waiver of the right to counsel or see to it that counsel is present, whether the defendant is in custody or at large.

---

2   *See* § 6.3 *infra*.

3   *See* § 6.5 *infra*.

4   **Miranda v. Arizona, 384 U.S. 436, 86 S. Ct. 1602, 16 L. Ed. 2d 694 (1966)**.

5   *See* §§ 6.6–6.8 *infra*.

6   *See* § 6.9 *infra*.

Confessions provide powerful evidence of guilt and are often necessary for a conviction. However, they are easily contaminated. Violation of the rules discussed in this chapter will result in suppression. Consequently, police officers must be thoroughly versed in the law of interrogations and confessions. Although restrictions on police interrogations are designed to protect the accused, compliance serves the interests of society by producing confessions that can be used as evidence.

Legally Relevant Phases in the Development of a Criminal Case

Police questioning may take place at different stages in the development of a criminal case, with the tone varying from inquisitive to accusatory. The legal requirements that police officers must observe are not the same across the entire spectrum of questioning situations. Although confessions must pass five legal hurdles in order to be admissible, all five do not materialize the instant a police officer asks a question. The requirements in effect during police questioning vary with the stage when questions are asked and the tone of the questioning. In developing an overview of the law of interrogations and confessions, it is useful to break down the development of criminal cases into three phases and focus on the legal requirements that police officers must observe during each stage. This will lead to a clearer understanding of what police officers are required to do, and when they are required to do it, in order to preserve the admissibility of confessions. The timeline at the top of Figure 7.2 identifies three legally relevant phases in the development of a criminal case. The first phase (noncustodial **investigative questioning**) spans the period between the unfolding of a hunch and the time when a suspect is placed under formal arrest or taken into custody. The tone of questioning is inquisitive during the first phase, but becomes accusatory once the case enters the second phase. The second phase (**custodial interrogation**) begins when the suspect is placed under formal arrest or is taken into custody and continues until formal charges have been made. Once formal charges are filed, the case enters the third phase, which continues until the trial. The five legal requirements discussed in this chapter are shown along the left-hand margin of Figure 7.2. The shaded areas show the periods during which each of them is in effect.

The typical criminal case begins when an officer develops a hunch that a person has committed, is committing, or is about to commit a crime, and decides to investigate further. The officer approaches the suspect, introduces him or herself, and asks whether the suspect would be willing to answer some questions. As long as a reasonable person in the suspect's position would feel free to decline the interview, terminate the encounter, and go about his or her business, the investigative encounter is consensual, and none of the five requirements applies. In Chapter 3, we used the phrase "free zone" to describe police activity that is not regulated by the Constitution.[7] The "free zone" concept applies here as well. Incriminating statements elicited during consensual investigative encounters will always be admissible.

However, investigative encounters are not always consensual. This is true of investigatory detentions and traffic stops. Although the suspect has not yet been arrested or taken into

---

7   For the characteristics of a voluntary investigative encounter, *see* Chapter 3, §§ 3.3–3.5.

Timeline	Phase 1: Noncustodial Investigative Questioning of Suspects Who Are Not in Custody		Phase II: Interrogation of Suspects Who Are in Custody	Phase III: Interrogation of Defendants After Formal Charges Have Been Filed
	Consensual encounter	Investigatory detentions and traffic stops		
Due process free and voluntary rule				
Fourth Amendment exclusionary rule				
McNabb-Mallory rule				
Miranda rule				
Sixth Amendment right to counsel				

FIGURE 7.2 Timeline in the Development of a Criminal Case Showing the Periods During Which Each of the Five Hurdles Operates

custody, investigatory detentions and traffic stops are not consensual because the suspect has been seized. Statements made during these encounters are capable of being contaminated because two of the five legal requirements—the due process free and voluntary rule and the Fourth Amendment exclusionary rule—are in effect.

The second phase, the *custodial interrogation phase*, begins when police officers place a suspect under formal arrest or take a suspect into custody. Once the investigation enters this phase, the tone of the questioning changes. The questioning is no longer inquisitive; it becomes accusatory. The mere fact of being in police custody puts pressure, both internal and external, on a suspect. As a result, restrictions on police questioning tighten and, as Figure 7.2 shows, four of the five requirements are now in effect.

At some point after the arrest, formal charges will be filed. When this happens, the suspect officially becomes an accused and the Sixth Amendment right to counsel attaches. The case now enters the third phase—the *prosecutorial* stage—and protection for the defendant's right to counsel broadens.

The Free and Voluntary Rule

At early common law, confessions were admissible as evidence of guilt even when they were tortured from suspects. As time passed, judges came to appreciate that coerced confessions are not reliable. Everyone has a breaking point. When exposed to extreme pressure, even an innocent person may confess. This insight led to the adoption, both in England and the United States, of the rule that confessions must be voluntary in order to be admissible as evidence of guilt. This requirement is incorporated into the Fifth and Fourteenth Amendment due process clauses. Suppression of coerced confessions serves three main purposes. It (1) protects against convictions based on unreliable evidence; (2) preserves a suspect's freedom of choice; and (3) deters police from engaging in interrogation practices our society does not tolerate.

Confessions are not voluntary and will be suppressed when: (1) coercive pressures exerted by the government (2) induce the making of a statement the suspect would not otherwise have made.

FIGURE 7.3 Due Process Free and Voluntary Requirement

The Two-Part Test of "Voluntariness"

A confession is involuntary under the due process clause if it results from coercive pressures exerted by the government that overcome the suspect's free will and induce the making of a statement the suspect would not otherwise have made.[8] The due process test of voluntariness has two components—the first is concerned with the source of the pressure and the second with its impact on the suspect.

The confession must derive from improper government activity to be involuntary in the constitutional sense. Internal pressures and external ones exerted without government complicity do not render a confession involuntary in the constitutional sense. Suppose that Sticky-Fingered Sam suffers a head injury in an auto accident that temporarily incapacitates the "lying" center of his brain. For a few (poorly-timed) moments, Sam is unable to speak anything but the truth. When the police reach the accident scene, Sam confesses to all of his past crimes. Although Sam's confession was not a product of his free will, his confession satisfies the due process test of voluntariness because the police did nothing improper to induce the confession.

The Supreme Court used this reasoning in a case in which a chronic schizophrenic suffering from auditory hallucinations walked into a police station and confessed to murdering a young girl.[9] The Supreme Court refused to suppress the confession, despite psychiatric testimony that

---

8   Nix v. Williams, 467 U.S. 431, 104 S. Ct. 2501, 81 L. Ed. 2d 377 (1984); Colorado v. Connelly, 479 U.S. 157, 107 S. Ct. 515, 93 L. Ed. 2d 473 (1986).

9   Colorado v. Connelly, *supra* note 8.

the deranged man believed that God's voice had ordered him to confess, because the confession was obtained without improper activity by the police. Improper police activity is necessary for a confession to be involuntary in a due process sense.

Factors Considered in Determining Voluntariness

Physical force and violence are so obviously coercive that confessions extracted through their use are involuntary as a matter of law.[10] When the pressures to confess are less extreme, voluntariness is determined by examining the circumstances surrounding the making of the confession, with emphasis on three factors: (1) the pressures exerted by the police; (2) the suspect's degree of susceptibility; and (3) the conditions under which the interrogation took place.[11]

Physical brutality and threats of violence render a confession involuntary as a matter of law. When the pressures are less extreme, voluntariness is determined by examining the totality of circumstances surrounding the confession, with emphasis on three factors:

1. the pressures exerted by the police;
2. the suspect's degree of susceptibility; and
3. the conditions under which the interrogation took place.

FIGURE 7.4 Factors Relevant to Voluntariness

Pressures exerted by the police. Courts first examine the methods used by the police to elicit the confession. Force and brutality render confessions involuntary as a matter of law. While "beating" confessions out of suspects is rare in modern times, it is unfortunately not rare enough. The following is an unnerving account of testimony given by a defendant in an Illinois case concerning the circumstances surrounding his confession.[12] The defendant testified that,

---

10   Beecher v. Alabama, 389 U.S. 35, 88 S. Ct. 189, 19 L. Ed. 2d 35 (1967) (statement obtained after police held a gun to suspect's head and threatened to kill him if he did not tell the truth); Brown v. Mississippi, 297 U.S. 278, 56 S. Ct. 461, 80 L. Ed. 682 (1936) (statement obtained after police whipped suspect).

11   **Arizona v. Fulminante, 499 U.S. 279, 111 S. Ct. 1246, 113 L. Ed. 2d 302 (1991)**; Schneckloth v. Bustamonte, 412 U.S. 218, 93 S. Ct. 2041, 36 L. Ed. 2d 854 (1973).

12   People v. Banks, 549 N.E.2d 766 (Ill. 1989). Cases like *People v. Banks* are not unique. On January 11, 2003, two days before leaving office, Illinois governor George Ryan pardoned four inmates on death row who were convicted on the basis of confessions tortured from them through tactics similar to those used in the Banks case. *See* James Webb, *Illinois Governor Pardons Four Inmates Condemned to Death*, COURIER JOURNAL A7 (Jan. 11, 2003). On the following day, Governor Ryan commuted all 167 remaining Illinois death sentences to prison terms, stating: "The facts that I have seen in reviewing each and every one of these cases raised questions not only about the innocence of people on death row, but about the fairness of the death penalty as a whole." Jodi Wilgoren, *Illinois Governor Cleans Out Death Row*, COURIER JOURNAL A1 (Jan. 12, 2003).

following his arrest, he was taken to an interrogation room where he was interrogated for six hours with his wrists handcuffed behind his back. When he persisted in denying knowledge of the crime, one of the detectives put a chrome .45 caliber automatic gun in his mouth and told him that he would blow off his head because he knew that the defendant was lying. The defendant further testified that the detective struck him in the stomach with a flashlight three or four times and, when he fell out of the chair, stomped on him and hit him with the flashlight. When he continued denying knowledge of the crime, the detective put a plastic bag over his head while another officer kicked him. Thereafter, three officers took him to another room and again placed a plastic bag over his head, this time for about two minutes. At this point, the defendant confessed.

Although the officers denied these incidents, their testimony was not convincing. A physician who examined the defendant found lacerations on both wrists, multiple scrapes and scratches on his chest and abdomen, bruises on both legs and upper thighs, swollen muscles, and a lump under the skin in his lower rib cage. Confessions procured through tactics like these are involuntary as a matter of law.

Threats and false promises also raise constitutional concerns.[13] Police may not threaten to arrest innocent family members or take the suspect's children away to induce a confession.[14] Nor may they promise immunity from prosecution, a lighter sentence, or another form of leniency.[15] However, it is not improper to tell suspects that the prosecutor will be informed of their

---

13   *See, e.g.,* Payne v. Arkansas, 356 U.S. 560, 78 S. Ct. 844, 2 L. Ed. 2d 975 (1958) (invalidating confession obtained after police threatened to turn the suspect over to an angry lynch mob); Rogers v. Richmond, 365 U.S. 534, 81 S. Ct. 735, 5 L. Ed. 2d 760 (1961) (invalidating confession made in response to bogus threat to arrest suspect's ailing wife); Lynum v. Illinois, 372 U.S. 528, 83 S. Ct. 917, 9 L. Ed. 2d 922 (1963) (invalidating confession made in response to bogus threat to take away suspect's children); Spano v. New York, 360 U.S. 315, 79 S. Ct. 1202, 3 L. Ed. 2d 1265 (1959) (invalidating confession where officer lied to childhood friend that he would lose his job and this would create a family hardship if suspect did not cooperate); Hopkins v. Cockrell, 325 F.3d 579 (5th Cir. 2003) (holding confession involuntary where the police detective conducting an interview with the defendant assured the defendant that "their conversation was confidential, telling [the defendant], 'This is for me and you. This is for me. Okay. This ain't for nobody else.' " The court stated that "[a]n officer cannot read the defendant his *Miranda* warnings and then turn around and tell him that despite those warnings, what the defendant tells the officer will be confidential and still use the resultant confession against the defendant"; Spence v. State, 281 Ga. 697, 642 S.E.2d 856 (2007) (same).

14   Rogers v. Richmond, *supra* note 13.

15   *See, e.g.,* United States v. LeBrun, 306 F.3d 545 (8th Cir. 2002); State v. Sturgill, 469 S.E.2d 557 (N.C. Ct. App. 1996); State v. Rush, 174 Md. App. 259, 921 A.2d 334 (2007) (holding that confessions are involuntary as a matter of law when they are induced by false promise that suspect will be given special consideration from a prosecuting authority or some other form of assistance in exchange for his confession). However, vague assurances that cooperation is in the suspect's best interest are not considered improper. *See, e.g.,* United States v. Ruggles, 70 F.3d 262 (2d Cir. 1995); United States v. Nash, 910 F.2d 749 (11th Cir. 1990); Collins v. State, 509 N.E.2d 827 (Ind. 1987).

cooperation,[16] or to refer to the jail time or maximum penalty they face.[17] Police officers are allowed to make truthful representations about the suspect's legal predicament.

Misrepresentations designed to convince suspects that the case against them is stronger than it really is, on the other hand, rarely cause constitutional concern because deceptions like this are unlikely to induce an innocent person to confess.[18]

If the court determines that the police used improper interrogation tactics, it will next consider whether the suspect's will was overborne. The suspect's degree of susceptibility is the central focus of this inquiry.

Suspect's degree of susceptibility. People vary in the degree and types of pressure they can withstand. The suspect's background, education, intellect, prior experience with the criminal justice system, physical and mental condition, ability to cope with stress, and other traits will be examined to decide whether the suspect's free will was overcome by the stresses that were placed on him or her.[19]

Conditions under which the interrogation took place. The details of the interrogation are the last consideration. Because a suspect's capacity to resist pressures can be eroded by factors, such as the location of the interrogation; the length, intensity, and frequency of the interrogation sessions; food and sleep deprivation; the intimidating presence of large numbers of police officers; and other factors that were part of the interrogation environment, these factors will be examined as well.[20]

---

16   United States v. Westbrook, 125 F.3d 996 (7th Cir. 1997).

17   United States v. Braxton, 112 F.3d 777 (4th Cir. 1997) (telling a suspect "if you don't come clean, you can get five years" is not improperly coercive).

18   For cases finding confession voluntary despite police deception, see Frazier v. Cupp, 394 U.S. 731, 89 S. Ct. 1420, 22 L. Ed. 2d 684 (1969) (misrepresentation that suspect's associate had confessed to the crime and implicated him); United States v. Rodgers, 186 F. Supp. 2d 971 (E.D. Wis. 2002) (misrepresentation that defendant's fingerprints had been found on the firearm); Sovalik v. State, 612 P.2d 1003 (Alaska 1980) (misrepresentation that defendant's fingerprints were found at the crime scene); Ledbetter v. Edwards, 35 F.3d 1062 (6th Cir. 1994) (misrepresentation that the victim and two witnesses had identified suspect); State v. Pitts, 936 So. 2d 1111 (Fla. App. 2006) (appeal to suspect for assistance in finding the victim's body so that the family can arrange a decent burial); State v. Woods, 280 Ga. 758, 632 S.E.2d 654 (2006) (same); People v. Dishaw, 30 A.D.3d 689, 816 N.Y.S.2d 235 (2006) (telling defendant that her actions were caught on video surveillance, and placing fake videotape on table in front of defendant); 2 WAYNE R. LAFAVE, JEROLD H. ISRAEL, & NANCY J. KING, CRIMINAL PROCEDURE (2d Ed. 1999) § 6.2(C), p. 456 ("as a general matter it may be said that the courts have not deemed [police trickery and deception] sufficient by itself to make a confession involuntary"). However, deceptive ploys like these may violate the Miranda rule, if they take place after suspects have invoked their right to counsel or to remain silent. See § 6.7(B)(2) infra.

19   See, e.g., **Arizona v. Fulminante**, supra note 11 (below-average intelligence, fourth-grade education, poor coping skills).

20   Mincey v. Arizona, 437 U.S. 385, 98 S. Ct. 2408, 57 L. Ed. 2d 290 (1978) (statement obtained from suspect under sedation in intensive care unit); Greenwald v. Wisconsin, 390 U.S. 519, 88 S. Ct. 1152, 20 L. Ed. 2d 77 (1968) (statement obtained from suspect interrogated nonstop for more than 18 hours without food or sleep); Reck v. Pate, 367 U.S. 433, 81 S. Ct. 1541, 6 L. Ed. 2d 948 (1961) (statement obtained after depriving suspect of adequate food, sleep, and contact with family); Malinski v. New York, 324 U.S. 401, 65 S. Ct. 781, 89 L. Ed. 1029 (1945) (statement obtained after forcing suspect to remain naked).

C. Procedures for Determining the Voluntariness of a Confession

The question of whether a confession is voluntary is one that the judge must decide before admitting the confession into evidence. The judge may not admit it and leave this question to the jury, with instructions to disregard the confession if the jury finds it involuntary.[21] It is unrealistic to expect lay jurors to disregard a confession once they have heard it. Consequently, when the voluntariness of a confession is challenged, the judge must hold a hearing outside the presence of the jury and take testimony about the circumstances surrounding the making of the confession.[22]

The burden of proof at the voluntariness hearing is on the government. To secure admission, the government must prove that the defendant confessed of his own free will. In *Lego v. Twomey*,[23] the defendant argued, without success, that the government should be required to prove this fact "beyond a reasonable doubt." The Court disagreed, holding that, while the government must establish guilt beyond a reasonable doubt, the Constitution does not require this degree of certainty to secure the admission of a confession. The Court adopted a "preponderance of the evidence" standard; the government must establish that it is more probable than not that the defendant confessed of his or her own free will. If the evidence at the suppression hearing is equally weighted, the government will lose because its burden of proof has not been carried.

Summarizing, involuntary confessions—confessions that are a product of police misconduct that overbears a suspect's free will—are inadmissible. Voluntariness is determined by examining the methods police used to elicit the confession, the suspect's degree of susceptibility, and the conditions under which the interrogation took place. The government bears the burden of proving by a preponderance of the evidence (i.e., that it is more probable than not) that the defendant confessed of his or her own free will.

The Fourth Amendment Exclusionary Rule

The second ground for challenging a confession stems from the Fourth Amendment exclusionary rule. The Fourth Amendment exclusionary rule applies to confessions as well as to physical evidence. If the police conduct an illegal search, find drugs, and the suspect confesses when confronted with the evidence, the confession will be suppressed even if it was otherwise voluntary. The same holds true for confessions caused by unconstitutional arrests and stops. Moreover, when a confession is contaminated by violation of the Fourth Amendment, the taint normally destroys the admissibility of **derivative evidence** discovered as a result of the confession.

This branch of the Fourth Amendment exclusionary rule is known as the "fruit of the poisonous tree" doctrine. The fruit of the poisonous tree doctrine derives from the case of *Wong Sun v.*

---

21   Jackson v. Denno, 378 U.S. 368, 84 S. Ct. 1774, 12 L. Ed. 2d 908 (1964).

22   This position is codified in 18 U.S.C.A. § 3501(a).

23   404 U.S. 477, 489, 92 S. Ct. 619, 626, 30 L. Ed. 2d 618 (1972).

United States.[24] The facts of *Wong Sun* are convoluted, but every fact is important. Narcotics agents barged into Blackie Toy's apartment and arrested him, without probable cause or a warrant. Toy confessed at the scene and implicated another man named Johnny Yee. The agents immediately went to Yee's home and arrested him. They found heroin in Yee's possession, which he said he got from Toy and Wong Sun. The agents next arrested Wong Sun. Wong Sun was released on his own recognizance and several days later voluntarily returned to the police station and confessed. The Supreme Court dealt with each confession separately. Concerning Blackie Toy, the Supreme Court ruled that Toy's confession given at the scene of his arrest and the heroin found in Johnny Yee's possession, which was discovered as a result of it, were the fruits of Toy's unconstitutional arrest and could not be used against him.

The Fourth Amendment exclusionary rule requires suppression of confessions that are: (1) causally connected (2) to a violation of the suspect's Fourth Amendment rights (i.e., illegal Terry stop, arrest, or search). Further, when a confession is tainted beyond use, derivative evidence that would not have been discovered without the confession will also be suppressed.

FIGURE 7.5 Fourth Amendment Exclusionary Rule

The Court, nevertheless, declined to hold that violation of a defendant's Fourth Amendment rights renders the defendant permanently incapable of making an admissible confession. The question turns on whether the illegal conduct caused the defendant to confess. Courts consider three factors in deciding this: (1) the length of time between the violation and the confession, (2) the presence of intervening circumstances, and (3) purpose and flagrancy of the violation.[25]

Length of time. The length of time between the Fourth Amendment violation and the confession is the first consideration. When the confession occurs at the scene of the violation, there is no break in the causal chain and suppression is required.[26] Blackie Toy's confession in Wong Sun, which occurred when the police barged into his home, was suppressed for this reason. When the confession occurs hours or days later, the remaining two factors will be examined.[27]

Presence of intervening circumstances. The passage of time alone is not enough to break the causal chain. There must be intervening circumstances that show that the suspect's decision to confess was an independent act of free will. Speaking with family members, consulting with an

---

24   371 U.S. 471, 83 S. Ct. 407, 9 L. Ed. 2d 441 (1963).

25   **Kaupp v. Texas**, 538 U.S. 626, 123 S. Ct. 1843, 155 L. Ed. 2d 814 (2003); New York v. Harris, 495 U.S. 14, 110 S. Ct. 1640, 109 L. Ed. 2d 13 (1990); Taylor v. Alabama, 457 U.S. 687, 102 S. Ct. 2664, 73 L. Ed. 2d 314 (1982); Dunaway v. New York, 442 U.S. 200, 99 S. Ct. 2248, 60 L. Ed. 2d 824 (1979); Brown v. Illinois, 422 U.S. 590, 95 S. Ct. 2254, 45 L. Ed. 2d 416 (1975).

26   Wong Sun v. United States, *supra* note 24, 371 U.S. at 484–488, 83 S. Ct. at 416.

27   *See* cases *supra* note 25.

attorney, and voluntarily returning to the police station after being released are the circumstances most often relied on to establish this.[28] The second factor was present in the *Wong Sun* case. The Supreme Court admitted Wong Sun's confession because he voluntarily returned to the police station to confess after being released. This showed that his decision was an independent act of free will, and not a panicked reaction to his illegal arrest. *Miranda* warnings, in contrast, do not break the causal chain.[29] The Supreme Court has entertained several cases in which suspects who were illegally arrested confessed at the police station after receiving *Miranda* warnings.[30] In only one case[31] was the confession admitted and it was for a different reason.

Purpose and flagrancy of the violation. The purpose and flagrancy of the violation is the last consideration. This factor is tied to the policy behind the exclusionary rule, which is to deter unconstitutional conduct by taking away the incentive.[32] The need for exclusionary sanctions is strongest when the violation enables police to obtain a confession they could not have obtained through lawful means. The Court relied on the absence of this factor in a case[33] in which the suspect confessed at the police station after being arrested inside his home, without a warrant, in violation of the *Payton* rule.[34] The Court admitted the confession because police did not profit from their *Payton* rule violation. Because they had probable cause for the arrest, they could have arrested the suspect lawfully had they waited for him to come outside.

This cannot be said for confessions obtained as a result of an arrest made without probable cause. Here, the violation enables the police to obtain a confession they could have obtained lawfully, and allowing them to keep it will encourage future violations. As a result, suppression is required unless there are intervening circumstances, such as in *Wong Sun*, that break the causal chain.[35]

The three factors used to determine causation—length of time between the violation and the confession, the presence of intervening circumstances, and the purpose and flagrancy of the police misconduct—admittedly do not yield a high degree of predictability. However, the lack of predictability will not prevent police from properly discharging their duties because causation analysis takes place after the Fourth Amendment violation has occurred. Police officers do not

---

28   Wong Sun v. United States, *supra* note 24; United States v. Patino, 862 F.2d 128 (7th Cir. 1988).

29   *See* authorities, *supra* note 25; State v. Ford, 30 S.W.3d 378 (Tenn. Crim. App. 2000).

30   *See* authorities *supra* note 25.

31   New York v. Harris, *supra* note 25.

32   *See, e.g.,* United States v. Leon, 468 U.S. 897, 906, 104 S. Ct. 3405, 3411, 82 L. Ed. 2d 677 (1984).

33   New York v. Harris, *supra* note 25 ("[W]here the police have probable cause to arrest a suspect, the exclusionary rule does not bar the State's use of a statement made by the defendant outside of his home, even though the statement is taken after an arrest made in the home in violation of *Payton*.").

34   The rule of *Payton v. New York*, 445 U.S. 573, 100 S. Ct. 1371, 63 L. Ed. 2d 639 (1980) requires an arrest warrant to make an arrest inside a home. This rule was discussed in § 3.15.

35   **Kaupp v. Texas**, *supra* note 25; Taylor v. Alabama, *supra* note 25; Dunaway v. New York, *supra* note 25; Brown v. Illinois, *supra* note 25.

need to know in advance how long the effects of their Fourth Amendment violation will linger in order to properly discharge the responsibilities of their job.

Overview of the Rules Governing Custodial Interrogation

At this point, two grounds for suppression have been discussed. First, confessions are inadmissible unless they are a product of the suspect's own free will. Second, they are inadmissible if a police violation of the suspect's Fourth Amendment rights caused the suspect to confess. Notice in Figure [7.5] that both grounds carry over and continue to provide the basis for challenging confessions made during the second and third phases of a criminal case. Notice further that confessions made during the second phase are vulnerable to challenge on two additional grounds: the *McNabb-Mallory* rule and the *Miranda* rule.

These requirements were developed to counterbalance the pressures that arise from the fact of being in police custody. Once a suspect is arrested or taken into custody, the tone of the questioning changes. The questions are no longer inquisitive; they are now accusatory. Moreover, once in custody, suspects find themselves in strange surroundings, often behind closed doors, and experience interrogation methods that may be new to them, but with which their interrogators have considerable expertise and experience. Most important, the suspect is alone, without an advocate or even an impartial witness. As a result, the atmosphere is inherently coercive, even when police interrogation methods are not. Consequently, there are fewer guarantees that confessions elicited during police custodial interrogations will be a product of the suspect's free will and voluntary choice. To counteract this danger, the Supreme Court has imposed two additional safeguards that become effective once the suspect is arrested or taken into custody—the *McNabb-Mallory* rule and the *Miranda* requirement.

The *McNabb-Mallory* rule seeks to alleviate the pressured atmosphere of a police custodial interrogation by requiring the police to present the arrested person to a magistrate promptly after the arrest. Presentment to a magistrate reassures the suspect that the outside world is aware that she is in police custody and that the police are accountable to the courts. This procedure also reinforces protection for an arrested person's constitutional rights. The magistrate will inform the suspect of her constitutional rights and confirm that she understands them and knows that she is free to exercise them. The *McNabb-Mallory* rule enforces compliance with this requirement by suppressing confessions obtained during a period of unnecessary delay in presenting the arrested person to a magistrate.

It is also at this point that the *Miranda* rule goes into effect. The *Miranda* rule requires the police to issue a detailed set of warnings—"you have the right to remain silent, anything you say can and will be used against you, you have a right to an attorney, and one will be appointed for you if you cannot afford one"—before initiating a custodial interrogation and to cease the interrogation if the suspect at any time thereafter expresses a desire to exercise her rights. Failure to give the required warnings or to cease interrogation if the suspect invokes her rights will result in the suppression of any resulting confession.

The *McNabb-Mallory* Delay in Arraignment Rule

Rule 5(a) of the Federal Rules of Criminal Procedure and the procedural rules of most, if not all, states, require officers to take persons under arrest "forthwith" or "without unnecessary delay" before the nearest available magistrate or other committing officer for an arraignment. The purpose of this requirement is to ensure that prisoners are given timely notice of their rights and are not subjected to lengthy secret interrogations. This requirement was routinely ignored in the period before the *McNabb-Mallory* rule because statutes requiring a prompt arraignment specified no penalties for their violation.

Statement and Discussion of the McNabb-Mallory Rule

The Supreme Court took steps to correct this problem in *McNabb v. United States*[36] by announcing that confessions obtained in violation of Rule 5(a) of the Federal Rules of Criminal Procedure (the federal prompt arraignment statute) would henceforth be inadmissible in federal criminal prosecutions, even if they were voluntary.

The Court reaffirmed this position in *Mallory v. United States*.[37] Mallory, a rape suspect, was arrested between 2:00 and 2:30 P.M. the day after the rape and taken to police headquarters, where he was questioned for about 30 minutes before agreeing to submit to a polygraph test. The polygraph operator was not located until later that evening. Mallory was detained at police headquarters for four hours while the police waited for the polygraph operator to arrive, even though several magistrates were available in the immediate vicinity. The polygraph questioning began at around 8:00 P.M. Approximately 90 minutes into the interview, Mallory stated that he "might" have done it. At this point, the police made their first attempt to reach a United States Commissioner, but when they were unsuccessful, asked Mallory to repeat his confession, which he agreed to do. Between 11:30 P.M. and 12:30 A.M., Mallory dictated his confession to a typist. Mallory was not brought before a United States Commissioner until the next morning. Notwithstanding the delay in taking him before a magistrate, his confession was admitted into evidence, he was found guilty, and sentenced to death. The Supreme Court reversed his conviction, stating:

> We cannot sanction this extended delay, resulting in a confession, without subordinating the general rule of prompt arraignment to the discretion of arresting officers. In every case where the police resort to interrogation of an arrested person and secure a confession, they may well claim, and quite sincerely, that they were merely trying to check the information given by him … . It is not the function of the police to arrest, as it were, at large and to use an interrogation process at police headquarters in order to determine whom they should charge … .

---

36   318 U.S. 332, 63 S. Ct. 608, 87 L. Ed. 819 (1943), *reh'g denied*, 319 U.S. 784, 63 S. Ct. 1322, 87 L. Ed. 1727 (1943).

37   354 U.S. 449, 77 S. Ct. 1356, 1 L. Ed. 2d 1479 (1957).

Determining Whether a Delay in Arraignment Is "Unnecessary"

The *McNabb-Mallory* rule does not impose a fixed time period within which arrested persons must be taken before a magistrate. The question turns on whether the confession was obtained during a period of "*unnecessary* delay." Each case is evaluated on its own facts. Delays due to causes beyond the government's control, such as lack of an available magistrate,[38] the distance that needs to be traveled,[39] transportation problems,[40] mechanical breakdowns, and hazardous weather conditions are disregarded in applying the *McNabb-Mallory* rule because they are unavoidable. The same holds true for delays needed to complete booking,[41] sober prisoners up,[42] or obtain needed medical treatment.[43]

The purpose of the *McNabb-Mallory* rule is to prevent prolonged questioning of suspects before bringing them into the open. When an arrest is made during normal business hours, a judicial officer is readily available, and police have no excuse for not taking the suspect before a magistrate other than a desire to question him, the delay is unnecessary and statements taken during the delay are generally inadmissible.[44]

The *McNabb-Mallory* or "delay in arraignment" rule requires suppression of confessions obtained during a period of unnecessary delay in presenting the suspect to a magistrate for arraignment.

FIGURE 7.6 *McNabb-Mallory* Rule

Current Status of the McNabb-Mallory Rule in Federal Courts

In 1968, Congress passed § 3501 of the Omnibus Crime Control and Safe Streets Act[45] in an effort to abolish the *Miranda* rule. While Congress was unsuccessful,[46] the statute also called the continued existence of the *McNabb-Mallory* rule into question. Subsection (a) provides that confessions "shall be admissible in evidence if voluntarily given." Subsection (b) lists several factors that are to be considered in determining whether a confession is voluntary, including

---

38   United States v. Gorel, 622 F.2d 100 (5th Cir. 1979).

39   United States v. McCormick, 468 F.2d 68 (10th Cir. 1972).

40   United States v. Odom, 526 F.2d 339 (5th Cir. 1976).

41   United States v. Rubio, 709 F.2d 146 (2d Cir. 1983); United States v. Johnson, 467 F.2d 630 (2d Cir. 1972).

42   United States v. Christopher, 956 F.2d 536 (6th Cir. 1991), *cert. denied*, 505 U.S. 1207, 112 S. Ct. 2999, 120 L. Ed. 2d 875 (1992); United States v. Bear Killer, 534 F.2d 1253 (8th Cir. 1976).

43   United States v. Isom, 588 F.2d 858 (2d Cir. 1978).

44   McNabb v. United States, *supra* note 36; Mallory v. United States, *supra* note 37.

45   **18 U.S.C. § 3501.** This statute is reproduced in Part II.

46   Dickerson v. United States, 530 U.S. 28, 120 S. Ct. 2326, 147 L. Ed. 2d 405 (2000) (holding that the *Miranda* decision is based on the Constitution and cannot be abrogated by statute).

whether there was unnecessary delay in presentment. Subsection (c) states that confessions made by a defendant under arrest "shall not be inadmissible solely because of delay in bringing such person before a magistrate judge ... if such confession was made or given by such person within six hours immediately following his arrest ... ."

There were two plausible interpretations of this language. The first was that § 3501 abolished the *McNabb-Mallory* rule by making voluntariness the sole test of admissibility in federal court and treating unnecessary delay in presentment as a factor bearing on voluntariness, but only if the confession is given more than six hours after the person's arrest.[47] The second was that § 3501 excluded the first six hours after an arrest from the operation of the *McNabb-Mallory* rule, but otherwise left the rule intact.

The Supreme Court adopted a second interpretation in *Corley v. United States*.[48] The Court held that § 3501 immunizes confessions taken during the first six hours after an arrest on federal charges from suppression based on unnecessary delay in presenting the suspect for arraignment, but once the six-hour safe harbor period expires, the rule springs back into full force and effect. Confessions obtained outside the six-hour period will be suppressed if they were given during a period of unnecessary delay in arraignment, even if they are voluntary.

The *McNabb-Mallory* rule, as modified by § 3501, requires suppression of confessions given more than six hours after an arrest during a period of unnecessary delay in presenting the defendant for arraignment, but immunizes confessions given during the first six hours from being challenged on this grounds.

Status of the McNabb-Mallory Rule in State Courts

The *McNabb-Mallory* exclusionary rule was promulgated by the Supreme Court under its supervisory authority to establish rules of evidence for the federal courts.[49] Because suppression is not mandated by the Constitution, state courts are not obliged to follow the rule. The same is true for § 3501. Being a federal statute, it establishes rules for federal courts, not state courts.

However, virtually all states have procedural rules requiring officers to act without unnecessary delay in presenting persons under arrest to a magistrate for arraignment. Some states have voluntarily adopted the *McNabb-Mallory* rule as a means of enforcing their speedy arraignment

---

47   United States v. Christopher, *supra* note 42 (interpreting § 3501 as abrogating the *McNabb-Mallory* rule); Glover v. United States, 104 F.3d 1570 (10th Cir. 1997) (same).

48   _____ U.S. _____, 129 S. Ct. 1558, 173 L. Ed. 2d. 443 (2009).

49   McNabb v. United States, *supra* note 36; Mallory v. United States, *supra* note 37; United States v. Alvarez-Sanchez, 511 U.S. 350, 114 S. Ct. 1599, 128 L. Ed. 2d 319 (1994).

statutes, but most treat unnecessary delay in presentment for arraignment as a factor bearing on whether the confession was voluntary.[50]

Protection for the Fifth Amendment Privilege against Self-Incrimination during Police Interrogations: The *Miranda* Rule

In 1966, the Supreme Court handed down the most famous of all criminal justice decisions—*Miranda v. Arizona*.[51] The decision was based on the Fifth Amendment privilege against self-incrimination, which the Court extended to police custodial interrogations. After surveying police interrogation manuals recommending strategies designed to capitalize on the isolated surroundings of a custodial interrogation to break down and overcome resistance to confess, the Court concluded that station house interrogations were inherently coercive and that special procedures were needed to ensure that suspects in police custody were aware of their constitutional rights and that the police respected their decision to exercise them. The Court laid out the procedures that the police henceforth would be required to follow in order to obtain an admissible confession during a police custodial interrogation.

The *Miranda* decision was so controversial in the beginning that Congress immediately tried to overturn it by enacting a statute, 18 U.S.C. § 3501, requiring federal judges to admit confessions

---

The *Miranda* rule is activated whenever police interrogate a suspect who is then in custody. To procure an admissible confession, police must:

1. warn the suspect of his or her Fifth Amendment rights;
2. secure a knowing, intelligent, and voluntary waiver before initiating questioning; and
3. cease interrogation if the suspect anytime thereafter manifests a desire to remain silent or to consult with an attorney.

FIGURE 7.7 Statement of the *Miranda* Rule

---

50   *See* Romualdo P. Eclavea, Annotation, *Admissibility of Confession or Other Statement Made by Defendant as Affected by Delay in Arraignment—Modern State Cases*, 28 A.L.R. 4TH 1121 (1984). While older cases tended to treat unnecessary delay in arraignment as automatic grounds for suppression, *see, e.g.*, Duncan v. State, 291 Ark. 521, 726 S. W. 2d 653 (1987), more recent cases generally treat it as a factor in evaluating the overall voluntariness of the confession and admit the confession if it was given voluntarily, *see, e.g.*, Commonwealth v. Perez, 577 Pa. 360, 845 A. 2d 779 (Pa. 2004); Williams v. State, 75 Md. 404, 825 A.2d 1078 (2003); Rhiney v. State, 935 P.2d 828 (Alaska Ct. App. 1997); Landrum v. State, 328 Ark. 361, 944 S.W.2d 101 (1997); People v. Cipriano, 431 Mich. 315, 429 N.W.2d 781 (1987).

51   384 U.S. 436, 86 S. Ct. 1602, 16 L. Ed. 2d 694 (1966).

made without the benefit of warnings that were voluntarily given. The statute was ignored on the assumption that it was unconstitutional, an assumption that was later borne out.[52] Although many predicted that *Miranda* would make it impossible for the police to obtain confessions, this has not turned out to be the case. Law enforcement officials have managed to live with the *Miranda* rule now for more than 40 years.

Overview of the Miranda Rule

There are two aspects of the *Miranda* rule that police officers must commit to memory—when it applies and what it requires. *Miranda* procedural safeguards must be observed only when the police **interrogate** a suspect who is then in police **custody**. Prior to initiating a custodial interrogation, the officer must warn the suspect: (1) that he has the right to remain silent, (2) that anything he says can be used against him in a court of law, (3) that he has the right to the presence of an attorney, and (4) that one will be appointed if he cannot afford one.[53] The officer must then make sure that the suspect understands his rights and determine whether he wishes to exercise them before proceeding with questioning.[54] Unless the prosecution can demonstrate that the required warnings were given and that the suspect made a voluntary and intelligent waiver of his *Miranda* rights, statements made during the custodial interrogation will be suppressed.[55]

Custodial Interrogation Defined

Two factors combine to determine when warnings are necessary. These factors are *custody* and *interrogation*. *Miranda* safeguards are necessary only when police interrogate a suspect who is then in custody. They are not required in any other situation.[56] For example, warnings do not have to be given to grand jury witnesses, even when they are the focus of the investigation, because grand jury proceedings do not have the coercive atmosphere of a police custodial interrogation.[57] Custodial interrogations are unique. Being questioned in police custody, with no one else around, brings into play feelings of fear, isolation, and vulnerability that place

---

52   Dickerson v. United States, *supra* note 46.

53   *Supra* note 51 at 467–474, 479, 86 S. Ct. at 1624–1628, 1630.

54   *Id.*, at 475, 86 S. Ct. at 1628.

55   Suppression of evidence is a criminal defendant's only remedy for Miranda violations. The defendant cannot bring a civil action for damages. Chavez v. Martinez, 538 U.S. 760, 123 S. Ct. 1994, 155 L. Ed. 2d 984 (2003) (plurality opinion); Olaniyi v. District of Columbia, 416 F. Supp. 2d 43 (D.D.C. 2006) (holding that failure to provide *Miranda* warnings, standing alone, cannot be the basis for a civil suit).

56   Minnesota v. Murphy, 465 U.S. 420, 104 S. Ct. 1136, 79 L. Ed. 2d 409 (1984) ("The mere fact that an investigation has focused on a suspect does not trigger the need for *Miranda* warnings in noncustodial settings. . .").

57   United States v. Washington, 431 U.S. 181, 97 S. Ct. 1814, 52 L. Ed. 2d 238 (1977); United States v. Mandujano, 425 U.S. 564, 96 S. Ct. 1768, 48 L. Ed. 2d 212 (1976); United States v. Wong, 431 U.S. 174, 97 S. Ct. 1823, 52 L. Ed. 2d 231 (1977).

suspects at a psychological disadvantage, making it difficult for them to resist the pressure to confess. *Miranda* warnings were developed to neutralize the inherently coercive atmosphere of a police custodial interrogation.

Miranda safeguards must be observed whenever police interrogate a suspect who is then in custody.

1. Custody requires a formal arrest or a restraint of the suspect's freedom of action to the degree associated with a formal arrest.
2. An interrogation occurs when the police ask investigative questions or engage in other words or actions they should know are reasonably likely to elicit an incriminating response from the suspect.

FIGURE 7.8 Definition of Custodial Interrogation

Custody Defined

A custodial interrogation has two components: *custody* and *interrogation*. When both are present, warnings are necessary whether the suspected offense is a felony or a misdemeanor.[58]

Objective Nature of the Inquiry

Custody requires either a formal arrest or a restraint of a suspect's freedom of action to the "degree associated with a formal arrest."[59] Whether a suspect is in custody is determined objectively based on how a reasonable person in the suspect's shoes would have experienced the encounter.[60] A suspect is in custody whenever the objective circumstances of an encounter would cause a reasonable person to experience it as an arrest.[61] When the circumstances of an encounter have the pressured atmosphere of an arrest, *Miranda* safeguards are necessary.[62] A

---

58 **Berkemer v. McCarty, 468 U.S. 420, 104 S. Ct. 3138, 82 L. Ed. 2d 317 (1984).**

59 Thompson v. Keohane, 511 U.S. 318, 116 S. Ct. 457, 133 L. Ed. 2d 383 (1995); Stansbury v. California, 511 U.S. 318, 114 S. Ct. 1526, 128 L. Ed. 2d 293 (1994).

60 Stansbury v. California, *supra* note 59; Yarborough v. Alvarado, 541 U.S. 652, 124 S. Ct. 2140, 158 L. Ed. 2d 311 (2004) (whether a suspect is in custody for warning purposes calls for objective inquiry into how a reasonable person would have experienced the encounter; the suspect's individual characteristics, such as youthful age and lack of prior experience with the criminal justice system are not relevant).

61 *See* cases *supra* note 59.

62 Stansbury v. California, supra note 59. Students should not confuse the *Miranda* test for when a suspect is in "custody" with the Fourth Amendment test for when a suspect is "seized." "Seizure" and "custody" are not congruent concepts. The "free to leave" test is used to determine when a suspect is seized. A suspect is seized when a reasonable person under the circumstances of the encounter would believe that he or she is no longer free to leave. At this point, the suspect acquires Fourth Amendment protection. If the seizure

police officer's uncommunicated intentions are not considered in *Miranda* analysis because they have no impact on a reasonable person's experience of the encounter.[63]

The time, place, and manner of the interrogation are the most important considerations. Although most custodial interrogations take place at a police station, questioning does not have to occur at the police station for a suspect to be in custody, and the converse is also true.[64] In *Oregon v. Mathiason*,[65] a suspect voluntarily went to the police station on his own after receiving a communication that the police wanted to talk to him. When he arrived, he was told that he was not under arrest and could leave at any time. He gave a confession after a brief interview, got up, and was allowed to leave. The Supreme Court held that the suspect was not in custody because his presence at the police station was voluntary throughout.

Custody Indicators

While there is no infallible checklist for when a suspect is in custody, a number of factors can contribute to the coercive atmosphere of an arrest, including:[66] (1) prolonged questioning; (2) isolated surroundings; (3) the threatening presence of several police officers; (4) weapon displays; (5) physical touching; (6) a hostile demeanor; (7) an intimidating tone of voice or language; (8) restrictions on movements, handcuffs, or other forms of restraint; and (9) confronting the suspect

---

was effected without reasonable suspicion, statements made during the encounter will be suppressed under the Fourth Amendment exclusionary rule. *See* § 6.3 *supra*. *Miranda* protection requires more than an objectively reasonable belief that one is not free to leave. A person is in custody for *Miranda* warning purposes only if the objective circumstances of the encounter are such that a reasonable person would experience the encounter as tantamount to an arrest. Accordingly, suspects can be seized in a Fourth Amendment sense without necessarily being in custody for *Miranda* purposes. This explains why suspects are generally not entitled to *Miranda* warnings during traffic stops and *Terry* stops. They are "seized," but they are not "in custody." Accordingly, warnings are not necessary. *See* § 6.7 (A)(3) *infra*.

63   Stansbury v. California, *supra* note 59.

64   *Compare* Oregon v. Mathiason, 429 U.S. 492, 97 S. Ct. 711, 50 L. Ed. 2d 714 (1977) *with* United States v. LeBrun, 306 F.3d 545 (8th Cir. 2002) (suspect was in custody during police station interview, even though he was told that he was not under arrest, where police drove him there under a false pretense and interrogated him in a highly coercive way); United States v. Wauneka, 770 F.2d 1434 (9th Cir. 1985) (custody found where suspect was brought to station by police, questioning was accusatory, suspect was without transportation to leave, and officers never offered him an opportunity to leave); Commonwealth v. Magee, 423 Mass. 381, 668 N.E.2d 339 (1996) (questioning was custodial for *Miranda* purposes even though suspect voluntarily came to police station, where suspect was questioned in closed room at police station by three officers for more than seven hours and was never told she could leave).

65   *Supra* note 64.

66   For Supreme Court decisions finding questioning custodial, *see, e.g.,* New York v. Quarles, 467 U.S. 649, 104 S. Ct. 2626, 81 L. Ed. 2d 550 (1984) (suspect surrounded by four police officers and handcuffed); Orozco v. Texas, 394 U.S. 324, 89 S. Ct. 1095, 22 L. Ed. 2d 311 (1969) (suspect awakened in middle of the night by four police officers who entered his bedroom); Mathis v. United States, 391 U.S. 1, 88 S. Ct. 1503, 20 L. Ed. 2d 381 (1968) (suspect questioned while incarcerated in jail for unrelated offense). For Supreme Court decisions finding questioning noncustodial, *see, e.g.,* **Berkemer v. McCarty, *supra* note 58** (motorist detained for routine traffic stop).

with evidence of guilt.[67] This is not an exhaustive list of factors and all of them need not be present; they are mentioned simply as factors to look out for. Deciding whether a suspect is in custody can be a tricky call.[68] Officers should consider whether they would feel intimidated, vulnerable, and under pressure to answer if the tables were reversed. If the answer is "yes," *Miranda* warnings should be given. If the answer is "perhaps," they should also be given because it is better to give them when they are not required than to neglect them when they are.

Suspect's Awareness that He Is Speaking with a Police Officer

Miranda warnings are not required when the suspect is unaware that the interrogator is a police officer.[69] In *Illinois v. Perkins*,[70] the Supreme Court rejected a *Miranda* challenge to a jailhouse confession made by an inmate to a police undercover agent who had been planted in his cell. The Court ruled that requiring warnings in this situation would thwart undercover operations without advancing the concerns behind the *Miranda* rule. The need to neutralize pressures to confess endemic in police-dominated settings is not present when a suspects speaks freely to a person whom he believes is a fellow inmate.[71]

Traffic Stops, Terry Stops, and the Miranda Rule

Have you ever been stopped for a traffic violation? If so, did the officer administer warnings? Our bet is that this did not happen. Roadside questioning during a traffic stop does not involve custody which means that there is no right to *Miranda* warnings.[72] How many of the factors listed

---

67   For cases containing a good general discussion of factors bearing on "custody," *see, e.g.,* United States v. Kim, 292 F.3d 969 (9th Cir. 2002) (suspect was in custody for *Miranda* purposes where police, while executing search warrant, locked door to shop with her inside, deliberately isolating her from her husband, before conducting lengthy interrogation session); United States v. Johnson, 64 F.3d 1120, 1126 (8th Cir. 1995), *cert. denied*, 516 U.S. 1139, 116 S. Ct. 971, 133 L. Ed. 2d 891 (1996) (defendant was in custody for *Miranda* purposes where he was ordered out of his vehicle at gunpoint, handcuffed, placed in the back of a patrol car, and questioned by detectives); United States v. Smith, 3 F.3d 1088 (7th Cir. 1993), *cert. denied*, 510 U.S. 1061, 114 S. Ct. 733, 126 L. Ed. 2d 696 (1994) (defendant was in custody for *Miranda* purposes where police stopped the cab in which defendant was riding and frisked, handcuffed, and surrounded him while he was questioned); State v. Rucker, 821 A.2d 439 (Md. 2003) (defendant was not "in custody" for *Miranda* purposes when he made incriminating statement during investigatory stop in public parking lot, detention was brief, no weapons were drawn, and defendant was not handcuffed or physically restrained until after he admitted having cocaine).

68   Oregon v. Elstad, 470 U.S. 298, 105 S. Ct. 1285, 84 L. Ed. 2d 222 (1985).

69   Illinois v. Perkins, 496 U.S. 292, 110 S. Ct. 2394, 110 L. Ed. 2d 243 (1990) ("*Miranda* forbids coercion, not mere strategic deception by taking advantage of a suspect's misplaced trust in one he supposes to be a fellow prisoner.")

70   *Id.*

71   In *Illinois v. Perkins*, the suspect had not been formally charged with the offense under investigation. The rules change once formal charges are lodged. Undercover questioning is no longer allowed. *See* § 6.9(C) *infra.*

72   **Berkemer v. McCarty,** *supra* **note 58** (holding that roadside questioning of a motorist detained for a routine traffic stop does not constitute a "custodial interrogation"). Traffic stops are discussed in Chapter 3, §§ 3.10–3.11.

on page 124 are present during the typical traffic stop? The answer is none of them. Traffic stops occur on a public street, generally with other people around, there is no prolonged questioning, the period of detention is brief, and the police do not draw weapons or use handcuffs. In fact, motorists are generally treated fairly courteously. Because the typical traffic stop lacks the coercive atmosphere of an arrest, there is no right to *Miranda* warnings.[73]

This is also true of most *Terry* stops. Brief *Terry* encounters in which the officer requests identification and asks a moderate number of questions do not equate to custody.[74] However, the situation can change. Police are permitted during *Terry* stops to draw weapons, use handcuffs, order detainees to lie prone on the ground, and place them in squad cars when they have reasonable concerns for their safety.[75] Intrusive precautions like these, nevertheless, render the detainee in custody, and makes warnings necessary.[76] As one court bluntly put it, "Police officers must make a choice—if they are going to take highly intrusive steps to protect themselves from danger, they must similarly provide protection to their suspects by advising them of their constitutional rights."[77]

Interrogation Defined

Interrogation is the second component. *Miranda* procedural safeguards come into play only when a person in custody is subjected to an interrogation. Suspects sometimes blurt out incriminating statements before the police have time to Mirandize them. While being taken into custody, they may say things like "How did you find me so quickly?" "Did Joe blow the whistle on me?" or

---

73   *See, e.g.,* **Berkemer v. McCarty,** *supra* **note 58**; United States v. Jones, 187 F.3d 210 (1st Cir. 1999) (*Terry* stop not custodial where it occurred on public highway, only one officer questioned each of the defendants, no physical restraints were used, the stop was brief, and the questions asked were few and specifically directed to the justification for making the stop); United States v. Burns, 37 F.3d 276 (7th Cir. 1994) (questioning noncustodial when suspect was detained for 10 minutes, without handcuffs or physical restraints, while two law enforcement officers searched premises). *Terry* stops are discussed in §§ 3.7–3.9.

74   **Berkemer v. McCarty,** *supra* **note 58**.

75   *See, e.g.,* United States. v. Perdue, 8 F.3d 1544 (10th Cir. 1993); United States v. Clemons, 201 F. Supp. 2d 142 (D.D.C. 2002).

76   *See, e.g.,* United States v. Foster, 70 Fed. Appx. 415 (9th Cir. 2003) (Defendant was in custody during *Terry* stop, requiring suppression of his statements made in absence of *Miranda* warning where he was (1) stopped by a combined unit of four armed federal and local officers on a remote rural highway, (2) had three police and Border Patrol vehicles positioned in single file behind him; (3) was accused by the officers of engaging in the trafficking of illegal narcotics; (4) was informed that the officers had discovered a large quantity of illegal drugs nearby and that they believed he was in the area to pick it up; (4) had his driver's license and car registration seized; and (5) was pressured by the officers to be "honest" and to confess that the marijuana belonged to him); United States v. Perdue, 8 F.3d 1455 (10th Cir. 1993) (officers who draw weapons and force detainees to the ground while conducting *Terry* stop create a custodial situation in which *Miranda* warnings are required); United States v. Clemons, 201 F. Supp. 2d 142 (D.D.C. 2002) (*Terry* detainee was in custody for *Miranda* purposes when he was removed from vehicle, handcuffed, and forced to lie on the ground); State v. Morgan, 254 Wis. 2d 602, 648 N.W.2d 23 (2002) (*Terry* detainee was in custody for *Miranda* purposes where police drew weapons, four officers were present, suspect was frisked and handcuffed, and the questioning occurred while suspect was detained in squad car).

77   United States v. Perdue, *supra* note 75.

"Why are you arresting both of us when I did it?"[78] Spontaneous, unsolicited statements are not affected by the *Miranda* rule because they are not the product of an interrogation.[79]

The test for what constitutes an interrogation was established in *Rhode Island v. Innis*.[80] The term interrogation includes both express questioning and any other words or actions that police should know are reasonably likely to elicit an incriminating response from the suspect.[81]

Express Questioning

Interrogations usually take the form of express questions, but express questions do not invariably involve an interrogation. "Would you like to make a phone call?" is an example. To constitute an interrogation, the officer must have reason to expect that the question is likely to elicit an incriminating response from the suspect.[82] Small talk about matters unrelated to the investigation and questions asked for administrative purposes are not treated as interrogations. For example, if Officer Quizzard, while driving Mary Wanna to the police station during a heavy snowstorm, attempts to make small talk by saying, "What do you think about this weather?" and she replies "Terrible! You caught me with two kilos because I haven't made a sale for the last two days," her unwarned statement is admissible because it is not the product of an interrogation.[83] The same is true for routine booking questions covering matters such as name, address, height, weight, eye color, date of birth, age, and the like.[84] Routine booking questions may be asked without administering *Miranda* warnings because they are not designed to elicit an incriminating response.[85] However, questions like how much alcohol a person arrested for drunk driving has consumed are not booking questions.[86] Police may not ask investigative questions, even during the booking process, without administering *Miranda* warnings.

---

78   United States v. Crowder, 62 F.3d 782 (6th Cir. 1995); United States v. Montano, 613 F.2d 147 (6th Cir. 1980); United States v. Gonzalez, 954 F. Supp. 48 (D. Conn. 1997).

79   *See, e.g.,* **Miranda v. Arizona, *supra* note 51**, 384 U.S. at 478, 86 S. Ct. at 1630; United States v. Hawkins, 102 F.3d 973 (8th Cir. 1996); United States v. Hayes, 120 F.3d 739 (8th Cir. 1997); United States v. Sherwood, 98 F.3d 402 (9th Cir. 1996). However, police must administer warnings before asking follow-up questions if the answers are likely to be incriminating. *See, e.g.,* State v. Walton, 41 S.W.3d 75 (Tenn. 2001).

80   **446 U.S. 291, 100 S. Ct. 1682, 64 L. Ed. 2d 297 (1980)** ("[T]he term "interrogation" under *Miranda* refers not only to express questioning but also to any words or actions on the part of the police (other than those normally attendant to arrest and custody) that the police should know are reasonably likely to elicit an incriminating response from the suspect.").

81   **Pennsylvania v. Muniz, 496 U.S. 582, 601, 110 S. Ct. 2638, 2650, 110 L. Ed. 2d 528 (1990); Rhode Island v. Innis,** supra **note 80.**

82   **Pennsylvania v. Muniz, *supra* note 81**; State v. Griffin, 814 A.2d 1003 (Me. 2003) ("Even in a custodial situation, an officer may, without giving *Miranda* warnings, ask questions designed to identify the suspect, check her identification and resolve any health or safety concerns regarding the suspect or others.").

83   *See, e.g.,* State v. Tucker, 81 Ohio St. 3d 431, 692 N.E.2d 171 (1998).

84   *See, e.g.,* **Pennsylvania v. Muniz, *supra* note 81**; Vasquez v. Filion, 210 F. Supp. 2d 194 (E.D.N.Y. 2002); Colon v. State, 568 S.E.2d 811 (Ga. Ct. App. 2002).

85   **Pennsylvania v. Muniz, *supra* note 81.**

86   State v. Chrisicos, 813 A.2d 513 (N.H. 2002) (booking officer's question how much alcohol defendant arrested for drunk driving had consumed was not routine booking question, but was instead designed to elicit incriminating statement).

Functional Equivalent of Express Questioning

The definition of interrogation also includes words or actions that are the "functional equivalent" of an express question. "Functional equivalent" covers maneuvers designed to trick suspects into confessing. The test for whether something is the "functional equivalent" of an express question is whether the police knew or should have known that their actions were reasonably likely to elicit an incriminating response from the suspect.[87] Any knowledge that police have about a suspect's unusual susceptibility to a particular form of persuasion is taken into consideration in deciding this.

In *Rhode Island v. Innis*,[88] two police officers, while transporting an armed robbery suspect to the police station, held a conversation between themselves concerning the missing shotgun. One of the officers mentioned to the other that there was a school for handicapped children near the vicinity of the robbery and said "God forbid one of the children should find the gun and hurt herself." The suspect, who was listening in the back seat, interrupted the conversation and told the officers to turn the squad car around and go back to the robbery scene so he could show them where the gun was located.

Were these officers engaged in the functional equivalent of express questioning? This depends on whether the officers should have anticipated that their actions were reasonably likely to elicit an incriminating response from the suspect. Had the officers known that the suspect was unusually susceptible to the theme of their conversation and staged this conversation to provoke an incriminating response, their actions would have constituted an interrogation. However, the Supreme Court did not read the facts this way. The Court viewed the conversation as "offhand remarks" between two police officers for which no response from the suspect was expected. Viewed this way, the police were not responsible for the suspect's unforeseen response.

However, the Supreme Court reached the opposite conclusion in a case in which the use of a similar strategy was deliberate. Police, knowing of the murder suspect's deep religious convictions, told him that the victim's missing body deserved a "Christian" burial. This statement prompted the suspect to tell the officers where the body was located.[89] The Supreme Court held that the statement was the product of a police interrogation.

Telling suspects that they have been implicated by someone else, identified by eyewitnesses, or that their alibi was not confirmed are examples of actions that are the functional equivalents of an express question because they represent attempts to elicit an incriminating response.[90] In

---

87 **Rhode Island v. Innis,** *supra* note 80.

88 *Id.*

89 Brewer v. Williams, 430 U.S. 387, 97 S. Ct. 1232, 51 L. Ed. 2d 424 (1977) (decided under the Sixth Amendment right to counsel).

90 *See, e.g.,* Drury v. State, 368 Md. 331, 793 A.2d 567 (2002) (officers engaged in functional equivalent of an interrogation when they confronted suspect with physical evidence of the crime and told him that they were going to send the evidence to be examined for fingerprints); United States v. Orso, 266 F.3d 1030 (9th Cir. 2001) (suspect subjected to the functional equivalent of an interrogation when officer engaged in detailed discussion of the evidence and witnesses against the suspect and penalties for the crime of which she was suspected, going so far as to make up some of the evidence); United States v. Collins,

one case, police falsely told a murder suspect that his father had lived long enough to identify him as the killer.[91] The son then admitted to the acts, explaining that he had performed them in a blacked-out state. "[I]t wasn't me, it was like another Marty Tankleff that killed them." Even though the son's unwarned confession was the product of an interrogation, it was admitted because the son had gone to the police station voluntarily and, consequently, was not in custody when he made the statement. When a suspect is interrogated without being in custody, warnings are not necessary.

Public Safety Exception

Police officers may dispense with *Miranda* safeguards before interrogating a suspect in custody when they are confronted with an emergency that requires immediate action to protect the public safety or their own safety.[92] This is known as the "public safety" exception. The Supreme Court articulated the public safety exception in a case in which two police officers on patrol encountered a woman who stated that she had just been raped by a man with a gun, and that he had gone into a nearby grocery store. The police entered the store and saw a man fitting the suspect's description approaching the checkout counter. When the suspect saw the police, he dropped his items and fled into the aisles. After the suspect was apprehended and frisked, the police discovered an empty shoulder holster, and before warning the suspect of his *Miranda* rights, asked him where the gun was. The suspect pointed to some empty cartons and said "The gun is over there." The officers retrieved a loaded .38-caliber revolver from one of the cartons.

The suspect was later prosecuted for possession of a weapon and moved to suppress his unwarned statement and the weapon discovered as a result of it. The Supreme Court ruled that *Miranda* warnings may be delayed temporarily when police officers are confronted with an immediate need for answers to questions in a situation posing a threat to the public safety or to the officer's safety. The Court was careful to limit this exception in order to prevent abuse. Warnings may be delayed without violating the *Miranda* rule only when the officer's perception

---

43 Fed. Appx. 99 (9th Cir. 2002) (defendant's statement "I've heard enough, you got me," in response to playing of incriminating audiotape was inadmissible because defendant was subjected to functional equivalent of an interrogation); United States v. Guerra, 237 F. Supp. 2d 795 (E.D. Mich. 2003) (*Miranda* violated where police told defendant that his accomplice had confessed and invited him to discuss the case after defendant had invoked his right to remain silent); State v. Brown, 592 So. 2d 308 (Fla. Dist. Ct. App. 1991) (confessions obtained in violation of *Miranda*, where, after defendant clearly invoked his rights, officer informed defendant that victim named him as suspect, that three witnesses placed him at scene of crime, that his girlfriend implicated him in burglary, and that he had been seen in possession of items stolen in burglary, causing defendant to state later that he wanted to tell "the truth" or "his side of the story.") *But see* White v. State, 374 Md. 232, 821 A.2d 459 (2003) (conduct of police in providing defendant with statement of charges, after he had invoked his Miranda rights, was not the functional equivalent of an interrogation where notification of the charges was a routine part of the booking process.).

91   Tankleff v. Senkowski, 993 F. Supp. 151 (E.D.N.Y. 1997).

92   New York v. Quarles, *supra* note 66.

of danger is "objectively reasonable."[93] Further, police are restricted to asking questions necessary to address the immediate danger.[94] They may ask an unwarned suspect "Where is the gun?"
but not "Who owns it?" "Where did you buy it?" or "Do you have a license for it?" Investigative
questions such as these must be postponed until after *Miranda* warnings have been administered.

Non-Police Interrogators

Private detectives and security officers are not bound by the *Miranda* rule[95] because the rule
is based on the Fifth Amendment and, like other portions of the Bill of Rights,[96] reaches only
the actions of the government.[97] However, the interrogator does not have to be a police officer.
Government officials employed in other capacities are required to administer warnings when they
conduct custodial interviews seeking information that could later be used against the person
in a criminal prosecution.[98] Prison psychiatrists, for example, are required to administer *Miranda*
warnings before eliciting information from prison inmates when the information is intended for
use at the trial, but not when seeking information that will be used for diagnosis or treatment.[99]

Summarizing, the *Miranda* rule applies only during custodial interrogations. A custodial interrogation has two ingredients: custody and interrogation. Custody requires a formal arrest or

---

93   *Id.* at 659 n. 8, 104 S. Ct. at 2633 n. 8; **Benson v. State, 698 So. 2d 333 (Fla. Dist. Ct. App. 1997)**
(warnings unnecessary when police need to ask questions to address what they reasonably believe is a
life-threatening emergency); United States v. Reyes, 249 F. Supp. 2d 277 (S.D.N.Y. 2003) (asking suspect
about to be searched about the possible presence of objects that could pose a danger to the officer comes
within the public safety exception only when officer has some genuine, particularized reason for believing
that dangerous, undetected objects might exist). *But see* United States v. Brathwaite, 458 F.3d 376 (5th
Cir. 2006) (The "public safety" exception to the *Miranda* rule did not apply to the defendant's unwarned
statement concerning the presence of guns in his house where, at time of questioning, agents had performed two sweeps of the house, and the only two occupants were both in handcuffs.).

94   United States v. Simpson, 974 F.2d 845, 845 (7th Cir. 1992).

95   United States v. Garlock, 19 F.3d 441 (8th Cir. 1994); United States v. Antonelli, 434 F.2d 335 (2d Cir.
1970); United States v. Birnstihl, 441 F.2d 368 (9th Cir. 1971); United States v. Bolden, 461 F.2d 998 (8th
Cir. 1972) (per curiam); United States v. Casteel, 476 F.2d 152 (10th Cir. 1973); Woods v. City of Tucson,
128 Ariz. 477, 626 P.2d 1109 (1981); State v. Brooks, 862 P.2d 57 (N.M. Ct. App. 1992).

96   *See, e.g.,* Burdeau v. McDowell, 256 U.S. 465, 475, 41 S. Ct. 574, 576, 65 L. Ed. 1048 (1921) (Fourth
Amendment provides no protection against private searches).

97   *See* cases *supra* note 95.

98   *See, e.g.,* Mathis v. United States, *supra* note 66 (*Miranda* violated by IRS civil investigator's failure
warn inmate before questioning him about matters that could lead to a criminal prosecution); Estelle v.
Smith, 451 U.S. 454, 101 S. Ct. 1866, 68 L. Ed. 2d 359 (1981) (unwarned statement made to psychiatrist
during court-ordered psychiatric evaluation inadmissible); State v. Bankes, 57 P.3d 284 (Wash. Ct. App.
2002) (same). *See also* 2 WAYNE R. LAFAVE ET AL., CRIMINAL PROCEDURE § 6.10(C), at 622–624 (2d ed.
1999) (custodial questioning by any government employee comes within *Miranda* whenever prosecution of
the defendant being questioned is among the purposes, definite or contingent, for which the information
is elicited; this is generally the case whenever the government questioner's duties include investigation
or reporting of crimes).

99   Estelle v. Smith, *supra* note 98 (interrogation conducted by a court-appointed competency psychiatrist
at the county jail implicates *Miranda* rights).

a restraint of the suspect's liberty to the degree usually associated with a formal arrest. The latter is determined from the vantage point of a reasonable person in the suspect's shoes. An interrogation includes not only express questions, but any words or actions on the part of the police that they should know are reasonably likely to elicit an incriminating response from the suspect. Volunteered statements are not subject to *Miranda* warnings because they are not elicited through interrogation. To constitute an interrogation, the questioning must be reasonably likely to elicit an incriminating response; routine booking questions are not considered interrogations and, consequently, do not have to be preceded by warnings. Undercover questioning is also not covered by the *Miranda* rule because the suspect must be aware that the other person is a police officer. Otherwise, the encounter lacks the coercive atmosphere of a police custodial interrogation. Police officers may temporarily postpone giving *Miranda* warnings before interrogating a suspect when they are confronted with an emergency that requires immediate action to protect their own safety or the safety of the public.

Procedural Requirements for Custodial Interrogations: *Miranda* Warnings and Waivers

The *Miranda* warnings are the best-known aspect of this Supreme Court opinion, but they are only part of the steps necessary to obtain an admissible statement. *Miranda* established a complete set of rules that remain in effect throughout the interrogation.[100] These rules are summarized in the next paragraph.

Once a complete set of warnings is administered, suspects must be afforded an opportunity to exercise their rights. Questioning may lawfully begin only if the suspect makes a knowing, intelligent, and voluntary waiver. Despite an initial waiver, suspects remain free to change their mind and stop the questioning at any time. If at any point during the interview the suspect expresses a desire to speak with an attorney, all questioning must cease and may not resume until counsel is available, unless the suspect—not the police—reopens the dialogue. If the suspect invokes the right to remain silent, questioning must also cease and may not resume unless the suspect reopens the dialogue. However, police may initiate questioning about an unrelated crime after a sufficient waiting period.

Violation of *Miranda* rules at any point in an interview will make statements obtained thereafter inadmissible. Consequently, police officers must be able to recognize when they may start questioning and when they must stop.

---

100   In a recent case, four Justices on the Supreme Court took the startling position that the rules established in *Miranda* do not function as a direct restraint on the police, but operate instead solely as a limitation on the admissibility of evidence. According to them, the administration of *Miranda* warnings is optional; police must give them if they want to use the confession as evidence, but not if they want to use it for leads or other purposes. *See* Chavez v. Martinez, *supra* note 55. *See generally* Steven D. Clymer, *Are the Police Free to Disregard* Miranda? 112 YALE L.J. 447 (2002).

The Requirement to Warn the Suspect

Required Content of Miranda Warnings

Anyone who regularly watches television or attends movies can probably recite from memory the *Miranda* warnings scripted by Chief Justice Warren:

> [You have] the right to remain silent, anything [you say] can and will be used against [you] in court. [You have] the right to consult with a lawyer and to have the lawyer with [you] during [questioning]. [If you are unable to afford] a lawyer, one will be appointed to represent [you].[101]

Four "warnings" or explanations are necessary. The suspect must be warned that:

1. She has the right to remain silent;
2. Anything she says can and will be used against her in a court of law;
3. She has the right to have an attorney present during interrogation; and
4. If she cannot afford an attorney, one will be appointed for her.[102]

Although police departments equip officers with *Miranda* script copies to carry with them and read at appropriate times, in the haste and confusion surrounding an arrest, they sometimes use their own wording. When this happens, a court must decide whether the officer's wording was legally sufficient. While departures from the Supreme Court's carefully scripted language are not fatal if the warnings given are adequate to advise the suspect of his or her rights,[103] deviations should be avoided because they engender needless controversy.

Frequency of Warnings

Miranda warnings are required on three occasions. First, warnings are always necessary before interrogating a suspect for the first time. The prevailing practice is to administer the first set of warnings immediately after the arrest. The reason is that police officers sometimes inadvertently elicit incriminating statements without being aware that they are engaged in an interrogation. The notion of an interrogation is not limited to formal interrogation sessions. An officer is engaged in an interrogation, for *Miranda* purposes, any time the officer asks a question, even a casual one, that the officer should know is reasonably likely to elicit an incriminating response. Saying to Sticky-Fingered Sam, "You look familiar. Weren't you the guy I stopped on Primrose Avenue about two months ago for questioning in connection with a burglary?" constitutes an interrogation. Consequently, to avoid slip-ups, police should issue the first set of *Miranda* warnings immediately after the arrest. Second, *Miranda* warnings can lose their efficacy and grow stale with the passage of time. To avoid controversies about whether earlier warnings had

---

101   Miranda v. Arizona, *supra* note 51.

102   *Id.*

103   Duckworth v. Eagan, 492 U.S. 195, 109 S. Ct. 2875, 106 L. Ed. 2d 166 (1989); California v. Prysock, 453 U.S. 355, 101 S. Ct. 2806, 69 L. Ed. 2d 696 (1981) (per curiam).

grown stale, police should issue a fresh set of *Miranda* warnings each time they initiate a new interrogation. Finally, warnings should be given before resuming interrogation of a suspect who initiates dialogue with the police after invoking *Miranda* rights.[104]

The Necessity of Waiver before Continuing with Custodial Interrogation

In order for statements made during custodial interrogations to be admitted as evidence, the prosecution must prove that the accused made a knowing, voluntary, and intelligent waiver of his or her *Miranda* rights before giving the statement.[105] It is up to the police to make sure that this evidence is available. If a suspect, after being advised of her *Miranda* rights, indicates a willingness to talk, the police should ask her to sign a written "advice of rights and waiver" form similar to the one below.

Prior to any questioning, I was advised that I have the right to remain silent, that whatever I say can or will be used against me in a court of law, that I have a right to speak with a lawyer and have a lawyer present during questioning, and that, if I cannot afford a lawyer, one will be appointed for me. I was further advised that, even if I sign this waiver, I have the right to stop the interview and refuse to answer further questions or ask to speak with an attorney at any time I so desire. I fully understand my rights. I am willing to answer questions and make a statement. I do not wish to consult with a lawyer or to have a lawyer present.

FIGURE 7.9 **Advice of Rights and Waiver**

While written waivers are not required, they are desirable because they aid the prosecution in proving that a confession was obtained properly. A suspect's oral statement that she understands her rights, does not wish to speak with a lawyer, and is willing to talk, while equally sufficient in a legal sense, is much more difficult to prove.[106]

An explicit waiver of *Miranda* rights it is not always necessary. A waiver may sometimes be inferred from conduct. For example, a suspect's participation in answering questions, after being

---

104   The rules concerning resumption of interrogation when the suspect seeks further communication with police after invoking *Miranda* rights are discussed below.

105   105 Withrow v. Williams, 507 U.S. 680, 113 S. Ct. 1745, 127 L. Ed. 2d 407 (1993); North Carolina v. Butler, 441 U.S. 369, 99 S. Ct. 1755, 60 L. Ed. 2d 286 (1979); Tague v. Louisiana, 444 U.S. 469, 100 S. Ct. 652, 62 L. Ed. 2d 622 (1980).

106   106 *See, e.g.,* United States v. Gaines, 295 F.3d 293, 298 (2d Cir. 2002) (declining to suppress defendant's statement, even though defendant did not sign form acknowledging that he received *Miranda* warnings, where arresting officer testified, inter alia, that he read warnings to defendant from a form and that defendant verbally acknowledged his understanding of each right).

warned of her *Miranda* rights, and asked whether she understands them is generally sufficient to support the finding of a waiver.[107] However, this is as far as courts are willing to go in inferring a waiver from silence. Proof that the officer administered warnings and that the suspect thereafter answered questions is not enough to show that a suspect understood her rights and intended to forego them.[108] If there is any doubt about a suspect's understanding of her rights or willingness to waive them, police should clarify these matters before asking any questions.

Police Duties When a Suspect Invokes Miranda Rights after Waiving Them

A suspect's waiver of *Miranda* rights is not a blanket authorization for police officers to continue an interrogation until they obtain all the information they need from the suspect. The suspect's waiver merely allows questioning to begin. However, the suspect remains free to change her mind at any time. If the suspect expresses a desire to invoke her right to remain silent or to speak with an attorney at any point in the interview, questioning must cease immediately.

However, once a suspect makes an initial waiver, the burden is on him to make known to his interrogators that he has changed his mind and now wants to exercise his rights.[109] Accordingly, police are at liberty to continue questioning a suspect who has waived his *Miranda* rights until the suspect makes a clear request to speak with a lawyer[110] or to end further questioning.[111] Ambiguous or equivocal statements such as "maybe I should talk to a lawyer," do not constitute a sufficiently clear request for an attorney to obligate the police to stop questioning.[112] Although it is good practice to clarify whether a suspect who makes an ambiguous request wants to speak to an attorney, this is not necessary. Police may ignore an ambiguous request and continue interrogating.

---

107   North Carolina v. Butler, *supra* note 105; United States v. Frankson, 83 F.3d 79 (4th Cir. 1996); United States v. Barahona, 990 F.2d 412 (8th Cir. 1993).

108   Tague v. Louisiana, *supra* note 105.

109   **Davis v. United States, 512 U.S. 452, 114 S. Ct. 2351, 129 L. Ed. 2d 362 (1994)**.

110   *Id.*

111   Medina v. Singletary, 59 F.3d 1095 (11th Cir. 1995).

112   112 **Davis v. United States, *supra* note 109**. The following statements have been found to constitute an insufficiently clear and unambiguous request for counsel to bar further questioning: Clark v. Murphy, 317 F.3d 1038 (9th Cir. 2003) ("I think I would like to talk to a lawyer" and "Should I be telling you, or should I talk to an attorney?"); United States v. Mendoza-Cecelia, 963 F.2d 1467 (11th Cir. 1992) ("I don't know if I need a lawyer, maybe I should have one, but I don't know if it would do me any good at this point."); Poyner v. Murray, 964 F.2d 1404 (4th Cir. 1992) ("Didn't you tell me I had the right to an attorney?"); Lord v. Duckworth, 29 F.3d 1216 (7th Cir. 1994) ("I can't afford a lawyer, but is there any way I can get one?"); State v. Harris, 741 N.W.2d 1 (Iowa 2007) ("If I need a lawyer, tell me now.") The following statements, in contrast, have been found sufficient: Alvarez v. Gomez, 185 F.3d 995 (9th Cir. 1999) ("Can I get an attorney right now, man?"); Com. v. Barros, 779 N.E.2d 693 (Mass. App. Ct. 2002) ("I don't think I want to talk to you anymore without a lawyer").

Resumption of Questioning After Miranda Rights Have Been Invoked

Once the suspect makes a clear request to speak with an attorney or to remain silent, the questioning must cease immediately.[113] If the police persist and the suspect gives in, a subsequent statement will be inadmissible.[114] This restriction is designed to prevent police from badgering suspects into waiving their previously invoked *Miranda* rights.

Resuming Questioning After a Suspect Has Invoked the Right to Counsel

After a suspect invokes the right to counsel, questioning may resume in only two instances—if the suspect reopens the dialogue or counsel is present.[115] This rule was announced in *Edwards v. Arizona*.[116] Edwards was questioned by the police until he said that he wanted an attorney. Questioning then ceased, but police came to the jail the following day and, after stating that they wanted to talk to Edwards and again informing of his *Miranda* rights, obtained a confession from him. The Supreme Court ruled that after a suspect expresses a desire to deal with the police only through counsel, no waiver of this right will be recognized during a police-initiated contact. Accordingly, police officers may not interrogate a suspect who has invoked the right to counsel without an attorney being present unless the suspect, without police prodding, reopens the dialogue.

To reopen the dialogue, the suspect must initiate further communications with the police in a manner that shows a willingness and desire to engage in a generalized discussion of the case. Breaking the silence with a statement like "What time is it?" or "May I have a drink of water?" does not indicate a desire to resume discussion of the crime and, consequently, does not authorize resumption of questioning. The clearest example of reopening the dialogue would be the case in which a suspect, who previously invoked the right to counsel, sends a message that he has changed his mind and now wants to tell his side of the story. However, this degree of clarity rarely exists and courts do not insist on it. Asking a question like "What is going to happen to me now?" after invoking the right to counsel, allows the police to explore whether the suspect wants to resume a generalized discussion of the crime.[117] However, in

---

113   Edwards v. Arizona, 451 U.S. 477, 101 S. Ct. 1880, 68 L. Ed. 2d 378 (1981) ("[A]n accused, ... having expressed his desire to deal with the police only through counsel, is not subject to further interrogation by the authorities until counsel has been made available to him, unless the accused himself initiates further communication, exchanges, or conversations with the police.").

114   *Id.*

115   *Id.*

116   *Id.*

117   Oregon v. Bradshaw, 462 U.S. 1039, 103 S. Ct. 2830, 77 L. Ed. 2d 405 (1983) (plurality opinion); Clayton v. Gibson, 199 F.3d 1162 (10th Cir. 1999) ("I have something I want to get off my chest" sufficient to reopen dialogue); Vann v. Small, 187 F.3d 650 (9th 1999) ("What is going to happen to me? What do you think I should do?" authorizes police to explore whether suspect wants to reopen dialogue); United States v. Michaud, 268 F.3d 728 (9th Cir. 2001) (contact reinitiated where defendant's cellmate told police, in the defendant's presence, that he wanted to speak to someone "about a murder" and defendant did not object).

order to avoid misunderstandings, police officers must issue a fresh set of *Miranda* warnings. Only if the suspect willingly participates after manifesting a desire to resume the discussion and receiving fresh a fresh set of *Miranda* warnings will the suspect be considered to have reopened the dialogue.

Resuming Questioning After a Suspect Has Invoked the Right to Remain Silent

After a suspect has invoked the right to remain silent, questioning must also cease. Police may not initiate contact to question the suspect about the same offense after the right to remain silent has been invoked; the only way questioning may resume is if the suspect reopens the dialogue. Police, nevertheless, may contact the suspect for questioning about an unrelated offense after waiting a sufficient period of time.[118] This option does not exist after a suspect has invoked the right to counsel. Once a suspect expresses a desire to deal with police only through counsel, the police may not question the suspect, even about an unrelated offense, during a police-initiated contact, until counsel is present.[119]

To summarize, *Miranda* warnings should be given each time a suspect is subjected to a custodial interrogation. Questioning may not begin unless the suspect makes a knowing, voluntary, and intelligent waiver of his or her *Miranda* rights. Ideally, the waiver should be in writing, but a suspect's express oral statement to this effect will also suffice. In certain situations, courts will infer an intent to waive *Miranda* rights from a suspect's conduct, but to avoid a misunderstanding, the officer should clarify whether the suspect wants to speak with an attorney or wants to remain silent before initiating questioning. Once *Miranda* rights have been waived, officers may begin questioning and may continue questioning unless or until the suspect makes a clear request for an attorney or expresses a clear desire to end the questioning. If the suspect, either before or during questioning, makes a clear request for an attorney, questioning must stop immediately and may not resume unless the suspect renews the dialogue or counsel is present. Questioning must also stop any time the suspect invokes his right to remain silent. The suspect may not be questioned about the same offense after invoking the right to remain silent unless the suspect initiates further discussion. However, the police may initiate questioning about an unrelated offense, after waiting a sufficient period.

---

118   Michigan v. Mosley, 423 U.S. 96, 96 S. Ct. 321, 46 L. Ed. 2d 313 (1975).

119   Edwards v. Arizona, *supra* note 113; Arizona v. Robertson, 486 U.S. 675, 108 S. Ct. 2093, 100 L. Ed. 2d 704 (1988).

The Sixth Amendment Right to Counsel during Interrogations Conducted after the Commencement of Adversary Judicial Proceedings

The Sixth Amendment provides that "[i]n all criminal prosecutions, the accused shall enjoy the right ... to have the assistance of counsel for his defense." Upon the lodging of formal charges, the suspect officially becomes an "accused" and the case enters the third phase. The system has now become fully adversarial and restrictions on engaging the accused at a time when counsel is not present tighten. Figure 7.10 summarizes the restrictions that go into effect when the case enters the third phase.

- The Sixth Amendment right to counsel attaches when adversary judicial proceedings are initiated.
- From this point forward, the government is prohibited from eliciting incriminating information outside counsel's presence unless the defendant gives a valid waiver of the right to counsel.
- Sixth Amendment restrictions apply only when the questions relate to the charged offense; they do not apply when the questions relate to other uncharged criminal activity.
- The Sixth Amendment right to counsel can be waived by a defendant after being informed of his rights, even though the defendant is already represented by counsel or has requested appointment.

FIGURE 7.10 **Sixth Amendment Restrictions on Police Questioning**

Attachment of the Sixth Amendment Right to Counsel

The Sixth Amendment right to counsel attaches when adversary judicial proceedings are commenced.[120] This generally occurs at the earliest of any of the following four events: (1) an **arraignment** (i.e., the defendant's initial appearance before a judicial officer where he is informed of the charges, a probable cause determination is made, and bail is set); (2) a **grand jury indictment**;

---

120   *See, e.g.,* Moran v. Burbine, 475 U.S. 412, 106 S. Ct. 1135, 89 L. Ed. 2d 410 (1986) (The Sixth Amendment, "[b]y its very terms ... becomes applicable only when the government's role shifts from investigation to accusation. For it is only then that the assistance of one versed in the 'intricacies ... of law' is needed to assure that the prosecution's case encounters 'the crucible of meaningful adversarial testing.' "); Kirby v. Illinois, 406 U.S. 682, 92 S. Ct. 1877, 32 L. Ed. 2d 411 (1972) (The right to counsel attaches only when "the government has committed itself to prosecute, [for it is] only then that the adverse positions of government and defendant have solidified."); **Rothgery v. Gillespie County, Tex., _____ U.S. _____, 128 S. Ct. 2578, 177 L. Ed. 2d 366 (2008)** (a criminal defendant's initial appearance before a magistrate is one of several events that trigger attachment of Sixth Amendment right to counsel).

(3) an **information** (i.e., a formal complaint filed by a prosecutor); or (4) a preliminary hearing (i.e., a hearing at which the judge finds that there is enough evidence to bind the accused for trial).[121] Criminal prosecutions are not commenced by the issuance of an arrest warrant[122] or the making of an arrest.[123] Although police have authority to conduct investigations and make arrests, only judges, prosecutors, and grand juries have the ability to initiate a criminal prosecution.

The most common way criminal prosecutions are initiated is at arraignments and preliminary hearings held after the police make an arrest. However, other sequences are possible. The prosecutor, for example, can convene a grand jury and seek an indictment without waiting for the police. If an indictment is returned, the judge will issue a warrant for the accused's arrest. When a prosecution is initiated in this manner, the Sixth Amendment right to counsel will already have attached at the time of arrest and there will be no *Miranda* phase.

Deliberate Elicitation Standard

Stronger protection exists for the Sixth Amendment right to counsel than the *Miranda* Fifth Amendment right. During the *Miranda* phase, protection is available only during *custodial interrogations*.[124] Once adversary criminal proceedings are commenced, the protection broadens. The Sixth Amendment standard is *"deliberate elicitation."*[125] Defendants have a right to have counsel present whenever the police deliberately elicit information from them pertaining to the charges, whether they are in custody, the interview constitutes an interrogation, or they are even aware that they are speaking with a police officer.[126]

The *deliberate elicitation* standard does not require custody or interrogation. In *Fellers v. United States*,[127] the Supreme Court held that this standard was met when police officers paid a post-indictment visit to the defendant's home and told him that they had come to discuss his involvement in drug distribution, that he had been indicted for conspiracy to distribute drugs,

---

121 *See* cases note 120 *supra*.

122 *See, e.g.,* United States v. D'Anjou, 16 F.3d 604, 608 (4th Cir.), *cert. denied,* 512 U.S. 1242, 114 S. Ct. 2754, 129 L. Ed. 2d 871 (1994).

123 *See, e.g.,* United States v. Langley, 848 F.2d 152 (11th Cir. 1988).

124 Review § 6.7 *supra*.

125 *See, e.g.,* Fellers v. United States, 540 U.S. 519, 124 S. Ct. 1019, 157 L. Ed. 2d 1016 (2004); **Kuhlmann v. Wilson, 477 U.S. 436, 106 S. Ct. 2616, 91 L. Ed. 2d 364 (1986)** ("[O]nce a defendant's Sixth Amendment right to counsel has attached, he is denied that right when federal agents 'deliberately elicit' incriminating statements from him in the absence of his lawyer.").

126 *See, e.g.,* Fellers v. United States, *supra* note 125 (holding that officers violated the Sixth Amendment by deliberately eliciting information from a defendant during a post-indictment visit to his home absent counsel or waiver of counsel, regardless of whether the officers' conduct constituted an "interrogation") ; United States v. Henry, 447 U.S. 264, 100 S. Ct. 2183, 65 L. Ed. 2d 115 (1980) (defendant's Sixth Amendment right to counsel was violated when a paid informant, planted in his cellblock, "deliberately elicited" incriminating statements from him, even though the defendant was unaware he was speaking with a police informant).

127 *Supra* note 126.

and that they had an arrest warrant for him. They went on to mention the names of four persons listed in the indictment. He responded that he knew the four persons, and that he had used methamphetamine with them. The officers then transported him to the county jail where they, for the first time, advised him of his *Miranda* rights." The Supreme Court held the police violated the defendant's Sixth Amendment rights because the discussion at his home took place after he was indicted, outside the presence of counsel, and in the absence of a valid waiver. The Court stated "there is no question that the officers in this case 'deliberately elicited' information from the petitioner. Indeed, the officers, upon arriving at petitioner's house, informed him that their purpose in coming was to discuss his involvement in the distribution of methamphetamine and his association with certain charged co-conspirators."

The lesson to be learned from *Fellers* is that police must administer *Miranda* warnings and obtain a valid waiver of the Sixth Amendment right to counsel before seeking to elicit information from a defendant under formal charges, whether their conduct constitutes an interrogation or the defendant is in custody or at large.

Secret Interrogations Using Police Undercover Agents, Paid Informants, and Jailhouse Snitches

The deliberate elicitation standard originated in cases in which the government conducted secret interrogations, using undercover agents, paid informants, and jailhouse snitches. *Massiah v. United States*[128] was the seminal case. Massiah was arrested and indicted on a federal narcotics charge. He retained a lawyer and was released on bail. Federal agents prevailed on his co-defendant to allow them to install a hidden radio transmitter in his car. The co-defendant engaged Massiah in an incriminating conversation while the federal agents secretly listened. The statements were admitted at Massiah's trial, over his objection, and he was convicted. The Supreme Court reversed, holding that Massiah's Sixth Amendment rights were violated when federal agents, acting in collusion with his co-defendant, deliberately elicited incriminating information from him, in the absence of his counsel, after his indictment. The Court stated that the surreptitious nature of the interrogation made the violation even more serious.[129]

The Sixth Amendment right to counsel is not violated if the undercover agent or informant does nothing to stimulate the conversation and merely functions as an attentive listener. In *Kuhlmann v. Wilson*,[130] police planted an inmate-informant in the defendant's jail cell, with instructions to "keep his ears open" and report what he heard, but not to ask questions. The informant did as

---

128   377 U.S. 201, 84 S. Ct. 1199, 12 L. Ed. 2d 246 (1964) (Sixth Amendment right to counsel was violated when informant working for police elicited incriminating statements subsequent to indictment).

129   The practice of conducting secret interrogations using undercover agents, paid informants, and jailhouse snitches, condemned in *Massiah*, is perfectly legal during the *Miranda* phase because a suspect is not "in custody" unless he is aware that the person questioning him is a police officer. *See* Illinois v. Perkins, *supra* note 69 (holding that a prisoner's *Miranda* rights were not violated when he was questioned, without warnings, by a government undercover agent posing as a fellow inmate). *Illinois v. Perkins* is discussed in § 6.7(A)(3).

130   ***Supra* note 125.**

instructed and, over time, the defendant made incriminating statements that were introduced against him at his trial. The Court held that "a defendant does not make out a violation [of the Sixth Amendment] by showing that an informant, either through prior arrangement or voluntarily, reported his incriminating statements to the police. Rather, the defendant must demonstrate that the police and their informant took some action, beyond merely listening, that was designed deliberately to elicit incriminating remarks."[131]

Requirements for Conducting Post-Attachment Interrogations

Miranda procedural requirements for conducting custodial interrogations have been incorporated into the Sixth Amendment right to counsel.[132] The requirements for conducting pre- and post-attachment interrogations are now the same.[133] The interview must be preceded by full set of *Miranda* warnings. Police must obtain a knowing, intelligent, and voluntary waiver of the right to counsel before questioning can begin. The interrogation must cease immediately any time thereafter that the defendant manifests a desire to remain silent or to consult with an attorney. If the defendant invokes the right to counsel, questioning cannot resume unless counsel is present or the defendant reinitiates the dialogue.[134]

Offense-Specific Nature of the Sixth Amendment Right to Counsel

The Sixth Amendment right to counsel is *offense-specific*. This means that it applies only when police question a defendant under formal charges about that offense.[135] They may question him about separate uncharged criminal activity, subject only to the *Miranda* rule.

In *Texas v. Cobb*,[136] the Supreme Court was asked to carve out an exception for crimes that are factually related. The police received a report that a home was burglarized and that a woman and child who occupied the home were missing. Acting on an anonymous tip that Cobb, who lived across the street, was involved in the burglary, the police questioned him about the events. Cobb gave a written confession to the burglary, but denied knowledge of the disappearances. He was subsequently indicted for the burglary and an attorney was appointed to represent him. While he was out on bail, Cobb admitted to his father that he had killed the missing woman and child, and his father contacted the police. Cobb was arrested, taken into custody, given *Miranda* warnings, and confessed to the murders. He later sought suppression, claiming that the police violated his Sixth Amendment right to counsel. His theory was that, when the Sixth Amendment right to counsel attaches, it attaches not only for the charged offense (i.e., the burglary), but also

---

131 *Id.*

132 **Montejo v. Louisiana, _____ U.S. _____, 129 S. Ct. 2079, 173 L. Ed. 2d 955 (2009),** *overruling* Michigan v. Jackson, 475 U.S. 625, 106 S. Ct. 1404, 89 L. Ed. 2d 631 (1986).

133 Review § 6.8.

134 *Id.*

135 McNeil v. Wisconsin, 501 U.S. 171, 111 S. Ct. 2204, 115 L. Ed. 2d 158 (1991); Texas v. Cobb, 532 U.S. 162, 121 S. Ct. 1335, 149 L. Ed. 2d 321 (2001) (same).

136 *Supra* note 135.

for other uncharged offenses that are "closely related factually" (i.e., the murders). The Supreme Court found this argument unpersuasive and reaffirmed that when a person under formal charges for one offense is questioned about a separate uncharged offense, the Sixth Amendment right to counsel has no application. Because Cobb had not yet been charged with the murders when he confessed to them, his only right was the right to *Miranda* warnings, and he received them. His confession was, therefore, admissible as evidence.

Obtaining a Waiver of the Sixth Amendment from a Defendant Who Has Already Retained Counsel or Requested a Court-Appointed Attorney

Under former rules, once a defendant was formally charged with an offense and retained or requested appointment of counsel, the police could not question him, outside his attorney's presence, unless the defendant initiated the contact.[137] The rationale was that the defendant, by obtaining representation, had manifested a desire to deal with the government only through counsel. If the police wanted to discuss the case with a defendant who was represented, they had to contact his attorney first.

The case that established this rule was *Michigan v. Jackson*.[138] Jackson requested appointment of counsel at his arraignment, but before he had an opportunity to consult with his attorney, the police contacted him in jail and advised him of his *Miranda* rights. He waived his rights and gave a confession. The Supreme Court held that the confession was illegally obtained because, once a defendant requests appointment of counsel at an arraignment, no valid waiver of the Sixth Amendment right to counsel can be given during a police-initiated interrogation.

Michigan v. Jackson was overturned in *Montejo v. Louisiana*.[139] In *Montejo*, the court appointed a public defender to represent the defendant, without his request. This was in accordance with Louisiana law, which required automatic appointment of counsel for indigent defendants. Later that day, two detectives visited him, read him his *Miranda* rights, and asked him to accompany them on a trip to locate the murder weapon. He agreed. During the excursion, Montejo wrote an inculpatory letter of apology to the widow of the murder victim. His letter was admitted at trial, over his objection. He was found guilty of first degree murder and sentenced to death. The Louisiana Supreme Court rejected Montejo's argument that the letter was subject to suppression under *Michigan v. Jackson* on the grounds that an affirmative request for appointment of counsel is necessary to trigger protection.

The Supreme Court found the position taken by the Louisiana Supreme Court unsound because it would lead to arbitrary distinctions between defendants in different states. Almost half the states, like Louisiana, automatically appoint counsel for indigent defendants without their request. The defendants in these states would be arbitrarily excluded from the claiming protection of

---

137 Michigan v. Jackson, 475 U.S. 625, 106 S. Ct. 1404, 89 L. Ed. 2d 631 (1986), *overruled* **Montejo v. Louisiana,** *supra* **note 132.**

138 *Supra* note 132.

139 *Supra* **note 132.**

Michigan v. Jackson because they are not given an opportunity to request counsel. At the same time, the Court was unwilling to make *Michigan v. Jackson* applicable to defendants who received representation without their request. "No reason exists," the Court wrote, "to assume that a defendant like Montejo, who has done *nothing at all* to express his intention with respect to his Sixth Amendment rights, would not be perfectly amenable to speaking with the police without having counsel present. And no reason exists to prohibit the police from inquiring."

Faced with two unacceptable choices, the Court solved the problem by overruling *Michigan v. Jackson*. The Court stated that *Miranda* procedural safeguards have proven adequate to protect the right to counsel in the Fifth Amendment context and there was no reason to suppose the same rules would not be equally so in the Sixth Amendment context. "Under the *Miranda-Edwards-Minnick* line of cases ..., a defendant who does not want to speak to the police without counsel present need only say as much when he is first approached and given the *Miranda* warnings. At that point, not only must the immediate contact end, but "badgering" by later requests is prohibited. If that regime suffices to protect the integrity of 'a suspect's voluntary choice not to speak outside his lawyer's presence' before his arraignment, it is hard to see why it would not also suffice to protect that same choice after arraignment, when Sixth Amendment rights have attached." The Court concluded that the policy behind *Michigan v. Jackson* "was being adequately served through other means" and that the case should be overruled because it caused more harm to the workings of the criminal justice system than the added layer of protection was worth.

Montejo v. Louisiana makes the transition from the *Miranda* phase to the Sixth Amendment phase smoother and easier for police. With the distinction between represented and unrepresented criminal defendants now eliminated, there are fewer rules and variations police have to remember.

Figure 7.11 summarizes the key points in this section.

- The *Miranda* right to counsel applies before formal charges are lodged, the Sixth Amendment right to counsel afterward.
- The *Miranda* right to counsel is available only during custodial interrogations. Protection for the Sixth Amendment right to counsel is available whenever the police deliberately elicit information about previously charged criminal activity, whether their action constitutes an interrogation or the defendant is in custody or at large.
- The *Miranda* right to counsel is not violated by surreptitious interrogations conducted through undercover agents, informants, and jailhouse snitches; the Sixth Amendment right to counsel is.
- The Sixth Amendment right to counsel is offense-specific; it applies only when a defendant under formal charges is questioned about that offense. The *Miranda* rule is not offense-specific; it applies whenever a suspect in custody is interrogated about any uncharged criminal activity.
- Both rights to counsel may be waived and the procedures for obtaining a valid waiver and conducting interrogations are the same for both.

FIGURE 7.11 **Comparison of the Right to Counsel Under the *Miranda* Rule and the Sixth Amendment**

Use of Inadmissible Confession for Impeachment

Confessions must be freely and voluntarily given, not caused by a violation of the accused's Fourth Amendment rights, and not obtained in violation of the *Miranda* rule or the Sixth Amendment right to counsel in order to be admissible as evidence of guilt. However, confessions that fail these requirements are not entirely useless. They can be used for a limited purpose—impeachment.[140]

Impeachment involves an attack on a witness's credibility. One way to attack a witness's credibility is to show that the witness previously made statements that are inconsistent with his trial testimony. If the accused takes the witness stand and tells the jurors a story different from the one he previously told the police, the prosecution may, during cross-examination, use an inadmissible confession as impeachment evidence. In *Walder v. United States*,[141] the Supreme Court explained that "it is one thing to say that the Government cannot make an affirmative use of evidence unlawfully obtained. It is quite another to say that the defendant can turn the illegal method by which evidence in the Government's possession was obtained to his own advantage, and provide himself with a shield against contradiction of his untruths."[142] However, even this use is prohibited if the confession was not voluntary.[143] Involuntary confessions are considered too unreliable to be used for any purpose, including impeachment.

An inadmissible confession may be used for impeachment only if:

1. the defendant takes the stand and testifies in her own behalf.
2. she tells the jurors a story different from the one she told the police, and
3. the confession was freely and voluntarily given.

When a confession is admitted for impeachment purposes, the jurors may consider it for the sake of evaluating the trustworthiness of the defendant's trial testimony, but not as evidence of guilt.

FIGURE 7.12 **Impeachment Use of Inadmissible Confessions**

---

140   Harris v. New York, 401 U.S. 222, 91 S. Ct. 643, 28 L. Ed. 2d 1 (1971) (voluntary statements obtained in violation of *Miranda* rule are admissible to impeach a defendant's inconsistent trial testimony); Michigan v. Harvey, 494 U.S. 344, 110 S. Ct. 1176, 108 L. Ed. 2d 293 (1990) (voluntary statements obtained in violation of the Sixth Amendment right to counsel may be used for impeachment purposes); Kansas v. Ventris, _____ U.S. _____, 129 S. Ct. 1841, 173 L. Ed. 2d 801 (2009) (statements elicited by police informant after attachment of Sixth Amendment right to counsel can be used to impeach the defendant's inconsistent trial testimony).

141   347 U.S. 62, 74 S. Ct. 354, 98 L. Ed. 503 (1954).

142   *Id.* 347 U.S. at 65, 74 S. Ct. at 356.

143   Harris v. New York, *supra* note 140; Michigan v. Harvey, *supra* note 140.

When a confession has been contaminated so that it can be used only for impeachment, its value to the government is greatly reduced. A confession is one of the most powerful pieces of evidence that can be put before a jury. When a confession is introduced as substantive evidence of guilt, the impact on the defense is devastating. However, only an admissible confession (i.e., one obtained in conformity with the requirements discussed in this chapter) may be introduced as evidence of guilt. The prosecution's potential gains from a contaminated confession are meager by comparison. First, it is the defense, not the prosecution, that controls whether an inadmissible confession can be introduced as impeachment evidence. The defense can thwart impeachment use by having the accused not testify, a right the accused enjoys under the Fifth Amendment. This generally happens in cases in which an accused has previously given an inadmissible confession because the accused now has little to gain and much to lose by testifying. Second, even if the accused takes the witness stand and tells the jurors a different story from the one he or she told the police, when a confession is used on cross-examination as impeachment evidence, the jurors may consider it for only one purpose—to evaluate whether the accused's trial testimony is trustworthy. The jurors will be instructed that they may not consider the confession as evidence of guilt.

Restrictions on the Use of Derivative Evidence

Statements given in response to an interrogation are often instrumental in uncovering other evidence. The suspect, for example, may tell the police the location of physical evidence, such as the murder weapon or drugs, or identify potential prosecution witnesses. The initial statement may also prompt the suspect to give a subsequent statement in which further damaging disclosures are made. Evidence that derives from a confession is called "**derivative evidence.**" Derivative evidence is generally treated the same as the confession. When a confession is obtained in compliance with all applicable legal requirements, the evidence is admissible. On the other hand, when a confession is tainted by illegal police practices, the taint generally carries over and destroys the admissibility of derivative evidence.[144]

The rule requiring suppression of derivative evidence is known as the "fruit of the poisonous tree" doctrine. The fruit of the poisonous tree doctrine was developed to destroy the incentive for police to violate the Constitution by taking away all gains.[145] Suppose Sticky-Fingered Sam is arrested on burglary charges and taken to the police station, where he is deprived of food and sleep for two days until he finally confesses. Sam admits to the crime, tells the police where he hid the stolen property, and names Joe as his accomplice. Several hours after he has eaten and slept, Sam, believing his situation is hopeless, gives a second confession, this time in writing.

---

144   Nardone v. United States, 308 U.S. 338, 60 S. Ct. 2663, 84 L. Ed. 307 (1939); Wong Sun v. United States, *supra* note 24. *See also generally* Yale Kamisar, *On the "Fruits" of Miranda Violations, Coerced Confessions, and Compelled Testimony*, 93 MICH. L. REV. 929 (1995).

145   *See* authorities *supra* note 144.

The police locate the stolen property where Sam said it was hidden, prevail on Joe to testify, and offer the stolen property, Joe's testimony, and Sam's second confession into evidence. None of this evidence can be used because it constitutes of the fruits of an involuntary confession.[146] Allowing police to benefit from the coercive interrogation practices used on Sam will operate as an incentive to continue using them. Consequently, when police use coercion to obtain a confession, courts will invoke the poisonous tree doctrine and suppress the fruits along with the confession.[147] The same generally also holds true for the fruits of statements obtained in violation of the Fourth Amendment search and seizure clause[148] and the Sixth Amendment right to counsel.[149]

---

1. The fruits of statements obtained in violation of the due process free and voluntary requirement, the Fourth Amendment search and seizure clause, and the Sixth Amendment right to counsel are inadmissible.
2. The fruits of statements obtained in violation of the *Miranda* rule are admissible, despite the violation, unless the statement was involuntary or the violation was deliberate.

FIGURE 7.13 **Restrictions on Admission of Derivative Evidence**

The fruit of the poisonous tree doctrine does not apply to *Miranda* warning violations. Although a failure to warn contaminates the unwarned statement, the fruits are admissible if the statement was voluntarily given.[150] This probably comes as a surprise. However, the fruits doctrine only

---

146   *See, e.g.,* Clewis v. Texas, 386 U.S. 707, 87 S. Ct. 1338, 18 L. Ed. 2d 423 (1967).

147   *Id.*

148   *See, e.g.,* Wong Sun v. United States, *supra* note 24 (physical evidence derived from confession procured in violation of suspect's Fourth Amendment rights inadmissible); Brown v. Illinois, *supra* note 25 (subsequent confession suppressed where police violation of suspect's Fourth Amendment rights caused suspect's initial confession).

149   *See, e.g.,* Brewer v. Williams, *supra* note 89; Nix v. Williams, *supra* note 8; United States v. Wade, 388 U.S. 218, 87 S. Ct. 1926, 18 L. Ed. 2d 1149 (1967) (same); United States v. Johnson, 196 F. Supp. 2d 795 (N.D. Iowa 2002).

150   *See, e.g.,* United States v. Patane, 542 U.S. 630, 124 S. Ct. 2620 159 L. Ed. 2d 667 (2004) (failure to warn does not require suppression of the physical fruits of a statement if the statement is voluntary); Michigan v. Tucker, 417 U.S. 433, 94 S. Ct. 2357, 41 L. Ed. 2d 182 (1990) (failure to warn does not require suppression of the testimony of witness whose identity is discovered as a result of an unwarned, voluntary statement); Oregon v. Elstad, *supra* note 68 (a noncoercive, unintentional failure to warn does not require suppression of a subsequent voluntary confession given after warnings are administered). *But see* **Missouri v. Seibert, 542 U.S. 600, 124 S. Ct. 2601, 159 L. Ed. 2d 643 (2004)** (deliberately interrogating a suspect about the same matters twice, the first time without *Miranda* warnings and the second time after warnings are administered as part of a calculated strategy to undermine the exercise of *Miranda* rights requires suppression of both confessions).

applies to evidence obtained in violation of the Constitution. The *Miranda* rule is based on the Fifth Amendment privilege against compulsory self-incrimination. However, a failure to warn, standing alone, does not violate a suspect's Fifth Amendment rights; the Fifth Amendment is violated only when a statement is compelled.[151] Consequently, the fruits of voluntary, unwarned statements can be used as evidence.

This does not mean that police can deliberately violate the *Miranda* rule and walk away with usable derivative evidence.[152] In *Oregon v. Elstad*,[153] the Supreme Court held that a simple failure to warn, unaccompanied by coercion or other improper conduct, does not destroy the admissibility of a subsequent statement given after warnings are administered. Specialists in police training read this decision as meaning that the only thing at risk in deliberately withholding *Miranda* warnings is loss of the original unwarned statement, but that subsequent repetitions of that statement and derivative evidence could still be used. As a result, they developed interrogation strategies based on deliberately failing to administer *Miranda* warnings. The Supreme Court put a stop to this in *Missouri v. Seibert*.[154] In that case, police deliberately withheld *Miranda* warnings and interrogated the suspect until she confessed, using a technique known as the "two-step" or "question first" interrogation strategy. The strategy consists of purposefully withholding *Miranda* warnings until a full confession is obtained, providing them, getting the suspect to re-confess, and offering the second confession into evidence. The officers in *Seibert* took a 15-minute break after the first confession, administered warnings, obtained a written waiver, turned the tape recorder on, and went over the details of the confession. The second confession was reduced to writing, signed, and offered into evidence. The Supreme Court held the two-step interrogation strategy was based on a misreading of *Oregon v. Elstad*. In that case, the failure to administer warnings the first time around resulted from an oversight, not a calculated strategy to deprive the warnings of their effectiveness by withholding them until after a full confession was obtained, as in this case. Police cannot magically transform inadmissible confessions into admissible ones by deliberately withholding warnings until the suspect confesses, administering them, and then

---

151 *See, e.g.,* Michigan v. Tucker, 417 U.S. 433, 444, 94 S. Ct. 2357, 2364, 41 L. Ed. 2d 182 (1974) ("[P] rophylactic *Miranda* warnings ... are 'not themselves rights protected by the Constitution but [are] instead measures to ensure that the right against compulsory self-incrimination [is] protected' ") Oregon v. Elstad, *supra* note 68 (same).

152 **Missouri v. Seibert**, *supra* note 150; United States v. Faulkingham, 295 F.3d 85 (1st Cir. 2002) (expressing view that suppression is required when police deliberately fail to give *Miranda* warnings in the hopes of obtaining admissible derivative or impeachment evidence or leads). *See also generally* Charles D. Weisselberg, *Deterring Police from Deliberately Violating* Miranda: *In The Stationhouse after Dickerson*, 99 MICH. L. REV. 1121 (2001).

153 *Supra* note 68 (holding that the existence of a prior statement obtained without warnings does not require suppression of a subsequent statement knowingly and voluntarily made after warnings are administered).

154 *Supra* note 150.

getting the suspect to repeat the confession. When police use calculated strategies designed to undermine the *Miranda* rule, derivative evidence will be suppressed, along with the confession.[155]

Restrictions on the Use of Confessions Given by Accomplices

This section begins with another story about Sticky-Fingered Sam. Sam pulled off a big "after hours" bank robbery by working a deal with Tillie Teller to share half the loot in exchange for keys to the bank vault. Unfortunately for Sam, his driver's license fell out while stuffing money into his pockets and the police quickly caught up with him. Sam was taken to the police station, where he was subjected to coercive interrogation methods. He confessed and named Tillie as his accomplice. Tillie is now facing trial. May she object to the prosecutor's introduction of Sam's confession as evidence against her?

This question raises a problem that prosecutors encounter when they try to introduce one accomplice's confession as evidence against another. There are two constitutional objections Tillie might raise—one valid and the other invalid. The most obvious objection—that the police violated Sam's constitutional rights to obtain the confession—is not valid. The problem is lack of standing. Only a person whose constitutional rights have been violated has standing to challenge the admissibility of evidence on the grounds that it was unconstitutionally obtained.[156] That the confession was coerced is an objection that only Sam can raise.

However, Tillie has a valid objection to the prosecutor's introduction of Sam's confession against her. The Sixth Amendment confrontation clause guarantees that "[i]n all criminal prosecutions, the accused shall enjoy the right ... to be confronted with the witnesses against him."[157] The purpose of this guarantee is to enable an accused to challenge the credibility of prosecution witnesses and expose inaccuracies in their testimony.

An accused's Sixth Amendment right to confront prosecution witnesses bars the government from using an out-of-court statement given by an accomplice, implicating the accused, as evidence against the latter unless the government can prevail on the accomplice who gave the statement to appear at the trial.[158] This means that Sam's confession cannot be introduced as evidence against Tillie unless Sam is willing to testify. Unfortunately for the prosecution, Sam can invoke the Fifth Amendment and refuse to testify because his testimony is self-incriminatory. Consequently, a prosecutor who wants to use one accomplice's confession as evidence against another is generally forced to grant immunity or work out some other deal in exchange for this testimony.

---

155   *See, e.g.,* United States. v. Gilkeson, 431 F. Supp. 2d 270 (N.D.N.Y. 2006) (holding that fruit of poisonous tree doctrine bars admission of evidence that derives from a deliberate violation of the *Miranda* rule); State v. Knapp, 285 Wis. 2d 86, 700 N.W.2d 899 (2005) (reaching same result under state constitutional provision).

156   Alderman v. United States, 394 U.S. 165, 89 S. Ct. 961, 22 L. Ed. 2d 176 (1969).

157   157 The Sixth Amendment confrontation clause applies to the states through the Fourteenth Amendment. Pointer v. Texas, 380 U.S. 400, 85 S. Ct. 1065, 13 L. Ed. 2d 923 (1965).

158   Lilly v. Virginia, 527 U.S. 116, 119 S. Ct. 1887, 144 L. Ed. 2d 117 (1999) (admission of nontestifying accomplice's confession violated defendant's confrontation clause rights).

The Requirement of Corroboration of Valid Confessions

In order to secure a conviction, the prosecution must prove that a crime was committed and that the defendant was the person who committed it. Under early English common law, the defendant's confession could be used to establish both elements. This practice increased the danger that an innocent person might be convicted—even of a crime that never happened. To combat this danger, most American jurisdictions adopted the rule that in order to secure a conviction based on a confession, the prosecution must produce some evidence independent of the confession that the crime was committed by someone or, in other words, that there was in fact a crime.[159] The independent proof requirement is known as the **corpus delicti** rule.

The phrase *corpus delicti* means the "body of the crime" (i.e., the fact that the crime charged was committed by someone). In the case of an unlawful homicide, for example, the prosecution would have to prove that a person is dead, and that his or her death was caused by a crime, before a confession given by the accused may be introduced as evidence. Courts differ on the amount of proof necessary to satisfy the foundation required by the corpus delicti rule. However, the modern tendency is to minimize this requirement by establishing a low threshold of proof.[160] The corpus delicti requirement is generally stated as demanding "some evidence" or "slight evidence," independent of the defendant's confession, that the confessed crime was committed.[161]

The corpus delicti requirement made sense when no safeguards existed against the admission of confessions secured by coercion. The danger that innocent people might be coerced into confessing to crimes that were never committed was real. However, with *Miranda* safeguards and the due process free and voluntary requirement, the legal situation has changed. With these changes, the original purpose of the corpus delicti requirement no longer exists[162] and some have expressed misgivings about whether this requirement should be retained.[163] Requiring the prosecution to present independent evidence that the confessed crime was in fact committed before introducing a confession rarely accomplishes anything other than allowing the guilty to go free.[164]

---

159   For a general discussion of the corroboration requirement, *see* Thomas A. Mullen, *Rule Without Reason: Requiring Independent Proof of the Corpus Delicti as a Condition of Admitting an Extrajudicial Confession*, 27 U.S.F. L. REV. 385 (1993) (recommending elimination of corpus delicti rule).

160   *Id*. at 390–391.

161   State v. Van Hook, 39 Ohio St. 3d 256, 261–262, 530 N.E.2d 883, 888–889 (1988); Thomas A. Mullen, *supra* note 159, at 390–391.

162   Willoughby v. State, 552 N.E.2d 462, 466 (Ind. 1990).

163   Thomas A. Mullen, *supra* note 159.

164   *See, e.g.,* State v. Thompson, 560 N.W.2d 535 (N.D. 1997) (confession insufficient to sustain conviction for sexual contact with young child when there was no independent evidence establishing the corpus delicti).

Summary and Practical Suggestions

A confession must pass at least four, and in some jurisdictions five, legal hurdles before it will be received as evidence of guilt. Voluntary confessions that fail some of these requirements may be used as impeachment evidence (i.e., to attack the credibility of the accused's trial testimony if he takes the witness stand and tells the jurors a different story from the one he told the police). However, this use is relatively unimportant. Consequently, students need a solid grounding in the requirements for a valid confession and the phases in the development of a criminal case when each applies.

Due process free and voluntary requirement. When a confession is offered as evidence, the government bears the burden of proving by a preponderance of the evidence that the confession was given voluntarily. A confession is considered involuntary under the due process clause when: (1) an agent of the government applies improper pressures that (2) overcome the suspect's free will. Voluntariness is determined by examining the totality of circumstances under which the confession was given, with emphasis on: (1) the interrogation methods used by the police; (2) the suspect's degree of susceptibility; and (3) the conditions under which the interrogation took place.

Fourth Amendment exclusionary rule. Confessions that are causally related to a police violation of the suspect's Fourth Amendment rights (i.e., unconstitutional investigatory stop, arrest, or search) are inadmissible, even if voluntary. Courts consider the following three factors in deciding whether a causal relationship exists: the length of time between the violation and the confession, the presence of intervening circumstances, and the purpose and flagrancy of the violation.

McNabb-Mallory rule. The *McNabb-Mallory* rule was developed to enforce compliance with Rule 5(a) of the Federal Rules of Criminal Procedure, which requires federal officers to act without unnecessary delay in presenting persons arrested on federal charges to a magistrate for arraignment. It does this by requiring suppression confessions obtained during a period of unnecessary delay in complying with this requirement. Section 3501 of Omnibus Crime Control and Safe Streets Act of 1968 limited the *McNabb-Mallory* rule by excluding confessions obtained during the first six hours after an arrest on federal charges from its operation. The *McNabb-Mallory* rule was based on the Supreme Court's supervisory powers to establish rules of evidence for federal courts and is not binding on state courts, though some have voluntarily adopted it.

Fifth Amendment/*Miranda* rule. The *Miranda* rule, which is grounded in the Fifth Amendment privilege against self-incrimination, was developed to counteract the coercive atmosphere of a police custodial interrogation. *Miranda* warnings must be administered whenever the police: (1) interrogate a suspect; (2) who is then in custody; (3) about an offense with which he has not yet been charged. (If the suspect has already been charged with the offense, police must observe Sixth Amendment right to counsel procedures, which are summarized below.) A suspect is considered "in custody" whenever the objective circumstances surrounding the encounter are such that a reasonable person would assess the situation as equivalent to an arrest. The suspect must be aware that the questioner is a police officer for custody to exist. An interrogation occurs when police ask questions or engage in other words or actions that they should know are reasonably likely to elicit an incriminating response from the suspect. Unless confronted with an emergency requiring immediate action to protect the public safety or their own safety, police must warn the suspect and obtain an intelligent and voluntary waiver before initiating questioning. If the suspect, either before or during the questioning, clearly expresses a desire to speak with an attorney or to remain silent, questioning must stop immediately and may resume only under narrowly defined circumstances. Failure to comply with *Miranda* requirements results in suppression of the confession, but not derivative evidence unless police are guilty of coercion.

Sixth Amendment right to counsel. The Sixth Amendment right to counsel attaches upon the initiation of adversary criminal proceedings by way of a preliminary hearing, indictment, information, or arraignment. Once the Sixth Amendment right to counsel attaches, police may not deliberately elicit incriminating statements from the accused at a time when counsel is not present, unless the accused gives a valid waiver. This restriction applies whether the accused is in custody or at large. However, it only applies when the questioning relates to the pending charges; it does not apply when police question an accused about other uncharged criminal activity. The Sixth Amendment right to counsel can be waived. The procedures for obtaining a valid waiver and for conducting the interrogation are the same as under the *Miranda* rule.

Chapter 2: Key Terms and Discussion Questions

Key Terms

Admission: a suspect's statement that he or she is involved in a crime

Chain of Custody: documentation about how and when evidence has been handled since it came into police custody

Confession: a suspect's statement that he or she committed a crime

Corroboration: the act of confirming a fact; evidence that supports a statement or finding

Derivative Evidence: evidence that has come from an illegal source

Evidence: anything used to prove or disprove a fact in a case

Exclusionary Rule: doctrine that prevents illegally obtained evidence from being admissible at trial

Fifth Amendment: "No person shall be held to answer for a capital, or otherwise infamous crime, unless on a presentment or indictment of a Grand Jury, except in cases arising in the land or naval forces, or in the Militia, when in actual service in time of War or public danger; nor shall any person be subject for the same offence to be twice put in jeopardy of life or limb; nor shall be compelled in any criminal case to be a witness against himself, nor be deprived of life, liberty, or property, without due process of law; nor shall private property be taken for public use, without just compensation."

Fourth Amendment: "The right of the people to be secure in their persons, houses, papers, and effects, against unreasonable searches and seizures, shall not be violated, and no Warrants shall issue, but upon probable cause, supported by Oath or affirmation, and particularly describing the place to be searched, and the persons or things to be seized."

Free and Voluntary Rule: rule that states a voluntary confession is a confession that is given out of a suspect's own free will and has not been obtained by force, coercion, or intimidation

Impeachment: challenging a witness's testimony in a trial; process of calling into question the credibility of a witness during a trial

Interrogation: intense and accusatory questioning sessions by the police while a suspect is in custody

Miranda Rule: from Miranda v. Arizona; prior to interrogation, law enforcement must read four warnings to suspects, informing them that (1) they have the right to remain silent; (2) anything said can and will be used against the suspect in a court of law; (3) they have the right to an attorney; (4) if the suspect cannot afford an attorney, one will be provided for him or her

Physical Evidence: tangible evidence at a crime scene; also called "real" or "material" evidence

Sixth Amendment: "In all criminal prosecutions, the accused shall enjoy the right to a speedy and public trial, by an impartial jury of the State and district wherein the crime shall have been committed, which district shall have been previously ascertained by law, and to be informed of the nature and cause of the accusation; to be confronted with the witnesses against him; to have compulsory process for obtaining witnesses in his favor, and to have the Assistance of Counsel for his defence."

Discussion Questions

1. Why does the buddy system work well in crime scene investigations?
2. What is the purpose of Miranda warnings?
3. What seems to be the best way to interrogate a suspect?
4. Why do some people give false confessions?
5. Do you believe it should be legal for law enforcement to lie to suspects during interrogation? Why?

Exclusionary Rule

The Exclusionary Rule

by Rolando V. del Carmen and Jeffrey T. Walker

Introduction

The exclusionary rule provides that any evidence obtained by the government in violation of the Fourth Amendment right against unreasonable searches and seizures is not admissible in a court of law. It is a judge-made rule whose purpose is to deter police misconduct; the assumption being that, if evidence obtained by the police in violation of the Fourth Amendment cannot be used in court, police misconduct will be minimized.

Evidence obtained by the police in violation of other rights under the Bill of Rights (such as the privilege against self-incrimination under the Fifth Amendment, or the right to counsel under the Sixth Amendment) is not admissible in court either, but that exclusion does not come under the exclusionary rule; rather, the evidence is excluded based on a violation of the constitutional right to due process. The exclusionary rule, therefore, is of limited application in that it applies only in cases involving violations of the prohibition against unreasonable searches and seizures under the Fourth Amendment.

The first exclusionary rule case decided by the United States Supreme Court was *Boyd v. United States* (116 U.S. 616) in 1886. In that case, the Court held that the forced disclosure of papers amounting to evidence of a crime violated the Fourth Amendment right of the suspect and, therefore, the evidence could not be used in court. In 1914, in *Weeks v. United States* (32 U.S. 383), the Court held that evidence illegally obtained by federal officers could not be used in federal criminal prosecutions. *Mapp v. Ohio*, 467 U.S. 643 (1961) is the leading and best-known case on the exclusionary rule. In *Mapp*, the Court held that the exclusionary rule also applied to state criminal prosecutions, thus extending the exclusionary rule to all federal and state criminal proceedings.

There are many exceptions to the exclusionary rule, as the cases briefed here show. The common theme in these cases is that the misconduct, mistake, or error was not committed by the police but by other government officials—in some cases judges, the legislature, or a court clerk. The evidence obtained can be used in court because the exclusionary rule was meant to deter police misconduct, not the misconduct of other government officials.

Although originally controversial, the exclusionary rule has been accepted and applied by the courts and is now an accepted part of policing. The United States Supreme Court continues to define exceptions, but the exclusionary rule is here to stay as a form of protection against violations by the police of the public's right against unreasonable searches and seizures.

The leading cases briefed in this chapter on the exclusionary rule are *Mapp v. Ohio* and *Weeks v. United States*.

Weeks v. United States 232 U.S. 383 (1914)

CAPSULE: Evidence illegally seized by federal law enforcement officers is not admissible in a federal criminal prosecution.

FACTS: Weeks was arrested for using the mail to transport tickets for a lottery. Other officers searched Weeks' home without a warrant and seized various articles and papers that were then turned over to the United States Marshals Service. Later in the day, police officers returned with a Marshal and again searched Weeks' home without a warrant and seized letters and other articles. Weeks was charged with and convicted of unlawful use of the mail.

ISSUE: Is evidence illegally obtained by federal law enforcement officers admissible in court? NO.

SUPREME COURT DECISION: Evidence illegally seized by federal law enforcement officers is not admissible in federal criminal prosecutions.

REASON: The Fourth Amendment freedom from unreasonable searches and seizures applies "... to all invasions on the part of the government and its employees of the sanctity of a man's home and the privacies of life. It is not the breaking of his doors and the rummaging of his drawers that constitutes the essence of the offense; but it is the invasion of his indefeasible right of personal security, personal liberty and private property."

CASE SIGNIFICANCE: This decision excluded illegally obtained evidence from use in federal prosecutions. This rule was extended to state criminal prosecutions in 1961 in *Mapp v. Ohio*, 367 U.S. 643 (1961), making illegally obtained evidence inadmissible in both state and federal courts. It is interesting to note that from 1914 to 1960, federal courts admitted evidence of a federal crime if it was obtained illegally by state officers, as long as there was no connivance with federal officers. This questionable practice was known as the "silver platter doctrine."

In 1960, the Court rejected the "silver platter doctrine" (*Elkins v. United States*, 364 U.S. 206), holding that the Fourth Amendment prohibited the use of illegally obtained evidence in federal prosecutions whether it was obtained by federal or state officers.

Rochin v. California 342 U.S. 165 (1952)

CAPSULE: Some searches are so "shocking to the conscience" that they require exclusion of the evidence seized based on due process.

FACTS: Having information that Rochin was selling narcotics, police officers entered his home and forced their way into the bedroom. When asked about two capsules lying beside the bed, Rochin put them in his mouth. After an unsuccessful attempt to recover them by force, the officers took Rochin to the hospital where his stomach was pumped. Two capsules containing morphine were recovered. A motion to suppress this evidence was denied and Rochin was convicted in a California state court of possession of morphine.

ISSUE: Were the capsules recovered as a result of pumping Rochin's stomach admissible as evidence in court? NO.

SUPREME COURT DECISION: Although searches by state law enforcement officers are not governed by the exclusionary rule, some searches are so "shocking to the conscience" as to require exclusion of the evidence seized based on the due process (fundamental fairness) clause of the Constitution. These cases are limited to acts of coercion, violence, and brutality.

REASON: "... [T]he proceedings by which this conviction was obtained do more than offend some fastidious squeamishness or private sentimentalism about combating crime too energetically. This is conduct that shocks the conscience. Illegally breaking into the privacy of the petitioner, the struggle to open his mouth and remove what was there, the forcible extraction of his stomach's contents—this course of proceeding by agents of the government to obtain evidence is bound to offend even hardened sensibilities. They are methods too close to the rack and screw to permit of constitutional differentiation."

CASE SIGNIFICANCE: This case was decided prior to the extension of the exclusionary rule to the states in 1961. In this state prosecution, however, the Court decided that the evidence obtained could not be used in court, not because of the exclusionary rule, but because the conduct of the police officers was shocking and therefore violated Rochin's right to due process guaranteed by the Fourteenth Amendment. If the case were to be decided today, the evidence would be excluded under the exclusionary rule, not under the due process clause.

Mapp v. Ohio 367 U.S. 643 (1961)

CAPSULE: The exclusionary rule applies to all state criminal proceedings.

FACTS: Mapp was convicted of possession of lewd and lascivious books, pictures, and photographs in violation of Ohio law. Three Cleveland police officers went to Mapp's residence based on information that a person who was wanted in connection with a recent bombing was hiding out in her home. The officers knocked on the door and demanded entrance, but Mapp, telephoning her attorney, refused to admit them without a warrant. The officers again sought entrance three hours later, after the arrival of more police. When Mapp did not respond, the officers broke the door open. Mapp's attorney arrived but was denied access to his client. Mapp demanded to see the search warrant the police claimed to possess. When a paper supposed to be the warrant was held up by one of the officers, Mapp grabbed the paper and placed it in her bosom. A struggle ensued and the paper was recovered after Mapp was handcuffed for being belligerent. A search of the house produced a trunk that contained obscene materials. The materials were admitted into evidence at the trial and Mapp was convicted of possession of obscene materials.

ISSUE: Is evidence obtained in violation of the Fourth Amendment protection from unreasonable searches and seizures admissible in state criminal prosecutions? NO.

SUPREME COURT DECISION: The exclusionary rule, applicable in federal cases, which prohibits the use of evidence obtained as a result of unreasonable searches and seizures also applies to state criminal proceedings.

REASON: "Since the Fourth Amendment's right of privacy has been declared enforceable against the States through the Due Process Clause of the Fourteenth [Amendment], it is enforceable against them by the same sanction of exclusion as is used against the Federal Government. Were it otherwise, then just as without the Weeks rule the assurance against unreasonable searches and seizures would be 'a form of words,' valueless and undeserving of mention in a perpetual charter of inestimable human liberties, so too, without that rule the freedom from state invasions of privacy would be ... ephemeral ..."

CASE SIGNIFICANCE: *Mapp* is significant because the Court held that the exclusionary rule was thereafter to be applied to all states, thus forbidding both state and federal courts from accepting evidence obtained in violation of the constitutional protection against unreasonable searches and seizures. In the mind of the Court, the facts in *Mapp* illustrate what can happen if police conduct is not restricted. *Mapp* was therefore an ideal case for the Court to use in settling an issue that had to be addressed: whether the exclusionary rule should apply to state criminal proceedings. The Court answered with a definite yes.

Wong Sun v. United States 371 U.S. 471 (1963)

CAPSULE: Evidence obtained as a result of illegal acts by the police must be excluded. In addition, the "fruit of the poisonous tree" of that illegal act must also be excluded. Evidence that has been purged of the primary taint, however, is admissible.

FACTS: Federal narcotics agents arrested Hom Way and found heroin in his possession. Although Way had not been an informant before, the agents went to "Oye's Laundry" based upon his statement that he had bought the heroin from "Blackie Toy," who owned the laundry. At the laundry, agent Wong got James Wah Toy to open the door by telling him that he was calling for dry cleaning. Upon announcing that he was a federal agent, Toy slammed the door and started running. The agents then broke open the door and began to chase Toy. Toy was placed under arrest in his bedroom. A search of the premises uncovered no drugs. There was nothing to link Toy to "Blackie Toy." Upon interrogation, he stated that he had not been selling narcotics but knew that an individual named Johnny had. He told the officers where Johnny lived, and described the bedroom where the heroin was kept and where he had smoked some of the heroin the night before. Based on this information, the agents went to the home of Johnny Yee and found him in possession of an ounce of heroin. Upon interrogation, Yee stated that he had bought the heroin from Toy and an individual named "Sea Dog." Further questioning of Toy revealed that "Sea Dog's" name was Wong Sun. Toy then took the agents to a multifamily dwelling where Wong Sun lived. After identifying himself, agent Wong was admitted by Wong Sun's wife who said he was in the back, asleep. Wong Sun was arrested by the agents. A search pursuant to the arrest found no narcotics. Each of the offenders was arraigned and released on his own recognizance. A few days later, Toy, Yee, and Wong Sun were interrogated again and written statements were made. Neither Toy nor Wong Sun signed their statements, but Wong Sun admitted to the accuracy of his statement. At the trial, the government's evidence consisted of: (1) the statements made by Toy at the time of his arrest; (2) the heroin taken from Yee; (3) Toy's pretrial statement; and (4) Wong Sun's pretrial statement. Wong Sun and Toy were convicted of transportation and concealment of heroin.

ISSUES: There were a number of issues in this case, but the important issues related to the exclusionary rule are:

1. Were the statements made by Toy after an unlawful arrest admissible? NO.
2. Were the narcotics taken from Yee after an unlawful arrest admissible? NO.
3. Was Wong Sun's statement admissible? YES.

SUPREME COURT DECISION: Statements or evidence obtained indirectly as a result of an unlawful arrest or search are not admissible in court because they are "tainted fruit of the poisonous tree." A suspect's intervening act of free will, however, breaks the chain of illegality, purges the evidence of the taint, and makes the evidence admissible.

REASON: The exclusionary rule has traditionally barred from trial physical, tangible materials obtained either during or as a direct result of an unlawful invasion. "... Thus, verbal evidence which derives so immediately from an unlawful entry and an unauthorized arrest as the officers' action in the present case is no less the 'fruit' of official illegality than the more common tangible fruits of the unwarranted intrusion ..."

"We turn now to the case of ... Wong Sun. We have no occasion to disagree with the finding of the Court of Appeals that his arrest, also, was without probable cause or reasonable grounds. For Wong Sun's unsigned confession was not the fruit of that arrest, and was therefore properly admitted at trial. On the evidence that Wong Sun had been released on his own recognizance after a lawful arraignment, and had returned voluntarily several days later to make the statement, we hold that the connection between the arrest and the statement had 'become so attenuated as to dissipate the taint.'"

CASE SIGNIFICANCE: This case addresses the "tainted fruit of the poisonous tree" aspect of the exclusionary rule. The exclusionary rule provides that evidence obtained in violation of the Fourth Amendment prohibition against unreasonable searches and seizures is not admissible in a court of law. The rule goes beyond that, however, and also says that any other evidence obtained directly or indirectly as a result of the illegal behavior is not admissible either. Hence, once an illegal act has been proved, any evidence obtained either directly or indirectly cannot be admitted in court either under the concept of the original illegality or as the "tainted fruit."

This case also carves out an exception to the exclusionary rule: the "purged taint" exception. What it says is that, despite the initial illegality, the evidence may nonetheless be admissible if it has been purged of the initial taint. An example is this case, in which the statement of Wong Sun, which initially was the product of unlawful behavior by the agents, was nonetheless admitted because of subsequent events. What happened was that after Wong Sun was released on his own recognizance and after lawful arraignment, he returned several days later and made a statement that was then admitted by the trial court. The Court said that the voluntary return by Wong Sun purged the evidence of the initial taint and therefore made the statement admissible.

Nix v. Williams 467 U.S. 431 (1984)

CAPSULE: Illegally obtained evidence may be admissible if the police can prove that they would have discovered the evidence anyway through lawful means.

FACTS: On December 24, a 10-year-old girl disappeared from a YMCA building in Des Moines, Iowa. A short time later, Williams was seen leaving the YMCA with a large bundle wrapped in a blanket. A 14-year-old boy who helped him carry the bundle reported that he had seen "two legs in it and they were skinny and white." William's car was found the next day, 160 miles east of Des Moines. Items of clothing belonging to the missing child and a blanket like the one used to wrap the bundle were found at a rest stop between the YMCA in Des Moines and where the car was found. Assuming that the girl's body could be found between the YMCA and the car, a massive search was conducted. Meanwhile, Williams was arrested by police in a town near where the car was found and was arraigned. Williams' counsel was informed that Williams would be returned to Des Moines without being interrogated. During the trip, an officer began a conversation with Williams in which he said the girl should be given a Christian burial before a snowstorm which might prevent the body from being found. As Williams and the officer neared the town where the body was hidden, Williams agreed to take the officer to the child's body. The body was found about two miles from one of the search teams. At the trial, a motion to suppress the evidence was denied and Williams was convicted of first degree murder. Williams sought release on habeas corpus in U.S. District Court. That court ruled that the evidence had been wrongly admitted at Williams' trial. At his second trial, the prosecutor did not offer Williams' statements into evidence and did not seek to show that Williams had led the police to the body. The trial court ruled that the state had proved that, even if Williams had not led the police to the body, it would have been found by the searchers anyway. Williams was again convicted of murder.

ISSUE: Was the evidence (the body) admissible in court on the theory that the body would ultimately have been discovered anyway because of the ongoing search? YES.

SUPREME COURT DECISION: Evidence that is obtained illegally may be admissible if the police can prove that they would have discovered the evidence anyway through lawful means.

REASON: "The independent source doctrine teaches us that the interest of society in deterring unlawful police conduct and the public interest in having juries receive all probative evidence of a crime are properly balanced by putting the police in the same, not a worse, position than they would have been in if no police error or misconduct had occurred."

CASE SIGNIFICANCE: This case illustrates the "inevitable discovery exception to the exclusionary rule." "Fruit of the poisonous tree" is evidence obtained indirectly as a result of illegal police behavior (such as the illegal discovery of a map that tells where contraband is hidden). This evidence is usually inadmissible due to the illegality of police actions. The exception set out in this case states that evidence that is the "fruit of the poisonous tree" is admissible if the police can prove that they would inevitably have discovered the evidence anyway by lawful means. In this case, no *Miranda* warnings were given to the suspect before he confessed; hence, the evidence obtained was excluded during the first trial. But because the evidence would have been discovered anyway as a result of the continued search, the Court said that the evidence could be admitted.

United States v. Leon 468 U.S. 897 (1984)

CAPSULE: The exclusionary rule allows the use of evidence obtained by officers who are acting in reasonable reliance on a search warrant that is later declared invalid.

FACTS: Acting on the basis of information from a confidential informant, officers initiated a drug trafficking investigation. Based on an affidavit summarizing the police officer's observation, a search warrant was prepared. The warrant was reviewed by three Deputy District Attorneys and issued by a state court judge. Ensuing searches produced large quantities of drugs. Leon was indicted on drug charges. Motions to suppress the evidence were granted in part because the affidavit was insufficient to establish probable cause. The court rejected the notion of good faith of the officer and acquitted the defendants.

ISSUE: Is evidence obtained as the result of a search conducted pursuant to a warrant that was issued by a neutral and detached magistrate admissible in court if the warrant is ultimately found invalid through no fault of the police officer? YES.

SUPREME COURT DECISION: The Fourth Amendment's exclusionary rule allows the use of evidence obtained by officers acting in reasonable reliance on a search warrant issued by a neutral and detached magistrate that is ultimately found invalid.

REASON: "In the ordinary case, an officer cannot be expected to question the magistrate's probable cause determination or his judgment that the form of the warrant is technically sufficient. '[O]nce the warrant issues, there is literally nothing more the policeman can do in seeking to comply with the law.' Penalizing the officer for the magistrate's error, rather than his own, cannot logically contribute to the deterrence of Fourth Amendment violations."

CASE SIGNIFICANCE: This case, together with *Massachusetts v. Sheppard*, 468 U.S. 981 (1984), which was decided on the same day, are arguably the most important cases decided on the exclusionary rule since *Mapp v. Ohio*, 367 U.S. 643 (1961). They represent a significant, although narrow, exception to that doctrine. In these two cases, the Court said that there were objectively reasonable grounds for the officers' mistaken belief that the warrants authorized the searches. The officers took every step that could reasonably have been taken to ensure that the warrants were valid. The difference between the *Leon* and *Sheppard* cases is that, in *Sheppard*, the issue was improper use of a search warrant form (the form used was used in another district to search for controlled substances, the judge telling the detective who filed the form that the necessary changes would be made by the judge), whereas in *Leon* the issue was the use of a questionable informant and stale information. The cases are similar, however, in that the mistakes were made by the judges, not the police. The Court said that the evidence in both cases was admissible because the judge, not the police, erred and the exclusionary rule is designed to control the conduct of the police, not the conduct of judges.

Massachusetts v. Sheppard 468 U.S. 981 (1984)

CAPSULE: Evidence obtained as a result of a search in which the police acted in reliance on a search warrant that was subsequently declared invalid by the court is admissible as an exception to the exclusionary rule.

FACTS: Based on evidence gathered in a homicide investigation, a police officer drafted an affidavit to support an application for a search warrant and an arrest warrant. The affidavit was reviewed and approved by the District Attorney. Because it was Sunday, the officer had difficulty finding a warrant application form. The officer ultimately found a used search warrant authorizing a search for controlled substances. After making some changes, the officer presented the warrant to a judge at his residence. The judge was informed that the warrant might need further changes. Concluding that the affidavit established probable cause for the search, the judge made some corrections and signed the warrant. He then returned the warrant to the officer with the assurance that it was sufficient authority to carry out the search. The ensuing search was limited to the items listed in the affidavit. Several pieces of incriminating evidence were found and Sheppard was arrested. At a pretrial motion to suppress, the judge ruled that the warrant was invalid, but the evidence was admitted based on the officer's good faith in executing what he believed to be a valid warrant. Sheppard was convicted of first degree murder.

ISSUE: Is evidence that is obtained from a search that is based on a warrant that is later declared invalid because of error by the issuing magistrate admissible in court? YES.

SUPREME COURT DECISION: Evidence obtained by the police acting in good faith, based on a search warrant that was issued by a neutral and detached magistrate, but that was later found to be invalid, is admissible in court as an exception to the exclusionary rule.

REASON: "Having already decided [in Leon] that the exclusionary rule should not be applied when the officer conducting the search acted in objectively reasonable reliance on a warrant issued by a detached and neutral magistrate that subsequently is determined to be invalid, the sole issue before us in this case is whether the officers reasonably believed that the search they conducted was authorized by a valid warrant. There is no dispute that the officers believed that the warrant authorized the search that they conducted. Thus, the only question is whether there was an objectively reasonable basis for the officers' mistaken belief ... . The officers in this case took every step that could reasonably be expected of them ... . [A] reasonable officer would have concluded, as O'Malley did, that the warrant authorized a search for the materials outlined in the affidavit ... . Sheppard contends that since O'Malley knew the warrant form was defective, he should have examined it to make sure that the necessary changes had been made. However, that argument is based on the premise that O'Malley had a duty to disregard the judge's assurances that the requested search would be authorized and the necessary changes would be made ... . [W]e refuse to rule that an officer is required to disbelieve a judge who has just advised him, by word and by action, that the warrant he possesses authorizes him to conduct the search he has requested."

CASE SIGNIFICANCE: As indicated in the *Leon* case, above, *Sheppard* was the second case involving the exclusionary rule decided by the Court on the same day. These cases dealt with incidents in which mistakes were made, not by the police, but by the magistrates who issued the warrants. Both cases carved out a significant exception to the exclusionary rule: that evidence is admissible if the mistake was made by a magistrate rather than by the police. Note, however, that this is a very narrow "good faith" exception. The police acted "in good faith" in these cases; but it cannot be said that evidence is admissible every time the police act "in good faith." For example, if the police acted illegally in obtaining evidence, they cannot later claim to have acted in good faith in arguing for the admissibility of the evidence obtained, even if they actually did act in good faith and can prove it. This is because the error was committed by the police, not a third person. In the *Sheppard* case, the error was committed by the magistrate, not the police[.] This is an important difference.

Murray v. United States 487 U.S. 533 (1988)

CAPSULE: The exclusionary rule allows the use of evidence obtained by officers who act in reasonable reliance on a search warrant that is later declared invalid.

FACTS: Suspecting illegal drug activities, federal agents followed Murray and several co-conspirators. At one point, Murray drove a truck and another person drove a camper into a warehouse. Twenty minutes later, when the two emerged from the warehouse, law enforcement agents could see a tractor-trailer bearing a long, dark container. The truck and camper were later turned over to other drivers who were arrested and found in possession of marijuana.

Upon receiving this information, the law enforcement agents returned to the warehouse, without a warrant, and forced entry. The warehouse was unoccupied but the agents observed, in plain view, several burlap-wrapped bales of marijuana. The law enforcement agents left the warehouse without disturbing the bales and did not reenter until they had a valid search warrant. In applying for the warrant, the agents did not mention the forced entry into the warehouse and did not rely on any information obtained during that search. After obtaining the warrant, law enforcement agents returned to the warehouse and seized numerous bales of marijuana and a notebook listing the destinations of the bales. Murray was arrested and convicted of conspiracy to possess and distribute illegal drugs.

ISSUE: Is evidence first observed in an illegal entry by officers but subsequently seized through a valid, independent, search warrant admissible in court? YES.

SUPREME COURT DECISION: Even if the police illegally enter private property, evidence initially discovered during that illegal entry may be admissible in court if it is later discovered during a valid search that is wholly unrelated to the illegal entry.

REASON: The Court reasoned that the evidence ought not to have been excluded just because of unrelated illegal conduct by the police. If probable cause for a search warrant can be established apart from any illegal activity by the police, the evidence obtained in the subsequent search should be admissible.

CASE SIGNIFICANCE: This case illustrates the "independent source" exception to the exclusionary rule. In this case, the police illegally entered the warehouse and discovered bales of marijuana. The Court said that the marijuana would be admissible if the officers later searched the warehouse pursuant to a valid warrant that was issued based on information that was not obtained during the illegal entry. An initial illegal entry, therefore, does not automatically exclude the evidence if the evidence is not seized at the time of the illegal entry, but pursuant to a valid warrant that is later obtained without relying on information obtained during the illegal entry.

Minnesota v. Olson 495 U.S. 91 (1989)

CAPSULE: Warrantless nonconsensual entry of a residence by police to arrest an overnight guest violates the Fourth Amendment.

FACTS: The police suspected Olson of being the driver of the getaway car involved in a robbery-murder. Based on an anonymous tip, the police surrounded the home of two women with whom they believed Olson had been staying as a guest. A detective then telephoned the home and told one of the women that Olson should come outside, whereupon he heard a male voice saying, "Tell them I left." When the woman told the detective this, he ordered the police to enter. Without permission or a search warrant, and with their weapons drawn, the police entered the house and arrested Olson, who was hiding in a closet. Based on an incriminating statement made by Olson, he was convicted of murder, armed robbery, and assault.

ISSUE: Is the Fourth Amendment violated when the police make a warrantless, nonconsensual entry and arrest without exigent (emergency) circumstances? YES.

SUPREME COURT DECISION: The warrantless non-consensual entry by the police of a residence to arrest an overnight guest violates the Fourth Amendment, unless justified by exigent circumstances.

REASON: "... [W]e think that society recognizes that a houseguest has a legitimate expectation of privacy in his host's home." An overnight guest "... seeks shelter in another's home precisely because it provides him with privacy, a place where he and his possessions will not be disturbed by anyone except his host and those his host allows inside ... . The houseguest is there with the permission of his host, who is willing to share his house and his privacy with the guest ... . The host may admit or exclude from the house as he prefers, but it is unlikely that he will admit someone who wants to see or meet with the guest over the objection of the guest." Hosts, therefore, "... will more likely than not respect the privacy interests of their guests, who are entitled to a legitimate expectation of privacy despite the fact that they have no legal interest in the premises and do not have the legal authority to determine who may or may not enter the household." Because Olson's "... expectation of privacy in the host's home was rooted in 'understandings that are recognized and permitted by society,' it was legitimate, and respondent can claim the protection of the Fourth Amendment."

CASE SIGNIFICANCE: This case establishes the principle that the arrest of a suspect in another person's home requires a warrant for entry into the home, except: (1) if exigent circumstances are present, or (2) if consent is given by the owner of the house. In this case, suspect Olson was an overnight guest in the home. There was no reason to believe that he would flee the premises, hence exigent circumstances were not deemed present. The Court ruled that the police should have obtained a search warrant to enable them to enter the house legally. An overnight guest has an expectation of privacy that society is prepared to recognize as reasonable, hence a warrant should have been obtained. The statement made after his arrest was not admissible in court.

Arizona v. Evans 514 U.S. 1 (1995)

CAPSULE: The exclusionary rule does not require suppression of evidence seized in violation of the Fourth Amendment where the erroneous information resulted from clerical errors of court employees.

FACTS: Police officers saw Evans going the wrong way on a one-way street in front of the police station. When Evans was stopped, officers determined that his driver's license had been suspended. When Evans' name was entered into a computer data terminal in the officer's patrol car, it indicated that there was an outstanding misdemeanor warrant for Evans' arrest. While being handcuffed, Evans dropped a hand-rolled cigarette that turned out to be marijuana. A search of Evans' car revealed more marijuana under the passenger's seat. At trial, Evans moved to suppress the evidence as fruit of an unlawful arrest because the arrest warrant for the misdemeanor had been quashed 17 days prior to his arrest but was not entered into the computer due to a clerical error of a court employee. Evans also argued that the good faith exception to the exclusionary rule was inapplicable in this case. These motions were denied and Evans was convicted.

ISSUE: Does the exclusionary rule require suppression of evidence that is seized by an officer acting in reliance on erroneous information resulting from clerical errors of court employees? NO.

SUPREME COURT DECISION: "The exclusionary rule does not require suppression of evidence seized in violation of the Fourth Amendment where the erroneous information resulted from clerical errors of court employees."

REASON: "The exclusionary rule operates as a judicially created remedy designed to safeguard against future violations [by police officers] of Fourth Amendment rights through the rule's deterrent effect." The application of the exclusionary rule was for police officers rather than court employees (see *United States v. Leon*, 468 U.S. 897 [1974]). The Court found "... no sound reason to apply the exclusionary rule as a means of deterring misconduct on the part of judicial officers" because application of the exclusionary rule to court personnel could not be expected to alter the behavior of the arresting officer. Furthermore "[t]here [was] no indication that the arresting officer was not acting objectively reasonably when he relied upon the police computer record. Application of the *Leon* framework supports a categorical exception to the exclusionary rule for clerical errors of court employees."

CASE SIGNIFICANCE: This case extends an exception to the exclusionary rule when an error is committed by court employees rather than the police. The exclusionary rule was fashioned to deter police misconduct, hence the Court refused to apply it to cases in which the error was not made by the police. Previous cases have held that if the error is made by a magistrate (as in *Massachusetts v. Sheppard* and *United States v. Leon*), or by the legislature (as in *Illinois v. Krull*), the exclusionary rule does not apply. The theme in these cases is that if the error is not committed by the police, then the exclusionary rule should not apply because it was meant to control the behavior of the police. Evans, therefore, is consistent with the Court's holdings in previous cases and came as no surprise. The unanswered question is whether error by any public officer other than the police would be an addition to this rule. The dissent in *Evans* argued that the Fourth Amendment prohibition against unreasonable searches and seizures applies to the conduct of all government officers, not just the police. The majority in *Evans* disagreed, preferring instead to focus on the original purpose of the exclusionary rule—which is to control police conduct.

Brigham City, Utah v. Stuart et al. 547 U.S. 47 (2006)

CAPSULE: "Police may enter a home without a warrant when they have an objectively reasonable basis for believing that an occupant is seriously injured or imminently threatened with such injury."

FACTS: Officers responded to a call regarding a loud party at a residence. Upon arriving at the house, they heard shouting from inside. They also observed two juveniles drinking beer in the backyard. They entered the backyard and saw through a screen door and windows a fight taking place in the kitchen of the home involving four adults and a juvenile. After observing several people being punched, the officers then opened the screen door and announced their presence with no response from the occupants. The officers entered the kitchen and again announced their presence, at which time the fight then ceased. The officers arrested the adults and charged them with contributing to the delinquency of a minor, disorderly conduct, and intoxication.

ISSUE: May the police enter a home without a warrant when they have an objectively reasonable belief that an occupant is seriously injured or imminently threatened with injury? Yes.

SUPREME COURT DECISION: "Police may enter a home without a warrant when they have an objectively reasonable basis for believing that an occupant is seriously injured or imminently threatened with such injury."

REASON: "It is a 'basic principle of Fourth Amendment law that searches and seizures inside a home without a warrant are presumptively unreasonable.'" [internal citations omitted]. "One exigency obviating the requirement of a warrant is the need to assist persons who are seriously injured or threatened with such injury." "Accordingly, law enforcement officers may enter a home without a warrant to render emergency assistance to an injured occupant or to protect an occupant from imminent injury."

CASE SIGNIFICANCE: In this case, the Court ruled that police may justifiably enter a home or building without a warrant if they have an "objectively reasonable" basis (lower than probable cause) to believe that somebody inside is "seriously injured or threatened with such injury." The Court added that "the need to protect or preserve life or avoid serious injury is justification for what would be otherwise illegal absent an exigency or emergency." This reiterates the "danger to third person" or "emergency aid" exception to the warrant requirement. The other notable instances when the police may enter a building or home without a warrant are: (1) when there is danger of physical harm to the officer or destruction of evidence, and (2) in cases of "hot pursuit." All three exceptions may be classified under "exigent circumstances."

Davis v. Washington 547 U.S. 813 (2006)

CAPSULE: "Statements are nontestimonial [and therefore admissible in court] when made in the course of police interrogation under circumstances objectively indicating that the primary purpose of interrogation is to enable police assistance to meet an ongoing emergency."

FACTS: After a call and hang-up to 911, the operator reversed the call and Michelle McCottry answered. Based on questioning McCottry, the operator determined she was involved in a domestic disturbance with her former boyfriend, Davis. The operator learned that Davis had just left in a car with another person after hitting McCottry. Officers arrived and observed the injuries to McCottry but had no way to determine the cause of the injuries. Davis was later charged with violating a domestic no-contact order. Over Davis's objection, the 911 tape was admitted into evidence and he was convicted. Davis appealed his conviction, saying that his constitutional right to cross-examination was violated by the admission of the tape-recording into evidence because there was no opportunity to cross-examine.

ISSUE: Are statements made to law enforcement personnel during a 911 call or at a crime scene "testimonial" and thus subject to the requirements of the Sixth Amendment's right to cross-examination and confrontation? No.

SUPREME COURT DECISION: "Statements are nontestimonial [and therefore admissible in court] when made in the course of police interrogation under circumstances objectively indicating that the primary purpose of interrogation is to enable police assistance to meet an ongoing emergency."

REASON: "The Confrontation Clause of the Sixth Amendment provides: 'In all criminal prosecutions, the accused shall enjoy the right ... to be confronted with the witnesses against him.' In *Crawford* v. *Washington*, 541 U.S. 36, 53–54 (2004), we held that this provision bars 'admission of testimonial statements of a witness who did not appear at trial unless he was unavailable to testify, and the defendant had had a prior opportunity for cross-examination.' A critical portion of this holding, and the portion central to resolution of the two cases now before us, is the phrase 'testimonial statements.' Only statements of this sort cause the declarant to be a 'witness' within the meaning of the Confrontation Clause. See *id.*, at 51. It is the testimonial character of the statement that separates it from other hearsay that, while subject to traditional limitations upon hearsay evidence, is not subject to the Confrontation Clause." "A 911 call ... and at least the initial interrogation conducted in connection with a 911 call, is ordinarily not designed primarily to 'establis[h] or prov[e]' some past fact, but to describe current circumstances requiring police assistance." "We conclude from all this that the circumstances of McCottry's interrogation objectively indicate its primary purpose was to enable police assistance to meet an ongoing emergency. She simply was not acting as a *witness*; she was not *testifying*." [emphasis in original].

CASE SIGNIFICANCE: This is an important case in police work because it holds that tape-recordings of calls to the police may be admissible in court during trial as evidence as long as they are non-testimonial. Every day the police, through the 911 service, receive all kinds of calls that are recorded, including those that may be incriminating to the accused, such as in this case. Davis claimed that admitting the recording violated his right to cross-examination because the taped evidence could not be cross-examined. The Court rejected that claim, ruling that for purposes of admissibility as evidence in court, a distinction should be made between non-testimonial and testimonial evidence. Non-testimonial statements recorded through 911 are admissible, whereas testimonial statements are not. The Court then gave this distinction: "Statements are non-testimonial when made in the course of police interrogation under circumstances objectively indicating that the primary purpose of interrogation is to enable police assistance to meet an ongoing emergency." By contrast, the Court stated that statements "are testimonial when the circumstances objectively indicate that there is no such ongoing emergency, and that the primary purpose of the interrogation is to establish or prove past events relevant to later criminal prosecution." This distinction gives general guidance to police and prosecution as to what statements are admissible and what are not.

A Reason to Doubt

The Suppression of Evidence and the Inference of Innocence

by Cynthia E. Jones

The government's duty to disclose favorable evidence to the defense under Brady v. Maryland *has become one of the most unenforced constitutional mandates in criminal law. The intentional or bad faith withholding of* Brady *evidence is by far the most egregious type of* Brady *violation and has led to wrongful convictions, near executions, and other miscarriages of justice. This Article suggests that two ramifications should flow from intentional* Brady *violations. First, courts should have the power to inform the jury of the government's* Brady *misconduct by imposing a specially crafted punitive jury instruction. Unlike the ineffective sanctioning scheme currently used to redress* Brady *violations, the proposed "*Brady *Instruction" could serve as a powerful deterrent against this virulent form of prosecutorial misconduct. Second, under well-established evidentiary principles, a litigant's intentional suppression of relevant evidence gives rise to an inference that the litigant's case is weak and that the litigant knew his case would not prevail if the evidence was presented at trial. The government's intentional* Brady *misconduct falls within the scope of the "consciousness of a weak case" inference. Given that the government always has the burden of proof in a criminal case, evidence that the government's case is weak is relevant to whether the government can prove guilt beyond a reasonable doubt.* Brady *misconduct evidence also meets all other requirements for admissibility under the rules of evidence. As such, the blanket exclusion of this evidence could infringe upon the defendant's constitutional right to present a defense.*

Cynthia E. Jones, "A Reason to Doubt: The Suppression of Evidence and the Inference of Innocence," *Journal of Criminal Law & Criminology*, vol. 100, no. 2, pp. 415-474. Copyright © 2010 by Northwestern University Press. Reprinted with permission. Provided by ProQuest LLC. All rights reserved.

I. Introduction

In a nationally televised press conference, the Department of Justice announced that a federal grand jury had returned a seven-count indictment against Alaska Senator Theodore "Ted" Stevens.[1] The eighty-four-year-old Senator was charged with violating federal ethics laws by failing to disclose thousands of dollars in gifts and services received from constituents.[2] After publicly announcing the charges, the Justice Department official thanked the lawyers in the Public Integrity Section, the division of the Department of Justice charged with investigating and prosecuting corruption by public officials.[3] Ironically, the Public Integrity Section lawyers who investigated and prosecuted Stevens for nondisclosure of information would later face investigation and possible prosecution for obstruction of justice due to their own acts of nondisclosure of information.[4] In fact, following the prosecutors' repeated acts of concealing, altering, and falsifying critical evidence in the Stevens case, the trial judge rhetorically asked the prosecutors, "*How does the court have confidence that the Public Integrity Section has public integrity?*"[5]

Once the government initiated the criminal case against Ted Stevens, the landmark Supreme Court decision in *Brady v. Maryland*[6] mandated that the trial prosecutors provide the defense with favorable information collected by the government during the course of its investigation, including information that either negated guilt or undermined the government's case. The same constitutional principles of due process that compel the disclosure of *Brady* evidence likewise prohibit the government from securing a conviction with false testimony or concealing the fact that such tainted evidence has been introduced at trial.[7]

The crux of the criminal charges against Senator Stevens was that VECO, an Alaska-based company, performed extensive renovations on a home Stevens owned in Alaska.[8] The government maintained that the free labor, building supplies, and related gifts bestowed upon Stevens totaled more than $100,000 over a seven-year period.[9] The indictment alleged that Stevens violated the criminal penalty provisions of the federal ethics law by neither paying for these services

---

1   *See DOJ Press Conference on Stevens' Indictment* (Fox News television broadcast July 29, 2008); *see also* U.S. Dep't of Justice, Transcript of Press Conference with Acting Assistant Attorney General Matthew Friedrich on Indictment of U.S. Senator 3 (July 29, 2008), *available at* http://www.usdoj.gov/opa/pr/2008/July/pin-stevens-pressconference transcript.pdf.

2   Indictment, United States v. Stevens, 593 F. Supp. 2d 177 (D.D.C. 2009) (No. 1), 2008 WL 284791.

3   *DOJ Press Conference on Stevens' Indictment, supra* note 1.

4   Transcript of Motion Hearing at 4–5, 45–46, United States v. Stevens, 593 F. Supp. 2d 177 (D.D.C. 2009) (No. 374).

5   Neil A. Lewis, *Justice Dept. Moves to Void Stevens Case*, N.Y. TIMES, Apr. 2, 2009, at A1, *available at* http://www.nytimes.com/2009/04/02/us/politics/02stevens.html.

6   373 U.S. 83 (1963).

7   Napue v. Illinois, 360 U.S. 264 (1959).

8   Indictment, *supra* note 2.

9   *Id.*

nor reporting them as gifts when he filed his annual financial disclosure statement.[10] Though it did not charge Stevens with accepting bribes, the indictment described Stevens' relationship with VECO as a "scheme" to accept the free services while VECO was soliciting the Senator's help with obtaining federal grants and seeking other federal government assistance with its foreign and domestic business matters.[11] In defense, Stevens maintained that he paid for the renovation services and was unaware that he was not billed for the full cost. Stevens argued that he never *knowingly* submitted false financial disclosure statements.[12]

As the Stevens litigation progressed, the government violated nearly every facet of the *Brady* doctrine. In fact, their *Brady* violations grew in number and egregiousness throughout the trial.[13] Specifically, the trial judge found that the government "used business records that the Government undeniably knew were false," suppressed "critical grand jury transcript[s] containing exculpatory information," "affirmatively redacted" exculpatory content from documents, and provided the defense with a series of intentionally inaccurate document summaries.[14] Moreover, when a prosecution witness flown in from Alaska made unanticipated exculpatory statements during a pretrial interview, the prosecutors secretly shipped him back to Alaska before the defense could subpoena him.[15]

The *Brady* violations only intensified after Ted Stevens was found guilty on all counts. Post-trial, the defense learned of a whistleblower complaint filed by an FBI agent assigned to the Stevens case. When the defense petitioned the court to order the government to disclose the facts of the complaint, the prosecutors intentionally misrepresented to the court that the FBI complaint was unrelated to the Stevens verdict. When the trial judge later learned that the FBI complaint involved allegations that the prosecutors had not turned over all evidence to Stevens's defense team, the court ordered the prosecutors to disclose all evidence related to the FBI complaint to

---

10   Specifically, Stevens was charged with violating 18 U.S.C. § 1001(a)(2) (2006), which penalizes any person "within the jurisdiction of the executive, legislative, or judicial branch of the Government of the United States, [who] knowingly and willfully ... makes any materially false, fictitious, or fraudulent statement or representation." The statute was enacted as part of the Ethics in Government Act of 1978 and requires every elected United States Senator to file a financial disclosure form every year they are in office. The purpose of the filing requirement is to monitor and deter conflicts of interest. Senators are required to disclose their income, assets, gifts, financial interests, and liabilities from the previous year, including gifts over $250 or $300, and liabilities in excess of $10,000. Indictment, *supra* note 2.

11   Indictment, *supra* note 2.

12   Moreover, Stevens maintained that his wife directly oversaw the renovation project and had taken out a second mortgage to pay over $160,000 to VECO for the renovations, an amount they believed was the full cost of the services provided. *See* Neil A. Lewis, *Closing Arguments in Stevens Trial*, N.Y. TIMES, Oct. 21, 2008, at A19, *available at* http://www.nytimes.com/2008/10/22/washington/22stevens.html; *Stevens Says, 'I am innocent' After Corruption Convictions*, CNNPOLITICS.COM, Oct. 27, 2008, http://www.cnn.com/2008/POLITICS/10/27/stevens.jurors/index.html.

13   Transcript of Motion Hearing, *supra* note 4, at 4–5.

14   *Id.*

15   Senator Stevens's Motion to Dismiss Indictment or For a Mistrial at 1–9, United States v. Stevens, 593 F. Supp. 2d 177 (D.D.C. 2009) (No. 08–231).

the defense. When prosecutors repeatedly failed to comply with the court order, the trial judge held three prosecutors in contempt.[16]

Thereafter, a new team of prosecutors was assigned to the Stevens case. The new prosecutors quickly uncovered and disclosed what the trial judge called "the most shocking and serious *Brady* violations of all."[17] Bill Allen, the Chief Executive Officer of VECO, was the star witness for the prosecution. Most of the *Brady* violations during the Stevens case involved information that either undermined Allen's credibility or information from Allen and others that affirmatively exculpated Senator Stevens. During the trial, Bill Allen admitted that he received a letter from Stevens requesting a bill for the renovation services. Allen testified, however, that he was subsequently contacted by a Stevens emissary, Bill Persons, who indicated that the Senator was only sending the letter to create a false record to protect himself.[18] This explosive revelation significantly bolstered the government's allegation that Stevens schemed to cover up his financial windfall. The government never informed the defense that, during a pretrial interview with the prosecutors, Allen stated that he did not recall having a conversation with Bill Persons regarding Ted Stevens's bill.[19] Allen's inconsistent statement was memorialized in handwritten notes prepared by the trial prosecutors.[20] Despite knowing that Allen's pretrial statement was either powerful impeachment evidence or that Allen's bombshell trial testimony was perjury, the prosecutors withheld their handwritten notes from the defense.

In the end, the Stevens case collapsed under the weight of the *Brady* misconduct. Newly appointed Attorney General Eric Holder took the extraordinary and virtually unprecedented step of requesting a postconviction dismissal of all charges with prejudice.[21] The Stevens prosecution is significant, however, for three reasons. First, unlike most criminal cases, when the *Brady* violations were discovered in *Stevens*, the prosecutor's office took affirmative steps to repair the damage to the defendant and initiated its own internal investigation of the trial prosecutors. In the overwhelming majority of cases, prosecutors face few, if any, adverse consequences for *Brady* violations either within their offices or from an outside entity with the power to address their misconduct.

---

16   *See* Minute Order, United States v. Stevens, 593 F. Supp. 2d 177 (D.D.C. 2009) (on file with author).

17   Transcript of Motion Hearing, *supra* note 4, at 6.

18   Actually, the testimony was that Allen should not worry about getting the letter requesting the bill because "Ted is just covering his ass." Transcript of Motion Hearing, *supra* note 4, at 21.

19   *Id.* at 21–22.

20   *Id.* at 24–25.

21   Specifically, the Attorney General stated:

> I have concluded that certain information should have been provided to the defense for use at trial. In light of this conclusion, and in consideration of the totality of the circumstances of this particular case, I have determined that it is in the interests of justice to dismiss the indictment and not proceed with a new trial.

Press Release, U.S. Dep't of Just., Statement of Attorney General Eric Holder Regarding United States v. Theodore F. Stevens (Apr. 1, 2009), *available at* http://www.usdoj.gov/opa/pr/2009/April/09-ag-288.html.

The Stevens prosecution is also notable because of the actions of Judge Emmet Sullivan who presided over the trial. While applauding the Justice Department's initiative in conducting an internal investigation of the *Brady* misconduct, the judge also noted that "the events and allegations in this case are too serious and too numerous to be left to an internal investigation that has no outside accountability."[22] For this reason, Judge Sullivan initiated criminal contempt proceedings against six of the Stevens prosecutors "based on failures of those prosecutors to comply with the Court's numerous orders and potential obstruction of justice."[23] Commonly, when *Brady* violations are discovered—even when the violations are intentional and blatant—trial judges focus on curing any harm suffered by the defendant but fail to take punitive measures against the offending prosecutor to deter future *Brady* violations.

Most significantly, the Stevens case is a sad testament to the relative ease with which over-zealous prosecutors can manipulate evidence and finagle a guilty verdict in our American justice system. Because the Stevens case was one of the most politically explosive cases of the decade,[24] there was intense media coverage. Members of the press packed the courtroom, and an even larger group of photographers and camera crews were positioned outside the courthouse to provide daily reports on the trial. The intense media coverage ensured that the trial would be more public than the typical criminal case. Also, the Stevens case was prosecuted by a team of veteran prosecutors from the premiere prosecution authority in the country and defended by a top-notch team of experienced and respected private defense attorneys.[25] If multiple intentional

---

22   Transcript of Motion Hearing, *supra* note 4, at 46. Judge Sullivan also remarked: "In nearly 25 years on the bench, I have never seen anything approaching the mishandling and misconduct I have seen in this case." James Oliphant, *Prosecutors Now Target of Inquiry*, L.A. TIMES, Apr. 8, 2009, at 1, *available at* http://articles.latimes.com/2009/apr/08/nation/ na-stevens8.

23   Transcript of Motion Hearing, *supra* note 4, at 46. The court acted pursuant to Federal Rule of Criminal Procedure 42, which also authorized the court to appoint an independent attorney to prosecute the case against the prosecutors. This rule of procedure states, in relevant part: "Any person who commits criminal contempt may be punished for that contempt after prosecution on notice ... . The court must request that the contempt be prosecuted by an attorney for the government, unless the interest of justice requires the appointment of another attorney." FED. R. CRIM. P. 42(a)(2).

24   Prior to being criminally charged, Stevens had served six terms in the U.S. Senate, winning re-election five times. Biographical Directory of the United States Congress, http://bioguide.congress.gov/scripts/biodis-play.pl?index=s000888. When the charges were filed in July 2008, Stevens was in the middle of re-election to his seventh term in office. It was widely believed that he would almost certainly be re-elected. Lewis, *supra* note 5. Even though the guilty verdict was announced less than two weeks before the election, he was only narrowly defeated by the democratic challenger, Mark Begich. William Yardley, *Senator Stevens Hanging by a Thread in Alaska as the Ballot Counting Continues*, N.Y. TIMES, Nov. 6, 2008, at P17, *available at* http://www.nytimes.com/2008/11/06/us/politics/06alaska.html. As was widely speculated prior to the election, the loss of the "reliably Republican" Stevens seat had a far greater impact on the national polit-ical landscape because the Democratic Party was poised to (and did) win a powerful sixty-seat majority in the Senate, a feat that would not have been possible if Stevens had won re-election. *Alaska Sen. Ted Stevens Loses Re-Election Bid to Mark Begich*, ABCNEWS.COM, Nov. 18, 2008, http://blogs.abcnews.com/politicalradar/2008/11/alaska-sen-ted.html.

25   Kim Eisler, *Sen. Ted Stevens Hires Super-Lawyer Brendan Sullivan*, WASHINGTONIAN.COM, July 1, 2007, http://www.washingtonian.com/articles/capitalcomment/4457.html.

Brady violations could occur under these conditions, it is not difficult to understand how *Brady* violations occur in run-of-the-mill criminal cases. As Judge Sullivan stated upon dismissing the charges against Stevens,

> [t]he fair administration of justice ... should not depend on who represents the [d]efendant, whether an FBI agent blows a whistle, a new administration, a new attorney general[,] or a new trial team. The fair administration of justice depends on the Government meeting its obligations to pursue convictions fairly and in accordance with the Constitution.[26]

Despite the nationwide epidemic of *Brady* violations and the magnitude of injustice that results from such misconduct, the criminal justice system has not developed effective reforms to provide a remedy for defendants or appropriately sanction prosecutors for concealing evidence favorable to the defense. Even though the disclosure duty is violated regardless of whether the nondisclosure is negligent or intentional, the most egregious *Brady* violations occur when prosecutors purposely withhold information that they know is clearly and unquestionably favorable to the defense. Shockingly, this level of willful misconduct—exemplified by the blatant arrogance of the Stevens prosecutors—is generally not met with harsh sanctions.

This Article presents two alternative proposals to remedy and deter intentional *Brady* violations. First, pursuant to the broad discretionary authority granted to courts to sanction *Brady* violations and other discovery misconduct, trial judges should redress intentional *Brady* violations with a strongly worded jury instruction. The proposed "*Brady* instruction" would inform the jury that the government intentionally withheld evidence favorable to the defense and would permit the jury to consider the impact of the *Brady* misconduct as part of its deliberations. While legal scholars have proposed the use of jury instructions to redress *Brady* violations, the instruction proposed here is designed to be a punitive sanction that would deter *Brady* violations by making the cost of *Brady* noncompliance too high for errant prosecutors.

Alternatively, even if the trial judge does not elect to impose a *Brady* instruction sanction, the defense is entitled to adduce facts at trial to show that the government intentionally suppressed vital evidence favorable to the defense. Under well-established evidentiary principles, the fact that a litigant has purposely withheld or destroyed key evidence gives rise to the inference that the litigant knows his case is weak and knows his cause will not prevail if the adverse evidence is presented at trial. This "consciousness of a weak case" inference falls under the broad umbrella of relevant circumstantial evidence. Applied in the context of intentional *Brady* violations, the defendant is entitled to show that the prosecutor—the person in the best possible position to assess the merits of the government's case—was conscious of the weakness of the government's case and purposely withheld evidence that bolstered the defense or undermined the government's case. In a criminal case in which the government always has the burden of proof,

---

26   Transcript of Motion Hearing, *supra* note 4, at 6–7. Stevens's lead defense lawyer, Brendan Sullivan, likewise lamented to the trial judge, "[A]s hard as you try to make it fair[,] ... we are no match for corrupt prosecutors if they want to hide information known only to them or they want to present false testimony." *Id.* at 30.

the "consciousness of a weak case" inference signals to the jury that the government's case is compromised and can provide the jury with reasonable doubt. Just as criminal courts have traditionally allowed the government to prove the defendant's consciousness of guilt with evidence that the defendant attempted to suppress or destroy incriminating evidence, the government's intentional *Brady* misconduct is likewise admissible to prove the prosecutor's "consciousness of a weak case." Accordingly, the trial court's exclusion of *Brady* misconduct evidence against the government is both counter to long-standing evidentiary principles and constitutes an arbitrary denial of a criminal defendant's constitutional right to present all relevant evidence in defense of criminal charges.

Part II of this Article discusses the foundation and scope of the *Brady* doctrine and some of the complex litigation and reform issues that arise under the current state of the law. Part III discusses the use of a *Brady* instruction as an appropriate sanction for the government's intentional suppression of material exculpatory and impeachment evidence. Part IV discusses the application of the "consciousness of a weak case" inference created by the intentional withholding of *Brady* evidence. Part V applies both the *Brady* instruction sanction and the "consciousness of a weak case" inference to the case of *United States v. Shelton*.[27]

II: The *Brady* Doctrine

More than seventy years ago, the Supreme Court stated that the role of the prosecution in the criminal justice system

> is not that it shall win a case, but that justice shall be done ... . [W]hile [the prosecutor] may strike hard blows, he is not at liberty to strike foul ones. It is as much his duty to refrain from improper methods calculated to produce a wrongful conviction as it is to use every legitimate means to bring about a just one.[28]

To that end, in *Brady v. Maryland*,[29] the Court held that "suppression by the prosecution of evidence favorable to an accused violates due process when the evidence is material to either guilt or punishment, irrespective of good faith or bad faith of the prosecutor."[30] The purpose of the *Brady* rule is to ensure that the defendant receives a fair trial in which all relevant evidence of guilt and innocence is presented to enable the fact-finder to reach a fair and just verdict.[31] The *Brady* doctrine imposes an affirmative duty on the trial prosecutor to investigate, preserve, and disclose favorable information located in the prosecutor's files, as well as information in the

---

27   983 A.2d 363 (D.C. 2009).

28   Berger v. United States, 295 U.S. 78, 88 (1935).

29   373 U.S. 83 (1963).

30   *Id.* at 87–88.

31   *Id.*

possession of any member of the prosecution team.[32] Recently, in *Banks v. Dretke*,[33] the Court reiterated that the "essential elements" of a *Brady* claim are suppression of "favorable" and "material" evidence that results in prejudice to the defense.

A. "Favorable" Evidence

The *Brady* disclosure duty is triggered by an initial determination that the government has evidence that is "favorable" to the accused. The Court has held that "favorable" evidence includes both exculpatory evidence that negates guilt and impeaching evidence that undermines the government's case.[34] Both exculpatory and impeachment evidence are treated equally under the *Brady* doctrine. According to a recent national report, most state and federal statutes and court rules designed to implement the *Brady* disclosure duty fail to delineate the different types of information subject to disclosure under *Brady*.[35] As a result, the scope of the constitutional disclosure duty has been developed in the volume of state and federal court cases decided in the forty-five years since the Court's decision in *Brady*.

1. Exculpatory Evidence

Evidence is deemed to be exculpatory if it tends to negate guilt, diminish culpability, support an affirmative defense (duress, self-defense),[36] or if the evidence could potentially reduce the severity of the sentence imposed. The clearest example of exculpatory evidence is information uncovered during the criminal investigation indicating that someone other than the defendant

---

32   Kyles v. Whitley, 514 U.S. 419, 436–38 (1995).

33   540 U.S. 668, 669 (2004).

34   United States v. Bagley, 473 U.S. 667, 675–76 (1985).

35   LAURAL L. HOOPER, JENNIFER E. MARSH & BRIAN YEH, FED. JUDICIAL CTR., TREATMENT OF *BRADY V. MARYLAND* MATERIAL IN UNITED STATES DISTRICT AND STATE COURTS' RULES, ORDERS, AND POLICIES 12–14, 25–38 (2007) [hereinafter *Brady* Report], *available at* http://www.fjc.gov/public/pdf.nsf/lookup/bradyma2.pdf/$file/bradyma2.pdf. *But see* DIST. MASS. LOCAL R. 116.2(A), *available at* http://www.mad.uscourts.gov/ general/pdf/combined01.pdf (providing a definition for "exculpatory evidence"); DIST. OF KAN., GENERAL ORDER OF DISCOVERY AND SCHEDULING, *available at* http://www.ksd.uscourts.gov/forms/index.php (listing specific categories of *Brady* evidence subject to disclosure); TASK FORCE ON WRONGFUL CONVICTIONS, N.Y. STATE BAR ASS'N, FINAL REPORT OF THE NEW YORK STATE BAR ASSOCIATION'S TASK FORCE ON WRONGFUL CONVICTIONS 23–24 (2009), *available at* http://www.nysba.org/Content/ContentFolders/ TaskForceonWrongfulConvictions/FinalWrongfulConvictionsReport.pdf (discussing various categories of *Brady* evidence).

36   *E.g.*, Arline v. State, 294 N.E.2d 840 (Ind. Ct. App. 1973) (ordering new trial in self-defense case where prosecution failed to disclose the weapon used by decedent during altercation); Branch v. State, 469 S.W.2d 533 (Tenn. Crim. App. 1969) (finding error where defendant claimed self-defense to murder charges and gave uncorroborated testimony that the knife-wielding decedent aggressively attacked him immediately before the fatal encounter, prosecution suppressed evidence that a citizen gave police a knife purportedly belonging to the decedent that was found at or near the crime scene, and prosecutor argued in closing that there was no evidence to support the defense claim that the decedent was armed); *Ex Parte* Mowbray, 943 S.W.2d 461 (Tex. Crim. App. 1996) (mandating a new trial where prosecution intentionally withheld a blood spatter expert's report supporting the defense's theory that the victim committed suicide).

committed the crime.[37] Exculpatory evidence must be disclosed even if the prosecutor does not find the information credible or has other contradictory information.[38] Exculpatory evidence includes third-party confessions, victim or complainant recantations, eyewitness identifications of another person as the perpetrator, as well as descriptions of the perpetrator that are inconsistent with the defendant's appearance.[39] Also included is forensic evidence that affirmatively excludes the defendant as the culprit or fails to link the defendant to crime scene evidence (including physical evidence such as DNA, fingerprints, or bite marks).[40] The government is also required to disclose evidence regarding the existence of other suspects who either have a *modus operandi* similar to the charged offense or who had the motive, means, and opportunity to commit the charged offense.[41]

---

37   *E.g.*, State v. Landano, 637 A.2d 1270 (N.J. Super. Ct. App. Div. 1994) (involving a *Brady* violation where defendant charged with killing a police officer and prosecutor concealed fingerprint and ballistics tests, which showed that the gun used to kill the police officer was used in an earlier armed robbery committed by state's chief witness).

38   *See, e.g.*, People v. Jackson, 637 N.Y.S.2d 158, 161–62 (N.Y. Sup. Ct. 1995) ("Even if the Assistant District Attorney 'had valid reasons to consider this witness to be unreliable, [he] should nonetheless have provided the defense with this important exculpatory information which was clearly *Brady* material.'" (quoting People v. Robinson, 133 A.D.2d 859, 860 (N.Y. App. Div. 1987))); People v. Springer, 122 A.D.2d 87, 88 (N.Y. App. Div. 1986) (reversing the conviction and dismissing the indictment where prosecutor intentionally destroyed surveillance videos relevant to the sole critical issue even though the prosecutor claimed that he believed "the photographs showed nothing that would be of value in an identification procedure").

39   *See, e.g.*, People v. Thomas, 71 A.D.2d 839 (N.Y. App. Div. 1979) (finding a *Brady* violation during prosecution of two African-American defendants where government suppressed witness statements describing perpetrators as two white males); *see also* cases cited *infra* note 44.

40   *See, e.g.*, Padgett v. State, 668 So. 2d 78 (Ala. Crim. App. 1995) (finding a *Brady* violation where prosecutor failed to timely disclose new blood test results revealing that the blood sample used to match defendant's DNA to the crime was inconsistent with defendant's blood); Nelson v. Zant, 405 S.E.2d 250, 252 (Ga. 1991) (reversing capital murder conviction where government knowingly suppressed exculpatory FBI forensic report which had concluded that the hair sample used to connect the defendant to the victim was "not suitable for significant comparison purposes"); *see also* Innocence Project, Know the Cases: Roy Brown, http://www.innocenceproject.org/Content/425.php (last visited Feb. 2, 2010). At trial, the government introduced testimony of an expert witness that a bite mark on the victim's body was "entirely consistent" with the defendant and suppressed the fact that another expert had examined the bite mark before trial and excluded the defendant as the source. *Id.*

41   *E.g.*, Bloodsworth v. State, 512 A.2d 1056 (Md. 1986) (reversing a murder conviction based on brutal rape and murder of small girl where government suppressed a police report discussing another suspect who was found in the woods near the body, had a red spot of blood on his shirt when interviewed by police, and who had the underwear of a small girl in his car); State v. Munson, 886 P.2d 999, 1003 (Okla. Crim. App. 1994) (reversing a conviction based in part on the failure to disclose existence of another prime suspect with a similar modus operandi who was seen at the scene of the crime on the night of the murder); Cook v. State, 940 S.W.2d 623, 625 (Tex. Crim. App. 1996) (finding that the government did not reveal the existence of a person who had a motive to kill victim and had threatened to kill victim shortly before her death).

2. Impeachment Evidence

Impeachment evidence encompasses a broad range of information that would expose weaknesses in the government's case or cast doubt on the credibility of government witnesses. The Supreme Court has observed that "[t]he jury's estimate of the truthfulness and reliability of a given witness may well be determinative of guilt or innocence, and it is upon such subtle factors as the possible interest of the witness in testifying falsely that a defendant's life or liberty may depend."[42] Impeachment evidence is especially valuable in a case "when it impugns the testimony of a witness who is critical to the prosecution's case."[43] Impeachment evidence includes any information regarding a witness's prior convictions, biases, prejudices, self-interests, or any motive to fabricate or curry favor with the government. Impeachment evidence also consists of prior inconsistent statements of the witness and any prior failure of the witness to identify the defendant.[44] The government must also disclose information that casts doubt on the ability of the witness to accurately perceive, recall, or report the facts related to the witness's testimony, including mental instability, substance abuse, memory loss, or any other physical or mental impairment.[45]

In addition, *Brady* impeachment evidence includes any positive or negative inducements used to motivate a witness to testify on behalf of the government. Inducements include promises, rewards, financial payments, and benefits, as well as threats, intimidation, and other forms of coercion used to secure testimony.[46] Chief among government inducements are offers of favor-

---

42   Napue v. Illinois, 360 U.S. 264, 269 (1959).

43   Silva v. Brown, 416 F.3d 980, 987 (9th Cir. 2005); *see, e.g.*, Carriger v. Stewart, 132 F.3d 463 (9th Cir. 1997) (granting habeas relief in murder case where state failed to disclose evidence that government's star witness was known to be a "pathological liar" and a "prolific career burglar"); *Cook*, 940 S.W.2d at 625 (finding a *Brady* violation where government failed to disclose that witness was believed to be "mentally and emotionally unstable" and "a pathological liar").

44   *E.g.*, Commonwealth v. Ellison, 379 N.E.2d 560 (Mass. 1978) (failing to disclose initial pretrial statements of co-defendants, which did not name the defendant as one of the participants in the crime and which contradicted their subsequent statements and trial testimony); State v. Landano, 637 A.2d 1270 (N.J. Super. Ct. App. Div. 1994) (finding a *Brady* violation where prosecutor suppressed evidence showing that the only eyewitness to the crime specifically eliminated the defendant as the perpetrator during pretrial photo identification procedure); Texas v. Adams, 768 S.W.2d 281 (Tex. Crim. App. 1989) (suppressing crime victim's pretrial statement that was diametrically opposed to her trial testimony as well as her failure to identify defendant at police line-up).

45   *E.g.*, Jean v. Rice, 945 F.2d 82, 87 (4th Cir. 1991) (failing to disclose records of the victim's hypnosis, which were used to enhance the victim's testimony); United States v. Sterba, 22 F. Supp. 2d 1333, 1334–40 (M.D. Fla. 1998) (failing to disclose "severe credibility problems" of key government witness, including a history of mental health and substance abuse, as well the witness' prior guilty plea to lying under oath in a case that led to the arrest of an innocent man); *Munson*, 886 P.2d at 1003 (failing to reveal the fact that testimony of one witness was hypnotically induced).

46   *E.g.*, Banks v. Dretke, 540 U.S. 668, 700 (2004) (vacating death sentence and remanding case based in part on prosecution's nondisclosure of financial payments, cooperation agreements, and other impeachment evidence involving the state's two chief witnesses); Guerra v. Johnson, 90 F.3d 1075, 1078–80 (5th Cir. 1996) (finding that prosecutor intimidated and threatened three juvenile witnesses to identify the defendant as the shooter); State v. Spurlock, 874 S.W.2d 602 (Tenn. Crim. App. 1993) (ordering a new trial

able treatment regarding the witness's own criminal matters. Commonly, the government must enter into plea deals, cooperation agreements, or immunity agreements with witnesses in order to secure their testimony against the defendant. The government violates *Brady* if the government does not disclose the existence of these agreements. This nondisclosure is exacerbated if the government allows these cooperating witnesses to falsely testify that no agreement with the government exists.[47] In some cases, prosecutors have even affirmatively used the witness's perjured testimony regarding the nonexistence of an agreement to bolster the credibility of the witness during closing arguments.[48] In addition to agreements, the *Brady* doctrine also mandates disclosure of both pending criminal cases and prosecutable offenses committed by any witness and known by the government.[49] The existence of these unresolved criminal cases could provide the witness with the expectation of favorable treatment even in the absence of a formal agreement with the government.[50]

B. "Material" Evidence

Non-disclosure of favorable evidence does not result in a *Brady* violation, however, unless the defense can establish that the withheld evidence was material or prejudicial to the defendant.[51] In *Kyles*, the Court held that the *Brady* materiality requirement is satisfied by a showing that "the favorable evidence could reasonably be taken to put the whole case in such a different light as to

---

where prosecution failed to disclose that a key witness implicated the defendant on recorded interview only after being promised release from jail); *Ex parte* Brandley, 781 S.W.2d 886 (Tex. Crim. App. 1989) (finding that key government witnesses were threatened, choked, and manhandled by law enforcement officers prior to falsely implicating the defendant in the murder).

47   *See, e.g., Napue*, 360 U.S. 264; Pyle v. Kansas, 317 U.S. 213 (1942); United States v. Kelly, 35 F.3d 929, 932–37 (4th Cir. 1994) (finding that prosecutor allowed key government witness to give unimpeached testimony that was either patently false or seriously misleading and which severely undercut the defense); United States v. Kojayan, 8 F.3d 1315, 1322 (9th Cir. 1993) (failing to disclose government informant status and cooperation agreement with a key government witness); People v. Jimerson, 652 N.E.2d 278 (Ill. 1995) (finding error where government witness who had agreement with government for reduced charges committed perjury in denying the existence of any inducement to testify at trial and prosecutor failed to correct the false testimony); People v. Perkins, 686 N.E.2d 663, 669 (Ill. App. Ct. 1997) (finding prosecution's failure to correct government witness' false testimony that he received no favorable treatment in exchange for his testimony was intentional where "[o]ne of the prosecutors who tried this case participated in the earlier negotiations" with the witness to secure testimony).

48   *See, e.g., Banks*, 540 U.S. at 700–02; *Carriger*, 132 F.3d at 470.

49   *E.g., Landano*, 637 A.2d at 1271 ("[The] State suppressed evidence that its principal identification witness was under investigation for having ties with organized crime, and was suspected of having engaged in loan sharking and money laundering, and further, that on the very day his earlier tentative identification of defendant became positive, he was questioned about whether he paid illegal gratuities to [murdered police officer] where defendant was convicted of killing a police officer.").

50   *See, e.g.*, Giglio v. United States, 405 U.S. 150, 154–55 (1972).

51   The Court has made clear that the materiality determination is synonymous with the prejudice analysis. *See* Kyles v. Whitley, 514 U.S. 419, 435–40 (1995); United States v. Bagley, 473 U.S. 667, 674–75 (1985).

undermine confidence in the verdict." [52] The defense must also show that, in light of the evidence of guilt adduced by the prosecution at trial, the withheld evidence was noncumulative, highly probative evidence that could have had an impact on the determination of guilt. [53] The Court has stated that the defendant does not have to prove that he would have been acquitted had the *Brady* evidence been presented at trial but must show that, in the absence of the evidence, he did not receive a fair trial "resulting in a verdict worthy of confidence." [54]

C. Intentional *Brady* Violations

From the inception of the *Brady* doctrine, the Court has consistently stated that the intent of the prosecutor is not determinative of whether a *Brady* violation has occurred. In *Agurs*, the Court stated:

> [n]or do we believe the constitutional obligation is measured by the moral culpability, or the willfulness, of the prosecutor. If evidence ... of innocence is in his file, he should be presumed to recognize its significance ... . If the suppression of evidence results in constitutional error, it is because of the character of the evidence, not the character of the prosecutor. [55]

Though *Brady* violations can occur when a prosecutor accidentally or negligently withholds favorable information, intent is not completely irrelevant. In determining whether to impose sanctions for *Brady* violations—particularly whether dismissal of the charges is warranted—courts frequently rely on the presence or absence of evidence that the government acted with purpose or in bad faith.

Intentional violations occur when the prosecutor fully understands the *Brady* disclosure duty, is aware of the existence of favorable evidence in the government's possession, appreciates the exculpatory or impeachment value of the evidence, but intentionally withholds the evidence to gain a tactical advantage in the litigation. Too frequently, the intentional withholding of *Brady* evidence has resulted in gross miscarriages of justice in state and federal courts across the country. As in the case of Ted Stevens, courts have found intentional *Brady* violations based on the blatant and egregious conduct of prosecutors who knowingly used perjured testimony at

---

52   *Kyles*, 514 U.S. at 435.

53   *E.g.*, United States v. Jackson, 345 F.3d 59, 73–74 (2d Cir. 2003) (finding no *Brady* violation where suppressed impeachment evidence merely furnished an additional basis on which to impeach a witness whose credibility had already been shown to be questionable); United State v. Gil, 297 F.3d 93, 103 (2d Cir. 2002) (holding that materiality standard is less likely met where evidence of guilt is overwhelming).

54   *Kyles*, 514 U.S. at 434. If the defendant does not make this showing, reviewing courts commonly rule that, although it was error for the prosecutor to suppress favorable evidence, in light of the evidence of guilt adduced at trial, the suppressed evidence was not material.

55   United States v. Agurs, 427 U.S. 97, 110 (1976).

trial,[56] deliberately shielded exculpatory evidence from disclosure,[57] purposely altered or falsified evidence,[58] and knowingly exploited the absence of the very evidence the state withheld.[59]

The impact of intentional *Brady* violations on the determination of guilt or innocence in criminal cases is significant. One early study found that *Brady* violations played a major role in the wrongful conviction of more than one-third of the prisoners later exonerated by DNA evidence.[60] Even in the absence of DNA evidence, postconviction reinvestigations of old cases have also resulted in the exoneration of many prisoners wrongly convicted in trials tainted by intentional *Brady* violations.[61] Most disturbing, however, is the undisputed fact that intentional *Brady* violations

---

56   *E.g.*, Brown v. Borg, 951 F.2d 1011, 1015 (9th Cir. 1991) ("The prosecutor's actions in this case are intolerable. Possessed of knowledge that destroyed her theory of the case ... she kept the facts secret ... and then presented testimony in such a way as to suggest the opposite of what she alone knew to be true."); People v. Perkins, 686 N.E.2d 663, 669 (Ill. App. Ct. 1997); State v. Spurlock, 874 S.W.2d 602, 620 (Tenn. Crim. App. 1993) ("[T]he prosecution made every effort to suppress the recordings. The prosecution knew if the material contained on these tapes was conveyed to defense counsel ... the credibility of [the prosecution's chief witness] would have been completely destroyed [and the defendant would have been acquitted].").

57   *E.g.*, United States v. Kojayan, 8 F.3d 1315, 1323 (9th Cir. 1993) (stating that the prosecutor "did everything he could to keep the defense from learning" of the existence and nature of the government's cooperation agreement with witness); State v. Landano, 637 A.2d 1270, 1287 (N.J. Super. Ct. App. Div. 1994) (holding that "it is apparent that the State deliberately concealed evidence" implicating the government's two witnesses in the crime the defendant was charged with committing).

58   *E.g.*, United States v. Sterba, 22 F. Supp. 2d 1333, 1334–40 (M.D. Fla. 1998) (finding that where the government "knowingly disguise[ed] the identity of a government witness and deceptively" allowed the witness to testify under oath and give a false name "[t]he conception and implementation of this plan was intentional and calculated to deprive the defense of its right of confrontation. It almost succeeded."); Price v. State Bar, 30 Cal. 3d 537 (Cal. 1982) (convicting defendant after prosecutor altered date and time of taxi cab receipt to place defendant at the scene of the crime, destroyed original evidence supporting the defendant's alibi, and introduced the false evidence at trial).

59   *E.g.*, Arline v. State, 294 N.E.2d 840, 844 (Ind. Ct. App. 1973) (finding that despite pretrial receipt of knife used by decedent to cut defendant during fatal encounter in self-defense case, prosecutor "exaggerated [the knife's] absence in evidence," strongly suggesting to the jury that the knife did not exist); *Ex parte* Mowbray, 943 S.W.2d 461, 465 (Tex. Crim. App. 1996) (finding that prosecutors "engaged in a deliberate course of conduct" to keep exculpatory evidence away from defense counsel).

60   In a study of the first seventy-four DNA-based exonerations, the Innocence Project found that the initial wrongful conviction was caused, in part, by *Brady* violations. Specifically, the study found that 37% of the cases involved the suppression of exculpatory evidence, 25% involved the knowing use of false testimony, and 11% involved the undisclosed use of coerced witness testimony. BARRY SCHECK, JIM DWYER & PETER NEUFELD, ACTUAL INNOCENCE (1st ed. 2001); Innocence Project, Understand the Causes, http://www.innocenceproject.org/understand/ (follow the Forensic Science Misconduct and Government Misconduct hyperlinks) (last visited Feb. 2, 2010); *see also* CTR. FOR PUB. INTEGRITY, HARMFUL ERROR: INVESTIGATING AMERICA'S LOCAL PROSECUTORS 91–100 (2003) [hereinafter HARMFUL ERROR] (citing twenty-eight cases where prosecutorial misconduct, most commonly *Brady* violations, significantly contributed to the wrongful conviction of people who were later exonerated).

61   *E.g.*, Carter v. Rafferty, 621 F. Supp. 533, 548 (D.N.J. 1985) (granting habeas relief in the case of famed boxer Rubin "Hurricane" Carter where the prosecution purposely misrepresented the results of a polygraph test given to its key witness in order to manipulate the witness into abandoning his recantation and giving

have resulted in near executions in numerous death penalty cases.[62] In one case, after twelve years on death row, a man came within fifteen hours of execution before being granted habeas relief.[63] More recently, Delma Banks was strapped to a gurney in the Texas death chamber and was within ten minutes of execution when the Supreme Court granted a stay of execution and ruled that he was entitled to habeas relief based on *Brady* violations that infected his trial.[64] There have been numerous other reversals of capital convictions based on intentional *Brady* violations.[65] In the overwhelming majority of capital murder cases, once *Brady* violations are exposed, the government opts not to retry the case,[66] or the formerly condemned prisoners are

---

the inculpatory testimony at the retrial that placed defendants at the scene of the crime); People v. Ramos, 614 N.Y.S.2d 977, 982–84 (N.Y. App. Div. 1994) (finding that defense was denied powerful impeachment evidence in child sexual assault trial where the government argued that the child's extensive knowledge of sexual activity stemmed from sexual abuse by defendant but suppressed documents showing that child had an unusually advanced knowledge and sophistication regarding sexual matters well before the alleged sexual assault); *Ex parte* Adams, 768 S.W.2d 281, 293 (Tex. Crim. App. 1989) (finding in murder case that "the State was guilty of suppressing evidence favorable to the accused, deceiving the trial court during [the] trial, and knowingly using perjured testimony").

62   *E.g.*, JAMES S. LIEBMAN, JEFFREY FAGAN & VALERIE WEST, A BROKEN SYSTEM: ERROR RATES IN CAPITAL CASES, 1973–1995 5 (2000), *available at* http://www2.law.columbia.edu/instructionalservices/liebman/liebman_final.pdf (documenting *Brady* violations in 16% to 19% of capital cases); DEBATING THE DEATH PENALTY (Hugo Adam Bedau & Paul G. Cassell eds., 2004) (finding that 35 out of 350 wrongful convictions based on wrongful suppression of evidence); Ames Alexander & Liz Chandler, *Errors, Inequities Often Cloud Capital Cases in the Carolinas*, CHARLOTTE OBSERVER, Sept. 10, 2000, at 1A (stating that in "North Carolina since 1977[,] … [c]ourts have overturned more than 25 death sentences, many based on findings that prosecutors hid evidence, made improper arguments, or broke other rules").

63   Brown v. Wainwright, 785 F.2d 1457, 1458–59 (11th Cir. 1986) (vacating 1974 capital murder convictions upon finding that the prosecutor failed to step forward when the only witness at trial to place the defendant at the scene of the crime and the only witness to testify to incriminating admissions by the defendant falsely testified that he had not received immunity from the government in exchange for his testimony).

64   *See* ANGELA J. DAVIS, ARBITRARY JUSTICE: THE POWER OF THE AMERICAN PROSECUTOR 133 (2007); *see also* Banks v. Dretke, 540 U.S. 668 (2004).

65   *E.g.*, State v. Moore, 969 So. 2d 169 (Ala. Crim. App. 2006) (vacating death sentence and ordering a new trial due to nondisclosure of exculpatory information in FBI reports); Commonwealth v. Smith, 615 A.2d 321, 322–25 (Pa. 1992) (reversing death sentence upon finding that the government's "intentional suppression" of extremely "exculpatory physical evidence" while arguing in favor of the death sentence on direct appeal "constitute[s] prosecutorial misconduct such as violat[ing] all principles of justice and fairness").

66   *See* Guerra v. Johnson, 90 F.3d 1075, 1078–80 (5th Cir. 1996); Brown v. Wainwright, 785 F.2d 1457, 1458–59 (11th Cir. 1986); Padgett v. State, 668 So. 2d 78 (Ala. Crim. App. 1995); Nelson v. Zant, 405 S.E.2d 250, 252–53 (Ga. 1991); Taylor Bright, *Guilty Until Proven Innocent?*, BIRMINGHAM POST-HERALD, Dec. 14, 2001, *available at* http://www.patrickcrusade.org/execution_2_5.htm (reporting that after court ordered a new trial, District Attorney decided not to prosecute former condemned prisoner); Jingle Davis & Mark Curriden, *Condemned Man Is Freed After Repeal*, ATLANTA J. CONST., Nov. 7, 1991, at E2 (reporting that prosecutors decided they could not re-prosecute Gary Zant following the reversal of his capital murder conviction for the rape and murder of a six-year-old girl); Sydney P. Freedberg, *Freed from Death Row*, ST. PETERSBURG TIMES, July 4, 1999, at 8A, *available at* http://www.sptimes.com/News/70499/State/yesangry.shtml (stating that after twelve years in prison, on remand, the prosecutor's office opted not

acquitted at a retrial.[67] In other cases, death row inmates are given parole,[68] allowed to plead guilty to a lesser charge and released based on time served,[69] or sentenced to life without parole.[70] Rarely are formerly condemned prisoners resentenced to death after the conviction is reversed based on *Brady* misconduct.[71] Thus *Brady* violations, if undetected and undeterred, could result in the death of people who, under the law, deserve either life or liberty.

D. Litigating *Brady* Violations

Under the current state of the law, several factors make pretrial litigation and adjudication of *Brady* violations extremely difficult. First, pretrial disclosure of *Brady* evidence is governed by an unrealistic "honor code" system. Prosecutors are in exclusive possession of the evidence collected during the criminal investigation. They alone are entrusted to exercise their discretion and make a subjective evaluation of the case to determine whether there is favorable evidence

---

to retry the case against Joseph Greene Brown and the former death row inmate was released after over five years on death row); *Mexican Long Held in Texas Murder Wins His Freedom*, N.Y. TIMES, Apr. 17, 1997, at A16, *available at* http://www.nytimes.com/1997/04/17/us/mexican-long-held-in-texas-murder-wins-his-freedom.html (reporting that Ricardo Aldape Guerra had spent over fifteen years in prison and, at one point, came within three days of execution); *see also* Chevel Johnson, *No Retrial in New Orleans Killing*, ASSOCIATED PRESS ONLINE, Jan. 9, 1999 (stating that the youngest person ever sentenced to death row at age seventeen, Shareef Cousins, was given a new trial in a case involving *Brady* violations, but the sentence was ultimately reversed on other grounds because prosecutors did not have enough evidence to pursue the case a second time).

67   *See, e.g.*, *Moore*, 969 So. 2d at 185; State v. Munson, 886 P.2d 999, 1003 (Okla. Crim. App. 1994); Richard L. Fricker, *State Falters in Retrial of Escaped Con*, A.B.A. J., June 1995, at 38 (describing the acquittal of Adolph Munson at re-trial after ten years on death row); Death Penalty Info. Ctr., Exonerations: Jury Acquits Former Death Row Inmate of All Charges, http://www.deathpenaltyinfo.org/exonerations-jury-acquits-former-death-row- inmate-all-charges (last visited Jan. 19, 2010) (describing the acquittal of a man on all counts in third trial after nearly ten years on death row).

68   *Ryan Issues Blanket Clemency*, CHI. TRIB., Jan. 12, 2003, at 14, *available at* http://www.chicagotribune.com/media/flash/2003-01/6205191.pdf. Madison Hobley, who spent eighteen years in prison, most of it on death row, was pardoned by Governor Ryan in Illinois during his mass purge of prisoners on death row. *Id.*

69   Dave Von Drehle, *Murder Suspects Will Plead Guilty, Leave Court Free*, SAN JOSE MERCURY NEWS, Jan. 15, 1988, at 2G, *available at* 1988 WLNR 468637 ("U.S. District Judge George Carr found that detectives deliberately suppressed evidence that might have pointed to the innocence of Jent and Miller ... [and that] [t]he State of Florida demonstrated 'a callous and deliberate disregard for the fundamental principles of truth and fairness that underlie our criminal system.'").

70   *Smith*, 615 A.2d 321; Death Penalty Info. Ctr., Innocence Cases: 1984–1993, http://www.deathpenaltyinfo.org/innocence-cases-1984-1993 (last visited Feb. 5, 2010) (describing the ultimate disposition in the *Smith* case where defendant's original death sentence was reduced to life in prison).

71   *See* Ken Armstrong & Maurice Possley, *The Verdict: Dishonor*, CHI. TRIB., Jan. 10, 1999, at 1, *available at* http://www.chicagotribune.com/news/nationworld/chi-dptrialerror-special,0,632955.special. Of the sixty-seven death row inmates granted new trials due to *Brady* violations, twenty-four were freed because charges were dropped, they were acquitted at re-trial, or they were given full pardons. Three plead guilty in return for their immediate release from prison, twenty-five others were convicted again (but did not receive the death penalty), and only four returned to death row. *Id.*

188 | Criminal Evidence

subject to disclosure.[72] Even if the prosecutor determines that favorable evidence exists, it is the prosecutor who is entrusted with determining when, if at all, that evidence will be disclosed to the defense. Lower courts charged with enforcing the *Brady* mandate have repeatedly ruled that *Brady* does not require pretrial disclosure even when the government is aware of the favorable evidence prior to trial.[73] Prosecutors need only disclose favorable evidence to the defense "in time for its effective use at trial."[74] Thus, prosecutors can (and do) purposely withhold *Brady* evidence until the last possible minute (and beyond) with full knowledge that the vital information in their exclusive possession could significantly bolster the defense case or seriously undermine the government's case.[75]

Moreover, prosecutors are also empowered to make the pretrial determination of whether a particular piece of favorable evidence meets the materiality standard. Many courts have observed that the impact-based analysis used to determine materiality is unworkable as a pretrial standard for prosecutors attempting in good faith to comply with *Brady*.[76] The Supreme Court also acknowledged as much in *Agurs*, when it stated that the pretrial materiality determination is "inevitably imprecise" and recognized that "the significance of an item of evidence can seldom be predicted accurately until the entire record is complete."[77] As Justice Marshall stated in his opinion in *Bagley*, rather than promoting full and complete disclosure, the materiality standard legitimizes nondisclosure by allowing prosecutors to determine which favorable evidence is material and will be disclosed and which favorable evidence is not material and can be constitutionally withheld.[78]

While the Court has expressed its hope that "the prudent prosecutor will resolve doubtful questions in favor of disclosure," there is no assurance that all prosecutors will heed the Court's caution and err on the side of disclosure.[79] Other than the unenforceable "honor code," there are few incentives for prosecutors to comply with *Brady* because there is no meaningful judicial

---

72   *See, e.g.*, *Moore*, 969 So. 2d at 175 (noting that the prosecutor testified that "he never intended to withhold exculpatory information and that he did not consider some of the materials to be exculpatory").

73   *See* United States v. Coppa, 267 F.3d 132, 135 (2d Cir. 2001); United States v. Presser, 844 F.2d 1275, 1283 n.9 (6th Cir. 1988) ("[D]isclosure in time for effective use at trial is all that the *Brady* doctrine requires."); WAYNE R. LAFAVE ET AL., CRIMINAL PROCEDURE 1143 (5th ed. 2009).

74   *Coppa*, 267 F.3d at 142.

75   *E.g.*, Padgett v. State, 668 So. 2d 78 (Ala. Crim. App. 1995) (finding that a mid-trial four-day delay prior to disclosure of exculpatory information constitutes a *Brady* violation); People v. Jackson, 637 N.Y.S.2d 158 (N.Y. Sup. Ct. 1995) (discussed *supra* notes 134–137 and accompanying text); Page v. Roberts, 611 N.Y.S.2d 214 (N.Y. App. Div. 1994) (granting new trial when district attorney kept exculpatory statement for over a year until the day prior to the start of trial when witness could no longer be found).

76   *See, e.g.*, United States v. Safavian, 233 F.R.D. 12, 16 (D.D.C. 2005) ("Most prosecutors are neither neutral (nor should they be) nor prescient, and any such judgment [on materiality] necessarily is speculative on so many matters that simply are unknown and unknowable before trial begins ... .").

77   United States v. Agurs, 427 U.S. 97, 108 (1976).

78   *See* United States v. Bagley, 473 U.S. 667, 700 (1985) (Marshall & Brennan, JJ., dissenting).

79   *Agurs*, 427 U.S. at 108; *see also* Kyles v. Whitley, 514 U.S. 419, 439 (1994).

oversight of the process.[80] The trial judge does not know what evidence exists in the government's files, what evidence the prosecutor has withheld, or why the prosecutor has unilaterally decided not to disclose certain evidence to the defense. Prosecutors do not have to keep a log of the evidence in the case. Nor are prosecutors required to seek an *in camera* review of potential *Brady* evidence prior to making the decision that evidence will not be disclosed. As a result, the trial court has only a limited ability to make a pretrial determinations of whether the prosecutor has fully complied with *Brady*.

The lack of judicial oversight of *Brady* disclosure decisions is compounded by the fact that, absent extraordinary circumstances, it is very likely that the defense will never learn of the existence of favorable evidence and cannot, therefore, seek leave of the court to compel disclosure. The very nature of the act of withholding evidence ensures that the defense does not know that such evidence is contained in the prosecutor's nonpublic case file. In the overwhelming majority of cases, the defense learns of *Brady* evidence by pure accident.[81] Sometimes the defense stumbles upon a lay witness who possesses the information.[82] Alternatively, as in the Stevens case, members of the prosecution team belatedly come forward and disclose the existence of favorable evidence. The constitutional right of criminal defendants to acquire exculpatory evidence for

---

80   LAFAVE, *supra* note 73, § 24.3(b) at 1147–48 (noting that trial courts are reluctant to review prosecutor's files to determine whether they have undisclosed *Brady* material); *cf.* Pennsylvania v. Ritchie, 480 U.S. 39, 59 (1987) (limiting authority of the court to impose in camera review for disputed *Brady* material).

81   United States v. Arnold, 117 F.3d 1308 (11th Cir. 1997) (stating that exculpatory contents of a tape recording were obtained by defense post-trial when prosecutor inadvertently sent transcripts of the tapes to the defense attorney); *see* McMillian v. State, 616 So. 2d 933, 945 (Ala. Crim. App. 1993) (involving a tape recording inadvertently given to defense counsel wherein the sheriff and other law enforcement officers were threatening the government's star witness to force him to falsely implicate McMillan); Armstrong & Possley, *supra* note 71 (discussing the case of James Richardson who was wrongly convicted in Florida and served twenty-one years in prison before exculpatory evidence was "stolen from a prosecutor's office by a man dating the prosecutor's secretary"; also reporting on other cases wherein exculpatory evidence was discovered after "a judge directed the U.S. marshal to seize the prosecutors' documents, or because newspapers sued under the Freedom of Information Act, or because of anonymous tips, conversations accidentally overheard or papers spied in a prosecutor's hand"); *see also* Joseph R. Weeks, *No Wrong Without a Remedy: The Effective Enforcement of the Duty of Prosecutors to Disclose Exculpatory Evidence*, 22 OKLA. CITY U. L. REV. 833, 869 (1997) (stating that judicial opinions involving *Brady* violations "appear in the reporters only because the criminal defendant, deprived of any knowledge of exculpatory evidence by the prosecutor's refusal to disclose it, was nevertheless able my some other means (often highly fortuitous) to discover its existence").

82   *E.g.*, Banks v. Dretke, 540 U.S. 668, 675 (2004) (noting that "long suppressed evidence came to light" after attorneys for death row defendant received affidavits from government witnesses detailing that, contrary to trial testimony, and the representations of prosecutors, witnesses were coached, paid for their testimony and threatened with incarceration if they did not provide false inculpatory testimony against the defendant); State v. Moore, 969 So. 2d 169, 173 (Ala. Crim. App. 2006) (stating that defense was alerted to exculpatory information by witness who contacted defense counsel after trial); State v. Cousin, 710 So. 2d 1065, 1067 n.2 (La. 1998) (stating that the defense learned "through an anonymous communication" during the penalty phase of a capital case that eyewitness who identified defendant as murderer previously told police that she could not identify the gunman because she did not get a good look at him, was not wearing her glasses, and could only see shapes and patterns).

use at trial should not depend on sheer luck or the industriousness of the defense investigative team. As the Court recognized in *Banks*: "[a] rule thus declaring 'prosecutor may hide, defendant must seek,' is not tenable in a system constitutionally bound to accord defendants due process."[83]

E. *Brady* Reform Proposals

Numerous *Brady* reforms have been proposed by jurists and legal scholars over the past two decades to address the myriad of problems associated with the enforcement of the *Brady* mandate. Notwithstanding these reform efforts, the *Brady* disclosure duty has become one of the most unenforced constitutional mandates in the criminal justice system.[84] According to several major national studies, *Brady* violations in state and federal courts have been continuous and persistent over the forty-five years since the *Brady* decision.[85] One landmark study found that during the first thirty-six years after *Brady*, 381 homicide cases across the country were reversed due to *Brady* violations.[86] A 2009 study further confirmed that *Brady* violations continue to be an on-going problem.[87]

Reform efforts to combat *Brady* violations are frequently stalled by non-reformers (usually prosecutors and former prosecutors) who persist in the assertion that *Brady* violations are an extremely rare occurrence.[88] Given the hundreds of thousands of cases prosecuted annually across the country, they argue that the number of reported *Brady* violations is *de minimis*.[89]

---

83   *Banks*, 540 U.S. at 696.

84   *See* BENNETT L. GERSHMAN, PROSECUTORIAL MISCONDUCT §§ 5:1, 5:3 (2d ed. 2002) ("Nondisclosure of exculpatory evidence by prosecutors ... account[s] for more miscarriages of justice than any other type of prosecutorial infraction.").

85   *See* Armstrong & Possley, *supra* note 71; *see also* HARMFUL ERROR, *supra* note 60, at i (reporting that a three-year study of over eleven thousand reported opinions involving prosecutorial misconduct (including *Brady* violations) found that over two thousand cases led to reversal of conviction and twenty-eight defendants were later exonerated); *see also* Bill Moushey, *Win at All Costs*, PITTSBURGH POST-GAZETTE, Nov. 22, 1998, at A1, *available at* http://www.post-gazette.com/win/ (documenting, in a ten-part series, a two-year investigation into prosecutorial misconduct (including *Brady* violations) across the country).

86   Armstrong & Possley, *supra* note 71.

87   TASK FORCE ON WRONGFUL CONVICTIONS, *supra* note 35, at 26 (citing numerous New York cases involving *Brady* violations and stating that "despite the clarity and longevity of the *Brady* rule, a sampling of recent published or otherwise available decisions show such conduct still occurs").

88   Randall D. Eliason, *The Prosecutor's Role: A Response to Professor Davis*, AM. U. CRIM. L. BRIEF, Fall 2006, at 15, 17–18, *available at* http://www.wcl.american.edu/journal/clb/documents/CriminalLawBrief-VolIIIssuel-Fall2006.pdf?rd=1 (commenting that given the number of prosecutors in the country (over 35,000) and the number of criminal cases prosecuted each year (twenty million in state courts and 70,000 in federal courts), the incidences of prosecutorial misconduct are extremely small).

89   *Id.* at 20 (dismissing statistics from Harmful Error study which found serious prosecutorial misconduct (including *Brady* violations) in a total of two thousand cases (average of sixty-six cases per year) as statistically insignificant because "sixty-six cases per year out of several million is a vanishingly small number. Even if the true incidence of prosecutorial misconduct, reported and unreported, were 500 times greater than what was found[,] ... it would still involve only about one percent of all serious criminal cases filed in a year." (emphasis omitted)).

Moreover, the small minority of prosecutors committing *Brady* violations are far outnumbered by the overwhelming number of ethical prosecutors committed to ensuring that justice is done and that all *Brady* evidence is properly disclosed to the defense.[90] Thus, non-reformers maintain that *Brady* violations are more "episodic" than "epidemic"[91] and that many of the proposed reforms unnecessarily interfere with the independence of the prosecution function. These proposed reforms, they contend, would curtail the broad discretion that prosecutors must have to perform their jobs effectively and free from undue judicial interference.[92] Non-reformers also steadfastly contend that when *Brady* violations do infrequently occur, the wrongful actions of these few errant prosecutors are adequately addressed by the current mechanisms in place within prosecution offices and the external sanctioning power of the state bar.[93]

The "epidemic" versus "episodic" debate, of course, misses the point. The problem with *Brady* violations is not the frequency with which they occur, it is the fact that they occur at all. By definition, *Brady* violations involve the withholding of material evidence that has a significant adverse impact on the accuracy of the guilt/innocence determination. Thus, even one *Brady* violation is too many when such misconduct can and does result in a wrongful conviction or a sentence of death. Just as it would be unacceptable to allow a preventable or curable disease to go untreated simply because it affects only a small number of people each year, we cannot allow *Brady* violations—even if infrequent and isolated—to remain "untreated." In the fair and just criminal justice system we strive to create, we should have zero tolerance for these preventable errors.

Against the backdrop of this ongoing reform debate, legal scholars and jurists have proposed a wide array of reforms. Some of the proposed reforms would simply mandate better enforcement and utilization of existing laws and standards. For example, many have proposed more aggressive use of the state bar disciplinary process to punish prosecutors for violating the professional standards that make it unethical for them to withhold favorable evidence.[94] While the use of

---

90   *Id.* at 17 ("[T]he vast majority of prosecutors are dedicated public servants striving to do a difficult job in an ethical and honorable way.").

91   HARMFUL ERROR, *supra* note 60, at 110 (providing a copy of a letter from an Oregon prosecutor stating that prosecutorial misconduct is "episodic" and not "epidemic," and stating that "prosecutors continue to be subject to the harshest sanctions on those truly rare occasions when they violate their oaths").

92   TASK FORCE ON WRONGFUL CONVICTIONS, *supra* note 35, at 36 n.11. In response to a proposal to have a mandatory *Brady* conference with the trial judge in criminal cases, dissenting Task Force members argued that "mandating a pretrial conference in every case for judicial review of the prosecutor's file impermissibly allows the judicial branch to intrude into the exclusive domain of a member of the executive branch, the prosecutor, in the advocacy determination of what to disclose and when; weakens the adversary system and the vigorous performance of the prosecutor's function." *Id.* (citations omitted).

93   Eliason, *supra* note 88, at 21 (citing the state bar disciplinary process and the Department of Justice Office of Professional Responsibility as powerful sources of "professional repercussions" for errant prosecutors who engage in misconduct).

94   *E.g.*, CAL. COMM'N ON THE FAIR ADMIN. OF JUSTICE, FINAL REPORT 77 (Gerald Uelmen ed., 2008) (discussing judicial reluctance to refer lawyers for professional discipline for *Brady* misconduct), *available at* http://www.ccfaj.org/documents/CCFAJFinalReport.pdf; *see also* TASK FORCE ON WRONGFUL

the state bar disciplinary process is a viable option, numerous studies and reports have shown that prosecutors are generally not referred for disciplinary action for *Brady* misconduct, and it is extremely rare that such a referral results in professional discipline.[95] Thus, without greater enforcement of ethical rules, reliance on the state bar disciplinary process to deter and punish *Brady* misconduct is misplaced.

A second category of proposed *Brady* reforms would require major changes in existing law to implement. Legal scholars have proposed subjecting prosecutors to civil liability for their actions by eliminating or reducing the broad immunity prosecutors currently enjoy.[96] In light of recent Supreme Court precedent upholding prosecutorial immunity, this proposal is not likely to succeed.[97] Other reform proposals, including the use of criminal sanctions and contempt citations against prosecutors, are also very rarely used.[98] Moreover, the effectiveness of these

---

CONVICTIONS, *supra* note 35, at 28–29; Robert P. Mosteller, *The Duke Lacrosse Case, Innocence, and False Identifications: A Fundamental Failure to "Do Justice"*, 76 FORDHAM L. REV. 1337 (2007); Paul J. Speigelman, *Prosecutorial Misconduct in Closing Argument: The Role of Intent in Appellate Review*, 1 J. APP. PRAC. & PROCESS 115, 170 (1999) (noting that of forty-five recent federal cases where convictions were reversed due to "intentional misconduct and extensive criticism of prosecutors' conduct, not one court ordered a prosecutor disciplined or referred a prosecutor for discipline"); Ellen Yaroshefsky, *Wrongful Convictions: It Is Time to Take Prosecution Discipline Seriously*, 8 UDC/DCSL L. REV. 275 (2004) (advocating the creation of an independent commission to examine wrongful convictions cases and enforce disciplinary rules for prosecutors).

95   Richard A. Rosen, *Disciplinary Sanctions Against Prosecutors for* Brady *Violations: A Paper Tiger*, 65 N.C. L. REV. 693 (1987) (discussing the results of a nation-wide empirical study of state bar disciplinary actions for *Brady* violations and finding few prosecutors are referred and even fewer are actually disciplined); *see* ABA Comm. on Ethics and Prof'l Responsibility, Formal Op. 09–454 (2009) (discussing Rule 3.8(d) of the Model Rules of Professional Conduct, which defines the scope of the prosecutor's duty to make timely disclosure of exculpatory evidence under ethics rules independent of the constitutional disclosure duty); *see also* HARMFUL ERROR, *supra* note 60, at 81–90. *But see* Amended Findings of Fact, Conclusions of Law and Order of Discipline, N.C. State Bar v. Nifong, No. 06 DHC 35 (Disciplinary Hearing Comm'n July 24, 2007), *available at* http://www.ncbar.gov/Nifong%20Final%20Order.pdf. In the high profile investigation of allegations that an African-American woman was gang-raped at an off-campus party hosted by college students who were members of the Duke University lacrosse team, the prosecutor violated *Brady* by suppressing exculpatory DNA results that excluded the defendants and by instructing a doctor to withhold such evidence from his medical report. The prosecutor was held in contempt following an independent investigation. *Id. See generally* Angela J. Davis, *The Legal Profession's Failure to Discipline Unethical Prosecutors*, 36 HOFSTRA L. REV. 275 (2007).

96   Walker v. City of New York, 974 F.2d 293, 301 (2d Cir. 1992) (finding that the district attorney's failure to train employees on their *Brady* obligations and "the duty not to lie or persecute the innocent" subjected her to liability under 28 U.S.C. § 1983); *see also* Yarris v. County of Delaware, 465 F.3d 129, 132, 137 (3d Cir. 2006) (following reprosecution of defendant by the same prosecutor who "allegedly slammed his case file against the courtroom wall, screamed at [the defendant Yarris], 'Motherfucker, you'll never leave the county alive!' and spat in Yarris's face," and finding that prosecutor's conduct in destroying exculpatory evidence was not covered by absolute immunity).

97   Van de Kamp v. Goldstein, 129 S. Ct. 855 (2009) (holding that the chief deputy district attorney and district attorney were entitled to absolute prosecutorial immunity).

98   Weeks, *supra* note 81, at 879 (dismissing as improbable "the alternative of criminal sanctions for civil rights violations" due to *Brady* violations). *But see* United States v. Jones, 609 F. Supp. 2d 113 (D. Mass.

measures depends on the willingness of individual judges and prosecution offices to take punitive measures against errant prosecutors. Judges have been reluctant to take action, and as one scholar noted, "[p]rosecutors simply will not prosecute other prosecutors."[99]

Similarly, some scholars and jurists have proposed amending Rule 16, the criminal discovery provision of the Federal Rules of Criminal Procedure, to include mandatory disclosure of *Brady* evidence.[100] Included among the provisions of the potential Rule 16 amendment is a requirement that prosecutors make timely disclosure of all favorable evidence, irrespective of any pretrial materiality determination they have made.[101] This *Brady* amendment to Rule 16 was vigorously opposed by the Department of Justice and ultimately defeated.[102]

The final category of *Brady* reforms involves administrative changes within prosecution offices to enhance compliance with the *Brady* disclosure duty. These reforms include improved training,

---

2009) (requiring the government to show cause why the court should not impose sanctions for *Brady* violation after the prosecutor failed to turn over the inconsistent statements of a police officer). Also, some state court rules and statutes expressly recognize contempt as a discovery sanction. *E.g.*, LA. CODE CRIM. PROC. ANN. Art. 729.5(B) (2003) (stating that willful violation of discovery rule "shall be deemed to be a constructive contempt of court"); *see also* ARK R. CRIM. P. 19.7(b); FLA. R. CRIM. P. 3.220(n)(2); HAW. R. PENAL P. 16(9)(ii); ILL. SUP. CT. R. 415(g)(ii); MINN. R. CRIM. P. 9.03(8); VT. R. CRIM. P. 16.2(g)(2); WASH. SUP. CT. CRIM. R. 4.7(h)(7)(ii).

99   Weeks, *supra* note 81, at 879.

100   *Brady* Report, supra note 35, at 6. The proposed "*Brady* Amendment" to Rule 16 provided:

> Exculpatory or Impeaching Information. Upon a defendant's request, the government must make available all information that is known to the attorney for the government or agents of law enforcement involved in the investigation of the case that is either exculpatory or impeaching. The court may not order disclosure of impeachment information earlier than 14 days before trial.

Id. at 23 app. A (emphasis omitted) (providing the text of the *Brady* Amendment); *see also* Am. Coll. of Trial Lawyers, *Proposed Codification of Disclosure of Favorable Information Under Federal Rules of Criminal Procedure 11 and 16*, 41 AM. CRIM. L. REV. 93 (2004).

101   Am. Coll. of Trial Lawyers, *supra* note 100, at 113.

102   *See Brady* Report, supra note 35, at 4. In opposition to the Rule 16 amendment, the Department of Justice (DOJ) argued before the Judicial Conference Advisory Committee on the Rules of Criminal Procedure ("Advisory Committee") that no codification of the *Brady* rule was warranted because the *Brady* disclosure obligation was already "clearly defined" under existing law. *Id.* at 6–7. Although DOJ opposed the amendment, DOJ representatives revised the Department of Justice Manual for United States Attorneys in an effort to more clearly define the scope of the *Brady* disclosure duty under existing law. *See also id.* at 6–7, 43 app. D (providing the text of United States Attorney's Policy Regarding Disclosure of Exculpatory and Impeachment Information, § 9–5.001). Following the Ted Stevens litigation, the federal judge who presided over the case, Judge Emmet Sullivan, wrote a letter to the Judicial Conference Advisory Committee urging reconsideration of the *Brady* Amendment to Rule 16. Letter from Judge Emmett G. Sullivan to Judge Richard C. Tallman, Chair, Judicial Conference Advisory Committee on the Rules of Criminal Procedure (Apr. 28, 2009) (on file with author). Judge Sullivan wrote: "An amendment to Rule 16 that requires the government to produce all exculpatory information to the defense serves the best interests of the court, the prosecution, the defense, and ultimately the public." *Id.*

the creation of detailed guidelines on *Brady* disclosure,[103] and administrative procedures to track and catalog *Brady* evidence to make disclosure more efficient.[104] Advocates of these internal reforms suggest that such measures would combat confusion over the scope of the disclosure duty and avoid carelessness or negligent nondisclosures.

While some of these proposals could potentially curb *Brady* violations when nondisclosure is the result of carelessness or negligence, it is unlikely that many of these measures would be sufficient to curb the more egregious, intentional *Brady* violations committed by prosecutors determined to "win at all costs." In numerous cases, nondisclosure is the result of a deliberate choice to withhold evidence that the prosecutor knows is subject to disclosure under *Brady*. The intentional, purposeful nature of the *Brady* violation in those cases is illustrated by the varied excuses articulated by prosecutors in defense of their decisions to conceal *Brady* evidence. For example, prosecutors have defended their intentional suppression of *Brady* evidence on the grounds that (1) the witness that provided an exculpatory pretrial statement was not, in the prosecutor's mind, a credible witness;[105] (2) the exculpatory evidence was not subject to disclo-

---

103   CAL. COMM'N ON THE FAIR ADMIN. OF JUSTICE, *supra* note 94, at 87–91 (recommending that State Attorney General formulate and disseminate a written office policy to govern *Brady* compliance, create a "*Brady* list" of impeachment evidence against law enforcement officers/witnesses, and hold training programs on *Brady* disclosure compliance); *see also* JOHN F. TERZANO ET AL., IMPROVING PROSECUTORIAL ACCOUNTABILITY: A POLICY REVIEW 3–6 (2009), *available at* http://www.thejusticeproject.org/wp-content/uploads/pr-improving-prosecutorial- accountability1.pdf (recommending increased training for line prosecutors on *Brady* disclosure duties); TASK FORCE ON WRONGFUL CONVICTIONS, *supra* note 35, at 37–38 (recommending same).

104   ABA CRIM. JUSTICE SECTION'S AD HOC INNOCENCE COMM. TO ENSURE THE INTEGRITY OF THE CRIM. PROCESS, ACHIEVING JUSTICE: FREEING THE INNOCENT, CONVICTING THE GUILTY 1, 103 (2006) ("In light of the prosecutor's on-going obligation to disclose Brady material and the desire to provide all defendants with fair trial, prosecutors should establish guidelines and procedures for turning Brady evidence over to the defense and for receiving that information from its partners and agents, including police departments and laboratories."); CAL. COMM'N ON THE FAIR ADMIN. OF JUSTICE, *supra* note 94, at 12–16; TERZANO ET AL., *supra* note 103, at 7–8; Peter A. Joy, Brady *and Jailhouse Informants: Responding to Injustice*, 57 CASE W. RES. L. REV. 619, 641 (2007) (advocating for the head prosecutor to provide "clearer guidance that ensures complete compliance with *Brady*," and proposing "open file" discovery to give defense attorneys greater access to discoverable materials); *see also* Robert P. Mosteller, *Exculpatory Evidence, Ethics, and the Road to the Disbarment of Mike Nifong: The Critical Importance of Full Open-File Discovery*, 15 GEO. MASON L. REV. 257 (2008).

105   In *United States v. Harrington*, the government failed to disclose the existence of a witness who contradicted the trial testimony of the government's star witness and implicated that witness as the true perpetrator of the crime. The government claimed that it did not disclose the witness's pretrial statements to the defense because the government did not find the witness to be credible. In reversing the murder conviction, the trial judge stated:

> [B]oth the identity and the testimony of Ms. Gibson, unquestionably, without any doubt, should have been turned over to the defense well in advance of trial … . [T]he information about Ms. Gibson's identity and her information and her grand jury testimony and her police statement was withheld from the defense consciously, deliberately, and as a tactic, because I think the Government probably recognized it as not particularly favorable to their case, at a minimum, and may have recognized it as something that could be mischievous in the hands of a good defense lawyer

sure because it would have been inadmissible at trial;[106] (3) the exculpatory statement was not *Brady* evidence because the same statement also contained other inculpatory information;[107] or (4) the prosecutor did not personally believe the witness's pretrial inconsistent statement was credible.[108] It is difficult to accept that prosecutors in possession of evidence that falls squarely within the scope of the *Brady* doctrine could honestly form the professional opinion that disclosure was not mandated for any of these reasons. As one court stated in rejecting a prosecutor's incredulous excuse for suppressing blatantly exculpatory evidence, "Such an explanation is laughable, offering it an effrontery. It does not wash, nor do we believe for a moment that the prosecutor could have been so simple-minded as to have believed it would."[109]

Thus, although the wide array of reform proposals that have been advanced by jurists and legal scholars have the potential to greatly improve the disclosure of *Brady* evidence, comprehensive *Brady* reform must also include measures specifically designed to address intentional, purposeful violations. The two proposals discussed in Parts III and IV below recommend the presentation of evidence of the *Brady* misconduct at trial either as a punitive sanction or as relevant circumstantial evidence of the government's consciousness of a weak case.

... . In my opinion, it was patently disclosable, not a debatable point ... . [T]he government's attempt to explain away the evidence that is, in my view obviously favorable to the accused, is unavailing largely for the reason pointed out by [defense counsel]: It's not for [the prosecutor] to decide whether Ms. Gibson would be believable ... it's for the jury to decide ... .

Transcript of Hearing on Post-Trial Motion to Dismiss at 9–10, 13, United States v. Harrington, No. 2007-CF1–22855 (D.C. Sup. Ct. Apr. 17, 2009) (on file with author) (emphasis added).

106   Branch v. State, 469 S.W.2d 533 (Tenn. Crim. App. 1969) (arguing that a lack of proper chain-of-custody excused the prosecutor's failure to disclose the knife purportedly belonging to decedent that was given to the police shortly after a fatal brawl).

107   Gwen Filosa, *Review Board Clears Prosecutor*, TIMES-PICAYUNE, Sept. 25, 2004, at B1 (discussing statements made by Roger Jordan, a seasoned prosecutor in New Orleans, during a state bar disciplinary proceeding related to his prosecution of Shareef Cousins for capital murder); *see also* State v. Cousins, 710 So. 2d 1065, 1066–67 (La. 1998) (discussed *supra* note 66).

108   Lindsey v. King, 769 F.2d 1034, 1040 (5th Cir. 1985) ("As for the prosecutor's attempted explanation of his refusal to produce the police report[,] ... [i]t was for the jury, not the prosecutor, to decide whether the contents of an official police record were credible, especially where—as here—they were in the nature of an admission against the state's interest in prosecuting Lindsey. On such grounds as these, prosecutors might, on a claim that they thought it unreliable, refuse to produce any matter whatever helpful to the defense."); *see, e.g.*, Shelton v. United States, 983 A.2d 363 (D.C. 2009) (discussed *infra* Part IV).

109   *King*, 769 F.2d at 1040.

Chapter 3: Key Terms and Discussion Questions

Key Terms

Brady Rule: from the holding in *Brady v. Maryland*; where the prosecution must disclose favorable information to the defense in a criminal case if requested to do so

Credibility: the quality of being convincing or believable

Culpability: responsibility for wrongdoing or a crime

Due Process: deals with the administration of justice; Fifth Amendment clause that holds that the government cannot arbitrarily deny life, liberty, or property in a legal manner

Exculpatory: evidence tending to clear an individual from alleged fault or guilt

Impeachment: challenging a witness's testimony in a trial; process of calling into question the credibility of a witness during a trial

Inculpatory: evidence tending to accuse an individual of fault or guilt

Inference: a conclusion reached on the basis of logic and reasoning as a result of circumstantial evidence

Jury Instruction: an instruction given by the judge to a jury at the end of a trial to advise the jury of the law that applies to the case and the manner in which the jury should conduct its deliberations

Litigation: taking legal action against a party

Sanction: a penalty for disobeying a law or rule

Suppression: the act of preventing evidence from being admissible

Discussion Questions

1. What was the holding in *Brady v. Maryland*?
2. Which is the better proposal to curb *Brady* violations: a jury instruction or the defense introducing evidence at trial of the prosecution's *Brady* violations? Why?
3. What is considered "favorable" evidence?
4. Does the prosecutor's intent factor in when the court determines whether a *Brady* violation occurred?
5. Why is litigation in *Brady* violations so difficult?

Evidentiary Basics

Relevancy. *Gardetto v. Mason*, 201 F.3d 447, (Cir. 1999)

Before BRORBY, LUCERO and WEST, [**] Circuit Judges.
ORDER AND JUDGMENT [*]
BRORBY.

Ann Gardetto appeals the district court's admission of evidence in her civil rights suit against Eastern Wyoming College (the college) and Roy Mason. She contends evidence concerning her acts of rude and abrasive behavior was improperly admitted in her suit against the college for the violation of her First Amendment rights of free speech and free association.

This appeal arises out of a judgment rendered after retrial pursuant to a reversal by this court in Gardetto v. Mason, 100 F .3d 803 (10th Cir. 1996.) In that case, Ms. Gardetto brought federal civil rights claims against her employer, Eastern Wyoming College and her supervisor, Mr. Roy Mason, pursuant to 42 U.S.C. § 1983. She claimed she was demoted and suspended for eleven days with pay in retaliation for her constitutionally protected public criticism of Mr. Mason and the policies of the college. She also brought claims under Wyoming law for defamation against Mr. Mason and against the college for breach of good faith and fair dealing. The jury returned a verdict in favor of Ms. Gardetto on the defamation claim, but found she had failed to prove damages resulting from the defamation. The jury returned a verdict in favor of the defendants on the duty of good faith and fair dealing claim and on the First Amendment claims. After receiving the verdict, Ms. Gardetto appealed to this court, claiming the trial court gave incorrect jury instructions and further erred by admitting evidence of her rude and abrasive behavior. This court concluded the jury instructions were improper because they allowed the jury to determine whether the speech in

Court of Appeals for the Tenth Circuit, "Gardetto v. Mason, 100 F.3d 803 (10th Cir. 1996)," 1996.

question was protected by the First Amendment. Because this court vacated the decision and remanded for a new trial based on the erroneous jury instructions, we did not address the evidentiary ground for appeal. See id. at 807–08, 818.

Prior to the second trial, Ms. Gardetto filed a motion in limine to exclude testimony concerning alleged verbal confrontations with a variety of persons both before and after the original case was tried. Her request was denied. The jury once again returned a verdict for the defense on the First Amendment issues. Ms. Gardetto now appeals that ruling and contends the trial court erred by admitting evidence of her behavior both before and after the first trial. We exercise jurisdiction pursuant to 28 U.S.C. § 1291 and affirm.

Background

The background of this case is fully set forth in our prior opinion, Gardetto, 100 F.3d at 808–10. The facts pertinent to this appeal are summarized as follows.

Ms. Gardetto began working for the college in 1974 as the Minority and Community Counselor. She was eventually promoted to Director of Non-Traditional Student Services/Special Services. In that position, she developed programs designed to provide support and guidance to adult students and supervised twelve peer counselors and four staff members at the Adult Reentry Center. When Mr. Mason first became the president of Eastern Wyoming College in 1990, he found Ms. Gardetto's work praiseworthy. However, his opinion of Ms. Gardetto's performance changed, and in April 1993, Ms. Gardetto was demoted and her staff was taken away. In May 1993 she was suspended for eleven days with pay. Ms. Gardetto filed suit against Mr. Mason and the college claiming these actions had been taken against her in retaliation for her criticisms of Mr. Mason and the college in violation of her constitutionally protected right to free speech.

Ms. Gardetto asserted she was suspended in retaliation for the following instances of the exercise of her right to free speech: (1) Ms. Gardetto spoke out against a program instituted by the college's Board of Trustees to reduce the work force of the college; (2) she opposed the termination of a fellow employee at the Adult Reentry Center under the reduction in work force program; (3) she supported three outside candidates for positions on the Board of Trustees; (4) she expressed her criticism of the Center's reorganization to Dr. Gonzales, a guest speaker at the college; (5) she accused Mr. Mason of holding himself out as a Ph.D. when he had not obtained that degree; (6) she called for a vote of "no confidence" in Mr. Mason by the faculty association.

In the prior appeal, we determined that four of the six asserted incidents of speech were entitled to First Amendment protection [1] and concluded the trial court erred by allowing the jury to determine which of these speech incidents were protected by the First Amendment. Gardetto, 100 F.3d at 815–16, 818. [2] Accordingly, we vacated the judgment below and remanded for a new trial on Ms. Gardetto's First Amendment claims.

Before the second trial, Ms. Gardetto filed a motion in limine seeking to exclude evidence of her abrasive attitude and poor ability to work with others. Ms. Gardetto argued this evidence was only being offered to attack her character, was not relevant to the First Amendment question and was therefore inadmissible under Federal Rules of Evidence 402. She also argued the evidence was more prejudicial than probative and should be excluded under Fed.R.Evid. 403. After hearing argument on the motion, the district court determined the evidence of her post-suspension behavior was relevant in light of Ms. Gardetto's contention the administration had continued to take retributive action against her following the first trial by deciding to leave her in her present position without secretarial support. As to the evidence of her behavior prior to the suspension, the court referred to a footnote in our previous opinion in this case and concluded this court had resolved the admissibility issue by indicating that the jury might find the evidence relevant in determining whether the defendants would have reached the same decision in the absence of the protected speech.

At the trial, the defense presented witnesses who testified Ms. Gardetto was a difficult person with whom to work and gave specific examples of her rude and abrasive behavior on numerous occasions both before and after the first trial. In addition, Mr. Mason testified he suspended Ms. Gardetto because she had acted in violation of the college's policies and against his directions when she applied for a grant to support the Adult Reentry Center without first obtaining his signature on the application, and when she failed to try to find grant money for another employee at the Center. He testified that her act of insubordination was the final act that triggered his decision to take action against Ms. Gardetto, but that this action had been taken in light of her history of behavior as an employee. Mr. Mason testified he was aware of her history of conflicts with other staff members and had received complaints concerning her behavior by staff members and by her supervisors. He had contemplated either suspending or dismissing her in the past and had warned her many times to change her behavior. The defendants also presented evidence that the members of the Board of Directors had been aware of Ms. Gardetto's behavior problems and had taken them into consideration in deciding to support the suspension.

The jury once again returned a verdict in favor of the defense. Ms. Gardetto appeals the evidentiary ruling of the court and asks for a new trial.

Waiver and Standard of Review

The defendants contend Ms. Gardetto's evidentiary objections were not preserved on appeal because she failed to make contemporaneous objections to the admission of this evidence. Ms. Gardetto contends her motion in limine was sufficient to preserve these issues for appellate review because the court ruled the evidence was admissible as a matter of law.

A. Objections

Although several witnesses testified concerning her rude behavior and conflicts with others, the record on appeal reveals Ms. Gardetto only made contemporaneous objections to the relevancy of Mr. Guido Smith's testimony. The court overruled Ms. Gardetto's particular objection to the testimony of Mr. Guido Smith, the former president of the college, concerning the means she used to contact Mr. Smith following her misuse of the college's postage meter to send political literature. Ms. Gardetto also objected to the relevancy of Mr. Smith's testimony concerning a dispute between Ms. Gardetto and another employee, Ms. Kathy France. The court overruled this objection, but allowed Ms. Gardetto a continuing objection to the relevancy of Mr. Smith's testimony concerning the dispute with Ms. France. Ms. Gardetto failed to make any objections based on Fed.R.Evid. 403, [3] which allows the trial court to exclude evidence that is unfairly prejudicial.

B. Standards

... .

C. Effect of the Motion in Limine on the Preservation of the Issues and Standard of Review.

A motion in limine is sufficient to preserve an objection to the admission of evidence, and thereby avoid application of the narrow, plain error standard of review, only if a three part test is satisfied. Pandit, 82 F.3d at 380 (citing Green Constr. Co. v. Kansas Power & Light Co., 1. F.3d 1005, 1013 (10th Cir.1993)). "To overcome the claim of waiver for failure to contemporaneously object, we must satisfy ourselves that (1) the matter was adequately presented to the district court; (2) the issue was of a type that can be finally decided prior to trial; and (3) the court's ruling was definitive." Id.; see also United States v. Mejia-Alarcon, 995 F.2d 982, 987–88 (10th Cir.) (establishing the rule), cert. denied, 510 U.S. 927 (1993). Because the issues of relevancy and prejudicial effect of the evidence were not of the type that could be finally decided prior to trial, we conclude the motion in limine was not sufficient to preserve the objections not raised at trial.

1. Sufficiency of the Motion in Limine to Preserve the Objections Based on Relevancy.

First, Ms. Gardetto's objection as to the relevancy of the evidence of her rude and unprofessional behavior did not raise an issue that was of the type that could be finally decided prior to the trial. Fed.R.Evid. 401 provides: " 'Relevant evidence' means evidence having any tendency to make the existence of any fact that is of consequence to the determination of the action more probable or less probable than it would be without the evidence." The relevancy of each piece of evidence concerning Ms. Gardetto's behavior was contingent upon other facts produced at trial concerning damages and the reasons for the actions taken against Ms. Gardetto. Only after hearing these facts, as introduced at trial, could the trial court make an informed decision as to the relevancy of Ms. Gardetto's unprofessional acts. For example, Mr. Mason testified that he was aware of conflicts between Ms. Gardetto and other staff members, and that he had taken these conflicts into consideration when he decided to suspend Ms. Gardetto. Mr. Mason testified that he knew about a particular conflict between Ms. Gardetto and Ms. Lynnea Bartlett. Ms. Bartlett testified concerning her conflict with Ms. Gardetto. The relevancy of this testimony to the issue of whether Ms. Gardetto had been suspended in violation of her Constitutional rights was apparent only after Mr. Mason testified he knew about this conflict and had taken Ms. Gardetto's conflicts with other staff members into consideration when he decided to suspend Ms. Gardetto. Thus, it was not the type of issue that could have been finally decided prior to trial. Therefore, except for the relevancy of Mr. Smith's testimony, which we review for abuse of discretion because Ms. Gardetto made a contemporaneous objection to that testimony, we review the court's determination as to the relevancy of the evidence of Ms. Gardetto's acts of rude and unprofessional behavior for plain error only.

2. Sufficiency of the Motion in Limine to Preserve the Rule 403 Objection.
Second, Ms. Gardetto's motion in limine did not preserve her objection concerning the prejudicial nature of the evidence. Federal Rule of Evidence 403 states, "[a]lthough relevant, evidence may be excluded if its probative value is substantially outweighed by the danger of unfair prejudice, confusion of the issues, or misleading the jury, or by considerations of undue delay, waste of time, or needless presentation of cumulative evidence." When the court performs the balancing test under Rule 403, the admissibility of the evidence depends on the specific facts adduced at trial and upon the context of those facts at trial. The balancing of the probative value and prejudicial effect of the evidence can only be properly performed after the trial court assesses the evidence introduced in the trial prior to its admission. See Mejia-Alarcon, 995 F.2d at 987–88 & n. 2; Green Constr. Co., 1. F.3d at 1013. Thus, this issue was not one that could be finally decided prior to trial and the motion was not sufficient to preserve it on appeal.

D. Conclusion.
Because the court was unable to properly assess the relevancy and the prejudicial effect of the evidence of Ms. Gardetto's rude and unprofessional behavior prior to trial, these issues were not of the type that could be fairly decided prior to trial and were not preserved by the motion in limine. Thus, even if Ms. Gardetto was correct in her belief that the court was ruling on the admission of the evidence of her rude and unprofessional behavior as a matter of law, making the ruling definitive, she nevertheless should have objected when the evidence was introduced because the issue did not satisfy the second inquiry set forth in Pandit. As most objections are dependent upon the trial context, and are waived if not renewed, we again strongly suggest counsel renew all objections when the evidence is introduced. Mejia-Alarcon, 995 F.2d at 988. [5] Because the motion in limine did not preserve the objections to the evidence based on Rules 402 and 403, we review the admission of the evidence of her rude and abrasive behavior for plain error only. Because Ms. Gardetto contemporaneously objected to the relevancy of Mr. Smith's testimony, we review the court's determination concerning the relevancy of Mr. Smith's testimony under the abuse of discretion standard.

Admission of the Evidence

Having determined the proper standards of review over the alleged evidentiary errors, we now turn to our substantive analysis of the court's introduction of the evidence of Ms. Gardetto's rude and abrasive behavior. Ms. Gardetto contends the court erred by failing to independently assess the admissibility of the evidence. She further contends the evidence was admitted only to attack her character, and thus was not relevant to any material issue in the case, was more prejudicial than probative, and was admitted in contravention of the Rules of Evidence.

Under the Federal Rules of Evidence, "[a]ll relevant evidence is admissible," except as limited by the Federal Rules and other laws. Fed.R.Evid. 402. "Evidence which is not relevant is not admissible." Id.

Thus, the threshold to admissibility is relevance. The scope of relevancy is bounded only by the liberal standard of Rule 401, which provides that evidence is relevant if it has any tendency to make the existence of any fact that is of consequence to the determination of the action more probable or less probable than it would be without the evidence. As commentators have noted, Rule 401's definition of relevancy incorporates notions of both materiality and probativity. As for materiality, under Rule 401 a fact is "of consequence" when its existence would provide the fact-finder with a basis for making some inference, or chain of inferences, about an issue that is necessary to a verdict.

McVeigh, 153 F.3d at 1190 (quotation marks and citation omitted). Only a minimal degree of probability is required. Id. The evidence is sufficiently probative if it tends to show the existence of the asserted fact is "more ...--probable than it would be without the evidence." Id. (quotation marks and citations omitted.) Even if the evidence meets the relevancy standard under Rule 401, and is thus tentatively admissible under Rule 402, Rule 403 allows the court to exclude the evidence if it determines "its probative value is substantially outweighed" by other factors. Fed.R.Evid. 403. Those factors include the "danger of unfair prejudice," "confusion of the issues," and "misleading the jury." Id.

A. Reliance on the Previous Opinion.

... .

B. Relevancy

Ms. Gardetto contends the court erred by admitting the evidence of her behavior because it was not relevant to any material issue in the case. Ms. Gardetto's argument concerning the relevancy of the evidence fails because the evidence of her behavior was relevant to the only issues remaining in the case on retrial.

In a First Amendment retaliation case, after the court has determined the speech involves a matter of public concern and the employee's interest in making the speech outweighs the employer's interest in preventing disruption of its public service under the Pickering/Connick test, the employee must show that the constitutionally protected conduct or speech "was a substantial factor or a motivating factor" in the employer's decision to take the detrimental action against the employee. Gardetto, 100 F.3d at 811 (citing Mt. Healthy City Sch. Dist. Bd. of Educ. v. Doyle, 429 U.S. 274 (1977)). The burden is then placed upon the employer to show " 'by a preponderance of evidence that it would have reached the same decision ... even in the absence of the protected conduct.' " Gardetto, 100 F.3d 15 811 (quoting Mt. Healthy, 429 U.S. at 287.) In the prior appeal, we determined four of the speech incidents were matters of public concern, and, because the defendants had failed to show any evidence of disruption resulting from those instances of protected speech, the balance of interests tipped in favor of Ms. Gardetto. Gardetto, 100 F.3d at 815–16. Consequently, the central issues remaining in the second trial were whether the defendants had taken action against Ms. Gardetto in retaliation for her protected speech, if such action would have been taken in the absence of that speech, and the nature and extent of her damages.

The defense contended Ms. Gardetto was not suspended in retaliation for her constitutionally protected speech and activities. They argued she was suspended as appropriate discipline for her insubordination and neglect of duty related to her submission of a grant application without Mr. Mason's signature and her failure to apply for grant monies to fund another employee's position at the Center. The defense presented evidence that Ms. Gardetto's suspension was triggered by the grant incident, but her history of uncooperative, rude and disruptive behavior was taken into consideration when the decision to suspend her was made. The evidence of her rude and abrasive behavior prior to the suspension was therefore relevant to the issues of whether her protected speech was the substantial factor in the decision to take disciplinary action against her, and whether these actions would have been taken in the absence of her speech.

Furthermore, Ms. Gardetto made the evidence of her unprofessional and rude behavior a material issue in the case by claiming damage to her professional reputation resulting from the continuing retributive actions taken against her by the administration prior to the second trial. She claimed she was being treated like a "pariah" at the college because she had been given work assignments without adequate staff and her accomplishments and ideas were ignored by the administration. She claimed these retributive activities continued up to the time of the second trial, and that she had been, and remained, isolated and "cast into operational outer darkness." Although the defamation claim was no longer a part of the case on retrial, Ms. Gardetto's claim for damages remained essentially reputational. She claimed her professional reputation was tarnished as a result of the retributive actions taken against her both before and after the first trial. Thus, the evidence concerning her abrasive behavior towards the members of the faculty and community both before and after the first trial was highly relevant to her claim that her reputation had been damaged among those groups. Accordingly, Ms. Gardetto did not suffer a miscarriage of justice and the court did not commit plain error by failing to exclude this evidence under Rule 402.

Likewise, the court did not abuse its discretion by overruling Ms. Gardetto's relevancy objections to Mr. Smith's testimony. Mr. Smith testified concerning incidents that took place several years prior to the first trial, when he was president of the college. Mr. Smith testified the Board of Directors instructed him to write a letter of discipline to Ms. Gardetto for using the college's postage meter to mail political literature. Ms. Gardetto objected to the relevancy of his testimony concerning the manner in which Ms. Gardetto attempted to contact him concerning this incident. The court overruled this objection, and Mr. Smith was allowed to testify that Ms. Gardetto had convinced a neighbor to let her into Ms. Smith's house so she could leave him a note asking him to contact Ms. Gardetto about the incident.

Ms. Gardetto also objected to Mr. Smith's testimony relating to a conflict between Ms. Gardetto and Ms. France, the director of computer services. The court overruled this objection as well, but allowed her a continuing objection. In overruling her objection, the court noted Ms. Gardetto had introduced evidence of this conflict during her examination of Mr. Mason. Ms. Gardetto asserted she had only asked Mr. Mason if this conflict had anything to do with the suspension. According to Mr. Smith's testimony, the conflict with Ms. France centered on Ms. Gardetto's use of the computer in the resource center. Ms. Gardetto went to Mr. Smith's house to complain about Ms. France and referred to her in vulgar terms. Mr. Smith attempted to mediate the dispute at a meeting with Ms. Gardetto, Ms. France, Mr. Marsh, who was Ms. Gardetto's supervisor at that time, and Larry Dodge, Ms. France's supervisor. Ms. Gardetto became "very emotional" at that meeting and accused Mr. Smith of supporting Ms. France. Mr. Smith asked Ms. France to repair the situation immediately and told Ms. Gardetto to apologize to Ms. France for calling her a liar. Ms. Gardetto slammed the door when she left the meeting.

Mr. Smith's testimony concerning the postage meter incident was relevant to the issue of damages. Ms. Gardetto was claiming damage to her professional reputation among her colleagues. Mr. Smith's testimony concerning her behavior at the mediation meeting served to illustrate the defense's contention that Ms. Gardetto did not have a good professional reputation among her colleagues prior to her suspension. The evidence concerning Ms. Gardetto's conflict with Ms. France was likewise relevant to the damages issue. Mr. Smith's testimony about the postage meter incident was also relevant to the defense's contention that they had not suspended Ms. Gardetto in retaliation for the exercise of her First Amendment rights, but had suspended her, in part, due to her history of unprofessional behavior. Although the testimony concerning the manner in which Ms. Gardetto chose to contact Mr. Mason about the postage meter incident, standing alone, was less relevant to the material issues in the case than was the fact that the incident occurred, in light of the abundance of other relevant evidence at trial concerning Ms. Gardetto's abrasive and unprofessional behavior, we do not conclude Ms. Gardetto's substantial rights were affected by the introduction of the evidence concerning the manner she used to contact Ms. Mason about the postage meter incident. We conclude the trial court did not abuse its discretion by overruling Ms. Gardetto's objection to this evidence based on relevancy.

C. Prejudicial Effect of the Evidence

Ms. Gardetto contends the court erred by admitting the evidence of her rude and abrasive behavior because its probative value was outweighed by its prejudicial effect and should have been excluded pursuant to Rule 403. As discussed above, the trial court erred by failing to conduct the balancing test under Rule 403. In cases where the court has overruled an objection based on Rule 403 but has failed to explicitly set forth its reasons for doing so, we have "authority to conduct a de novo balancing where the trial court failed to make explicit findings to support a Rule 403 ruling." Lazcano-Villalobos, 175 F.3d 838, 846–47 (10th Cir.1999). However, in the present case, because the court relied upon our prior opinion to determine the evidence was admissible, it simply did not conduct the balancing test under Rule 403. Thus, this is not an obvious case in which we may reweigh the evidence de novo to determine whether the trial court was correct in its assessment. Cf. Lazcano-Villalobos, 175 F.3d at 847 (where the court noted the district court record "sheds sufficient light on how the district court viewed the evidence" and concluded the district court "must have implicitly made a Rule 403 finding when it contemplated [the defendant's] unfair prejudice and probative value argument.") Furthermore, because the motion in limine did not preserve her Rule 403 objection to the evidence, and because Ms. Gardetto never renewed her objection to the admission of the evidence under Rule 403, we review the trial court's decision to admit the evidence under the plain error standard. See Fed.R.Evid. 103(d). Although the evidence was allegedly prejudicial and the court erred by failing to conduct the balancing test required by Rule 403, we cannot say the error seriously affected the integrity or fairness of the proceedings. Considering the probative value of the evidence on the central issues of the case, we conclude the prejudicial effect of the introduction of the evidence was not such that it resulted in a miscarriage of justice. [7]

Ms. Gardetto has failed to show the evidentiary errors entitle her to a new trial. AFFIRMED.

[**] The Honorable Lee R. West, Senior United States District Judge for the Western District of Oklahoma, sitting by designation.

[Footnotes omitted].

Gardetto v. Mason, 201 F.3d 447, (Cir. 1999)

Materiality. *Hager v. Astrue*, Civil Action 2:09-cv-01357

THOMAS E. JOHNSTON, District Judge.

Pending before the Court is Plaintiff's Motion to Remand [Docket 14]. For the reasons stated below, Plaintiff's motion is GRANTED.

Background

On December 14, 2009, Plaintiff Roger Hager filed his complaint in this Court seeking a review of the Commissioner of Social Security's final decision denying his application for supplemental security income (SSI). (Docket 2.) By Standing Order entered August 1, 2006, and filed in this case on December 14, 2009, this action was referred to United States Magistrate Judge Mary E. Stanley for submission of proposed findings and a recommendation (PF&R). Magistrate Judge Stanley filed a PF&R (Docket 13) on January 6, 2011, recommending that this Court affirm the final decision of the Commissioner and dismiss this matter from the Court's docket. Objections to the PF&R in this case were due on January 24, 2011. Although Plaintiff filed a document on January 24, 2011, entitled "Plaintiff's Objections to the Defendant's Proposed Findings and Recommendation," the substance of this document is actually a motion to remand pursuant to the sixth sentence of 42 U.S.C. § 405(g), and the Court construes it as such. On January 28, 2011, Defendant replied in opposition of the motion. Plaintiff filed a response on February 4, 2011. The motion is now ripe for review.

United States District Court, S.D. West Virginia, Charleston Division, "Hager v. Astrue, Civil Action 2:09-cv-01357," 2011.

Applicable Law

The Court may remand a case to the Commissioner when additional evidence is presented, "but only upon a showing that there is new evidence which is material and that there is good cause for the failure to incorporate such evidence into the record in a prior proceeding." 42 U.S.C. § 405(g). Accordingly, the Court may remand the case if the following four prerequisites are met: (1) the evidence must be relevant to the determination of disability at the time the application was first filed and not merely cumulative; (2) the evidence must be material to the extent that the Commissioner's decision might reasonably have been different; (3) there must be good cause for the claimant's failure to submit the evidence when the claim was before the Commissioner; and (4) the claimant must present to the remanding court at least a general showing of the nature of the new evidence. Borders v. Heckler, 777 F.2d 954 (4th Cir. 1985), superseded by statute, 42 U.S.C. § 405(g), as recognized in Wilkins v. Sec'y, Dept. of Health & Human Servs., 925 F.2d 769 (4th Cir. 1991), vacated on rehearing, 935 F.2d 93 (4th Cir. 1991) (en banc), superseded by statute on other grounds, 20 C.F.R. § 404.1527.[1]

Discussion

In his objections to the PF&R, Plaintiff references his recent receipt of "education records," which show (1) one IQ test with "valid IQ scores from 1984, with a full scale IQ of 65 when the Plaintiff [was] 9 years old" and (2) a second IQ test with "a valid IQ score with a verbal IQ of 68 in 1987, when the Plaintiff was 12 years old." (Docket 14 at 2.) Plaintiff argues that the education records, coupled with the administrative record on review, demonstrate that he suffers from mental retardation, a condition that was not presented to or considered by the ALJ. As such, Plaintiff requests that the Court remand under § 405(g) for consideration of this evidence.

A. Relevancy

First, the evidence must be "relevant to the determination of disability at the time the application was first filed and not merely cumulative." Borders, 777 F.2d at 955 (citing Mitchell v. Schweiker, 699 F.2d 185, 188 (4th Cir. 1983)). In this case, the relevant time period is from Plaintiff's alleged disability onset date, June 1, 1995, to the ALJ's decision date, December 11, 2008. See Salling v. Apfel, No. 99–1772, 1999 WL 1032616, at *2 (4th Cir. Nov. 15, 1999). Plaintiff alleges that the evidence shows that he has suffered from mental retardation, which is considered "a lifelong condition," since childhood. Branham v. Heckler, 775 F.2d 1271, 1274 (4th Cir. 1985) (quoting 20 C.F.R. subpart P, Appendix 1 § 12.00(B)(4)). Accordingly, the educational records are relevant to the initial disability determination period. Further, the proffered evidence is clearly not cumulative or duplicative because it relates to a condition that was not presented before the ALJ.

B. Materiality

Second, the evidence "must be material to the extent that the Secretary's decision might reasonably have been different' had the new evidence been before her." Borders, 777 F.2d at 955 (citing King v. Califano, 599 F.2d 597, 599 (4th Cir.1979); Sims v. Harris, 631 F.2d 26, 28 (4th Cir.1980)). As such, Plaintiff must establish that the new evidence, "when considered in conjunction with all evidence," would lead to the conclusion that he disabled as defined by the Act. McAbee v. Halter, No. 00–2198, 2010 WL 1251452, at *3 (4th Cir. Oct. 19, 2001) (citing 42 U.S.C. § 423(d)(5) (A)). Defendant did not brief the issue of whether the new evidence, if considered, could have affected the Secretary's decision.[2]

Plaintiff asserts that the recently acquired education records demonstrate that he suffers from mental retardation as listed in 20 C.F.R. pt. 404, subpt. P, app. 1, § 12.05(C) ("12.05(C)"), rendering him disabled within the meaning of the Act.[3] Listing 12.05 "contains an introductory paragraph with the diagnostic description for mental retardation... [and] four sets of criteria (paragraphs A through D)." 20 C.F.R. pt. 404, subpt. P, app. 1 § 12.00(A). Plaintiff is within 12.05(C) if his impairment satisfies the "diagnostic description in the introductory paragraph" of 12.05 as well as the specific criteria listed in 12.05(C). Id. As such, Plaintiff must demonstrate (1) "significantly subaverage general intellectual function with deficits in adaptive functioning initially manifested... before age 22," (2) "[a] valid verbal, performance, or full scale IQ of 60 through 70," and (3) "a physical or other mental impairment imposing additional and significant work-related limitation or function." §§ 12.05; 12.05(C).

First, the introductory "diagnostic" paragraph of listing 12.05 requires both "subaverage general intellectual function" as well as "deficits in adaptive functioning" that manifested at an early age. Although these terms are not explicitly defined, "adaptive activities" are described elsewhere in the Listing as "[a]ctivities of daily living" such as "cleaning, shopping, cooking, taking public transportation, paying bills, maintaining a residence, caring appropriately for your grooming and hygiene, using telephones and directories, and using a post office." § 12.00(C)(1). In support of this prong of the test, Plaintiff points the Court to his low childhood IQ scores and several incidents reported in his administrative record in support of the proposition that he has subaverage intellectual function and "difficulty dealing with ordinary everyday life." (Docket 14 at 3.) Specifically, Plaintiff argues that his record of hospitalizations, incarcerations, and suicide attempts indicate significant deficits in adaptive functioning.

The Court's evaluation of this case is complicated by Plaintiff's substance abuse, specifically alcoholism, which the ALJ determined was a material factor in Plaintiff's initial disability determination. See 42 U.S.C. § 423(d)(2)(C); 20 C.F.R. § 404.1535(a) (precludes an award of disability benefits if alcohol or drug abuse was "a contributing factor material to the Commissioner's determination that the individual is disabled"). It is unclear how many of the alleged incidents reflecting "deficits in adaptive functioning" identified in Plaintiff's motion simply reflect his periods of decomposition from alcohol abuse. The administrative record is only slightly more illuminating. For example, the ALJ noted that Plaintiff would, in the absence of substance abuse, have a "moderate restriction" in the activities of daily living. (Docket 9 at 22.) Further, the ALJ found that he had "moderate difficulties" with "concentration, persistence, or pace" and "social functioning." (Id.) Although the record below is far from conclusive, given these findings and the fact that Defendant did not brief this issue, the Court is inclined to give Plaintiff the benefit of the doubt that there is at least a "reasonable possibility" that Plaintiff could meet this prong of the test. Borders, 777 F.2d at 955.

Second, the newly offered evidence purports to meet the prong of the test which requires "[a] valid verbal, performance, or full scale IQ of 60 through 70." 20 C.F.R. pt. 404, subpt. P, app. 1 § 12.05(C). The recently-acquired IQ tests were administered in 1984 (when the Plaintiff was 9 years old),[4] resulting in a score of 65, and 1987 (when the Plaintiff was 12 years old), resulting in score of 68. According to the regulations pertaining to children's mental retardation, these tests are too old to be considered accurate:

> IQ test results must also be sufficiently current for accurate assessment under [20 C.F.R. pt. 404, subpt. P, app. 1, §] 112.05. Generally, the results of IQ tests tend to stabilize by the age of 16. Therefore, IQ test results obtained at age 16 or older should be viewed as a valid indication of the child's current status, provided they are compatible with the child's current behavior. IQ test results obtained between ages 7 and 16 should be considered current for 4 years when the tested IQ is less than 40, and for 2 years when the IQ is 40 or above. IQ test results obtained before age 7 are current for 2 years if the tested IQ is less than 40 and 1 year if at 40 or above. 20 C.F.R. pt. 404, subpt. P, app. 1, § 112.00(D)(10). The application of this provision to the adult mental retardation description is unclear.[5] However, given that there is no express prohibition on the consideration of these tests, the Court cannot hold that they would be considered invalid as a matter of law. Again, there is at least a reasonable possibility that Plaintiff could meet this prong of the test. Borders, 777 F.2d at 955.

For the final prong of the test, Plaintiff would need to establish a "physical or mental impairment imposing additional and significant work-related limitation or function." § 12.05(C). What constitutes a "significant" impairment is not defined in the Act's regulations; however, the Fourth Circuit has noted that "the significant limitation under section 12.05(C) need not be disabling in and of itself." Branham, 775 F.2d at 1273. The ALJ determined that Plaintiff has several "severe impairments": alcohol dependence, antisocial personality disorder, and alcohol-induced mood disorder. (Docket 9 at 20.) Although the ALJ found that these impairments were non-disabling because, in the absence of substance use, they would not meet or medically equal the impairments listed in 20 C.F.R. pt. 404, subpt. P, app. 1, he noted that even in the absence of substance use, "the claimant would continue to have a severe impairment or combination of impairments." (Docket 9 at 21.) For the purposes of 12.05(C), a "severe impairment," by definition, imposes a significant work-related limitation of function. Compare 20 C.F.R. Pt. 404, Subpt. P, App. 1, § 12.00(A), with 20 C.F.R. § 416.920(c); see also Luckey v. U.S. Dept. of Health & Human Serv., 890 F.2d 666, 669 (4th Cir. 1989) (per curiam). Therefore, it seems that there is a reasonable possibility that Plaintiff could meet this prong of the test. Borders, 777 F.2d at 955.

Although the impact that this new evidence will have on Plaintiff's disability determination is uncertain, as described above, there is at least a possibility that the Secretary's decision "might reasonably have been different" had this evidence been before her. Borders, 777 F.2d at 955.

C. Good Cause

Under the third prong of the Borders test, Plaintiff has to show "good cause" for failing to submit the evidence to the commissioner. Borders, 777 F.2d at 955. Plaintiff argues that the records were unavailable at the time of the administrative proceeding because his previous school had closed and the records were stored at an unknown location until Dec. 27, 2010. The Court accepts the representations of counsel that the location of the evidence was unknown at the time of the administrative hearing and finds that there is sufficient good cause for the failure to submit the additional evidence when the case was before the Commissioner.

D. General Showing

The final prong of the Borders test requires that the Plaintiff make at least a "general showing" of the new evidence. Borders, 777 F.2d at 955. Any deficiency in this area was corrected when the Plaintiff attached the educational records in question to its reply. (Docket 16–1.) As Plaintiff has provided the Court with a copy of these records, this element of the Borders test is satisfied.

Conclusions

As evidenced by Plaintiff's satisfaction of the four prerequisites identified in Borders , Plaintiff has made the appropriate "showing that there is new evidence which is material and that there is good cause for the failure to incorporate such evidence into the record in a prior proceeding." 42 U.S.C. § 405(g). Accordingly, Plaintiff's Motion to Remand [Docket 14] is GRANTED. A separate Judgment Order will be entered this day implementing the rulings contained herein. The Court hereby REMANDS this case to the Commissioner of Social Security for further proceedings and ORDERS the Commissioner to consider Plaintiff's additional evidence.

IT IS SO ORDERED.

   The Court DIRECTS the Clerk to send a copy of this Order to counsel of record and any unrepresented party.

[Footnotes omitted].

Hager v. Astrue, Civil Action 2:09-cv-01357

Competence. *Jones v. Warden Lebanon Correctional Institution*, 2:14-cv-1218

GEORGE C. SMITH JUDGE.
REPORT AND RECOMMENDATION AND ORDER
Terence P. Kemp United States Magistrate Judge.

Petitioner, a state prisoner, filed this action seeking a writ of habeas corpus pursuant to 28 U.S.C. §2254. This matter is before the Court on the Respondent's Supplemental Return of Writ and the Petitioner's Traverse (Docs. 21 and 26) as well as two motions filed by Petitioner. Petitioner's motion to delete claim one of the petition (Doc. 19), which claim has already been denied by the Court, is DENIED AS MOOT. His other motion (Doc. 20), which asks, as substantive relief, for an order directing that he not be transferred to another prison during the pendency of this action, is also DENIED AS MOOT, it appearing that the transfer has already taken place. For the reasons that follow, it is recommended that the Court deny the petition and dismiss this action.

Background

For ease of reference, the Court will restate the brief factual background included in the Court's prior Report and Recommendation (Doc. 12), which concluded that ground one of the petition had been procedurally defaulted, and recommended that a supplemental return of writ be filed with respect to ground two. That recommendation was adopted on December 4, 2015 (Doc. 18). As the Court said in the prior Report and Recommendation, at 4:

United States District Court, S.D. Ohio, Eastern Division, "Jones v. Warden Lebanon Correctional Institution, 2:14-cv-1218 ", 2016.

The alleged victim in the case was a daughter of Petitioner's then-girlfriend, Danielle Inskeep (she and Petitioner subsequently married). Ms. Inskeep had shared custody of her two daughters. In September of 2011, the younger of the two told her father that Petitioner had been sexually abusing her. She repeated these allegations to workers at Nationwide Children's Hospital. The victim was nine years old at the time of trial. The trial court held a hearing to determine if she was competent to testify. After finding that she was, the trial judge allowed her to testify by closed circuit video. She repeated her allegations to the jury. The jury was also permitted to hear that she had told the same story to a caseworker at Children's Hospital. Petitioner took the stand and denied that he had ever sexually abused the victim. As noted above, the jury convicted him despite his denials.

In his petition for writ of habeas corpus, Petitioner raised two claims:

1. The trial court abused its discretion when it found the child was competent to testify, which violated Petitioner's right to due process of law; and
2. The state failed to prove the existence of one or more of three factors contained in O.R.C. §2945.481, for the court to permit the child witness to testify via closed circuit video.

By Order dated December 4, 2014, adopting the Magistrate Judge's Report and Recommendation, the Court dismissed Claim One as procedurally defaulted. (Doc. 18). Respondent's supplemental return was filed on December 23, 2015. (Doc. 21). Petitioner filed a supplemental traverse on February 5, 2016. (Doc. 26).

Standard of Review

Petitioner seeks habeas relief under 28 U.S.C. §2254. The Antiterrorism and Effective Death Penalty Act ("AEDPA") sets forth standards governing this Court's review of state-court determinations. The United State Supreme Court recently described AEDPA as "a formidable barrier to federal habeas relief for prisoners whose claims have been adjudicated in state court" and emphasized that courts must not "lightly conclude that a State's criminal justice system has experienced the 'extreme malfunction' for which federal habeas relief is the remedy." Burt v. Titlow, ___ U.S. ___, ___, 134 S.Ct. 10, 16 (2013) (quoting Harrington v. Richter, 562 U.S. 86, 102 (2011)); see also Renico v. Lett, 559 U.S. 766, 773 (2010) ("AEDPA... imposes a highly deferential standard for evaluating state-court rulings, and demands that state-court decisions be given the benefit of the doubt.") (internal quotation marks, citations, and footnote omitted). The factual findings of the state appellate court are presumed to be correct:

> In a proceeding instituted by an application for a writ of habeas corpus by a person in custody pursuant to the judgment of a State court, a determination of a factual issue made by a State court shall be presumed to be correct. The applicant shall have the burden of rebutting the presumption of correctness by clear and convincing evidence.
>   28 U.S.C. §2254(e)(1).

Habeas corpus should be denied unless the state court decision was contrary to, or involved an unreasonable application of, clearly established federal law as determined by the Supreme Court, or based on an unreasonable determination of the facts in light of the evidence presented to the state courts. 28 U.S.C. §2254(d)(1); Coley v. Bagley, 706 F.3d 741, 748 (6th Cir. 2013) (citing Slagle v. Bagley, 457 F.3d 501, 513 (6th Cir. 2006)); see also 28 U.S.C. §2254(d)(2) (a petitioner must show that the state court relied on an "unreasonable determination of the facts in light of the evidence presented in the State court proceeding"). The United States Court of Appeals for the Sixth Circuit explained these standards as follows:

> A state court's decision is "contrary to" Supreme Court precedent if (1) "the state court arrives at a conclusion opposite to that reached by [the Supreme] Court on a question of law[,]" or (2) "the state court confronts facts that are materially indistinguishable from a relevant Supreme Court precedent and arrives" at a different result. Williams v. Taylor, 529 U.S. 362, 405 (2000). A state court's decision is an "unreasonable application" under 28 U.S.C. § 2254(d)(1) if it "identifies the correct governing legal rule from [the Supreme] Court's cases but unreasonably applies it to the facts of the particular ...case" or either unreasonably extends or unreasonably refuses to extend a legal principle from Supreme Court precedent to a new context. Id. at 407. ... Coley, supra, at 748–49. The burden of satisfying the standards set forth in § 2254 rests with the petitioner. Cullen v. Pinholster, 563 U.S. 170, 181 (2011).

"In order for a federal court to find a state court's application of [Supreme Court precedent] unreasonable, ... [t]he state court's application must have been objectively unreasonable, " not merely "incorrect or erroneous." Wiggins v. Smith, 539 U.S. 510, 520–21, (2003) (internal quotation marks omitted) (citing Williams v. Taylor, 529. U.S. at 409 and Lockyer v. Andrade, 538 U.S. 63, 76 (2003)). See also Harrington v. Richter, 131 S.Ct. at 786 ("A state court's determination that a claim lacks merit precludes federal habeas relief so long as 'fairminded jurists could disagree' on the correctness of the state court's decision.") (quoting Yarborough v. Alvarado, 541 U.S. 652, 664 (2004)). In considering a claim of "unreasonable application" under § 2254(d)(1), courts must focus on the reasonableness of the result, not on the reasonableness of the state court's analysis. "'[O]ur focus on the 'unreasonable application' test under Section 2254(d) should be on the ultimate legal conclusion that the state court reached and not whether the state court considered and discussed every angle of the evidence.' " Holder v. Palmer, 588 F.3d 328, 341 (6th Cir. 2009) (quoting Neal v. Puckett, 286 F.3d 230, 246 (5th Cir. 2002) (en banc)). See also Nicely v. Mills, 521 Fed.Appx. 398, 403 (6th Cir. 2013) (considering evidence in the state court record that was "not expressly considered by the state court in its opinion" to evaluate the reasonableness of state court's decision). Moreover, in evaluating the reasonableness of a state court's ultimate legal conclusion under § 2254(d)(1), a federal habeas court must review the state court's decision based solely on the record that was before the state court at the time that it rendered its decision. Put simply, "review under § 2254(d)(1) focuses on what a state court knew and did." Pinholster, supra at 1398.

Discussion

In ground two, Petitioner alleges that his Sixth Amendment right to confront the witnesses against him was violated when the trial court permitted the alleged child victim to testify at trial outside the courtroom by way of two-way closed circuit video. As noted above, on appeal, the appellate court addressed only a claim based on state law, and because it found that Petitioner had not properly objected to the procedure used by the trial court, reviewed that claim only for plain error. This Court, however, has concluded that Petitioner both fairly presented a federal constitutional claim, as well as a claim under Ohio law, to the state court of appeals, and that he had not waived that claim on appeal. Doc. 18, at 5. Consequently, this Court must resolve the Sixth Amendment claim on its merits. Under the standard of review set forth above, however, even though the state court did not address the federal claim, this Court can grant Petitioner relief only if the result of the state court proceedings—that is, the affirmance of his conviction despite his objection to allowing the victim to testify by two-way closed circuit television—represents an unreasonable application of clearly established federal law. For the following reasons, the Court cannot reach that conclusion.

It is helpful to begin with some basic principles. The Sixth Amendment right to be confronted with one's accusers requires, absent special circumstances, that the witnesses personally appear at the defendant's trial and be subject to live cross-examination. Crawford v. Washington, 541 U.S. 36, 51 (2004). Stated a different way, testimonial statements of a witness who does not appear personally at trial may not be admitted or used against a criminal defendant unless the witness is unavailable to testify and the defendant had a prior opportunity to cross-examine that witness. Id. However, a defendant's right to face-to-face confrontation is not absolute. Rather, as the Supreme Court said in Maryland v. Craig, 497 U.S. 836, 849–50 (1990) "we cannot say that [face-to-face] confrontation is an indispensable element of the Sixth Amendment's guarantee of the right to confront one's accusers" and that this right, like other rights found in the Sixth Amendment, must "be interpreted in the context of the necessities of trial and the adversary process." Nevertheless, the Supreme Court noted that "[t]hat the face-to-face confrontation requirement is not absolute does not, of course, mean that it may easily be dispensed with." Id. at 850. The Supreme Court then held that a defendant's right to confront accusatory witnesses may be satisfied absent a physical confrontation at trial only where "denial of such confrontation is necessary to further an important public policy and only where the reliability of the testimony is otherwise assured." Id.

In Craig, the Supreme Court was faced with the question of whether a Maryland statutory procedure which allowed a victim to testify by one-way closed circuit video violated the Sixth Amendment. The procedure was described in this way:

> The child witness is ... examined and cross-examined in the separate room, while a video monitor records and displays the witness' testimony to those in the courtroom. During this time the witness cannot see the defendant. The defendant remains in electronic communication with defense counsel, and objections may be made and ruled on as if the witness were testifying in the courtroom.

Id. at 842. In support of its motion to allow testimony to be provided in this way, the State presented expert testimony that the named victim would suffer "serious emotional distress such that [the victim could not] reasonably communicate if required to testify in the courtroom." Id. at 841. The Supreme Court, based on that testimony, found no Sixth Amendment violation, noting that the purpose of the Confrontation Clause is "ensuring that evidence admitted against an accused is reliable and subject to the rigorous adversarial testing that is the norm of Anglo-American criminal proceedings." Id. at 846, and concluding that the Maryland procedure "preserves all of the other elements of the confrontation right: The child witness must be competent to testify and must testify under oath; the defendant retains full opportunity for contemporaneous cross-examination; and the judge, jury, and defendant are able to view (albeit by video monitor) the demeanor (and body) of the witness as he or she testifies." Id. at 851.

The Craig court set out three factors that must be considered in order to justify allowing the witness to testify by closed-circuit video and held that these factors must be evaluated in relation to the specific facts of each case. Those factors are: (1) whether "the use of the one-way closed circuit television procedure is necessary to protect the welfare of the particular child witness who seeks to testify"; (2) whether "the child witness would be traumatized, not by the courtroom generally, but by the presence of the defendant"; and (3) whether "the emotional distress suffered by the child witness in the presence of the defendant is more than de minimis, i.e., more than "mere nervousness or excitement or some reluctance to testify." Craig, supra, at 855–56.

In his petition and traverse, Petitioner argues that allowing the child to testify via two-way closed circuit video constituted "theatrics" and prejudiced the jury against him. He also argues that the witness was lying, and that the trial court made no finding that the witness had refused to testify in person, that she would have been unable to communicate, had she been present in the courtroom, due to extreme fear, or that she would suffer emotional trauma if she were required to testify in person. (Docs. 1 and 25). Respondent argues that Petitioner has failed to demonstrate that "the Ohio Court of Appeals' decision to reject his claim involved an unreasonable application of or was contrary to clearly established Supreme Court law." (Doc. 21 at 3).

The Court first examines the factual background of this case, keeping in mind the Supreme Court's admonition that each case where face-to-face confrontation of an accusing witness is not permitted is to be judged on its individual facts. Here, before making its ruling, the trial court held a hearing. At that hearing, social worker Elizabeth Ramsey, who treated the victim, was called to testify in support of the State's motion to present the victim's testimony by closed-circuit television. She first testified that the child was "scared" about testifying in general. Further, the child was mildly to moderately anxious about being in the presence of Petitioner. Ms. Ramsey was asked her opinion about how testifying in the courtroom with Petitioner present might affect the child. She said that it might cause the child to regress in coping with the incident itself, which had caused her to suffer nightmares and to struggle with her schoolwork. Ms. Ramsey also said that testifying in person would likely be "more than she [the child] can handle" and that "it would be very difficult for her and the potential risk is great." On cross-examination, Ms. Ramsey admitted that she was predisposed to be on the safe side with respect to the child because she was concerned for the child's well-being, but reiterated that if the child testified in a "safe setting that separates her from Mr. Jones, I think there is a potential for less emotional trauma than if she has to sit in the same room. See Transcript of August 8, 2012 Motions Hearing, Doc. 7–2, at 46–55). The trial court accepted her testimony and ordered that the two-way video procedure be used at trial.

When the child was testifying, Petitioner, the jury, the trial judge, and counsel were all able to observe, on video monitors, the child's demeanor, and counsel was able to question her in real time through the two-way closed circuit television connection. She could also see them. The child testified that Petitioner came into the bottom bunk of the bed she shared with her sister on a number of occasions and raped her while her sister was on the top bunk. She stated that Petitioner also threatened to hurt her if she told anyone about his behavior. The child acknowledged seeing Petitioner on the monitor in front of her and correctly identified Petitioner as Terry Jones. See Transcript of Jury Trial, Doc. 7–3, at 137–55. The Sixth Amendment claim in this case must be judged with this background in mind.

The first reason that Petitioner has not demonstrated that the state court's decision to allow the victim to testify in this way is that there is no well-settled Supreme Court precedent dealing with testimony given by way of two-way (as opposed to oneway) closed-circuit television. As the court observed in Horn v. Quarterman, 508 F.3d 306, 318 (5th Cir. 2007), "our independent search has not found[] any post-Craig decision by a federal appellate court that squarely states that introduction of testimony through two-way closed-circuit television violates the Confrontation Clause." In reaching that conclusion, the court cited to, among other decisions, Fuster-Escalona v. Florida Dept. Of Corrections, 170 Fed.Appx. 627, 629–30 (11th Cir. 2006), which held that it was "not contrary to, or an unreasonable application of, established federal law to hold that no case-specific findings were required prior to [ ] four children testifying via two-way closed television." See also Johnson v. Warden, Lebanon Correctional Institution, 2014 WL 4829592 (S.D. Ohio Sept. 29, 2014), adopted and affirmed 2015 WL 268924 (S.D. Ohio, Jan. 21, 2015)(discussing the case law on this subject, including United States v. Gigante, 166 F.3d 75, 81 (2nd Cir. 1999), which held that it was not necessary to apply Craig when the trial judge "employed a two-way system that preserved the face-to-face confrontation, " but ultimately finding it unnecessary to resolve the issue because the state court had made findings that satisfied Craig). In light of this unsettled state of the law, Petitioner would not be entitled to habeas corpus relief even if the state courts had made no findings at all concerning the need to have the child testify via two-way closed circuit television.

This conclusion is bolstered by the fact that the trial court did, in fact, make its decision based on a factual record that addressed the Craig factors. There was testimony that not just being a witness in the courtroom setting, but being in the physical presence of Petitioner, would be harmful to the child. Ms. Ramsey detailed her concerns about that, and the trial court credited her testimony. Such factual findings are binding on this Court. See 28 U.S.C. §2254(e)(1)("In a proceeding instituted by an application for a writ of habeas corpus by a person in custody pursuant to the judgment of a State court, a determination of a factual issue made by a State court shall be presumed to be correct"). Whether this Court would have made the same findings or reached the same conclusions as did the state trial judge is not the issue. It would be extremely difficult to characterize his ruling as contrary to, or an unreasonable application of, Craig to this set of facts. For both of these reasons, the Court concludes that Petitioner has not demonstrated that the result of the state court proceedings represents an unreasonable application of clearly established federal law. Therefore, it is recommended that the petition be DENIED and that this case be DISMISSED.

Procedure on Objections

If any party objects to this Report and Recommendation, that party may, within fourteen (14) days of the date of this Report, file and serve on all parties written objections to those specific proposed findings or recommendations to which objection is made, together with supporting authority for the objection(s). A judge of this Court shall make a de novo determination of those portions of the report or specified proposed findings or recommendations to which objection is made. Upon proper objections, a judge of this Court may accept, reject, or modify, in whole or in part, the findings or recommendations made herein, may receive further evidence or may recommit this matter to the magistrate judge with instructions. 28 U.S.C. §636(b)(1).

The parties are specifically advised that failure to object to the Report and Recommendation will result in a waiver of the right to have the district judge review the Report and Recommendation de novo, and also operates as a waiver of the right to appeal the decision of the District Court adopting the Report and Recommendation. See Thomas v. Arn, 474 U.S. 140 (1985); United States v. Walters, 638 F.2d 947 (6th Cir. 1981).

Jones v. Warden Lebanon Correctional Institution, 2:14-cv-1218

Chapter 4: Key Terms and Discussion Questions

Key Terms

Arrest: the act of taking an individual into custody in a manner such that the individual would reasonably disbelieve that he or she is free to leave in order to charge the individual with a criminal offense

Consent: permission

Electronic Surveillance: the monitoring of a home, business, or individual using a variety of devices, such as CCTV, legal wiretapping, cameras, digital video equipment, and other electronic, digital, and audio-visual means

Entrapment: a defense to criminal charges; when police use coercion to induce an individual to commit a crime when he or she was not already predisposed to committing the crime charged

Exclusionary Rule: doctrine that prevents illegally obtained evidence from being admissible at trial

Forfeiture: the loss of any property without compensation as a penalty for illegal conduct

Frisk: a superficial search of an individual's person; a pat-down

Interrogation: intense and accusatory questioning sessions by the police while a suspect is in custody

Lineup: a group of individuals that may or may not include a suspect in the crime; usually a witness or victim is present to identify whether the suspect is one of the individuals in the group

Miranda Rule: from *Miranda v. Arizona*; prior to interrogation, law enforcement must read four warnings to suspects, informing them that (1) they have the right to remain silent; (2) anything said can and will be used against the suspect in a court of law; (3) they have the right to an attorney; (4) if the suspect cannot afford an attorney, one will be provided for him/her

Open Fields Doctrine: the legal doctrine that a warrantless search of the area outside a property owner's curtilage does not violate the Fourth Amendment

Photo Array: suspect lineup contained in photographs of suspects instead of the suspects appearing in person

Plain View Doctrine: allows a police officer to seize objects not included in a warrant when executing a lawful search or seizure if he or she observes the object in plain view and has probable cause to believe that it is connected with criminal activities

Probable Cause: justification for police action that is based on more than 50 percent certainty that a crime has been or is being committed; more than reasonable suspicion, less than beyond a reasonable doubt

Search: an exploratory investigation of an individual or location by the government that infringes on the individual's reasonable expectation of privacy

Seizure of a Person: when law enforcement intentionally restrains an individual's liberty such that the individual would not believe that he or she is free to leave

Seizure of Property: when law enforcement meaningfully interferes with an individual's possessory interest in property

Showup: a one-on-one lineup

Stop: a detention of an individual for the purpose of investigation; a brief nonconsensual encounter between the police and an individual that does not rise to the level of an arrest

Discussion Questions

1. Give an example of entrapment.
2. What is the difference between a search incident to arrest and a frisk?
3. Why should the government be worried about legal liability?
4. Explain the fruit of the poisonous tree doctrine.
5. How often do you believe police violate constitutional rights? Explain.

Witnesses

"A Lay Witness, You Say!"

Fed. R. Ev. 701 and 702

by Lawrence C. Brown

Commercial practitioners, particularly those involved in the prosecution and defense of claims in federal courts (including the bankruptcy courts) and in state courts operating in states utilizing procedural rules based upon the Federal Rules of Civil Procedure ("Fed. R. Civ. Proc.") and the Federal Rules of Evidence (F.R.Ev.), are often confronted with issues presented by the interaction of F.R.Ev. 701[1] and 702[2] concerning lay opinion and expert testimony. A basic understanding of the interaction between F.R.Ev. 701 and 702 may be critical to a crafting of a party's case.

The proving of a claim or defense usually contemplates the use of witness testimony, whether by testimony in open court, deposition testimony, or by affidavits, the last often in the context of summary judgment motions. The testimony will have to be presented in a form that is admissible and characterized as to whether it is testimony about facts (the "fact" witness) or whether the testimony will be, in part, in the form of an opinion. An example of fact testimony is the testimony of fraud victims concerning the price they received on resale of coins which were represented as rare when sold

---

1   Rule 701. Opinion Testimony by Lay Witnesses. If the witness is not testifying as an expert, the witness' testimony in the form of opinions or inferences is limited to those opinions or inferences which are (a) rationally based on the perception of the witness, (b) helpful to a clear understanding of the witness' testimony or the determination of a fact in issue, and (c) not based on scientific, technical, or other specialized knowledge within the scope of Rule 702.

2   Rule 702. Testimony by Experts. If scientific, technical or other specialized knowledge will assist the trier of fact to understand the evidence or to determine a fact in issue, a witness qualified as an expert by knowledge, skill, experience, training, or education, may testify thereto in the form of an opinion or otherwise, if (1) the testimony is based upon sufficient facts or data, (2) the testimony is the product of reliable principles and methods, and (3) the witness has applied the principles and methods reliably to the facts of the case.

to the victims. The court, observing that no opinion testimony was involved said that this was, "but a simple recitation of an observed phenomenon; the price paid for the coins." *U.S. v. Kayne*, 90 F.3d 7, 12 (1st Cir.), *cert den.*, 519 U.S. 1055, 117 S. Ct. 681 (1996).

Opinion testimony is of two forms, lay opinion and expert opinion, addressed respectively by Fed. R. Ev. 701 and 702. The analysis of the testimony type desired to be elicited from a witness is of particular importance not only because its admissibility is based partly on the applicable evidence rule, but because there are disclosure rules which must be properly followed before the testimony may be used.

Disclosure rules relating to expert and lay witnesses are contained in Fed. R. Civ. P. 26(a), and in similar state procedural rules. A party, unless otherwise agreed to or ordered by the court, must disclose the identity of any person who may present evidence at trial under F.R.Ev. 702, 703 or 705. Fed. R. Civ. P. 26(a) (2)(A). The party must provide a written report prepared and signed by a witness who has been "retained or specially employed to provide expert testimony in the case or whose duties as an employee of the party regularly involve giving expert testimony." Fed. R. Civ. P. 26(a)(2)(B). The report must contain the detail and information required by the rule.

Lay witness disclosure, whether or not testimony could also be offered under F.R.Ev. 701, requires that the witness be identified, contact information be provided and a statement of the type of information the witness is likely to have without a written report requirement. Fed. R. Civ. P. 26 (a)(1)(A) (i) and 26 (a)(2)(A). The distinction between the disclosure requirements lies in whether the witness giving "expert" testimony under F.R.Ev. 702 is a witness either retained by the party for that purpose or employed by the party whose duties regularly involve testifying for the party employer. The lay witness testifying under F.R.Ev. 702 is often an employee having specialized knowledge but whose duties do not involve regularly testifying for the party employer. The consequences of not properly analyzing the testimony to be elicited and the person from whom it is being elicited can be damaging to a party's case, particularly where a party employee's testimony may involve matters engaging both F.R.Ev. 701 and 702. An example of such a situation follows.

A Second Circuit case, *Bank of China, New York Branch v. NBM LLC, et al,* 359 F.3d 171 (2d Cir. 2004), *cert granted in part,* 545 U.S. 1138, 125 S.Ct. 2956, *cert dismissed,* 126 S. Ct. 675 (2005) presents an example of the issues faced by a practitioner in the context of a party employee's testimony being provided under F.R.Ev. 701 when part of the testimony was within F.R.Ev. 702's ambit. *Bank of China* concerned a fraudulent scheme in which the bank was presented with trust receipts representing sales transactions that, in fact, involved no real goods. A Bank of China employee ("E") had been assigned to investigate the defendants' activities after the bank ceased doing business with them. E was a senior bank employee well experienced in international transactions.

The trial court allowed E to testify about—(1) certain transactions between specified defendants that were not normal buyer-seller transactions as understood by the business community; (2) the concept of a "trust receipt" and its use in international commercial transaction; and (3) that it is considered fraudulent for an importer to use a trust receipt to obtain a loan knowing there are no real goods involved. E's testimony was admitted as lay opinion testimony under F.R.Ev. 701 based upon E's many years of experience in international banking and trade.[3]

The Second Circuit disagreed with the trial court, explaining that F.R.Ev. 701 (c) explicitly bars admission of lay opinions that are "based on scientific, technical, or other specialized knowledge within the scope of Rule 702 [concerning expert testimony]". The appellate court observed that F.R.Ev. 701(a) requires lay opinion testimony to be "rationally based upon the perception of the witness", but that E's testimony was only partly so based, some qualifying for admission under F.R.Ev. 701, and some under F. R.Ev. 702. Distinguishing the testimony admissible under Rule 701, the Second Circuit stated—

> "To some extent, [E's] testimony was based on his perceptions. As a Bank of China employee, [E] was assigned to investigate... [E]'s senior role at the Bank and his years of experience in international banking made him particularly well-suited to undertake such an investigation... The fact that [E] has specialized knowledge, or that he carried out the investigation because of that knowledge, does not preclude him from testifying pursuant to Rule 701, so long as the testimony was based on the investigation and reflected his investigatory findings and conclusions, and was not rooted exclusively in his expertise in international banking. Such opinion testimony is admitted not because of experience, training or specialized knowledge within the realm of an expert, but because of particularized knowledge that the witness has by virtue of his [] position in the business. Fed. R. Evid. 701 advisory committee's note. Thus, to the extent [E's] testimony was grounded in the investigation he undertook in his [bank employee role], it was admissible pursuant to Rule 701 of the Federal Rules of Evidence because it was based on his *perceptions* (cite omitted, emphasis in original)."[4]

Continuing, describing that [E] testimony which was not admissible under F.R.Ev. 701, the Court of Appeals stated—

> "However, to the extent [E]'s testimony was not a product of his investigation, but rather reflected specialized knowledge he has because of his extensive experience in international banking, its admission pursuant to Rule 701 was error. Thus, [E]'s explanations regarding typical international banking transactions or definitions of banking terms, and any conclusions he made which were not a result of his investigation, were improperly admitted. Of course, these opinions may, nonetheless, have been admissible pursuant to Rule 702 because '[c]ertainly it is possible for the same witness to provide lay and expert testimony in a single case.' Fed. R. Evid. 701, advisory committee's note. (cite omitted). But before such testimony could have been proffered pursuant to Rule 702, Bank of China was obligated to satisfy the reliability requirements set forth in that rule, and disclose [E] as an expert ... . pursuant to Rule 26(a)(2) (A) of the Federal Rules of Civil Procedure, (ftnt reference omitted)[5]

The *Bank of China* case is instructive on a number of matters. Initially, practitioners must consider whether any part of a witness' testimony is based on scientific, technical or other

3   359 F.3d at 181–182

4   359 F.3dat 181.

5   359 F.3d at 182.

specialized knowledge. F.R.Ev. 701(c) provides that a lay witness' testimony is limited to opinions or inferences "not based on scientific, technical, or other specialized knowledge within the scope of Rule 702." The implication of such language is that if testimony can qualify under F.R.Ev. 702, then it cannot qualify under F.R.Ev. 701. Although the subject matter of testimony is said to be the focus of a query concerning whether testimony is within the scope of F.R.Ev. 701[6], the evaluation of testimony to be given can be problematic.

An example of fine distinctions made by the courts is, for example, where an outside accounting professional was permitted to testify as a lay witness about the effects of disputed debt reclassifications. The testimony was determined to have been based upon the accountant's observations during his twenty-months' engagement involving review of corporate books and the accounting procedures used by the company. The Second Circuit commented that a witness' specialized knowledge does not render his testimony "expert" as long as it was based on his investigation and reflected his investigatory findings and conclusions, and was not rooted exclusively in his expertise. *United States v. Rigas,* 490 F.3d 208, 224–225 (2d Cir. 2007). This suggests that there is careful analysis required of the foundation for the witness' testimony in terms of relationship between expertise and first hand knowledge when the witness's testimony may require the application of expertise to personally observed activities. Reading *Rigas* with *Bank of China,* the common theme seems to be that a witness may testify as to a lay opinion based upon first hand knowledge or observation providing a rational basis for the opinion, but may not do so as to testimony exclusively reliant on expertise for the opinion stated.

Courts addressing the F.R.Ev. 701 change in 2000, to add the present F.R.Ev. 701(c) prohibiting lay witness opinions where based on scientific, technical or other specialized knowledge, have observed, that "the amendment did not place any restrictions on the pre-amendment practice of allowing business *owners or officers* to testify based on *particularized knowledge* derived from their position."[7] Such testimony has been described as prototypical lay opinion evidence, not precluded by the F.R.Ev. 701(c) amendment, such as where a company's employees were permitted to testify on the reasonableness of charges for repairs.[8]

However, personal knowledge of a business' operation does not appear to be a requirement where third-party analysis of business documents requires calculations or evaluations of business records by procedures understandable by a lay person. In a bank fraud prosecution, a financial analyst summarized financial document content following processes of addition and subtraction and summary comparison of the resulting numbers, a procedure determined understandable by a reasonable lay person.[9] Similarly, the computation of the average of 103 numbers, though tech-

---

6   Advisory committee Note to Fed. R. Evid. 701.

7   E g., Texas A&M *Research Foundation v. Magna Transp. Inc.,* 338 F.3d 394, 403 n.12 (5th Cir. 2003) (emphasis in original)

8   *Tampa Bay Shipbuilding & Repair v. Cedar* Shipping, 320 F.3d 1213, 1222 (11th Cir. 2003).

9   *U.S.* v. *Hamaker,* 455 F.3d 1316. 1331–1332 (11th Cir. 2006)

nically a mathematical determination, was deemed within ability of a lay person to comprehend, allowing its use in a summary judgment affidavit.[10]

In understanding F.R.Ev. 701, the practitioner should note that the rule applies only to testimony in opinion form, based on personal knowledge of the facts on which the opinion is expressed. Second, the witness must not be testifying as an expert. Third, where an opinion is not based on specialized knowledge, it must be regarded as a lay opinion.[11] While the preceding three points appear clear, their application in practice can resemble a metaphysical exercise. For example, where an accountant was engaged to assist in the restatement or correction of financial statements of a company, and obtained a thorough knowledge of the company's books and its computerized accounting system, the accountant testified concerning a chart that summarized receivable transactions between the company and its affiliates. The accountant, who was described as a fact witness by the government, was determined by the trial and appellate courts to be testifying about records with which he had become acquainted, and addressed what would actually be owed if debt reclassifications, that others testified were fraudulent, had not occurred.[12] The appellate court observed that had the accountant been testifying that the reclassifications were fraudulent, the testimony would have partly fallen within F.R.Ev. 702.[13]

The interplay between F.R.Ev. 701 and 702 must be addressed in commercial cases when the practitioner seeks to elicit an opinion from a witness, particularly an employee of a party or a party witness. The admonition of F.R.Ev. 701(c) that a lay opinion may not be based on scientific, technical, or other specialized knowledge is particularly difficult to apply where distinction is to be made concerning perception (observations) based on first hand knowledge and investigation, and not based wholly on expertise. The Bank of China case supplies a cautionary analysis concerning party employees who are providing both lay opinion (ER.Ev.701) and expert testimony (F.R.Ev. 702) predicated upon the same investigation and transactional facts, with the party employee improperly not disclosed as providing testimony under F.R.Ev. 702 as required by Fed. R. Civ. P. 26(a)(2)(A). However, expert disclosure of a party employee witness does not require the production of an expert written report where the employee's duties do not regularly involve giving expert testimony suggesting an advantage in using such an employee witness as distinguished from a non-employee expert. Fed. R. Civ. P. 26 (a)(2)(B).

Counsel, when evaluating whether testimony and evidence to support a case falls within the scope of F. R.Ev. 701 and 702, and the applicability of disclosure rules, may consider the wisdom of Jomini's comment concerning Napoleon's invasion of Russia, that "Russia is a country which is easy to get into, but very difficult to get out of." The type of testimony, the background of witnesses and the types of proof required to establish claims or defenses must be considered in the initial stages of case preparation. Portions of the proof requiring fact and opinion testimony need to be identified. Where opinion testimony is suggested or required, does the client have

---

10   Bryan v. Farmers Ins. Exchange, 432 F.3d 1114, 1124 (11th Cir. 2005)

11   Wright & Gold, Federal Practice and Procedure: Evidence §6253 (1997; Supp. 2008)

12   *U.S. v. Rigas,* 490 F3d at 224–225

13   Id.

employees or independent contractors that can provide that testimony? What are these persons' backgrounds? Will the opinion testimony fall within F.R.Ev. 701, 702 or both? What disclosure will be necessary if F.R.Ev. 702 is applicable?

The impact of F.R.Ev. 701 and 702 upon case preparation cannot be underestimated. Testimony on subjects such as valuations and appraisals, causation, damages, solvency, fair consideration/ value for transfers, and industry business practices often involve opinion testimony. Careful analysis must be performed concerning the testimony a lay witness can offer. Elements of analysis include a witness' opportunity to observe first hand the facts or events which will be the testimony's subject. The quality of the first hand observations will likely affect the opinions or inferences to which the witness may testify, as the latter must be rationally related to the former.

In conclusion, the key concepts expressed by F.R.Ev. 701 are that a lay witness opinion must be based on first hand observation from which a conclusion can be rationally drawn. F.R.Ev. 701(a) and (b). The prohibition expressed by F.R.Ev. 701(c) relates two concepts; that an opinion not based on specialized knowledge must be regarded as a lay opinion and that the witness not be testifying as an expert.[14] Application of the concepts in case preparation will aid both counsel and courts in avoiding disputes and the parties in preserving their claims and defenses.

---

14   E.g. *Lifewise Master Funding v. Telebank,* 374 F.3d 917, 929–930 (10th Cir. 2004) (plaintiffs officer's testimony on damages not admissible based on acquaintance with business, but upon mathematical models deemed expert testimony the witness was not qualified to give).

In the Courtroom with the Expert Witness

Collaboration Between Testimony and Technology

by Timothy A. Piganelli

Introduction

Trial verdicts can and have turned on the testimony of the Expert Witness. Preparation of the testimony, supporting evidence, and demonstratives can make the difference between a win and a loss. Enhancing the testimony of the expert witness with technology tools can give you an advantage in the courtroom.

Retaining an expert witness to assist with evaluating and explaining case issues is a common occurrence in litigation. In almost every case, the expert's testimony is a necessity and is expected by jurors and judges. This is especially true in cases where the issues are difficult to interpret and define. Most jurors don't have the topical depth of knowledge needed to sort through the myriad of concepts or ideas they must consider in order to properly render a verdict for the most complex or technical cases. In order to assist in that effort, the expert witness is a critical component to advancing the party's theories in trial or at various stages of the case.

Most cases call for the opinion of an expert on specific issues of the case. The end result is the testimony and presentation of your expert's findings to an audience, judge, jury, mediator, arbitrator and even the opposition. All the time, effort, energy and money spent preparing the expert for the presentation should ultimately enhance your case.

Many times in court, I have seen the direct examination of an expert witness and the method of demonstrating the expert's opinions result in a complicated testimony that runs the risk of "talking over the heads" of the audience. Juries often become confused by the testimony and have trouble sorting through all the details. In response, the jurors' attention tends to wander off, and as their ability to comprehend drops, they become frustrated. The testimony about the expert's findings and opinions runs the risk of having a negative effect on your case or the jury's perception of the case.

Unexpected challenges occur during trial. The amount of time the judge allows for direct examination may be limited, or the areas you need to cover with your expert may have to be adjusted due to rulings in court. Both of these can cause last minute changes while standing at the podium. This can often throw you and your expert off, ultimately diffusing the impact and importance of your expert's work. Some resulting problems can be poor methodology of presentation, confusing graphics, loss of continuity and too many long winded oral answers with no supplemental visuals. The result is a jury who never gets the story or "sees the picture" that you thought was powerful and persuasive. Hence, it never makes it out of the starting blocks and the impact you were hoping for is gone.

Let's examine some common problems and discuss suggestions on how to enhance and clarify your expert's "presentation" and testimony that will guarantee an impacting and memorable result for the jury or audience.

The Expert's Tutorial

In general, when conducting a direct examination of an expert, the first thing you should do in an effort to enhance your expert's presentation is to slowly and clearly introduce the audience to the general issues on which your expert will be testifying. To do this effectively, I recommend a tutorial using visual aids.

One of the first steps you will want to take during the examination of your expert is to cover the basics of the topic at hand. This is what I call "The Expert's Tutorial".

The tutorial is the part of the testimony that gives the audience an overview of the area on which the expert will testify. Most expert direct examinations cover this; but, the problem is the lack of use of visuals. These visual aids may be a series of graphics that do nothing more than give the jury a crash course on the area on which your expert is about to testify. This tutorial usually addresses areas that are so basic they are not disputed and thus this part of your presentation never draws objections. The advantages in doing a tutorial with visual aids are:

1. You can teach or educate the jury your way, using your graphics. This is especially true if you are the plaintiff in the case and you go first. A crash course on your "terms" helps define your theories and put them into context for the jury. Using graphics will dramatically reduce the time it takes to teach your jury the expert's topic.
2. You can use the same set of graphics to aid in explaining the expert's opinion, your position of the case, and how it differs from your adversary. Using the same "style" of graphics for the expert's testimony that were used in the tutorial further "links" the expert's testimony with perceived "industry standards". Thus, the jury gets accustomed to that "look and feel" you portrayed during your tutorial with the case-specific graphics.

3. Try to use as many stipulated or admitted exhibits in the expert's examination as possible and reasonable. Incorporating real exhibits, such as document or photographs into demonstratives to bolster the expert's opinions serves to authenticate that expert's opinions and demonstrate that the opinion is based on real case facts and evidence and not a made up or "bought and paid for" art.

The jury generally appreciates the "crash course" on the basics so that they know what to measure the expert's testimony against. Then, when you dig deep into the issues with the expert's testimony and the differences in contrast to the opposing position, especially in a strongly disputed area, the jury has a base point from which to evaluate the expert's opinions.

The Academia Expert

In many instances, an expert witness comes to the lawyer from the world of academia. Presentations these experts traditionally give in their daily lives are vastly different than the one you will ask them to perform in court. Most of these academic experts are accustomed to teaching in a classroom or lecture hall, or delivering a speech at a conference. In these linear environments they are allowed to "'lecture" in a free format. These audiences are different from a jury mainly in two ways: 1) their audience is already, to some degree, educated on the topic that is being presented, and 2) their audience is very eager to learn the material that is being presented. Neither of these scenarios is commonly true with a jury.

In addition, the presentation format in the courtroom is completely different. You are all familiar with the Rules of Evidence and Civil Procedure regarding the examination of a witness. Once on the witness stand, most academic experts forget that they cannot begin speaking freely about a topic or issue. They need to be reminded that they are "fed" the question and then must give a specific answer. Often they tend to carry on with an explanation of their opinion or position, ultimately resulting in a narrative objection by an attentive opposing counsel.

One of the ways to overcome this problem is by using illustrative aids or graphics. Using demonstratives is always a good idea to assist in conducting the examination of your expert witness. Visual aids can assist with the testimony of your expert regardless of the topic to which they are testifying. Not only can graphics and demonstratives assist in the testimony, but the graphic can also be used as a "visual outline" for the expert who may have difficulty remembering "where we are going next."

In most cases, experts need to tone down their testimony as they speak to a layman jury. Demonstratives and graphics assist with this task by adding the "visual component" to the presentation. Carefully conceived and prepared graphics can assist in breaking down the topic to understandable levels.

A suggestion is to create graphics using a "build technique." Briefly, "animate" your graphics so that they build one step at a time. Placing an entire graphic with many objects on the screen at once has been found to confuse jurors as to the message of the graphic. In using this build technique, your expert can walk the jury through each point of the graphic, giving the expert the opportunity to "lecture" their way as each build of the graphics is revealed.

Another suggestion is to have the expert get up out of the witness chair (with the court's approval) and move to the display screen to testify to the jury in a more personal and interactive manner. This can also be done even when showing your case evidence such as documents or photographs. Using this method will leave the impression that the expert is part of the graphic or evidence. We want the jury to remember the testimony as well as what is displayed to give both a more impacting impression.

Another technique we use is to provide the expert with a hard copy of the fully built demonstrative before they begin their testimony about the graphic. Once you overcome any objections, whether you are using a graphic demonstrative or an exhibit, you can then proceed with the testimony. Your expert can review the graphic from the hard copy showing it fully built. They are reminded in advance of each step that is coming and can mentally prepare what they are going to say before the question is posed.

The result is more concise testimony from your expert witness in an environment which is often uncomfortable and intimidating, even for the most seasoned academic lecturer.

Real Science vs. Jury Science

Cases that involve very complex and/or technical issues can sometimes get to a point where trying to explain every detail to a jury is a daunting, if not impossible, task. Although the need to make the record complete and clear for appellate purposes causes most trial teams to try to explain every little last detail, you may need to consider a different approach. Even the best graphics, 3-D animation and compelling testimony can sometimes confuse the jury. Time spent trying to convey a complex detail is wasted and your jury will soon get frustrated, lost, and disinterested. Ultimately, the results will have a negative effect on your case and cause you to waste precious court time.

The decision that needs to be made is whether you "teach" real science or jury science, real technology or jury technology, real medicine or jury medicine. The concept of Real Science vs. Jury Science is simply a suggestion to simplify a concept to its basic terms. Once you have simplified the concept, use a simple analogy to help teach it to your jury or other audience. Then, create a set of graphics to illustrate the analogy or simpler concepts. I am not suggesting that you "teach" or present inaccurate facts but merely trim the explanation, giving the audience only enough information so that they can grasp the concept to assist them in making a decision.

For example, you don't need to explain the derivation of the complete mathematical set of equations of motion to a jury to explain to how gravity works. Recently in a case, we were faced with a situation on how to explain Alternating Current used in Residential Power Distribution from a utility company to a jury. Real Science might explain Alternating Current like this:

An alternating current (AC) is an electrical current, where the magnitude and direction of the current varies cyclically, as opposed to direct current, where the direction of the current stays constant. The usual waveform of an AC circuit is generally that of a sine wave, as this results in the most efficient transmission of energy. However in certain applications different waveforms are used, such as triangular or square waves. The "effective voltage " is known as the RMS or Root Mean Square Voltage.

The diagram below illustrates AC current and the applicable equations.

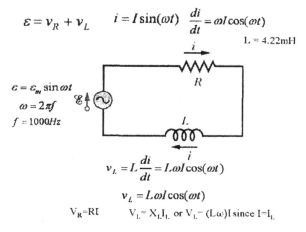

$$\varepsilon = v_R + v_L \qquad i = I\sin(\omega t) \qquad \frac{di}{dt} = \omega I\cos(\omega t)$$

$$L = 4.22\text{mH}$$

$$\varepsilon = \varepsilon_m \sin \omega t$$
$$\omega = 2\pi f$$
$$f = 1000Hz$$

$$v_L = L\frac{di}{dt} = L\omega I\cos(\omega t)$$

$$v_L = L\omega I\cos(\omega t)$$

$$V_R = RI \qquad V_L = X_L I_L \text{ or } V_L = (L\omega)I \text{ since } I = I_L$$

Jury science would say:

"Electricity or current flows in a circle from point A to point B, and then back to point A. The diagram below illustrates a "water analogy" to explain how current flows through a circuit.

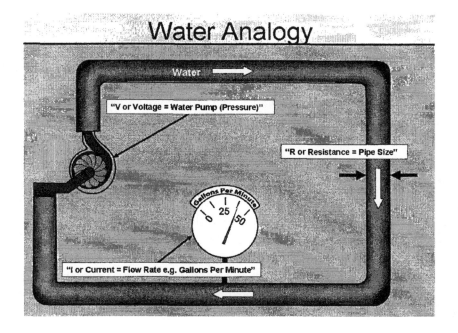

Probably the best example is the analogy of electricity to water. When describing how some basic electricity works it makes sense to use a water analogy and describe how electrons can flow and act just like water in a pipe. To explain how electricity flows in a circuit is like explaining how water will flow through two pipes, or what a plumber calls "flow rate". The bigger the pipe, the more water flows through it. The "bigger" the circuit (or least amount of resistance), the more electricity, or current, flows through it.

Thus, a set of graphics made to show a jury the water flow analogy, something they can better visualize and thereby are more familiar with, increases their ability to understand invisible electricity, rather than trying to create graphics that depict why more current flows through a better conductor.

In the above example, the simplified explanation of electricity and current through a circuit is all a jury needs to know to understand these concepts. Electricity was not on trial in this case. Rather, understanding the real world analogy of it helped the jury make a determination of liability. Using this methodology, expert testimony graphics only need to illustrate concepts, they don't need to explain every last detail.

How to create and present these simple analogies requires a team effort. This is sometimes easier said than done. Working with an expert on how to simplify a particular issue comes with its own set of challenges. Some experts can do this with some guidance from the trial lawyer. Once the trial lawyer and the expert come up with a simplified version, make sure that:

1. The examining lawyer fully understands the application of the simplified issue or analogy to the specific topic and its "big picture" purposes. This exercise will be a good indicator whether or not the approach will work with the jury. It also will assist the trial lawyer in developing the examination outline that will be used during the actual direct examination, and;

2. The expert feels comfortable testifying to this simplified version. When the expert has a major role in the conceptual creation of the simplified graphics, agrees with the illustrations, she will understand how to use the graphics effectively as an aid to her testimony. Also, make certain that the expert understands how the computerized presentation of the graphics will work in the courtroom, i.e., with slide animation steps, changing colors, etc.

The Expert Report

In most cases where an expert is retained, after analysis, the expert generates a written report. This same report is often offered as an exhibit at trial and is most certainly referenced in depositions, briefs and motions. Often times, experts' reports need some kind of visual or graphic enhancement because most experts are not presentation specialists, rather they are professionals in such specialties as electrical engineering, finance or economy or medical disciplines. They are not experts at the best way to illustratively depict their work. As thorough as the expert's report may be, the way in which the expert chooses to illustrate certain themes of the report can sometimes be very confusing to a layman. This may become very critical when presenting to a layman jury. Here are some tips to enhance the experts' reports before you produce them.

In addition to obtaining a printed hard copy of the report, try to get a digital copy from the expert. For example, if the report was created on a word processor using Microsoft Word, then try to get a copy of the original ".DOC" file. Ask to receive a copy of the report on a floppy disk, CD, DVD, or e-mail. In addition to the report, there may be supporting data which has also been generated and/or stored on a computer, such as charts, graphs, or scientific data. If that is the case, then ask for that information in its original digital format. These digital versions of the "raw data" can then be imported into a variety of graphic programs such as Microsoft Excel, PowerPoint, or Adobe Photoshop. The software applications have many features that allow you to take otherwise "raw", boring data and liven it up for demonstrative purposes to assist the jury or audience in comprehension of the total report. For instance, raw numbers taken by a technical expert can easily be imported into Microsoft Excel to be later presented as a bar chart. The illustration below shows a comparison of raw data vs. a bar chart.

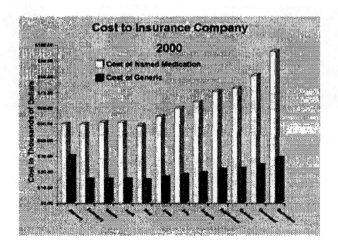

The two charts show the same information. The one on the left shows the raw numbers. The chart on the right shows the difference between the first and second columns of data. The objective of this data is to show the difference between the first and second column. The graphical bar chart on the right gives a better way to visually compare the two sets of numbers rather than simply observing the columns of numbers shown on the left. Juries appreciate a graphic look at a set of numbers rather than trying to study and analyze rows of numbers in spreadsheet cells.

Having the expert's report in a digital file format allows you to easily prepare it for presentation purposes. Too many times I see a trial team take the hard copy of the expert's report, scan it, then display charts and graphs or collections of numerical date directly from the scanned version. Charts and graphs presented in this manner lose color quality and the ability to animate or "build" the graph. A better method is to begin with the electronic files of the report, underlying supporting data, and graphic summaries of the findings and build demonstratives from that which replicate those in the report. The exception to this is displaying in court the written text of the report to a jury. To display those textual portions of the report, you can scan the report and use the image files to create specialized document slides or use your favorite trial presentation software to zoom in, "tear out" and highlight relevant portions of the report. This method is shown below.

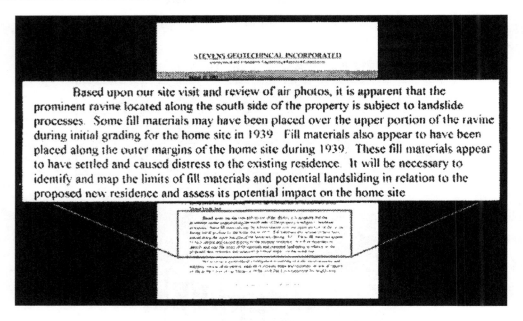

Finally, I will repeat this suggestion because I believe it merits repeating. Use the build or animation technique. Taking the bar charts or graphs and having the chart or graph "build" one step at a time focuses the testimony and the jury's attention on those specific points demonstrated on the chart as they are discussed.

Using Full Motion Animation with a Technical Expert

Arguably, the best graphical way to demonstrate a process, event or simulation is through the use of Full Motion 3-Dimensional Animation (3-D Animation). Using this method is by far the best way to educate and help a jury understand technical or mechanical issues and concepts. Typically there must be testimony provided to substantiate accuracy and lay the foundation for the animation. Typically, that witness is your technical or mechanical expert. Likely it is this expert's work or research that supports the data from which the animation is derived. Here are some tips and suggestions about using this type of technology to enhance an expert's testimony.

First, your expert must be the "designer" and "director" of the animation. They may not necessarily be an expert in the mechanical creation of the animation, but they should be somewhat familiar with how the hardware and software creates the end product. Many times in court the question is posed to the expert about how the animation was created. The expert fumbles a bit and answers that they are not aware of exactly how the animation is created but rather they agree with the results. This looks bad to a jury and makes it seem like the lawyer created the animation and has instructed the expert to testify to it, and you risk your expert losing credibility with the jury. You must make sure your expert is well-versed on what software was used, the process involved and how the file or video was ultimately created. As long as they can answer one or two of these questions, your jury will know that the expert's work is behind the animation and not just the lawyer. In addition, there is a chance that the expert's lack of knowledge on how exactly the animation was created could cause the presentation of the animation to be excluded.

When preparing to present an animation, take some time to plan and rehearse how and when the animation will be played during the expert's examination. For example, when playing an animation, you will likely want to pause at certain intervals to allow the expert to comment on the animation as well as allow the attorney to ask questions specific to the animation and the expert's opinions. A plan should be established between the lawyer, the expert and the system operator defining when the animation will be paused and, if necessary, to be reversed for clarity. Consideration should be given to the method of playing the animation. Animation files are typically produced as a computer file. Sometimes they are transferred to a DVD for playback on a commercial DVD player or they are produced as a standard digital computer file for MAC or Windows. In some instances, they are produced onto an analog video tape for playback on a standard VCR or video tape player.

Coordinating the Technology Team with the Expert

When computerized trial presentation is used in a case, a team of professionals are assigned the task of managing and applying the technology. One of the many tasks the technology team is responsible for is the operation of the computer system that ultimately displays evidence in court. The system typically consists of a laptop PC or Macintosh computer, a display system, usually a projector and screen, and a series of flat panel monitors located throughout the courtroom. This task can be accomplished by an outside consultant or an appropriately trained and experienced staff member from the party's counsel. In either case, time must be allocated to the rehearsal and coordination of the display of evidence and demonstratives.

The coordination between the presentation system operator, the lawyer and the expert is critical during the direct examination of the expert. This is particularly true during the presentation of an animation. Selection of the proper hardware and software will guarantee the operator's ability to effectively display the animation. There are a variety of software packages to display animation files. One of the most important features to have is the ability to pause, re-wind, fast forward and move frame by frame during the playback of the animation. This flexibility will allow the lawyer and expert to move freely during the examination and allow a good thorough explanation of the animated demonstrative. Inevitably, the animation will need to be re-wound or played repeatedly. It is here that the operator will need that flexibility to react to the request by the expert on the stand or the examining attorney. A brief meeting and rehearsal at some time before the expert's testimony will help insure a flawless collaboration between testimony and technology in court.

Chapter 5: Key Terms and Discussion Questions

Key Terms

Affidavit: a sworn, written statement made under oath

Credibility: the quality of being convincing or believable

Deposition: where an individual testifies under oath outside of the court room

Expert Witness: a witness who is qualified to testify because he or she has specialized knowledge that exceeds common knowledge

Impeach: to challenge a witness's testimony in a trial; questioning the credibility of a witness during a trial

Lay Witness: a witness who is not an expert witness

Opinion Testimony: a belief stronger than impression and less than certainty; expression of judgment by an expert witness

Testimony: oral or written evidence given by a witness under oath

Witness: an individual who gives evidence of a fact based on his or her own observations

Discussion Questions

1. Which is preferable: witness testimony or deposition testimony?
2. Explain the difference between a fact and an opinion.
3. When can a lay witness testify about his or her opinion?
4. When is expert testimony allowed?
5. What do you consider to be "specialized knowledge"?

Hearsay

Hearsay Rule and Exceptions

by Jefferson L. Ingram

> The determination that a statement is hearsay does not end the inquiry into admissibility; there must still be a further examination of the need for the statement at trial and the circumstantial guaranty of trustworthiness surrounding the making of the statement.
>
> *Zippo Mfg. Co. v. Rogers Imports, Inc.,*
> 216 F. Supp. 670 (S.D.N.Y. 1963)

Introduction

While virtually everyone has heard of the concept of hearsay evidence, whether from books, films, television shows, and newspapers, most people do not know how it operates in court and fewer still understand the rationale behind the hearsay rule. Even those who have some understanding of the rule are probably unaware that the exceptions to the hearsay rule allow may allow more evidence to be admitted than the rule excludes. When a court recognizes an exception and admits hearsay evidence, there are usually powerful reasons and other justifications for trusting the truthfulness of the evidence. If the hearsay rule were applied without exceptions, it would be very difficult in many criminal cases to present sufficient facts to prove guilt, and certainly much reliable evidence would be excluded from consideration.

As a practical matter, determining what kind of testimony can be considered hearsay provides the starting point for developing an understanding of this rule of exclusion. When an out-of-court statement is repeated in court by a person who overheard another person outside of court make a statement, the evidence that the witness utters in court may be excluded on the ground that it constitutes hearsay evidence. To be properly considered hearsay evidence, the substance of the out-of-court statement must have been offered in court to prove its truth. When an out-of-court statement is repeated in court and the purpose of offering the statement was merely to demonstrate that a particular person was physically present to be able to make the statement, the internal contents of the statement have not been offered for the proof of the truth contained within the words. In that situation, the out-of-court statement is not considered hearsay evidence. Courts tend to exclude hearsay evidence because subtle alterations in wording, demeanor, or inflection may change the meaning of spoken words. Every time a story is retold to a new person, the essence of the story alters slightly, with a detail added or unconsciously deleted, causing the meaning to shift. The general rule excluding hearsay statements is justified on these and other grounds. It is important to be aware of the historical justifications for the rule in order to understand the exceptions. If the reasons for the rule do not exist in a particular situation, then the evidence should be admitted to assist in determining the facts of the case. Some of the reasons for the exclusion of evidence under the hearsay rule are discussed in the following paragraphs.

1. "Traditionally, testimony that is given by a witness who relates not what he or she knows personally, but what others have said, and that is therefore dependent on the credibility of someone other than the witness."[1]

2. "Hearsay evidence is objectionable because the person who makes the offered statement is not under oath and is not subject to cross-examination."[2] Although the witness in court who has repeated what someone else has said will be under oath, the person who actually made the statement was not under oath so that hearsay statements generally lack trustworthiness.

3. The demeanor or conduct of the person who actually makes the statement cannot be observed by the judge and jury when the witness comes to court to tell what was stated outside the court. Evaluating demeanor proves important when judging credibility of witnesses and is an important aspect of the right of confrontation.[3]

4. There is a danger that the in-court witness who is reporting what was said by an out-of-court declarant may repeat the statement inaccurately. The proponent of the evidence "essentially asks the jury to assume that the out-of-court declarant was not lying or mistaken when the statement was made."[4]

5. One of the principal reasons for the hearsay rule is to exclude declarations whose veracity or truthfulness cannot be tested by cross-examination. Because the

---

1   *Black's Law Dictionary* (2004).

2   Missouri v. Mozee, 2003 Mo. App. LEXIS 940 (2003), quoting State v. Bowens, 964 S.W. 2d 232, 240, 1998 Mo. App. LEXIS 383 (1998).

3   *See* In re Kentron D., 101 Cal. App. 4th 1381, 125 Cal. Rptr. 2d 260, 2002 Cal. App. LEXIS 4629 (2002).

4   Armstead v. State, 255 Ga. App. 385, 389, 565 S.E.2d 579, 582, 2002 Ga. App. LEXIS 633 (2002).

declarant's statement was made out of court, the declarant cannot be cross-examined and the adverse party against whom the evidence is offered is deprived of the opportunity to challenge his memory or sincerity.[5]

In explaining some of the reasons for excluding hearsay evidence from court, one reviewing court noted that "[h]earsay evidence is excluded because the value of the statement rests on the credibility of the out-of-court asserter who is not subject to cross-examination and other safeguards of reliability."[6] Similarly, the Supreme Court of Connecticut offered related reasons for the hearsay rule when it stated:

> The declarant might be lying; he might have misperceived the events which he relates; he might have faulty memory; his words might be misunderstood or taken out of context by the listener. And the ways in which these dangers are minimized for in-court statements—the oath, the witness' awareness of the gravity of the proceedings, the jury's ability to observe the witness' demeanor, and, most importantly, the right of the opponent to cross-examine—are generally absent for things said out of court.[7]

Some forms of hearsay evidence prove more reliable than others and for that reason some hearsay will be admitted based on recognized and standardized hearsay exceptions. The courts, in seeking to allow as much evidence into court as possible while sifting out unreliable evidence, have developed many exceptions to the hearsay rule. For each exception, however, there is a clear justification designed to assure the trustworthiness of the evidence. In situations involving hearsay in which none of the well-known hearsay exceptions permits admission of the evidence, the federal rules allow a party to argue that the interests of justice would be promoted by admission of the hearsay evidence where there are guarantees that the evidence sought to be introduced would be trustworthy and probative on the point for which it is offered.[8]

While this chapter emphasizes many hearsay exceptions, some types of evidence that may be challenged as excludable hearsay have been discussed in other chapters of the book. For example, an out-of-court confession that is repeated by another person in a court is, technically, hearsay. However, this evidence is often admissible under one of the exceptions discussed in Chapter 16. The hearsay exception of "past recollection recorded" and its rationale were discussed in Chapter 9. Official records, ancient documents, and learned treatises are generally admissible as hearsay exceptions and will be considered in Chapter 13.

This chapter discusses and defines the hearsay rule of exclusion and introduces the important exceptions that permit hearsay evidence to be admitted in criminal courts. Among the exceptions treated within this chapter are declarations against interest, the business records exception, dying declarations, spontaneous and excited utterances, and family history.

---

5   Iowa v. Dullard, 2003 Iowa Sup. LEXIS 169 (2003).

6   State v. Taylor, 999 So. 2d 1262, 2009 La. App. Unpub. LEXIS 45 (La. 2009).

7   Connecticut v. Cruz, 260 Conn. 1, 792 A.2d 823, 2002 Conn. LEXIS 127 (2002).

8   *See* Fed. R. Evid. 807.

Definitions and Statement of the Hearsay Rule

Rule 801

Definitions

The following definitions apply under this article:

(a) Statement. A "statement" is (1) an oral or written assertion or (2) nonverbal conduct of a person, if it is intended by the person as an assertion.

(b) Declarant. A "declarant" is a person who makes a statement.

(c) Hearsay. "Hearsay" is a statement, other than one made by the declarant while testifying at the trial or hearing, offered in evidence to prove the truth of the matter asserted.

(d) Statements which are not hearsay. A statement is not hearsay if—

1. **Prior statement by witness.**—The declarant testifies at the trial or hearing and is subject to cross-examination concerning the statement, and the statement is (A) inconsistent with the declarant's testimony, and was given under oath subject to the penalty of perjury at a trial, hearing, or other proceeding, or in a deposition, or (B) consistent with the declarant's testimony and is offered to rebut an express or implied charge against the declarant of recent fabrication or improper influence or motive, or (C) one of identification of a person made after perceiving the person; or

2. **Admission by party-opponent.**—The statement is offered against a party and is (A) the party's own statement in either an individual or a representative capacity or (B) a statement of which the party has manifested an adoption or belief in its truth, or (C) a statement by a person authorized by the party to make a statement concerning the subject, or (D) a statement by the party's agent or servant concerning a matter within the scope of the agency or employment, made during the existence of the relationship, or (E) a statement by a co-conspirator of a party during the course and in furtherance of the conspiracy. The contents of the statement shall be considered but are not alone sufficient to establish the declarant's authority under subdivision (C), the agency or employment relationship and scope thereof under subdivision (D), or the existence of the conspiracy and the participation therein of the declarant and the party against whom the statement is offered under subdivision (E).[9]

During the course of both civil and criminal litigation, many courts have resolved and refined hearsay problems by explaining the concepts and defining hearsay and evaluating the admissibility

---

9   Fed. R. Evid. 801.

of hearsay evidence. Although these explanations are worded differently, the general meaning of hearsay concepts emerges. Some of these definitions are included here as examples:

> Evidence of a statement which is made other than by the witness while testifying at a hearing, offered to prove the truth of the matter stated, is hearsay evidence and inadmissible, subject to certain statutory exceptions.[10]
>
> "'Hearsay' is a statement, other than one made by the declarant while testifying at the trial or hearing, offered in evidence to prove the truth of the matter asserted."[11]
>
> "Hearsay" is a statement, other than one made by the declarant while testifying at the trial or hearing, offered in evidence to prove the truth of the matter asserted.[12]
>
> "Hearsay testimony" is an out-of-court statement offered to prove the truth of a matter asserted and is dependent on the credibility of the out-of-court declarant.[13]

The federal courts have interpreted and explained the Federal Rules of Evidence as litigants have raised legal questions and identified problems. For example, one court decided that evidence was "not hearsay" as defined in Rule 801(d)(1)(A) when a witness, although present and testifying at the trial, claimed no recollection of either the underlying events described in his prior grand jury testimony or of the giving of the testimony itself.[14] The trial court did not abuse its discretion in admitting the witness's grand jury testimony under Rule 801(d)(1)(A), which pertains to prior inconsistent statements. When prior inconsistent statements come within the rule, they are not considered hearsay and may be admitted as substantive evidence.

Under Rule 801(d)(1)(A), if an out-of-court statement is inconsistent with the declarant's trial testimony and was given under the penalty of perjury at a deposition, trial, hearing, or similar proceeding, the prior statement may be received as evidence and is not considered hearsay. For purposes of this rule, the word "inconsistent" does not include only statements diametrically opposed or logically incompatible, but also evasive answers, silence, changes in position, or in a reported change in memory.[15]

According to one court, the rationale for the admission of prior consistent statements as provided in Rule 801(d)(1)(B) is that the statements are considered relevant and necessary.[16] Where there is a charge of recent fabrication, a witness's prior deposition testimony is admissible to refute these charges of fabrication.[17] However, a sexual assault victim's videotaped statements

---

10   State v. Clark, 949 P.2d 1099 (Kan. 1997).

11   Perkins v. State, 2009 Ala. Crim. App. LEXIS 12 (Ala. 2009).

12   Ind. R. Evid. 801(c) (Matthew Bender 2009).

13   People v. Schoultz, 224 Ill. Dec. 885, 682 N.E.2d 446 (1997).

14   United States v. DiCaro, 772 F.2d 1314 (7th Cir. 1985).

15   United States v. Williams, 737 F.2d 594 (7th Cir. 1984). *See also* State v. Pusyka, 592 A.2d 850 (R.I. 1991), in which the court held that a witness's prior statement must be sufficiently inconsistent with the witness's in-court testimony to be admissible. This determination is within the sound discretion of the trial judge.

16   State v. Gardner, 490 N.W.2d 838 (Iowa 1992).

17   State v. Deases, 479 N.W.2d 597 (Iowa 1991).

were not admissible under this exception for prior statements by the witness when the victim was never subjected to cross-examination about the prior statements.[18]

The purpose of Rule 801(d)(1)(C) is to permit introduction of identifications made by a witness when the witness's memory was fresh and there was less opportunity for influence to be exerted upon him.[19]

The United States Supreme Court has determined that an out-of-court identification by the victim, naming the defendant as the assailant, was admissible as nonhearsay although the victim could not remember seeing the assailant.[20]

Section 801(d)(1)(B) of the Federal Rules of Evidence provides that a statement is not hearsay if consistent with the declarant's testimony and offered to rebut an express or implied charge against the declarant of recent fabrication or improper influence or motive. In a case that reached the United States Supreme Court, Tome v. United States, the interpretation of this provision was debated.[21] In Tome, the government initiated charges against the defendant involving the sexual abuse of his four-year-old daughter. The prosecution's theory was that the defendant committed the assaults while the child was with the defendant and disclosed the crime when she was spending vacation time with her mother. The defense argued that the allegations were concocted so that the mother would obtain custody and the child would not be returned to her father. After the alleged motive to fabricate arose, the child made out-of-court statements to witnesses. At the trial, the judge permitted the admission of the statements of some of these witness statements, despite the fact that they were introduced after charges of recent fabrication had been made. The United States Supreme Court reversed the conviction, deciding that Rule 801(d)(1)(B) permitted the introduction of a declarant's consistent out-of-court statements to rebut a charge of recent fabrication or improper influence, or motive only when those statements were made before the fabrication, influence, or motive arose.

Determining that the statements made by the child to other witnesses were made after the defendant's charge of fabrication, the Supreme Court remanded the case for further proceedings. The majority explained that to allow the out-of-court statements made after the in-court charge of fabrication would shift the emphasis of the trial to the out-of-court statements rather than the in-court statements.

Rule 801(d)(2)(E) of the Federal Rules, which has been made part of the rules of evidence in many states, provides that a statement is not hearsay if made by a conspirator during the course of and in furtherance of the conspiracy. Changes made to Federal Rule 801(d)(2)(E) in 1997 noted that the contents of a statement made by a conspirator are insufficient to establish that the conspirator can speak for the other conspirators. While an out-of-court statement made by a conspirator fits the traditional definition of hearsay, this rule of evidence simply declares that it shall not be deemed to be hearsay. In explaining the rule's purpose, a federal court noted that

18   State v. Palabay, 844 P.2d 1 (Wash. 1992).

19   United States v. Marchand, 564 F.2d 983 (2d Cir. 1977).

20   United States v. Owens, 484 U.S. 554, 108 S. Ct. 838, 98 L. Ed. 2d 951 (1988).

21   Tome v. United States, 513 U.S. 150, 115 S. Ct. 696, 130 L. Ed. 2d 574 (1995).

statements made by conspirators during the course of and in furtherance of a conspiracy do not fit within the definition of hearsay; rather, the court views these statements as party admissions.[22] A conspirator's statement is made in furtherance of the conspiracy (so as to be admissible as) when the statement is part of the information flow between the conspirators, intended to help each perform his or her role.[23] However, a mere conversation between the conspirators or merely narrative declarations among them would not constitute conversations made "in furtherance of a conspiracy" and would not be admissible under this provision.[24]

In case in which a doctor wanted to hire a hit man to kill his wife, the trial court refused to allow the doctor's son to testify, under Rule 801(d)(1)(B), that the doctor really only wanted the hit man to follow his wife and conduct some surveillance. The doctor told the son the surveillance story only after being arrested in the plot, and therefore he had a motive to fabricate despite his assertion to the contrary. Because the motive to fabricate arose before the statement to his son, the son could be prohibited from testifying about his father's statement because it would not meet Rule 801's requirements and would be considered inadmissible hearsay.[25]

Rule 802

Hearsay Rule

Hearsay is not admissible except as provided by these rules or by other rules prescribed by the Supreme Court pursuant to statutory authority or by Act of Congress.[26]

As defined in Rule 801 of the Federal Rules of Evidence, hearsay is "a statement other than one made by the declarant while testifying at the trial or hearing offered in evidence to prove the truth of the matter asserted."[27] Another definition is that hearsay evidence is evidence that derives its value not from the credit to be given to the witness upon the stand, but at least in part from the veracity and competency of another person who is not testifying. One court stated that "Hearsay is testimony of an out-of-court statement offered to establish the truth of the matter asserted therein and whose value thus depends upon the credibility of the out-of-court declarant."[28] For example, if a police officer were to testify concerning the meaning of numbers

---

22   United States v. Powell, 973 F.2d 885 (10th Cir. 1992), *cert. denied*, 507 U.S. 1161, 113 S. Ct. 1598, 123 L. Ed. 2d 161 (1992).

23   United State v. Godinez, 110 F.3d 448 (7th Cir. 1997).

24   United State v. Nazemian, 748 F.2d 552 (9th Cir. 1991).

25   United States v. Drury, 2003 U.S. App. LEXIS 18152 (11th Cir. 2003).

26   Fed. R. Evid. 802.

27   *Id.*

28   Illinois v. Thompson, 327 Ill. App. 3d 1061, 765 N.E.2d 1203, 2002 Ill. App. LEXIS 162 (2002).

on a fast food receipt when the officer gathered his understanding of the significance of the numbers by speaking with an employee of the fast food establishment, the officer's testimony would constitute hearsay evidence because it depends on the veracity and credibility of the fast food employee who was not in court or under oath.

While hearsay evidence may be excluded, out-of-court statements that are not offered for their substantive truth may be admissible because they do not meet the definition of hearsay. Where police arrested a suspected drug dealer after observing a sale, they found two cell phones during the post-arrest search of his person. When phones rang on two occasions, the officer answered the calls and had conversations with unknown persons who wanted to buy drugs. The trial court permitted the substance of the conversations to be admitted against the defendant because the statements were not offered to prove their substantive truth, only that other people thought they could buy drugs by phoning the defendant's cell phones. These phone conversations were circumstantial evidence that the defendant had the intent to distribute drugs.[29]

The term "statement," as used in the hearsay definition, consists of: (1) an oral or written assertion or (2) nonverbal conduct of a person, if it is intended by him or her as an assertion or is a substitute for speech. Therefore, a statement may be an actual verbal statement, a written statement, or nonverbal conduct, such as pointing, to identify a suspect in a lineup. The act of pointing to indicate a choice in a lineup context operates as a substitute for speech and when a police officer subsequently testifies in court about the out-of-court witness's indication, the officer has brought the out-of-court, nonverbal assertion into court as a hearsay statement. A "declarant," as used in the hearsay definition, is a person who makes a statement.

Admitting hearsay evidence generally involves having the out-of-court declarant's statement or evidence introduced in court with the result that the defendant cannot actually cross-examine that actual declarant. Cross-examination of the witness in court is certainly possible, but the person actually offering the evidence is not in court, a fact that creates constitutional issues that intermix with hearsay jurisprudence. In interpreting the Sixth Amendment right of confrontation and cross-examination, the Supreme Court overruled a case that allowed testimonial evidence without personal confrontation with the adverse witness. The older case, *Ohio v. Roberts*,[30] permitted the admission of prior testimony against the defendant when the witness was unavailable and when the prior testimony bore some "indicia of reliability." Unavailability was a fairly easy determination, but "indicia of reliability" seemed to invite judicial determination on uncertain terms. When the confrontation issue came to the Court in *Crawford v. Washington*,[31] the Court took the opportunity to overrule *Ohio v. Roberts* and to clearly enforce the original concept of the Sixth Amendment confrontation clause.

In *Crawford*, the defendant had been convicted of assaulting a man who attempted to rape his wife, using evidence given by the wife in a statement to police. The defendant's wife invoked her marital testimonial privilege and did not testify against the defendant, with the result being

---

29   Commonwealth v. Vasquez, 20 Mass. L. Rep. 319, 2005 Mass. Super. LEXIS 656 (Mass. 2005).

30   Ohio v. Roberts, 448 U.S. 56, 1980 U.S. LEXIS 140 (1980).

31   541 U.S. 36, 2004 U.S. LEXIS 1838 (2004).

that the trial judge allowed the wife's statement to the police to be used against the defendant. The judge followed the *Ohio v. Roberts* view and allowed the testimony because the judge viewed the defendant's wife as unavailable and considered the wife's out-of-court statement to be "reliable." The statement called into question the defendant's contention of self-defense. The Supreme Court reversed the decision of the Supreme Court of Washington that reinstated the trial court conviction and held that Crawford's Sixth Amendment right to confront and cross-examine adverse witnesses had been violated. The Court found a Sixth Amendment violation because, where testimonial evidence was at issue, the playing of the wife's testimony by audiotape prevented the defendant from confronting or conducting any cross-examination of the wife. The Court held that the Sixth Amendment demanded both unavailability and at least a prior opportunity to cross-examine the witness. In this case, the defendant had no opportunity to ever cross-examine his wife. The rule to be distilled from the *Crawford* case is that when testimonial evidence is involved, there must be a trial opportunity to cross-examine the witness or a proper earlier proceeding where the right of cross-examination existed and there must be proof of unavailability of the witness.[32] The case did not put an end to hearsay exceptions, but reinstated the right to confront and cross-examine witnesses where prior testimony is involved.

In a later Washington case,[33] the alleged victim in a domestic violence case made a 911 call to report an assault by her former boyfriend, who was under a no-contact order and who had just fled the victim's dwelling. The former girlfriend-victim did not testify against her attacker, but the trial court admitted an audiotape of the 911 call against the defendant, over his Sixth Amendment objection. The defendant appealed his resulting conviction through Washington courts with unsuccessful results. The Supreme Court of the United States affirmed after determining that the 911 call was not testimonial in nature and the use of the audiotape did not create a confrontation and cross-examination issue under the Sixth Amendment. The victim was speaking with an emergency operator while the events were in progress, describing current circumstances that necessitated a police response. As the Court noted in making a distinction between testimonial statements and nontestimonial statements, "Statements are nontestimonial when made in the course of police interrogation under circumstances objectively indicating that the primary purpose of the interrogation is to enable police assistance to meet an ongoing emergency. They are testimonial when the circumstances objectively indicate that there is no such ongoing emergency, and that the primary purpose of the interrogation is to establish or prove past events potentially relevant to later criminal prosecution."[34] The victim's statements were not testimonial because the statements were necessary to enable the police to resolve the ongoing emergency rather than to reconstruct what had happened in the past. Because the Court characterized the 911 call as nontestimonial, the Sixth Amendment was not implicated.

---

32   *Id.*

33   Davis v. Washington, 547 U.S. 813, 2006 U.S. LEXIS 4886 (2006).

34   *Id.* at 822.

In *Hammon v. Indiana*,[35] a companion case to *Davis v. Washington*, police responded to a domestic disturbance at the home of a married couple. The wife told officers that nothing was wrong, but invited the police inside the home, where they separately questioned each spouse. The wife signed an affidavit indicating that she had been the victim of a battery at the hands of her husband. The wife did not appear to testify at the bench trial. Over the defendant-husband's Sixth Amendment cross-examination objection, the trial court admitted the affidavit and other information that the wife had given to one of the officers. The prosecution put the officer who had questioned the wife on the stand and asked him to testify to what the wife-victim told him and to authenticate her affidavit. In relevant parts, the Indiana court all affirmed the conviction. The Supreme Court found that the wife's statements to police were testimonial in nature and the admission of the wife's statements violated the defendant's Sixth Amendment right of confrontation and cross-examination. According to the *Hammon* Court, the officer's questions were directed at determining what had happened and was part of an investigation into alleged criminal conduct. The more formal features of the investigation and the affidavit strengthened the testimonial aspects of the testimony given by police and through the introduction of the affidavit at trial. The Court reversed the defendant's conviction and remanded the case.

Although the rule that hearsay evidence is inadmissible is generally true, significant hearsay evidence is admitted based on exceptions to the general rule of exclusion and despite Sixth Amendment confrontation and cross-examination issues. The exceptions to the hearsay rule are so numerous that the argument could be made that most hearsay evidence may be admissible while some hearsay evidence may be excluded. This chapter considers some of the well-recognized exceptions and the reasoning for those exceptions in the sections that follow.

History and Development of the Hearsay Rule

In an article that appeared in the *Minnesota Law Review*, the authors included a thumbnail sketch of the history of the use of the hearsay rule.[36] This article included the following history:

> The hearsay rule was not the creation of some clever legal philosopher or rules-drafting committee. Rather, it was a byproduct of jury-based common law adjudication. It was molded and remolded over the course of more than four centuries by lawyers pursuing the business of representing clients and by judges seeking to ensure proper verdicts. As a consequence of its incremental development, the rule, like so much in Anglo-American jurisprudence, does not have a single goal or express a single viewpoint. It reflects a variety of objectives sought at different times by participants in the courtroom contests.
>
> Medieval English jury adjudication was, in essence, based upon hearsay. Juries in the thirteenth and fourteenth centuries decided cases on the basis of rumor, gossip, and community opinion to which they were exposed before the trial commenced. While reservations

---

35   547 U.S. 813, 2006 U.S. LEXIS 4886 (2006). Companion case to *Davis v. Washington*.

36   Richard F. Rakos and Stephen Landsman, *The Hearsay Rule as the Focus of Empirical Investigation,* 76 Minn. L. Rev. 655 (1992).

about hearsay were articulated as early as 1202, it was not until the latter half of the 1500s that serious concerns were voiced about its use in litigation.

The hearsay rule as we know it had its origin in England in the sixteenth century. Prior to that time, juries were permitted to obtain evidence by consulting persons who were not called as witnesses. Jurors did not decide the case on the basis of testimony given in open court, but were in fact chosen because they had some knowledge of the case.

In 1813, Chief Justice Marshall, in explaining the justification for the hearsay rule, stated, "Our lives, our liberty, and our property, are all concerned in the support of these rules, which have been matured by the wisdom of ages, and are now revered from their antiquity and the good sense in which they are founded. One of these rules is that hearsay evidence is by its own nature inadmissible." Justice Marshall went on to say that "[i]ts intrinsic weakness, its incompetency to satisfy the mind of the existence of the fact, and the frauds which might be practiced under its cover, combine to support the rule that hearsay evidence is totally inadmissible."[37]

As jurors began to be chosen only if they had no knowledge of the case that would influence their decision, the hearsay rule began to develop. By 1700, the rule prohibiting the admission of hearsay statements was formulated in criminal cases. Over the centuries, exceptions to the hearsay rule have developed because of the strict exclusionary nature of the rule.

Exceptions to the Hearsay Rule—General

Although Chief Justice John Marshall argued that hearsay evidence should not be admitted in federal courts because of its intrinsic weakness and incompetency, and despite the fact that he concluded that "[t]his court is not inclined to extend the exceptions further than they have already been carried,"[38] state and federal courts have made exceptions and the exceptions have been extended over the years in all American courts.

In Rules 803 and 804 of the Federal Rules of Evidence there are at least 28 specific exceptions, and Rule 807 contains one broad category of residual exceptions for situations not specifically covered by Rule 803 or Rule 804. Rule 807 provides for recognition of other exceptions when there are "equivalent circumstantial guarantees of trustworthiness."[39]

The reasons for the hearsay rule in the first instance are based on the facts that: (1) the declarant was not under oath to speak the truth; (2) the demeanor of the person who actually made the statement cannot be observed by the judge and jury; (3) there is danger that the statement may be repeated inaccurately; and (4) generally the declarant cannot be cross-examined despite

---

37   Mima Queen and Child v. Hepburn, 7 U.S. (3 Cranch) 290 (1813). *See also* Donnelly v. United States, 288 U.S. 243, 33 S. Ct. 449, 57 L. Ed. 820 (1913) for a discussion of the history of the rules.

38   Mima Queen and Child v. Hepburn, *supra* note 31.

39   Fed. R. Evid. 807. The exceptions noted in Rules 803 and 804 are not included in this section. Rule 807 covers situations that are not specifically mentioned in Rules 803 and 804. These rules are included in the Appendix, and they should be reviewed before continuing.

the defendant's rights under the Sixth Amendment. The argument for admitting evidence under exceptions to the rule holds that if the purpose and rationale for excluding evidence under the hearsay rule do not exist in a specific case and if the interests of justice will be best served by admitting the statement into evidence, then the evidence should be admitted as an exception to the hearsay rule.

As a general rule, most hearsay exceptions have been categorized into fairly recognizable and repeating fact patterns addressed by the rules of evidence. Attorneys are able to intelligently argue the advantages and disadvantages of following a well-known exception by arguing the merits of the introduction of hearsay evidence. Thus, when hearsay statements fall within firmly rooted hearsay exceptions, or occur under circumstances with particularized guarantees of trustworthiness,[40] such statements are adequately reliable to be admissible in criminal cases.[41]

In the following sections, the text discusses some of the hearsay exceptions that are most frequently encountered by criminal justice personnel and explains the rationales for the exceptions.

Spontaneous and Excited Utterances

Rule 803

Hearsay Exceptions; Availability of Declarant Immaterial

* * *

The following are not excluded by the hearsay rule, even though the declarant is available as a witness:

* * *

(2) Excited utterance. A statement relating to a startling event or condition made while the declarant was under the stress of excitement caused by the event or condition.[42]

* * *

Where hearsay evidence will be admitted as substantive evidence, as a general rule facts and circumstances that demonstrate the reliability and trustworthiness of the evidence must be present. Speech prompted in a declarant by an exciting event may be admissible as a hearsay exception if it qualifies as a spontaneous exclamation. The circumstances under which spontaneous declarations or excited utterances occur offer reasons to believe that a statement made

---

40   *See* Fed. R. Evid. 807.

41   United States v. Barrett, 8 F.3d 1296 (8th Cir. 1993); United States v. Matthews, 20 F.3d 358 (2d Cir. 1994).

42   Fed. R. Evid. 803(2).

under severe stress will be truthful. "Rule 803(2) allows the admission of excited utterances based on the theory that a person speaking about a startling event, while still under the stress of experiencing or observing that event, normally does not have either the capacity or the incentive to prevaricate."[43] The theory of this exception is that circumstances produce a condition of excitement that temporarily halts the capacity for reflection and produces utterances that are free of conscious and considered fabrication. Another way to indicate the spontaneity of such speech is to think of a stimulus that produces an instant human response without an opportunity for significant reflection. As one court properly described this hearsay exception, "An excited utterance is the event speaking and not the speaker."[44] "The crucial question, regardless of the time lapse, is whether, at the time the statement is made, the nervous excitement continues to dominate while the reflective processes remain in abeyance."[45] In order for a spontaneous or excited utterance to be admissible, a Wisconsin court noted that there must be: (a) proof of a startling event or experience, (b) the statement made by the declarant must relate to the startling event or situation, and (c) the statement must be made while the declarant is still under the stress or the excitement caused by the event or condition.[46] The court approved the admission of a victim's spontaneous statement offered to police after being hit in the head by a tire iron during a robbery perpetrated by the defendant. The victim knew the defendant, experienced the injury at the hands of the defendant, and gave his account concerning his injuries to the police within 10 minutes of being injured.[47] Following a similar rationale, a Washington court noted that for excited utterances to be admissible under the state's adaptation of the Federal Rules of Evidence, "A statement relating to 'a startling event or condition' made while the declarant was under the stress of excitement caused by the event or condition' is admissible as an excited utterance. ER 803(a)(2). An excited utterance has three closely related elements: First, a startling event or condition must have occurred. Second, the statement must have been made while the declarant was under the stress or excitement caused by the startling event or condition. Third, the statement must relate to the startling event or condition."[48] The statement in this case qualified as an excited utterance because the declarant had just been assaulted, had seen her vehicle destroyed, and seen a man's finger nearly bitten away from the hand. The declarant was under extreme stress and little time passed between the event and her statement to police officers.[49]

In another case, the victim was walking along a street and the defendant drove over to her in an attempt to pick her up. When she ultimately rebuffed his advances, he pulled his van ahead of her and was standing on the sidewalk when he grabbed her and tried to throw her into the

---

43   United States v. Brito, 427 F.3d 53, 61, 2005 U.S. App. LEXIS 22525 (1st Cir. 2006).

44   Pennsylvania v. Zukauskas, 501 Pa. 500, 503, 462 A.2d 236, 237, 1983 Pa. LEXIS 620 (1983).

45   Pennsylvania v. Keys, 2003 Pa. Super. 5, 814 A.2d 1256, 1258, 2003 Pa. Super. LEXIS 4 (2003).

46   State v. Mayo, 2006 Wis. App. 78, 713 N.W.2d 191, 2006 Wis. App. LEXIS 276 (Wis. 2006).

47   Id.

48   Washington v. Grzogorek, 2002 Wash. App. LEXIS 598 (2002).

49   Id.

van. The victim managed to get away and ran through traffic, pounding on cars trying to get help. The defendant stood nearby, pointed a gun at her, and threatened to shoot her. The victim managed to get to her house and call 911, but when police arrived she was hysterical and could not speak coherently. It took the officers 15 or 20 minutes to calm her down to the point where she could speak with them. Over the defendant's objection, the officers were permitted to render to the court what the hysterical victim had said to them while under the stress and the excitement following her assault. The reviewing court upheld the admission as an excited utterance, noting that there was a startling event, there was no time to contrive or misrepresent, and the statement was made while the victim was certainly under stress.[50]

Similar to the prior case, when police arrived in response to two 911 calls involving a domestic disturbance with a gun, the defendant's wife ran out of the home in a hurry shouting to police that "he's got a gun" and "he's going to kill me." The wife told the officers that her husband, at one point, had a gun to her head. During this time she appeared hysterical and in a state of panic. When the officers could not find the gun in the marital bedroom, they requested the wife's assistance in securing the firearm, but she was reluctant to help, appearing frantic and frightened to the officers. She told them that she did not want to go back in the house. Shortly after, the officers calmed her and took a detailed statement. At the defendant's federal trial for being a felon in possession of a firearm, the court admitted the spontaneous statements given by the wife upon the arrival of the police officers, over the defendant's objection. The Court of Appeals sustained the admission of the wife's excited utterance on the theory that the domestic disturbance constituted an exciting event, especially because the fight generated two 911 calls in rapid succession, the wife's statement was about the events in the home concerning the gun and the husband's threats, and she made them immediately after the events before she had a chance to calm herself or reflect on the events.[51]

In an Indiana case, police arrived at the scene of a reported criminal battery. The victim was crying and shaking, and her appearance and overall demeanor indicated that she was very upset. She was talking rapidly and showed signs of fresh physical injuries, including a bleeding cut above her eye. Her left eye was swollen and she was holding an ice pack to her eye. The attack had left marks on her neck that appeared to have been caused by someone grabbing her around the neck. Over the defendant's objection that the woman's story as told to an officer was not a spontaneous utterance, the trial court permitted the police officer to tell the court what the victim had told him at the scene concerning her injuries. The trial court noted that for a hearsay statement to be admitted as an excited utterance under Indiana's version of Rule 803(2), three elements must be shown: (1) a startling event occurs; (2) a statement is made by a declarant while under the stress of excitement caused by the event; and (3) the statement relates to the event. An Indiana appellate court held that the woman's statement to police met all the requirements and was properly admitted.[52]

---

50   Bell v. State, 847 So. 2d 558, 2003 Fla. App. LEXIS 8767 (Fla. 2003). *See* case in Part II.

51   United States v. Hadley, 431 F.3d 484, 496, 2005 U.S. App. LEXIS 26526 (6th Cir. 2005).

52   Cox v. State, 774 N.E.2d 1025, 2002 Ind. App. LEXIS 1533 (2002). *See* case in Part II.

The exciting event must affect the declarant with sufficient stress to remove or inhibit reflective ability. In sustaining a conviction for third-degree assault, the reviewing court approved the admission of a series of excited utterances made by the victim to a friend. The husband had been threatening his wife at their joint business when the wife phoned a friend for assistance in leaving the workplace, noting in a fearful voice that she was afraid her husband would hit her. A second call to the same friend requested that the friend rescue the wife immediately because her husband had beaten her and, when the rescuer arrived, the wife was crying and her face and arms were red. The wife did not testify at the trial, but the court permitted the wife's friend to relate virtually everything that the frightened and fearful wife told the rescuing friend about the ordeal at the time of the rescue. The Supreme Court of Colorado approved the admission of the rescuing friend's testimony because there was a startling event with the beating that created stress, the victim's spontaneous statement concerned the events and described them, and the wife related the story to her friend while still under the stress of the beating from her husband.[53]

As a general rule, to be admissible a spontaneous statement need not be completely spontaneous and may be made in response to a question by a police officer or other person.[54] The fact that the statement goes beyond a mere description of the event may be considered in deciding whether the statement was sufficiently related to the event to be spontaneous, as required by the excited utterance exception to the hearsay rule, or whether the statement was a product of conscious reflection.[55]

The fact that the excited witness was a law enforcement agent does not exclude the admissibility of statements under the excited utterance exception to the hearsay rule.[56] A prostitute who had been kidnapped and held for six hours in the back of a van where she was forced to commit sexual acts with the strangers who had taken her made an excited utterance to several District of Columbia police officers. The woman gained her freedom following a shootout with the police officers after they overcame the resistance of the armed men. She had undergone a stressful kidnapping where the men threatened her with death if she did not have sex with them, forced her to drive the van while they committed at least two robberies, and was present in the van during the shootout. As the reviewing court noted, "Being inside a van that becomes the target of police gunfire certainly qualifies as a serious occurrence."[57] Her first words to an officer involved her rape allegations, even though those acts occurred earlier than the shootout. The trial court admitted her first statement made to police under the excited utterances exception to the hearsay rule on the theory that it was her first opportunity to comment about her ordeal, that there were sufficient events to cause stress, that she had not had an opportunity to fabricate, and that her remarks indicated the spontaneity of her speech. Her comment to another officer a

---

53   Compan v. People, 121 P.3d 876, 882, 2005 Colo. LEXIS 873 (2005).

54   Washington v. Fikre, 2003 Wash. App. LEXIS 191 (2003); *see also* Massachusetts v. Ivy, 55 Mass. App. 851, 855, 774 N.E.2d 1100, 1104, 2002 Mass. App. LEXIS 1175 (2002).

55   United States v. More, 791 F.2d 566 (7th Cir. 1986).

56   Bryant v. United States, 859 A.2d 1093, 1106, 2004 D.C. App. LEXIS 526 (2004).

57   *Id.*

few minutes later that she had been kidnapped and repeatedly raped were not inadmissible due to a lapse of time. The court held that the lapse of time is a factor to consider in determining spontaneity, but in this case, the lapse was rather short for both utterances to the police. Under the circumstances, the reviewing court affirmed the admission of the victim's excited utterances.

According to accepted practice, there is no definite time interval following an exciting event that will make the utterance either fall under the exception to the hearsay rule. The general rule is that an utterance following an exciting event must be made soon enough thereafter so that it can reasonably be considered a product of the stress of the excitement, rather than of reflection or deliberation. In a Massachusetts case, the reviewing court affirmed a conviction of digital rape when the victim awoke to find the defendant's finger inside her private area and his mouth on her breast. She became so upset that her frantic, screaming, and crying awakened everyone in the house and the victim made her statements describing the events while under the stress of the rape. In approving the admissibility of the victim's stressful utterances, the court noted that there was an exciting or startling event (awakening to digital rape) that caused a high degree of agitation in the declarant and that the statements were made while the victim was under the stress or influence of the exciting event (immediately) and before she had time to fabricate. The eyewitnesses universally described the victim as being upset to the point of being frantic. The trial court properly allowed witnesses to testify concerning the substance of what the victim stated following the rape.[58] A different court, in a case with some distinguishing facts, held that when a woman alleged that her husband had beaten her, dragged by the hair, and had held her captive overnight, such information did not fall under the excited utterance exception. The victim had walked eight or ten blocks to find a police officer after she escaped the next morning and told the officer her story. The appellate court reversed the trial court's admission of the officer's rendition of the beating because the court did not concur that the woman's story to the officer met the requirements for a spontaneous utterance. According to the appellate court, the utterances were offered as a narrative of overnight events and were not given as a reaction to a single startling episode and failed as an excited utterance. The reviewing court held that the admission of the statement denied the defendant the right to cross-examine the victim, who did not testify against the defendant.[59]

In making an evaluation concerning whether the elapsed time between the startling event and the declaration to another is too long that the statement is not an excited utterance, the trial court will focus on the declarant's state of mind at the time the alleged excited statement was made. To be deemed admissible, the stress and influence of the event must be present at the time that a declarant makes a statement to a third party. For example, in a case in which the defendant had been charged with lewd conduct with a minor under 16 years of age, the trial court permitted a sister of the victim to tell the court what the victim told her.[60] In a later

---

58   Massachusetts v. Davis, 54 Mass. App. Ct. 756, 762, 767 N.E.2d 1110, 1116, 2002 Mass. App. LEXIS 674 (2002).

59   See Pennsylvania v. Keys, 2003 Pa. Super. 5, 814 A.2d 1256, 2003 Pa. Super. LEXIS 4 (2003).

60   State v. Field, 2006 Idaho App. LEXIS 44 (2006).

conversation, the child told her mother substantially the same story. According to the evidence, the conduct occurred while the defendant was babysitting the victim when he placed his finger in her private area. The child stayed at the defendant's home that night, went to school the next day, and returned to stay at the defendant's house the next night. On the second day, the child's father picked her up and drove her to her mother's home. The child disclosed no details of the incident to anyone until the evening when her sister questioned her concerning whether something was wrong. At that time, the child told her sister about the illegal conduct, and subsequently she told her mother about the encounter with the defendant. Over an objection by the defendant's attorney, the judge permitted the sister and the mother of the victim to tell the jury what the victim told them on the theory that the excited utterance exception to the hearsay rule permitted admission of their testimony. In finding error in the admission of the child's story through the sister and mother, the reviewing court noted that an excited utterance requires that the declarant be under the stress of the event when making the statement. The court stated that:

> "[i]n considering whether a statement constitutes an excited utterance, the totality of the circumstances must be considered, including the nature of the startling condition or event, the amount of time that elapsed between the startling event and the statement, the age and condition of the declarant, the presence or absence of self-interest, and whether the statement was volunteered or made in response to a question."[61]

The reviewing court agreed with the prosecution that the event would be classified as startling or shocking, but that stress would, for the purposes of the excited utterance exception, last for hours but and not days, as was contended in this case. In finding that the declarant was not offering an excited utterance, the court stated that "at some point, the time span between a startling event and a subsequent statement simply becomes too great for the statement to be considered an excited utterance even when the declarant is a child."[62] If the situation indicates a lapse of time sufficient to manufacture or formulate a statement and if a statement lacks spontaneity, a trial court should not admit the alleged spontaneous statement.[63]

---

61   *Id.*

62   *Id.*

63   North Carolina v. Riley, 54 N.C. App. 692, 695, 572 S.E.2d 857, 859, 2002 N.C. App. LEXIS 1531 (2002).

Business and Public Records

Rule 803

Hearsay Exceptions; Availability of Declarant Immaterial

* * *

The following are not excluded by the hearsay rule, even though the declarant is available as a witness:

* * *

(6) Records of regularly conducted activity. A memorandum, report, record, or data compilation, in any form, of acts, events, conditions, opinions, or diagnoses, made at or near the time by, or from information transmitted by, a person with knowledge, if kept in the course of a regularly conducted business activity, and if it was the regular practice of that business activity to make the memorandum, report, record, or data compilation, all as shown by the testimony of the custodian or other qualified witness, or by certification that complies with Rule 902(11), Rule 902(12), or a statute permitting certification, unless the source of information or the method or circumstances of preparation indicate lack of trustworthiness. The term "business" as used in this paragraph includes business, institution, association, profession, occupation, and calling of every kind, whether or not conducted for profit.

(7) Absence of entry in records kept in accordance with the provisions of paragraph (6). Evidence that a matter is not included in the memoranda, reports, records, or data compilations, in any form, kept in accordance with the provisions of paragraph (6), to prove the nonoccurrence or nonexistence of the matter, if the matter was of a kind of which a memorandum, report, record, or data compilation was regularly made and preserved, unless the sources of information or other circumstances indicate lack of trustworthiness.

(8) Public records and reports. Records, reports, statements, or data compilations, in any form, of public offices or agencies, setting forth (A) the activities of the office or agency, or (B) matters observed pursuant to duty imposed by law as to which matters there was a duty to report, excluding, however, in criminal cases matters observed by police officers and other law enforcement personnel, or (C) in civil actions and proceedings and against the Government in criminal cases, factual findings resulting from an investigation made pursuant to authority granted by law, unless the sources of information or other circumstances indicate lack of trustworthiness.[64]

* * *

---

64   Fed. R. Evid. 803. See also Fed. R. Evid. 803(9) and (10) in Appendix I.

Businesses, organizations, and government agencies collect and compile records generated during their ordinary and usual operations. Because businesses create these records with a view toward accuracy and with no motive to falsify, there is a presumption that they contain true and reliable information. Recognizing the accuracy principle, many states have adopted the Uniform Business Records Act, which facilitates the admission into evidence of records of regularly conducted operations of government and private entities. Demonstrative of the Uniform Business Records Act is the version adopted by the state of Washington, which provides that the "record of an act, condition or event, shall in so far as relevant, be competent evidence if the custodian or other qualified witness testifies to its identity and the mode of its preparation, and if it was made in the regular course of business, at or near the time of the act, condition or event, and if, in the opinion of the court, the sources of information, method and time of preparation were such as to justify its admission."[65]

The purpose of the statute is to provide, as an exception to the hearsay rule, an acceptable substitute for the specific authentication of records kept in the ordinary course of business. The underlying rationale permitting this exception is that business records have the "earmark of reliability" or "probability of trustworthiness," because they reflect events occurring in the day-to-day operations of the enterprise, and business entities rely on their ordinary records in the conduct of business.

Under the Federal Rules of Evidence, the uniform law regarding records has been greatly expanded. According to these rules, various business and public records may be the source of evidence as exceptions to the hearsay rule. Some of these are records of regularly conducted activity, public records and reports, records of vital statistics, etc. Not only is information from the records admissible, but evidence also may be introduced to prove the absence of public records or entries or the absence of an entry in records of regularly conducted activities.[66]

All such records are admissible under this rule, but they are subject to exclusion if the sources of the information or other circumstances indicate a lack of trustworthiness. In interpreting the Arizona Rules of Evidence, one court approved the admission as business records of quality assurance records of calibrations for machines that detect alcohol intoxication. Where technicians had calibrated the Intoxilyzer 5000 and kept public records of the results for each machine, the records could be admitted as an exception to the hearsay rule under Rule 803(6). There is every reason to trust the results of the tests because no technician knows whether a given machine will be used and the technician has no motive to falsify or otherwise misstate the truth concerning which machines pass or failed the calibration tests.[67]

Although in a slightly different context, a secondary school might not seem like a business, but an Indiana court held that computer-stored school attendance records were admissible as a record of regularly conducted activity. The Indiana court noted that "data compilation, in any form" is a

---

65   Wash. Rev. Code § 5.45.020, Uniform Business Records As Evidence Act. (Matthew Bender 2006).

66   Fed. R. Evid. 803.

67   *See* Bohsancurt v. Eisenberg, 129 P.3d 471, 2006 Ariz. App. LEXIS 26 (2006).

sufficiently broad category to include school records stored on a computer system.[68] An Arkansas court held that a state court did not commit error in a theft case by permitting the prosecution to introduce a state sales receipt that purported to establish the value of a stolen vehicle the defendant was alleged to have received. The vehicle was owned by the state and was sold at auction after recovery for fair market value. The office that oversaw Arkansas vehicles regularly kept appropriate records of sales of excess vehicles and had custody of the bill of sale that was properly introduced as a business record kept by a government agency in its regular course of business.[69]

Business records that have been created with litigation in mind may potentially reflect some bias of the preparer and do not generally qualify for admission under the business records exception to the hearsay rule. In a New York prosecution for driving while impaired, the defendant had given a urine sample that was subsequently tested for drug metabolites. The doctor testified at the trial that he was a general supervisor at his lab and also indicated that his laboratory and other subordinate staff prepared reports in anticipation of litigation that were transmitted to the local prosecutor. The doctor testified that he had no personal knowledge concerning the tests performed on the sample from the urine container. The prosecutor attempted to get the litigation package that the lab had prepared into evidence and the trial judge rejected the 300-page litigation package. The case had to be dismissed because there was no admissible proof that the urine had prohibited substances contained within the sample and the business record prepared for litigation by the laboratory could not be introduced.[70] Similarly, in a Florida DUI case,[71] the defendant objected to a technician testifying to what tests were conducted on a blood sample and what results a colleague recorded in a report. The colleague had retired and the employee technician had not performed the lab work but reported the results obtained by the retired colleague. Another Florida court had determined that "a lab report prepared pursuant to police investigation and admitted to establish an element of a crime is testimonial hearsay even if it is admitted as a business record."[72] The reviewing court concluded that the hearsay evidence should not have been admitted because there was no proof that the retired employee who conducted the tests was unavailable.

Some types of business records that are routinely created as a usual business practice fail to qualify for admission under the business records exception, especially when they may include hearsay on hearsay. In a prosecution for spousal battery, the trial court permitted the admission of client intake data from a crisis intervention center log. The information included the specific reason the person needed shelter and detailed past crimes and stresses in the client's relationships. Employees routinely took information from women needing shelter from domestic problems and used the information in counseling the women during their stay. The custodian of the records explained the routine of collecting the information and how that data was stored.

---

68   J.L. v. Indiana, 789 N.E.2d 961, 963, 964, 2003 Ind. App. LEXIS 921 (2003).

69   Ervin v. State, 2006 Ark. App. LEXIS 95 (2006).

70   People v. Levy, 2008 NY Slip Op 51878U (N.Y. 2008).

71   Sabota v. State, 2006 Fla. App. LEXIS 12505 (2006).

72   Johnson v. State, 929 So. 2d 4, 7, 2005 Fla. App. LEXIS 20 (2005).

The appellate court agreed that the admission of the intake forms to prove the truth of the contents was erroneous because the form's contents were derived from hearsay statements that contained multiple layers of hearsay. The client's offering of facts for the form was the first layer of hearsay; the employee's recording of the facts constituted another layer; and the rendering of the form at the trial was a third layer. The trial court should have rejected the records because they failed to meet the business records hearsay exception.[73]

Although police reports containing statements concerning the cause of or responsibility for an accident are in a sense business or public records, they are often excluded because the person making the report is relying on what someone else told him or her and the record does not reflect what the officer personally observed from firsthand perception. For example, in a case in which a man was convicted of three counts of violating the animal control ordinance, the trial court refused to allow him to introduce police reports of incidents that he had reported to show that he and his neighbors had problems getting along.[74] Proof of the prior difficulties could show the motivation for the present complaints against him. The appellate court noted that "police reports showing prior incidents are generally, by themselves, inadmissible hearsay with no probative value" and that the narrative parts of a police report do not contain facts that should be admissible under the business records exception to the hearsay rule.[75] Police reports that contain admissible evidence personally observed by the officer, as well as inadmissible evidence obtained from other eyewitnesses and included within the report, can be received in evidence if the inadmissible portions are redacted from the report.[76] Some public record police reports may be admissible where they contain only firsthand information or have been prepared in the usual course of business. For example, when police had prepared typical repair and cost reports concerning damage done to a holding cell by a prisoner, the reports constituted a business record and could be admitted against a defendant because the report had been prepared in the ordinary course of the business of running a jail.[77]

In determining whether a proffered government document is either an investigative report or a compilation of factual findings that do not come within the public record exception of the hearsay rule, the court considers: (1) whether the document contains findings that address materially contested issues in the case; (2) whether the record or report contains factual findings; and (3) whether the report was prepared for advocacy purposes or in anticipation of litigation.[78]

Applying this test, an Indiana court agreed that a diagram of the scene of a single-vehicle accident in which the passenger died, which was prepared by the accident investigator for the state police, did not contain any interpretative factual findings, and thus was admissible under

---

73   People v. Ayers, 125 Cal. App. 4th 988, 994, 23 Cal. Rptr. 3d 242, 245, 2005 Cal. App. LEXIS 50 (2005).

74   Pless v. State, 2006 Ga. App. LEXIS 523 (2006).

75   *Id.*

76   Pottorf v. Bray, 2003 Ohio 4255 (2003).

77   Williams v. State, 2003 Alaska App. LEXIS 136 (2003).

78   Shepherd v. State, 690 N.E.2d 318 (Ind. 1997).

the public records exception to the hearsay rule in the prosecution of a motorist for operating the vehicle while intoxicated. The court explained that the diagram was merely a recording of physical conditions that were observed by the investigator, and the fact that the statute, which makes accident reports filed by persons involved in automobile accidents confidential, did not bar the admission of a Standard Crash Report filed by the officer who investigated the accident, because the statute contains an exception for such reports.

A police report may be admitted as an exception to the hearsay rule where the report is required to be recorded as part of a police department's regularly conducted activities. In Louisiana, a parish sheriff has a duty to seek out and obtain fingerprint evidence and record them as part of criminal investigations. In a case involving attempted armed robbery,[79] a defendant contended that the officer who lifted a latent fingerprint from the crime scene had to personally testify to that fact and that any other expert who so testified would be offering hearsay evidence. In rejecting the defendant's contention that the testifying officer would be offering hearsay, the reviewing court noted that the Supreme Court of Louisiana previously ruled that fingerprints on file with a police agency fall under the public documents exception to the hearsay rule and, in this case, the fingerprint evidence was properly introduced to show that the crime scene fingerprint matched the print of the defendant.

In some jurisdictions, police reports and other public records may be admissible as business or public records in civil cases, but inadmissible in criminal cases.[80] In a Texas case, a criminal defendant wanted the court to admit police records of other similar accidents that occurred on the same road following his vehicle accident. The defendant had been drinking alcohol and subsequently drove into a tree. The accident resulted in criminal charges. The defendant wanted to introduce evidence of other accidents on the wet highway that occurred the same night in order to mitigate his criminal responsibility. The trial court refused to admit any police reports of the other accidents because Texas law excluded police reports from admission in all criminal cases on the ground that such evidence constituted hearsay.[81] An autopsy report may meet the requirements of a business record exception to the hearsay rule but may be excluded on constitutional grounds. In an Alabama homicide case,[82] the defendant objected to the introduction of an autopsy report when it was introduced by a doctor who had not performed the autopsy, but had read the public records generated by the actual autopsy doctor. Under Alabama law, an autopsy report is generally admissible as a business records exception to the hearsay rule.[83] However, the defendant made a Sixth Amendment right of confrontation argument that the actual declarant doctor giving the information was not present in court for cross-examination.

---

79   State v. Arita, 900 So. 2d 37, 44, 2005 La. App. LEXIS 501 (2005).

80   *See* Tex. Evid. R. 803(8) Hearsay Exceptions; Availability of Declarant Immaterial (Matthew Bender 2009).

81   McCumber v. Texas, 202 Tex. App. LEXIS 7351 (2002). Police reports may be admissible at suppression hearings because the formal rules of evidence do not apply. *See* Caballero v. State, 2005 Tex. App. LEXIS 1865 (2005).

82   Smith v. State, 898 So. 2d 907, 2004 Ala. Crim. App. LEXIS 93 (2004).

83   *Id.* at 916.

In holding that the trial court committed error in admitting the autopsy report, the appellate court noted that the Sixth Amendment confrontation clause prevents a prosecutor from proving an essential element of the crime by hearsay evidence alone. According to the reviewing court, if the prosecution had only to introduce an autopsy report and shift the burden to the defendant to refute the hearsay facts contained within, the report would not be consistent with due process of law. So while an autopsy report might be admissible as a business record exception in a civil case, the effect of the Sixth Amendment prevents the admission of an autopsy report in criminal cases when it is not offered by the doctor who performed the procedure.

It is well-known that business and public records are commonly entered and stored on computer systems and that police departments are moving toward generating fewer paper records. Computer records stored on servers or personal computers are unavailable and useless except by accessing the data on a display or printing the data on paper. In admitting computer-generated printouts, which reflect the records stored on the computer, courts are actually following the best evidence rule. This is not departing from the business records hearsay rule, because the data contained must meet any hearsay hurdles that are presented, as well as meeting the requirements of authentication of a writing. In a Virginia case[84] in which the defendants were observed committing theft from a retail store, the trial court admitted a computer-generated inventory report as an exception to the hearsay rule under the business records theory. In the past, Virginia courts have admitted business records into evidence even though the witness did not prepare them, because their trustworthiness or reliability is guaranteed by the regularity of preparation and the records are used by the business in transacting business. As the reviewing court noted, "[t]he evidence proved that Rite-Aid maintained a computerized inventory in the regular course of its business, and regularly used the Telethon device to determine the status of its inventory."[85] Following the observed theft, a loss prevention officer used a hand-held scanner to take inventory of the remaining products on the shelf to determine what items had been stolen and the computer system generated a report that was admitted into evidence.

Computer-generated maps may fall under the definition of business records stored on electronic computing equipment and should admissible in evidence if they are relevant and material, without the necessity of identifying, locating, and producing as witnesses the individuals who made the entries in the regular course of business. In a prosecution for manufacturing crack cocaine within 1,500 feet of a school zone, the trial court allowed the introduction into evidence of a computer-generated map of the jurisdiction purporting to demonstrate that a school existed within 1,500 feet of the crack laboratory. To be admissible as a business record, the evidence must have been made in the regular course of business, that it was the regular course of business to produce this record (a map), and that it must have been prepared at the time described in the report. In this case, the custodian of the map data personally prepared the map from computer-stored data, had sufficient knowledge of the methods used to generate city maps, and was well acquainted with the technology used to produce city maps. Thus, the trial court held

---

84   McDowell v. Commonwealth, 48 Va. App. 104, 628 S.E.2d 542, 2006 Va. App. LEXIS 229 (2006).

85   *Id.*

that the city map produced by the witness in the usual course of business could be admitted as a hearsay exception under the business records exception to help prove that the crack lab was within 1,500 feet of a school.[86]

The absence of a business record when it normally would have been recorded may constitute negative evidence of an event or evidence that the event most likely did not happen. The foundational showing that the business or entity normally recorded and kept such records and that a due diligence search has not revealed the entry where it would normally have been entered allows the custodian of the records to note the nonexistence of the data.[87]

Family History and Records (Pedigree)

Rule 803

Hearsay Exceptions; Availability of Declarant Immaterial

The following are not excluded by the hearsay rule, even though the declarant is available as a witness:

* * *

(11) Records of religious organizations. Statements of births, marriages, divorces, deaths, legitimacy, ancestry, relationship by blood or marriage, or other similar facts of personal or family history, contained in a regularly kept record of a religious organization.

(12) Marriage, baptismal, and similar certificates. Statements of fact contained in a certificate that the maker performed a marriage or other ceremony or administered a sacrament, made by a clergyman, public official, or other person authorized by the rules or practices of a religious organization or by law to perform the act certified, and purporting to have been issued at the time of the act or within a reasonable time thereafter.

(13) Family records. Statements of fact concerning personal or family history contained in family Bibles, genealogies, charts, engravings on rings, inscriptions on family portraits, engravings on urns, crypts, or tombstones, or the like.

(19) Reputation among members of a person's family by blood, adoption, or marriage, or among a person's associates, or in the community, concerning a person's birth, adoption, marriage, divorce, death, legitimacy, relationship by blood, adoption, or marriage, ancestry, or other similar fact of personal or family.[88]

* * *

---

86   *See* Connecticut v. Polanco, 69 Conn. App. 169, 797 A.2d 523, 2002 Conn. App. LEXIS 187 (2002).

87   Washington v. Knott, 2002 Wash. App. LEXIS 392 (2002).

88   Fed. R. Evid. 803.

Evidence of one's family information that occurred or existed prior to the declarant's birth by its nature involves hearsay. No person has an actual awareness of his or her date of birth except through hearsay information, and most family history falls into the same category. Almost all evidence relating to pedigree, genealogy, and family history consists of hearsay but usually will be admissible as an exception to the general rule excluding hearsay evidence. The family history exception to the hearsay rule is based in part on the inherent trustworthiness of a declaration by a family member regarding matters of family history and on the usual unavailability of other evidence. For example, in one case in which the defendant had been charged with incest and the rape of his daughter, the prosecution sought to prove that the victim was actually his daughter. The defendant had accepted the girl as his daughter; the mother testified that the defendant was the biological father of the victim; the victim called the defendant "Daddy;" and the entire family had accepted the girl as his daughter. In addition, a civil court entered a judgment of paternity against the defendant finding that the victim was his child. According to the trial court, the hearsay exception under the Louisiana equivalent of Federal Rule 803(19) governing reputation concerning family history and family relationship proved that the defendant was the father of the victim sufficient to support a conviction of aggravated incest.[89]

The family history exception does not extend to every facet of a defendant's life or his family history in a way that would allow every piece of exculpatory evidence to be admitted. In a death penalty case, in an effort to have the jury spare the life of her son, the mother of the defendant gave a videotaped interview covering many facts of the family in Cuba, her son's lack of problems with the law, and some additional inculpatory family history evidence. The defendant appealed the exclusion by the trial court of portions of the audio of the video as well the transcript of the same information. According to the defendant, the video contained sound information that should have been admitted under the family history exception of Rule 804. The court noted that the unavailability of the witness (she could not travel from Cuba) was clear, but the exception to the hearsay rule for family matters did not extend so far as to cover testimony about the mother's own medical problems, appellant's difficulties with the Texas Youth Commission, the defendant's desire to leave Cuba, his clean record in Cuba, and child abuse inflicted upon appellant by his stepfather. The Texas Court of Criminal Appeals affirmed the conviction and death sentence.[90]

Oral declarations by a family member regarding matters of family history are admissible as an exception to the hearsay rule, while other evidence of family history may be admissible where the information has been recorded in a manner that suggests reliability. Oral declarations of the names of uncles, aunts, and cousins and their point of origin in Eastern Europe may be accepted as family history sufficient to make a claim to an intestate relative's estate.[91] Virtually no family would record a birth record in a family bible if the birth never occurred, a factor that gives

---

89   Louisiana v. Scott, 823 So. 2d 960, 968, 2002 La. App. LEXIS 93 (2002), *remedial writ denied*, 843 So. 2d 1122, 2003 La. LEXIS 1653 (2003).

90   *See* Valle v. Texas, 109 S.W.3d 500, 2003 Tex. Crim. App. LEXIS 143 (2003).

91   *See* In re Estate of Doris Rosen, Deceased, 2003 Pa. Super. 96, 819 A.2d 585, 2003 Pa. Super. LEXIS 364 (2003).

reliability to family histories contained within religious books. Family records contained within the family bible are admissible when a proper showing is made as to the authority or authenticity of entries of the family record, especially when better evidence is not available. Such matters as births, deaths, and marriages are competent as evidence.

Some jurisdictions permit the entry of family history when it has been entered in a family Bible even where the persons who know the history remain alive. In a polygamy investigation, there was some belief that proof of the multiple marriages and sexual activity with underage wives resulting in live births would be found in a family Bible. The result of a search warrant revealed a bible with missing pages that were alleged to contain the intimate and illegal family history. The focus of the prosecution changed to tampering with evidence with the Bible being admitted in evidence against the defendant.[92] In some instances, the absence from the jurisdiction of the person who made the statements or the entries in the Bible, or insanity or illness hindering his or her presence at the trial is enough to make the evidence admissible. In some jurisdictions, entries in family Bibles are declared admissible by statute,[93] while some states recognize the hearsay exception for family records that have been included in family Bibles.[94]

Federal Rule of Evidence 803(11) provides that regularly kept records of a religious organization may be consulted in order to find family information, and if this information meets the legal requirements, it should be admissible as an exception to the hearsay rule. Although many people do not have close ties to organized religion, many people are intimately involved with their religion in situations in which careful records of church membership, birth, baptism, bar mitzvah, and wedding information are generated. Because there is every desire to record this information in an accurate manner and no reason to erroneously enter the information, there is a presumption that the records are accurate. In interpreting this rule, one federal court explained that the exception is limited to personal information and does not authorize evidence of statements of monetary contributions to a church, because these do not fall within the religious records exception to the hearsay rule.[95]

Under Federal Rule of Evidence 803(19) and its state equivalents, family relationships that exist by blood, adoption, or marriage may be proved by persons who have intimate knowledge of the family or by associates of family members concerning family history. For example, a father or mother could give the date of birth of their respective parents, even though they could not possibly know this information from firsthand knowledge. And a father could testify to the birth date of his son or daughter, even thought the father was not present at the birth or even in the geographical area of the birth. In a case in which a defendant was accused of harboring an illegal alien, among other crimes, a trial court permitted the illegal alien's aunt to testify that he was from El Salvador

---

92   State v. Sliwinski, 2004 Mont. 1221, 2004 Mont. Dist. LEXIS 2119 (2004).

93   Fed. R. Evid. 803.

94   Estate of Earl Wallace, Deceased, 2004 Phila. Ct. Com. Pl. LEXIS 134 (Pa. 2004).

95   Hall v. C.I.R., 729 F.2d 632 (9th Cir. 1984).

and was not a United States citizen.[96] People who do not have a close association with the family or group are not permitted to offer this sort of hearsay in court. For example, in a prosecution for aggravating driving under the influence of an intoxicant while a person under 15 years of age was in the vehicle,[97] the trial court permitted the arresting officer to relate to the court the fact that he had heard the putative father of the 15-year-old state that the boy passenger was only 13. While the investigation was ongoing, a different adult male came to take charge of the child and noted to the officer that the boy was his 13-year-old son. Police proved unable to locate the boy or his father prior to trial, so the trial judge permitted the police officer to state the age of the child, an element of the aggravating driving under the influence charge. At trial, the defendant entered a hearsay objection that the trial court rejected. The appellate court determined that the trial court committed reversible error in allowing the officer to give an age to the boy by stating that he looked young and that the putative father had stated to the officer that the boy was 13. The officer who testified had no personal knowledge concerning the age of the child, had not been a member of the family community, and was a stranger to the child and his father. Because the family history related to an element of the crime, the appellate court reversed the conviction.

Former Testimony

Rule 804

Hearsay Exceptions; Declarant Unavailable

* * *

(b) Hearsay exceptions.—The following are not excluded by the hearsay rule if the declarant is unavailable as a witness:

(1) Former testimony. Testimony given as a witness at another hearing of the same or a different proceeding, or in a deposition taken in compliance with law in the course of the same or another proceeding, if the party against whom the testimony is now offered, or, in a civil action or proceeding, a predecessor in interest, had an opportunity and similar motive to develop the testimony by direct, cross, or redirect examination.[98]

* * *

Every criminal defendant has a Sixth Amendment right to confront and cross-examine adverse witnesses and not having the opportunity to confront a witness will likely lead to the reversal

---

96   United States v. Garcia-Flores, 136 Fed. Appx. 685; 2005 U.S. App. LEXIS 12732 (5th Cir. 2005).

97   State v. May, 210 Ariz. 452, 455, 112 P.3d 39, 42, 2005 Ariz. App. LEXIS 73 (2005).

98   Fed. R. Evid. 804.

of a conviction. Therefore, when evidence is introduced against a defendant in a manner that has the effect of preventing meaningful cross-examination, the trial judge should exclude the evidence. A literal construction of the Sixth Amendment would prevent virtually all hearsay evidence from being considered for admission, and have the effect of making trials difficult. Where a substitute for cross-examination exists or where the defendant originally had motive, opportunity, and incentive to conduct cross-examination at a prior proceeding between the same parties, the evidence may be admitted even though it constitutes hearsay testimony. This exception does not require that the defendant have conducted cross-examination of the witness at the earlier proceeding, only that the defendant had the opportunity. As a general rule, to have an opportunity to use testimony given in a prior proceeding, the parties to the lawsuit must be identical, the now-absent witness must have been under oath in the first proceeding, the absent witness must now be unavailable for testimony, and the lawsuit must cover the same issues covered in the first proceeding. Under Rule 804, the declarant must be unavailable for testimony where unavailability may involve an assertion of a constitutional or other privilege, when the witness is beyond the power of the court to command attendance, or when the witness simply refuses to testify through no fault of the offering party, or when the witness testifies to a lack of memory, or when the witness is dead. If a hearsay exception absolutely conflicts with the Sixth Amendment provision that states: "in all criminal prosecutions, the accused shall enjoy the right to be confronted with the witnesses against him," the evidence will not be admissible.

In a case in which the witness had disappeared after the first trial and prior to the second trial, the defendant objected, complaining that his rights under the Sixth Amendment to confront and cross-examine adverse witnesses and Federal Rule of Evidence 804(b)(1) were violated.[99] The defendant objected to the prosecution using the transcript of the witness from the first trial. In order for the prior testimony to be used at a second trial, the party against whom the evidence is to be admitted must have had an opportunity and similar motive to conduct cross-examination at the first proceeding. Reviewing courts have looked at transcripts of the original cross-examination to determine whether the trial counsel had a full opportunity to probe and expose the witness's testimony and undermine its credibility where appropriate. In holding that the former testimony could be constitutionally used against the defendant at his second trial on the same issue, the Court of Appeals concluded:

> that this prior cross-examination sufficiently allowed the jury at the second trial to evaluate the truth of [the missing witness'] testimony, and that [the defendant] had a similar motive in both trials. This conclusion is further strengthened by the facts that evidence of [the missing witness'] flight was put before the jury in the second trial, defense counsel emphasized the flight in his summation, and the district court specifically referred to it in the charge to the jury. Therefore, the admission of [the missing witness'] prior testimony at [the defendant's] second trial did not violate [the defendant's] right to confrontation under the Sixth Amendment nor was it contrary to Federal Rule of Evidence 804(b)(1).[100]

---

99   United States v. Garcia, 117 Fed. Appx. 162, 2004 U.S. App. LEXIS 25480 (2d Cir. 2004).

100   *Id.* at 164.

In affirming the conviction, the Court of Appeals was satisfied that the defendant had suffi-cient reason conduct appropriate cross-examination of the missing prosecution witness at the prior trial and that it would not be unfair to allow evidence of what the witness said at the first trial into evidence at the second trial.

In one case, the defense wanted to use former testimony in favor of a defendant.[101] The trial issue involved missing witnesses who testified at a grand jury proceeding and then disappeared. The prosecution successfully contended that it did not have the same incentive, motive, and intent to examine the witnesses at the grand jury stage of the criminal process as it would have at a trial. The defendant wanted the grand jury testimony of the two missing witnesses to be admitted at trial because their evidence would deflect the responsibility for the crime from the defendant and place it on a third party. The parties were in agreement that the witnesses were missing and unavailable, but the quality and thrust of the questions asked of the missing grand jury witness was simply different than if the prosecution were to have cross-examined them at trial. The Court of Appeals agreed with the federal prosecutor and upheld the refusal to admit the evidence.[102] Not argued in the case was the concept that the government did not ever cross-examine the witnesses because they were called to the grand jury by the prosecution as grand jury witnesses and the prior grand jury proceeding was not an adversarial one.

Some jurisdictions and legal authorities assert that former testimony is actually not hearsay, because it was given under oath and subject to cross-examination. The Federal Rules of Evi-dence and derivative state adopters recognize former testimony as hearsay, but hold that it is admissible under an exception to the hearsay rule. Under either approach, when a witness for the prosecution or defense is unavailable and cannot be produced at the present trial or, being present, refuses to testify, courts will generally admit the recorded testimony of such witness from a prior criminal proceeding where it meets the other qualifications for this hearsay exception. A witness who is expected to assert some constitutional or statutory privilege is not considered to be unavailable until the witness is placed on the witness stand and formally asserts a privilege not to testify or simply refuses to testify even though no legal basis exists for the refusal.[103]

In admitting reported testimony, a Tennessee reviewing court approved the admission into evidence of prior testimony from a witness who had testified at the preliminary hearing but was deceased at the time of the trial.[104] The court noted that two issues were involved—the right of confrontation and whether a hearsay exception applied. The court noted that the defendant had ample opportunity and motive to conduct effective cross-examination of the witness at the preliminary hearing and that a preliminary hearing is precisely what the rules of evidence contemplate when Rule 804 mentions former testimony.

---

101   United States v. Carson, 455 F.3d 336, 2006 U.S. App. LEXIS 18361 (D.C. Cir. 2006).

102   *Id.*

103   *See* Edmonds v. State, 2006 Miss. App. LEXIS 311 (Miss. 2006).

104   State v. Bowman, 2009 Tenn. Crim. App. LEXIS 35 (Tenn. 2009).

In an Arkansas criminal case[105] in which there was a companion civil case that had been filed, an attorney for the civil plaintiff deposed a witness in the homosexual rape case and the witness died prior to the date of the criminal trial. The judge permitted the evidence from the deceased witness to be admitted into evidence because the declarant was deceased and the court found that the defendant's civil attorney had an opportunity that he did not exercise to cross-examine the now-dead witness. Additionally, the defendant's criminal attorney could have deposed the adverse witness but chose not to do so. In upholding the admission into evidence of the earlier deposition testimony, the reviewing court noted that the civil trial and criminal trial involved the same facts and same participants, giving the defendant's civil attorney proper motive and incentive to cross-examine at the earlier proceeding. An important concept that the appellate court may have missed is that the parties were different in the civil trial from the criminal trial because the plaintiff in the civil trial was the injured party and the plaintiff in the criminal trial was the prosecution.

In summary, when a party wants to admit into evidence earlier testimony offered at prior proceedings, there should be an identity of parties, and identity of issues between the prior proceeding and the present one. There must have been ample motive, incentive, and opportunity for the adverse party to have developed sufficient cross-examination of a witness who must have been under oath for the former testimony exception to be permitted. Where all the statutory and legal issues are met involving former testimony, "[o]nly the absence of an opportunity for the trier to observe the witness's demeanor detracts from the ideal conditions for giving testimony."[106]

Dying Declarations

Rule 803

Hearsay Exceptions; Declarant Unavailable

* * *

(b) Hearsay exceptions.—The following are not excluded by the hearsay rule if the declarant is unavailable as a witness:

* * *

(2) Statement under belief of impending death. In a prosecution for homicide or in a civil action or proceeding, a statement made by a declarant while believing that the declarant's death was imminent, concerning the cause or circumstances of what the declarant believed to be impending death.[107]

---

105   Simmons v. State, 2006 Ark. App. LEXIS 276 (2006).

106   5–804 Weinstein's Federal Evidence § 804.04. Chapter 804 Hearsay Exceptions; Declarant Unavailable (Matthew Bender 2009).

107   Fed. R. Evid. 804.

To qualify as a dying declaration, the victim must have made a statement concerning the cause and circumstances of his or her own impending death by homicide and the statement must have been made with a clear understanding that death was imminent. The victim must have given up all hope of recovery or living any appreciable length of time. Dying declarations in homicide cases have from ancient times been admitted in evidence either: (1) because of solemnity—the solemnity of the occasion and the fear that one would not want to meet one's maker with a lie on one's lips, or (2) because of necessity—because the victim of the homicide cannot testify, it is necessary to protect the public against homicidal criminals and prevent a miscarriage of justice. Under the common law, the person making the dying declaration must actually die,[108] but the federal courts do not require death in order for the declaration to be admissible. Consistent with the position of many states, a Tennessee appellate court noted the five requirements for the admissibility of a dying declaration:

> (1) The declarant must be dead at the time of the trial; (2) the statement is admissible only in the prosecution of a criminal homicide; (3) the declarant must be the victim of the homicide; (4) the statement must concern the cause or the circumstances of the death; and (5) the declarant must have made the statement under the belief that death was imminent.[109]

From the legal perspective, the dying declaration has the same effect and carries the same presumptive weight as if it were testimony given under oath, although a jury is free to give any weight it might desire to such evidence.

In order for a judge to admit a dying declaration, the declarant's statement must describe the circumstances and events immediately surrounding or leading up to the defendant's conduct that caused death of the declarant. Under current hearsay and Sixth Amendment standards, a dying declaration has a better chance of admission when the declarant makes a spontaneous statement rather than answering questions from a police officer.[110] To meet a defendant's objection to the admission of a dying declaration under the Sixth Amendment, the Commonwealth of Virginia takes the position that a defendant forfeits the right of confrontation and cross-examination when there is proof by a preponderance of the evidence that the defendant's act has caused the absence of the dying declarant.[111] Similarly, in Texas, one court permitted a dying declaration to be admitted against the a defendant who was on trial for killing the dying declarant.[112] The person making a dying declaration generally does not have to unequivocally and unambiguously state that the victim knows death is imminent but the awareness of impending death may be inferred from the character of the wounds, the language used by the declarant, from the facts

---

108   If the person survived, the individual could personally testify or the statement might be admissible as an excited utterance.

109   State v. Mayes, 2004 Tenn. Crim. App. LEXIS 9 (2004) and State v. Lewis, 2006 Tenn. Crim. App. LEXIS 237 (2006).

110   See Crawford v. Washington, 541 U.S. 36, 2004 U.S. LEXIS 1838 (2004).

111   Commonwealth v. Morgan, 69 Va. Cir. 228, 232, 2005 Va. Cir. LEXIS 189 (Va. 2005).

112   Gonzalez v. State, 195 S.W.3d 114, 2006 Tex. Crim. App. LEXIS 1129 (Tex. 2006). *See* case in Part II.

and surrounding circumstances, or from what has been told to the victim by medical personnel. The expectation of imminent demise may be shown by the circumstances of his or her condition or by his or her acts, such as sending for a minister or rabbi before making the declaration or requesting last rites from a minister or priest.

In an old case, *Mattox v. United States*, the Supreme Court of the United States succinctly stated conditions under which the dying declaration exception to the hearsay rule applied in federal criminal trials and set forth the justification for the rule:[113]

> Dying declarations are admissible in a trial for murder, as to the fact of the homicide and the person by whom it was committed, in favor of the defendant as well as against him. ... But it must be shown by the party offering them in evidence that they were made under a sense of impending death. This may be made to appear from what the injured person said; or from the nature and extent of the wounds inflicted, being obviously such that he must have felt or known that he could not survive; as well as from his conduct at the time and the communications, if any, made to him by medical advisors, if assented to or understandingly acquiesced in by him. The length of the time elapsing between the making of the declaration and the death is one of the elements to be considered ...

Approving the admission of the dying declarations in the case, the Court commented further:

> The admission of the testimony is justified on the ground of necessity, and in view of the consideration that certain expectation of almost immediate death will remove all temptation to falsehood and enforce as strict adherence to the truth as the obligation of an oath could impose. But the evidence must be received with the utmost caution, and, if the circumstances do not satisfactorily disclose that the awful and solemn situation in which he is placed is realized by the dying man because of the hope of recovery, it ought to be rejected.

Under the modern Federal Rules of Evidence, the dying declarant need not actually die, but many states still hold that or the dying declaration is not admissible unless the declarant has died. Even with the guidelines established by federal and state statutes and the Supreme Court of the United States and state supreme courts, lower courts are required to apply the test to specific cases. For example, are the victim's statements admitted as dying declarations if they are elicited by questions? Must the victim affirmatively state that he or she is dying? Is the length of time the declarant lives after making a dying declaration material? Must the person actually die?

In a New York murder prosecution,[114] the trial court admitted a series of comments and responses to questions as a dying declaration. The decedent's wife heard gunshots and found her husband on the sidewalk bleeding from two shots in his back. He told her that "it hurt" and to call an ambulance. He subsequently told her that "I'm dying" as the police arrived. Police asked his wife to inquire of the decedent as to who shot him because the victim spoke only Spanish. He replied by giving the defendant's name, who he identified by using a nickname. He died a few hours later. At trial, the dying declaration was admitted against the defendant. Years later, on the strength

---

113   Mattox v. United States, 146 U.S. 140, 13 S. Ct. 50, 36 L. Ed. 917 (1892).

114   People v. Durio, 7 Misc. 3d 729, 731, 794 N.Y.S.2d 863, 685, 2005 N.Y. Misc. LEXIS 398 (N.Y. 2005).

of *Crawford v. Washington*,[115] the defendant contended that the statements should not have been used as a dying declaration because the statements were "testimonial in nature" and he was not be able to exercise his Sixth Amendment right to confront and cross-examine the dead declarant. The New York court that reviewed the defendant's motion to vacate his homicide conviction noted that dying declarations constitute an exception to the ban on testimonial evidence that cannot be subjected to cross-examination. The court mentioned that the Supreme Court of the United States recently referred to dying declarations and noted that many dying declarations may not be testimonial in nature but that even those that were could be admitted.[116]

An Illinois court, in deciding whether a dying declarant possessed a belief that imminent death was a virtual certainty, held that a trial court could have inferred that the decedent knew death was approaching when he knew that he had been shot twice, he mentioned that he could not move his legs, he was gasping for air, he appeared to be in pain, and he told a friend that he was dying. At the hospital the dying victim told a doctor that he was not doing well and the doctor agreed with him that he was in "bad shape." At the hospital, the victim gave police a description of the defendant. The victim had been in an altercation the evening prior to the shooting with the defendant after the defendant forced the victim's girlfriend to have sex with him. The defendant was alleged to have shot the victim as the victim answered his front door. The reviewing court agreed with the trial court that the victim's statements were properly admitted as a dying declaration because the victim's words pertained to the cause or circumstances of the victim's receipt of final injuries, the victim knew he was dying, and the victim possessed the mental faculties to offer an accurate statement or statements concerning how his injuries were received.[117]

When an injured person does not believe that he or she is going to die or the proof may be uncertain that the victim has that belief, the statement may be admissible as an excited utterance. In a Texas case, in the victim was found by friends in a parking lot suffering from a tremendous beating that included a broken neck. In the parking lot, six witnesses heard the victim say in response to a question that the defendant had done this to him. The appellate court approved the admission into evidence of the victim statement as an excited utterance or as a dying declaration. It was clear that the victim had suffered an exciting traumatic event and other evidence indicated that he knew he was in precarious shape. When the victim was about to be removed from a ventilator, he indicated to others that the defendant had given him his final injuries and it was clear to the victim that he would not live very long once removed from the ventilator.[118]

As a matter of logic, a dying declaration must be made between the infliction of the fatal injury and the death of the declarant. For admission as a dying declaration, the length of time

---

115   541 U.S. 36, 2004 U.S. LEXIS 1838 (2004). *See* the material on this case in § 12.8—Former Testimony. The Supreme Court of California held that *Crawford v. Washington* and its Sixth Amendment concerns did not apply to dying declarations. *See* People v. Monterroso, 34 Cal. 743, 22 Cal. Rptr. 3d 1, 101 P.3d 956 (2004).

116   *Id.*

117   People v. Gilmore, 356 Ill. App. 3d 1023, 1031, 828 N.E.2d 293, 301, 2005 Ill. App. LEXIS 314 (2005).

118   Sadlier v. State, 2009 Tex. App. LEXIS 2962 (Tex. 2009). *See* case in Part II.

a declarant lives after making a dying declaration is immaterial in determining whether the statement qualifies a dying declaration for purposes of the hearsay exception. In a California case, the dying declarant was well aware of his impending death and despite the fact that he lived 11 more days was not material to the determination of whether the statement was admissible as a dying declaration.[119]

While the typical dying declaration is usually offered orally and later reduced to a writing, a dying declaration may be either written or oral but must relate to final injuries suffered by the declarant prior to his or her death and may never explain the death of a third party. Due to the typical police response to reported homicides, in many instances the dying statements are made to law enforcement officers and emergency medical responders. Law enforcement officers are generally trained to recognize that while a statement by a declarant may not qualify as a dying declaration, it may be admissible under the hearsay exception known as the excited utterance exception. Police officers should take care to record the substance of a statement and the circumstances under which it was uttered as soon as possible in order to clearly convey the final statements regarding a victim's final injuries. Cross-examination by defense attorneys should also be anticipated at the time the dying declaration is offered in court by the police officer or other third party so that the witness will be prepared to give accurate testimony about what he or she heard.

Declarations Against Interest

Rule 804

Hearsay Exceptions; Declarant Unavailable

* * *

(b) Hearsay exceptions.—The following are not excluded by the hearsay rule if the declarant is unavailable as a witness:

* * *

(3) Statement against interest. A statement which was at the time of its making so far contrary to the declarant's pecuniary or proprietary interest, or so far tended to subject the declarant to civil or criminal liability, or to render invalid a claim by the declarant against another, that a reasonable person in the declarant's position would not have made the statement unless believing it to be true. A statement tending to expose the declarant to criminal liability and offered to exculpate the accused is not admissible unless corroborating circumstances clearly indicate the trustworthiness of the statement.[120]

---

119   People v. Monterroso, 34 Cal. 4th 743, 763, 101 P.3d 956, 971, 22 Cal. Rptr. 3d 1, 18, 2004 Cal. LEXIS 11763 (2004).

120   Fed. R. Evid. 804.

A. Declarations Against Pecuniary Interests

Any time a person makes an oral or written statement that could have the effect of harming his or her pecuniary or monetary interests, such statement may qualify as an exception to the hearsay rule. Because most individuals are somewhat self-serving, when people make declarations against pecuniary interests that are out of line with typical statements, they are probably being truthful. A statement qualifying as a declaration against interest may be admissible as an exception to the hearsay rule because declarations against interest have been found to offer a high probability of truthfulness. Admission into evidence has become acceptable out of necessity, because most individuals decline to repeat such statements while under oath in a court of law because admitting a declaration against interest may have an adverse result. The legal theory holds that a person does not make statements against his or her own pecuniary interest unless the statements generally are true and have thus considered such statements trustworthy, even though there may be no opportunity to confront or to cross-examine the witness.

A declaration against interest by a person who is not a party nor in privity with a party to an action is admissible in evidence when: (1) the person making such declaration is either dead or unavailable as a witness due to sickness, insanity, or absence from the jurisdiction; (2) the declarant had peculiar means of knowing the facts that he or she stated; (3) the declaration was against his or her pecuniary or proprietary interest; and (4) he or she had no probable motive to falsify the facts stated.[121] Applying the declaration against interest theory, an Arkansas court revoked a prior judgment ordering a trustee to pay child support to a child beneficiary's custodian.[122] The trustee refused to comply with the court's original order when the trustee gained knowledge that the custodian-father and the non-custodial mother appeared to have colluded to defraud the court and the trust. The mother, who could not be found for the hearing, told the trustee that she and the custodian father had concocted a scheme to get $2,000 per month from the trustee for the benefit of the child and that the mother and father were planning on splitting the $2,000 each month. At the time of the court's hearing, the mother was absent and the statement clearly was against her pecuniary interest because if the trustee acted properly knowing the truth about the fraud, her share of the monthly child support would not likely be paid. She must have known that the statement was against her pecuniary interest when it was made and her absence permitted the hearsay use of her statement. As the appellate court noted in approving the trial court admission of the mother's declaration against interest, "Here, Ms. Salmon was unavailable because no one knew her location and attempts to find her had proved unavailing. Ark. R. Evid. 804(a)(4). Moreover, Ms. Salmon's statements that she had colluded with Mr. Osborne (the father) were admissible because such statements were declarations against the pecuniary interest of her estate.[123]

A hearsay statement may qualify as a declaration against interest if the statement, at the time of its original utterance, was contrary to the declarant's pecuniary, proprietary, or social

---

121   Gichner v. Antonio Troiano Tile Co., 410 F.2d 238 (D.C. Cir. 1969).

122   Osborne v. Salmon, 2006 Ark. App. LEXIS 266 (2006).

123   *Id.*

interest, or tended to subject the declarant to civil or criminal liability, or to render invalid the declarant's claim against another, so that a reasonable person in the declarant's position would not have uttered the statement unless that person believed the statement to be true.[124] A statement may qualify as a declaration against the interest when the statement threatens loss of employment or reduces chances for future employment. For example, a hearsay statement made by the lessee's employee to a fire investigator that he and others were smoking on the leased premises a few hours before the fire started was against the employee's pecuniary and proprietary interests, and because the statement also concerned a subject of which the employee was personally cognizant and there was no conceivable motive to falsify, the statement was admitted as a declaration against the interest of the employee. The court in that case agreed, however, that the statement would not be admitted unless the employee was unavailable to testify at the trial.[125]

In a Texas case, the trial court first acknowledged the rule relating to declarations against interest and reviewed the admissibility requirements, including the fact that the statement must have adverse consequences to the one making the statement. When police executed a search warrant of a residence where the defendant was present, the police discovered a quantity of cocaine in the presence of the defendant and a friend. Several days later, after posting bail for an associate, the defendant stated to his girlfriend that he knew the cocaine belonged to the friend who had been present during the search because the defendant admitted selling the cocaine to the same friend. In approving the admission of the declaration made to his girlfriend, the reviewing court noted that: "The voluntary statement, although made several days after the arrest, was not the product of coercion or questioning. ... McElroy's incriminating statements were made to his live-in girlfriend, and thus, he had no reason to believe that statements made to her would be used against him."[126] In this case, the original declarant, the defendant, was unwilling to repeat his statement on the witness stand and therefore was "unavailable" to testify within the meaning of the statute governing the inadmissibility of declarations against interest.

B. Statements Against Penal Interests—Confessions and Admissions

Included within the general exception introduced above is the hearsay exception concerning admissions and confessions. A confession, as it is used in criminal law, consists of a suspect admitting responsibility for all the elements of the crime or crimes, and constitutes a complete acknowledgment of guilt by one who has committed a crime or crimes. The confession is the admission of the criminal act itself, not an admission of a fact or circumstances from which guilt may be inferred. An admission, as distinguished from a confession, consists of the suspect admitting to some involvement or having responsibility for some elements of a crime or admitting to facts that, when linked to other facts, may show guilt. However, the statement falls short of a complete confession for the criminal act itself. An admission may consist of a partial

---

124   New Jersey v. Brown, 170 N.J. 138, 148, 784 A.2d 1244, 1251, 2001 N.J. LEXIS 1409 (2001).

125   Gichner v. Antonio Troiano Tile Co., *supra* note 125.

126   Risher v. Texas, 85 S.W.3d 839, 842, 2002 Tex. App. LEXIS 6086 (2002).

confession, but the admission fails to take complete responsibility for committing incriminating acts or conduct that equals guilt. In a Tennessee murder case, police videotaped a voluntary statement of the eventual defendant, in which she admitted being at the scene of the homicide, but denying any involvement. This kind of statement qualifies as an admission, but not a full confession, because it only placed her at the crime scene, and nothing more.[127]

In a Michigan case, a man was robbed at gunpoint while using a public phone. The two assailants went through the victim's pockets and took his watch and pager but were upset when he did not have anything else of value. At that moment, one of the felons shot the victim in the back. Police officers encountered the defendants within a few minutes after the incident because they appeared to be acting in a suspicious fashion. At this moment a radio broadcast alerted police of the robbery and shooting and when one of the officers asked to have the robbers' descriptions repeated, the defendant blurted out, "I did it—I'm the shooter!" According to the Supreme Court of Michigan, the defendant's statement was properly introduced against the defendants as a declaration against penal interest because at that time the defendant knew that it was not in his best interests to admit to a robbery and a shooting.[128]

Consistent with the Maryland practice, under the Federal Rules of Evidence the statement against interest exception includes statements that are against penal interest as well as those against pecuniary and proprietary interests.[129] In a federal prosecution, the defendant had been caught with a firearm under the seat of the car in which he was a passenger and suffered a federal conviction for being a felon in possession of a firearm.[130] One of the points of his appeal involved the fact that the trial court refused to allow his girlfriend to testify that a third-party friend of the defendant admitted to her that the gun belonged to the third party and that the third party admitted placing it under the car seat in which the defendant was riding at the time of his arrest. The appellate court noted that the declaration against interest (penal) was subject to two conditions. The first condition required that the person making the declaration be unavailable for testimony, a fact clearly present in this case because the third party asserted the Fifth Amendment privilege against self-incrimination at the trial. The second requirement for admission failed because the trial court did not find corroborating circumstances that could indicate the trustworthiness of the declaration against interest and the trustworthiness of the declarant. The girlfriend would like to see her boyfriend before he finished a prison term, so there was a motive for her to be less than honest. The third party had denied that he ever admitted to having the gun to his own parole officer. Under the circumstances, the reviewing court agreed with the trial court that the declaration against interest failed the tests of admissibility under the rules of evidence.[131]

---

127   State v. Lewis, 2006 Tenn. Crim. App. LEXIS 237 (2006).

128   *See* State v. Washington, 664 N.W.2d 203, 2003 Mich. LEXIS1465 (Mich. 2003). *See* case in Part II.

129   Fed. R. Evid. 804(b)(3).

130   United States v. Johnson, 121 Fed. Appx. 912, 2005 U.S. App. LEXIS 2533 (2d Cir. 2005).

131   *Id.*

When declarants make out-of-court confessions that could subject them to criminal prosecution and who are not defendants in a case, the confessions qualify as hearsay evidence and may be admitted as declarations against the interests of the people making the declarations. Such evidence may be admissible as an exception to the hearsay rule when the evidence meets the requirements of the declaration against interest.[132] The reason for admitting the confession as an exception to the hearsay rule is that a reasonable person in such a position would not have made the incriminating statement constituting a confession unless he believed it to be true, and if the confession is not true, the defendant is free to explain why he or she made a false confession. Confessions are made for a variety of reasons and may involve efforts to protect other people or by an attack of conscience and honesty, and for other unknown reasons.

In interpreting Federal Rule 804(b)(3), Statement against interest, the District of Columbia Court of Appeals observed that the Rule requires a three-step process to determine whether an admissible statement against penal interest has been made.[133] The court should consider whether the alleged declarant actually made a statement, determine whether the declarant actually is unavailable for testimony, and evaluate whether there are corroborating circumstances that support the trustworthiness of the statement. Of course, the statement must have had the tendency to subject the declarant to some sort of criminal penalty and the declarant must have been aware of that fact. There must be some proof that the declarant understood that the statement was against his or her penal interest at the time it was made. Corroboration need not be as strong as having a second person overhear the declarant; it just must appear that under the circumstances, the statement meets a threshold of believability or plausibility sufficient to admit the statement.[134]

In a case in which the declarant had a motive to falsify a declaration against interest, the trial court properly refused to admit the hearsay statement. During a murder prosecution, the defendant attempted to have the court admit the declaration against penal interest made by his father for jury consideration. In addition to the usual considerations concerning admissibility, the court evaluated whether the out-of-court declaration of the father would have been influenced by any motive to falsify. The father's statement did not fully incriminate him, but it was designed to remove suspicion from his son. According to the court, there were inconsistencies in the father's statement that created a credibility question concerning the trustworthiness of his statement. In addition, the father knew that police were looking for his son in connection with the killing, and the court expressed concern that the father's statement was not credible. The effort by the father to accept complete responsibility for attacks on three people half his age whom he did not know, and who were seriously wounded or killed, proved implausible to the court. After considering the appeal, the reviewing court upheld the convictions and agreed that the trial court was correct in refusing to admit the father's alleged declaration against penal interest.[135]

---

132   *See* Chapter 16 for a discussion of the constitutional issues concerning confessions and admissions. *See also* Kansas Annotated Statutes, K.S.A. § 60–460(j) Hearsay evidence excluded; exceptions. (2006).

133   Ingram v. United States, 885 A.2d 257, 264, 2005 D.C. App. LEXIS 533 (2005).

134   *Id.*

135   *See* Stewart v. Maryland, 151 Md. App. 425, 827 A.2d 850, 2003 Md. App. LEXIS 75 (2003).

Before leaving the declaration against interest exception to the hearsay rule, a couple of caveats should be noted. First, the federal rule, as well as most state rules, requires corroboration of both the declarant's trustworthiness as well as the statement's trustworthiness. The party who seeks to introduce the unavailable witness's statement against penal interest has a duty to introduce sufficient proof that a rational juror could believe in its truth. In order to determine whether a declarant's statement is sufficiently trustworthy, a judge should focus on whether there are corroborating circumstances that clearly demonstrate the trustworthiness of the declarant's statement.[136] In other words, the proponent must demonstrate sufficient corroboration of the statement in context with other facts in the case in order for the declaration to be admissible.

Moreover, there is no declaration against penal interest if the declarant has not mentioned facts that, if true, would most assuredly implicate the declarant in crime. Early stage criminal planning or merely thinking about a crime is not a crime in itself. In a Michigan case, the court held that a declarant's statements implicating the defendant in a scheme to burn down the defendant's house were not against the declarant's penal interest as required for admission under the hearsay exception. Because the arson had not yet taken place and significant steps toward completion had not taken place, the statements only demonstrated an intent to commit a crime in the future.[137]

Other Exceptions—Residual Exceptions

Rule 807

Residual Exception

A statement not specifically covered by Rule 803 or 804 but having equivalent circumstantial guarantees of trustworthiness, is not excluded by the hearsay rule, if the court determines that (A) the statement is offered as evidence of a material fact; (B) the statement is more probative on the point for which it is offered than any other evidence which the proponent can procure through reasonable efforts; and (C) the general purposes of these rules and the interests of justice will best be served by admission of the statement into evidence. However, a statement may not be admitted under this exception unless the proponent of it makes known to the adverse party sufficiently in advance of the trial or hearing to provide the adverse party with a fair opportunity to prepare to meet it, the proponent's intention to offer the statement and the particulars of it, including the name and address of the declarant.[138]

---

136   United States v. Franklin, 415 F.3d 537, 547, 2005 U.S. App. LEXIS 14540 (5th Cir. 2005).

137   People v. Brownridge, 225 Mich. App. 291, 570 N.W.2d 672 (1997).

138   Fed. R. Evid. 807.

While there are other specific exceptions, including those listed in Federal Rules 803 and 804, that cover the typical hearsay exceptions, Rule 807 regulates the admission into evidence of hearsay evidence that is not regulated by other rules governing hearsay. The rules have made it clear that merely because some of the exceptions are listed, such listing does not close the door to the use of other non-typical hearsay evidence as exceptions to the hearsay rule. It would be presumptuous to assume that all possible desirable exceptions to the hearsay rule have been catalogued or that accused individuals might never create any new situations in which there is reason to trust hearsay evidence will never arise. Therefore, Rule 807 specifically provides for other exceptions when certain conditions are met.[139]

In order to admit a statement under Rule 807, one court noted that:

> [T]here must be a showing that (1) the statement has equivalent circumstantial guarantees of trustworthiness to the other hearsay exceptions; (2) the statement is offered as evidence of a material fact; (3) the statement is more probative on the point for which it is offered than any other evidence which the proponent can procure through reasonable efforts; (4) the general purposes of the rules and the interests of justice will best be served by its admission; and (5) adequate notice must be given to the opposing party.[140]

To summarize, admissibility under Rule 807 must overcome five hurdles, including trustworthiness, materiality, probative importance, the interests of justice, and timely notice to the opposing party. In fact, the Second Circuit noted that the residual exception of Rule 807 is to be used "very rarely, and only in exceptional circumstances."[141]

Interpreting the rule authorizing evidence to be admitted under the exceptions of Rule 807, one commentator noted that they exist to provide some flexibility for the courts to deal with unique situations; they preserve the integrity of the specifically listed exceptions under Rules 803 and 804; and ultimately facilitate the basic goal of the Federals of evidence which is to determine the truth and fairly adjudicate controversies that come before the courts.[142] Courts in a variety of jurisdictions have repeatedly indicated that the residual hearsay exception under rule 807 should be used only rarely and for especially exceptional circumstances.[143]

In a case in which the defendant attempted to introduce hearsay evidence under Rule 807, the trial judge denied his efforts.[144] In the case, the defendant, who served in the military in Iraq, had been accused of selling military body armor on E-bay. Among other offenses, he had been charged with mail fraud and unauthorized sale of government property. During the inves-

---

139   The provisions of former Rule 803 (24) and former Rule 804(b)(5) have effectively been transferred to Rule 807 effective December 1, 1997 and remain in the latest 2008 version of the federal rules.

140   United States v. Peneaux, 432 F.3d 882, 891, 2005 U.S. App. LEXIS 28877 (8th Cir. 2005).

141   McGory v. City of New York, 2002 U.S. Dist. LEXIS 20177 (S.D.N.Y. 2002), quoting Parsons v. Honeywell, 929 F.2d 901, 907 (2d Cir. 1991).

142   Weinstein's Federal Evidence § 807.02 (Matthew Bender 2009).

143   United States v. Wilson, 281 Fed. Appx. 96, 2008 LEXIS 12302 (3rd Cir. 2008).

144   United States v. Avery, 2005 U.S. Dist. LEXIS 15979 (E.D. Pa. 2005).

tigation, a Defense Department employee interviewed the defendant in Iraq in the presence of two superior noncommissioned officers when the defendant, in response to a question, denied selling government body armor on E-bay. At the trial, the prosecution put one of the noncommissioned officers on the stand and he testified that he had been present when the defendant denied selling the armor. On cross-examination of the witness, when the witness admitted that he could not remember every detail of the meeting, the defense attorney sought to refresh the witness's memory by using a report of the meeting that had been prepared by the Defense Department employee. When the prosecution objected, the judge had the witness silently read the report to himself. The report contained the defendant's assertion that he purchased boots and body armor from a man in North Carolina. Defense counsel attempted to further cross-examine the witness with the Defense Department report in an effort to rebut the prosecutor's theory that the defendant had stolen the armor from the federal government. When the prosecutor complained that the report was hearsay evidence, the judge agreed and would not allow the statement to be used as evidence. The defendant's counsel sought to have the statement admitted under the residual exception covered by Rule 807. The trial court refused on the ground that to be admissible under Rule 807, a statement must meet five requirements: trustworthiness, materiality, probative importance, interests of justice and notice to the opposing party. According to the trial court,

> The trustworthiness of [the] statement is compromised, however, by the fact that his statement concerned events that took place, at the very at least, ten months earlier, and while he was deployed in Iraq. Moreover, [the declarant's] statement is contained in an interview report that he did not himself prepare, and there is no indication that the information he provided during the interview was made under oath and subject to the penalty of perjury.[145]

The court rejected the efforts of the defendant to have the statement-report admitted as an exception to the hearsay rule under Rule 807 because its trustworthiness could not be substantiated.

In applying Rule 807, a federal district court properly excluded an investigator's report from evidence when the report was designed to help the remaining defendant.[146] One conspirator pleaded guilty to robbery charges and testified against the other conspirator in the robbery of an armored truck driver. An investigator for the defendant had conversations with a third Brinks employee, which could have been used to impeach the government's conspirator witnesses who had already pled guilty. The conversations that the investigator wanted to relate to the jury were hearsay, but the defendant did not effectively show why the words spoken to the defendant's investigator would have any independent indicia of reliability or trustworthiness. There was no proof that the statements had been made under oath, and no proof that they were videotaped or voluntarily made. The reviewing court upheld the trial court's determination that the hearsay evidence should not having been admitted under Rule 807.

---

145   *Id.*

146   United States v. Rodriguez, 2009 U.S. App. LEXIS 4506 (9th Cir. 2009).

In a landmark case, *Crawford v. Washington*,[147] the Supreme Court of the United States dealt a harsh blow to prosecution efforts to successfully get evidence admitted under Rule 807 and related state evidence rules. In the *Crawford* case, a trial court convicted the defendant of assault of a man who had tried to rape the defendant's wife. At trial, the court permitted his wife's recorded out-of-court statement given to police to be admitted against him. The defendant's wife did not testify at trial after defendant invoked his state marital privilege to prevent her testimony, but the prosecution used her out-of-court recorded statements as substantive evidence against him. Because his wife did not testify, he was effectively prevented from confronting and cross-examining her. The Supreme Court reversed the assault conviction with the view that allowing the wife's statement against him that contained testimonial evidence, the trial court prevented the defendant's exercise of his Sixth Amendment right to confront and cross-examine an adverse witness. Only in exceptional situations will testimonial evidence be admitted when confrontation and cross-examination are impossible. In the *Crawford* case, the court noted that statements taken by police during investigations are generally considered testimonial in nature and can be excluded on Sixth Amendment grounds.[148]

Even before the *Crawford* case, courts hesitated to admit evidence under the residual exception unless all of the conditions were met. In a federal case that involved the admission of evidence under Rule 807, the defendant had been charged and convicted of kidnapping resulting in death based upon the disappearance of his ex-wife.[149] He filed a motion for a new trial based partly on the fact that the jury had seen and considered some evidence that the judge had not formally admitted into evidence and the defendant argued that it could not have been admitted even under the residual exception of Rule 807. The evidence that is contested by the defendant consisted of two day planner books that belonged to the defendant's ex-wife in which she penned some of her thoughts as an unhappy wife prior to the divorce. According to the trial court, the day planners were intentionally supplied to the jury by the government. The inadmissible evidence included notes within the day planners in which the deceased ex-wife mentioned harassing or threatening telephone calls by the defendant, referred to a protective order that she had sought at an earlier time, and included her cryptic notations about conversations she had with the defendant's daughter. The day planners also contained telephone numbers for a police detective who worked with protective orders and the number for a domestic violence support group. The trial judge found that the evidence contained in the day planners was virtually all hearsay and some of it had multiple layers of hearsay to which the defendant could obtain no cross-examination even if they had been admitted by the judge. There were also "moving and powerful" notes in the planners in the decedent's own handwriting. As the judge noted, "[t]his evidence, although compelling, bears no indicia of reliability because these statements do not fall within any of the twenty-three recognized exceptions to the hearsay rule, nor do they indicate any particularized

---

147   Crawford v. Washington, 541 U.S. 36, 52, 2004 U.S. LEXIS 1838 (2004).

148   *Id.*

149   United States v. Lentz, 2004 U.S. Dist. LEXIS 29650 (E.D. Va. 2004).

guarantees of trustworthiness."[150] According to the judge's reasoning, the fact that the jury saw and evaluated unadmitted hearsay evidence constituted a violation of the defendant's right to confrontation. In resolving whether the evidence could have been admitted, the judge considered that the decedent was unavailable, that there were no circumstantial guarantees of trustworthiness, that the evidence might relate to a material fact, whether the evidence was probative, whether admission would serve justice, and whether the opposing side had received notice. The court evaluated and rejected the government's contention that the day planner evidence could be admitted under the residual exception of Rule 807 and reversed the conviction.

In a different situation, a trial judge allowed evidence under the residual exception of Rule 807 when one minor was accused of the aggravated sexual battery of another minor.[151] At a bench trial, the judged adjudicated the alleged juvenile aggressor, a minor, as a juvenile delinquent. The evidence against the defendant consisted of some testimony from the minor victim and evidence presented by a forensic examiner who had questioned the victim. The forensic examiner followed proper interrogation protocols in interviewing the minor victim. As is required under Rule 807, the government gave the defendant notice that the forensic examiner would be called as a prosecution witness. Over the defendant's objection, the forensic questioner answered some foundational questions and explained the techniques used in talking to the juvenile victim. Over the juvenile defendant's objections on Rule 807 and Sixth Amendment confrontation grounds, the court allowed the forensic examiner to tell the court what the girl-victim told the forensic examiner concerning when the events occurred and how the defendant's and the victim's private areas had been joined together, among other relevant facts. Specifically, the court considered that the forensic examiner's evidence was material to the case, and, because the victim's testimony was unclear on some matters in court that she had freely mentioned out of court, the forensic examiner's testimony was the most probative available. The court found the examiner's testimony trustworthy when considered with other evidence in the case and proper notice had been given to the defendant. Admitting the evidence under the residual exception to the hearsay rule appeared to serve the interests of justice, so the court affirmed the juvenile adjudication.

If the reasons for excluding hearsay evidence are not strong and the interests of justice would best be served by admission of a hearsay statement into evidence, the proponent must assert logical rationales that support admitting the evidence under the residual exception theory to the hearsay rule. Admitting evidence under the residual exception rule had a chance of court approval where there are special cases involving unique circumstances.

Nontestimonial Utterances

The previous sections discussed the hearsay rule and demonstrated some of the well-known exceptions that allow admission of evidence in contravention of the general rule. Courts recognize

---

150   *Id.*

151   United States v. W.B., 452 F.3d 1002, 2006 U.S. App. LEXIS 17378 (8th Cir. 2006).

the legal principle that states that if an out-of-court statement is offered to show what was said, rather than for the truth of the matter stated, the out-of-court statements are not considered hearsay.[152] Demonstrative of this principle is a situation in which an officer believed that stolen property had been hidden in a wooded area, but he was not certain. When he asked the defendant's son where the stolen goods were located, the son pointed to the woods behind a motel, but did not speak. The trial court allowed the officer to testify concerning the one-sided conversation he had with the defendant's son over the defense objection that the evidence constituted inadmissible hearsay. The boy's gesture, or verbal act, conveyed information but the gesture was not used to prove the truth of the matters visually asserted by the boy. His gesture was admitted to show why the officer walked into the wooded area where he found the stolen goods. The court of appeals held that the testimony of the officer explaining the boy's gesture, did not qualify as hearsay because it was not offered for its truth.[153]

A Virginia court advised that whether an out-of-court statement or act constituted hearsay depended on the purpose for which the statement was offered at trial; a statement that was offered for proof of its truth qualified as hearsay, but a statement or act that has been offered to the purpose of explaining or throwing light on the conduct of an individual to whom the statement was directed is not considered hearsay.[154] Where a witness testified that she called police after observing a larcenist leaving her store and mentioned that the reason the man piqued her interest was because another store employee gave her a detailed description of the repeat larcenist. The statement describing the appearance of the repeat larcenist was not offered for proof of its truth; it was offered only to explain why the witness scrutinized the behavior of the particularly described customer.[155] However, "a nod of the head in response to a question calling for a "yes" or "no" answer, or a gesture pointing to a particular person when asked to identify a perpetrator, are examples of assertive conduct"[156] that qualifies as hearsay evidence.

A Florida trial court committed reversible error resulting in the wrongful conviction of a defendant for grand theft of a motor vehicle. The defendant's position was that another person told the defendant that the other person was the owner of the van and that the defendant had permission to drive it. If this were true, the defendant's necessary state of mind for larceny would have been lacking. The testimony was not hearsay and should not have been excluded because the defendant did not offer it for the truth of the matter asserted within the statement. The defendant's purpose in offering the evidence was to show that because he heard the statement by the alleged owner, the defendant possessed a good faith belief that the other person owned the van, and that he had lawful permission to drive it.[157]

---

152   Cormier v. State, 955 S.W.2d 161 (Tex. 1997).

153   Saunders v. Commonwealth, 2003 Va. App. LEXIS 394 (2003).

154   Farrar v. Commonwealth, 2006 Va. App. LEXIS 301 (2006).

155   *Id.*

156   People v. Jurado, 38 Cal. 4th 72, 129, 131 P.3d 400, 438, 41 Cal. Rptr. 3d 319, 365, 2006 Cal. LEXIS 4391 (2006).

157   Alfaro v. Florida, 837 So. 2d 429, 2002 Fla. App. LEXIS 13992 (2002).

"A verbal act is an utterance of an operative fact that gives rise to legal consequences."[158] The hearsay rule does not apply to verbal acts when the evidence has not been offered for its truth. In one case, a defendant contended on appeal that his counsel failed to object to inadmissible hearsay offered by the prosecution. A police officer testified that he asked the defendant for permission to search his apartment and the officer stated that the defendant answered in the affirmative. The defendant's statement could be called a verbal act "because the statement [was] admitted merely to show that it was actually made, not to prove the truth of what was asserted."[159] The trial court held, and the appellate court agreed, that no hearsay evidence had been permitted in that context because the officer was not offering the defendant's positive answer for its truth, only to indicate that the defendant had made a statement that would indicate to the officer that he had the legal authority to make a lawful entry and search of the apartment.[160]

Under what is sometimes referred to as the verbal act doctrine, a statement that accompanies conduct is admissible because it gives legal significance to the act. The Florida Supreme Court explained a verbal act as:

> an utterance of an operative fact that gives rise to legal consequences. Verbal acts, also known as statements of legal consequence, are not hearsay, because the statement is admitted merely to show that it was actually made, not to prove the truth of what was asserted in it.[161]

The Florida court noted that in order for verbal acts to be admissible, the conduct that is explained by the words must be independently material or important to the issue at hand, the conduct that occurs must be equivocal, and the words uttered must assist in giving legal context or significance to the conduct, and the words must be spoken with the conduct.[162] Where the evidence is offered only to show that words were spoken and not for proof of the truth of what was said, the evidence is not hearsay. For example, in a case in which a trial court convicted the defendant of the sale and delivery of cannabis and possession of cannabis, the case depended upon the testimony of a confidential informant.[163] The trial court refused to allow a separate witness to offer the defendant's response to a question from the confidential informant. One of the witnesses who had been present at the crime scene was prepared to tell the court that when the defendant had been asked to sell marijuana by the prosecution's confidential informant, the defendant told her, "I don't do that kind of stuff."[164] The trial court rejected allowing the witness to tell what the defendant answered to the confidential informant on the ground that it was

---

158   5–801 Weinstein's Federal Evidence § 801.11[3] Verbal Acts (Matthew Bender 2009).

159   *Id.*

160   Dragani v. Bryant, 2005 U.S. Dist. LEXIS 38057, n. 7 (M.D. Fla. 2005).

161   Banks v. Florida, 790 So. 2d 1094, 2001 Fla. LEXIS 1411 (2001).

162   *Id.*

163   Burkey v. State, 922 So. 2d 1033, 1035, 2006 Fla. App. LEXIS 2772 (2006).

164   *Id.*

hearsay. The appellate court held that the trial court should have allowed the witness to state what the defendant had said in response to an offer to commit a crime from the confidential informant. The statement was a verbal act of the defendant that was not hearsay and it should have been admitted just to show that he made the statement. The fact that the defendant would refuse an offer to commit drug selling is material for his defense that he was not involved in the drug sale that occurred within the home. In a different case, a "waitress" at a bar/club came over to where an undercover officer was sitting and rubbed her buttocks on his lap as an invitation to a free lap dance and said that the fun did not have to end there, that there was a private room. The undercover officer paid $50 to the proprietor and the "waitress" said the $50 would pay for oral sex but that a tip would be nice. The appellate court held that the words of the "waitress" were verbal acts because the statements were made merely to demonstrate that the operative words were uttered and not to prove their substantive truth. In this case, the words explain why the undercover officer wanted to go to the private room. The nonverbal conduct of the "waitress" was equivocal, the words spoken were important to understanding the situation, and the words accompanied her conduct and were admissible under the verbal act doctrine.[165]

Summary

The general rule is that once evidence is identified as hearsay it should not be admissible in court because of the concern that hearsay evidence may not be reliable or truthful and may not have been given under oath. Hearsay evidence is defined as oral testimony or written evidence presented in court from a statement uttered or written out of court, when the statement is offered in court to prove the truth of matters asserted therein. Thus, evidence that relies on the credibility of the out-of-court declarant will be classified as hearsay and excluded. Although this general rule is universally applied and based on sound reasoning, there are many exceptions. If evidence meets the requirements of a recognized exception or the residual exception, it may be admissible, even though it is classified as hearsay.

Examples of exceptions to the hearsay rule include spontaneous and excited utterances, some business and public records, family history and records, former testimony, dying declarations, declarations against interest, and exceptions under the residual exception rule. Under each of the traditional hearsay exceptions evidence may be admitted for substantive proof; however, it must meet the specific requirements that have been established for the particular exception because these requirements help assure trustworthiness.

The Sixth Amendment to the U.S. Constitution guarantees defendants the right to confront and cross-examine the witnesses against them. When out-of-court hearsay statements are admitted as evidence in court, the defendant may not have the opportunity to cross-examine or even confront the adverse declarant whose evidence is introduced by the one who overheard the declarant speak. Since the Supreme Court recently held that testimonial evidence normally

---

165   Pronesti v. Florida, 847 So. 2d 1165, 1166, 2003 Fla. App. LEXIS 9472 (2003).

requires that actual confrontation and cross-examination must be permitted, some hearsay exceptions have come under more intense scrutiny by trial courts.[166] While preserving of the rights of
confrontation for defendants, the interests of justice require that a balance exist between the
rights of defendants and the necessities of justice and fairness for society.

The hearsay rule does not exclude evidence when the out-of-court statements are offered solely
as evidence that a statement was made, and not for the substantive content of the statement.
Witnesses to out-of-court statements who repeat them in court, not for the substantive truth
of the statement, but to indicate the person's physical or mental condition, will be permitted
to offer evidence.

From the foregoing discussion, it is clear that although some hearsay evidence is not admissible in court, there are many exceptions to the hearsay rule. The exceptions to the rule may
result in most evidence classified as hearsay being admitted and very little evidence being
excluded, but where courts admit hearsay evidence, the requirements of the exceptions assure
truthfulness. In order to offer the greatest level of admissible evidence to the prosecutor, good
practice dictates that criminal justice personnel be familiar not only with the rules that exclude
hearsay evidence, but also with the hearsay exceptions and their individual requirements, which
permit the admission of hearsay evidence in court.

---

166   *See* Crawford v. Washington, 541 U.S. 36, 2004 U.S. LEXIS 1838 (2004).

Chapter 6: Key Terms and Discussion Questions

Key Terms

Business Records: records kept by a business in the course of operating the business

Declarant: an individual who makes a statement

Declarations Against Interest: a statement made by an unavailable individual that is against that individual's own personal interest

Dying Declaration: a statement made by an individual who believes he or she is at death's door

Excited Utterance: a statement made under the stress or excitement of a surprising event

Former Testimony: testimony that a declarant made in a previous court case

Hearsay: a statement made out of court that is offered in court for the truth of the matter asserted

Nontestimonial Evidence: a statement that is not made for the purpose of going in a record of a government agent or agency.

Prejudicial Evidence: evidence that is introduced with the sole role of wrongfully influencing the jury

Present Sense Impression: a statement that describes an event while it was occurring or immediately afterward

Probative Value: evidence that is sufficiently useful to prove something material in a trial

Statement: an oral or written assertion, including gestures

Testimony: oral or written evidence given by a witness under oath

Discussion Questions

1. What is the distinction between an excited utterance and a present sense impression?
2. Explain the rules of a dying declaration. Does the declarant actually have to die to use this exception?
3. When is a statement nontestimonial?
4. Where do family records fit in with the Hearsay Rule?
5. List and explain residual exceptions.

CONCLUSION

This book is primarily an effort to educate college-level students on the importance of evidence and evidentiary rules. It achieved this purpose by taking out the extraneous material one would find in an evidence casebook for law students and focused on the necessary basics for criminal justice majors, whether they be interested in a career in crime scene investigation, law enforcement, or law. Students should take away general knowledge of criminal evidence and a specific understanding of how evidentiary law works in the criminal justice system.

The principles in this book relate to real-world events, which is evidenced by the cases included in different chapters. These principles and concepts should be applied once students are in the field. They will aid students transitioning into their careers with strong ethics, critical thinking skills, and a solid background in evidentiary law.

I hope that students will keep and continue to use this book as a resource once they graduate from college and begin their adventures in the criminal justice system to make it a fairer organization as a whole, even if administered in small doses. The criminal justice system in the United States needs an overhaul, and I sincerely pray that I am supporting that change through compiling this book. Whenever you land, students, my best wishes to you!

INDEX

CPSIA information can be obtained
at www.ICGtesting.com
Printed in the USA
LVHW052152230821
695917LV00005B/98